**Women and Gender Equity in
Development Theory and Practice**

Women and Gender Equity in Development Theory and Practice

Institutions, Resources, and Mobilization

Edited by

Jane S. Jaquette and

Gale Summerfield

Duke University Press | Durham and London 2006

© 2006 Duke University Press
All rights reserved
Printed in the United States of America on acid-free paper ⊗
Designed by Heather Hensley
Typeset in Janson by Tseng Information Systems, Inc.
Library of Congress Cataloging-in-Publication Data appear
on the last printed page of this book.

Contents

Preface and Acknowledgments

We dedicate this volume to Irene Tinker (author of the final essay in Part III) in recognition of her role as a key intellectual provocateur of the field of women/gender and development. A scholar-activist who taught at Howard University, American University, and Berkeley, Irene helped make a focus on women part of U.S. aid policy through her role in formulating and lobbying for the Percy Amendment, which established the Women and Development Office at USAID. She co-founded several institutions, including the Wellesley Center on Women, the International Center for Research on Women, and the Equity Policy Center. For many years she headed the U.S. Council for INSTRAW (the UN International Research and Training Institute for the Advancement of Women).

Throughout her career, Irene has traveled widely, seeking out activists and scholars and bringing to the fore issues that were on the minds of women in the global South, but which were not yet part of the development debate. She ran the first conference on women and development issues in Mexico City, just before the first UN Conference on Women in 1975. In the 1970s she brought to the fore issues of women, energy, and technology at the household level; her work in the 1980s made the role of street foods visible to scholars and planners; in the 1990s she helped pioneer work on women and property rights, looking especially at the implications for women of the privatization of land and housing. Her most recent work returns to her earliest research—on electoral politics—looking at the impact of gender quotas and the election of women to national legislatures.

Irene has encouraged and mentored many scholars and practitioners, including the authors in this volume, over a wide range of topics and concerns. They in turn have been inspired—and pushed—by her to think more deeply and act more effectively to make change happen. This project gives us an opportunity to recognize Irene's unique role in multiplying the impact, enhancing the vision, and expanding the agenda of the field.

The editors of this volume first met in Bangkok in 1994 at a workshop on women and socioeconomic transitions in East/Southeast Asia. Irene, at the University of California, Berkeley, and Amara Pongsapich, at Chulalongkorn (see chapter entitled "Women's Movements in the Globalizing World" in this book), organized the meeting. Irene contacted Jane and Gale separately to help with parts of the workshop which brought together specialists from China, Laos, Vietnam, Thailand, the United States, and several other countries to identify the key issues for women in the countries undergoing transitions from socialist planning to market-oriented economies. Most countries sent four or five representatives, but the Laotian delegation amazed all of us when fourteen women in traditional dress walked into the conference room, the first meeting outside their country for most. After the requisite formal statements from each delegation, we had a lively discussion about the need to address families as well as individuals, housing, education, employment and microenterprise, and much more. Our hosts at Chulalongkorn arranged several visits to sites in Bangkok. We walked through the lanes of the one-room apartments that had originally been set up for servants of the adjacent gold-roofed palace. Although the lanes ran into the bay and were partially filled with water, the rooms had electricity and some had televisions where groups cheered their favorite soccer teams playing in the World Cup, which was being held in California. Local planners talked about the importance of a participatory approach to eliminating the slum-like conditions and relocating these people. When they listened to the residents, they found that a planned relocation would have cut the low incomes they managed to earn from selling to rush-hour passersby since the proposed new location would be too far from the commuters. We went to a large red-light district which was partly transforming into a night bazaar lined with stalls selling knockoffs of Rolex watches and Polo T-shirts. During the breaks, we discussed future collaborations on research projects. The next one would be at the NGO forum of the Fourth World Conference on Women in

China in 1995 and would focus on land and housing. We also held meetings in Berkeley and Monterey, California; published a special issue of the *Review of Social Economy* in 1997; an edited volume, *Women's Rights to House and Land: China, Laos, Vietnam* (Lynne Rienner Publishers, 1999); and this book, a decade after the initial workshop in Bangkok. The editors and contributors to this volume owe a great deal to Irene Tinker's mentorship, research, and energy.

A volume of this ambition has many sources and owes many debts. We would like to single out a few: the chapter authors themselves, who stayed with us through the several stages of planning and editing; Valerie Mulholland and Miriam Angress at Duke University Press, who recognized the value of the project and helped us carry it through, and Mark Mastromarino and Heather Hensley, who invested so much in its quality; the anonymous readers whose efforts greatly improved the text; and Kathy Martin of the Women and Gender in Global Perspectives Program at the University of Illinois, who helped with proofreading and preparation of the manuscript. We thank our families, whose patience and commitment made the effort possible and kept us grounded.

In 1991, Irene edited *Persistent Inequalities*, celebrating Ester Boserup's role as the inspiration for what became a field and a movement. We would like to acknowledge Irene whose initiatives, and the debates these have engendered, are still at the cutting edge.

Introduction

Jane S. Jaquette and Gale Summerfield

This collection of essays arose out of our perception that as the field of women and gender issues in development has expanded and grown more complex, it may be losing its momentum. We invited several people to use their research and experience to reflect on where they think the field is today and where it is going. We looked for authors from a variety of roles, from scholars and policy makers to advocates and those who do fieldwork in specific sectors. We sought perspectives from different regions, including Latin America, Asia, and Africa, and from men as well as women. Some of our writers accept, if they do not champion, globalization; others are quite critical of it.

This volume offers a rich menu of views. It is appearing at a time when the international political system is being rapidly restructured, with important implications for multilateral approaches, development models, and resource flows. We are no longer living in a "post–Cold War" world, which was characterized by the unquestioned dominance of neoliberal economics and a rising wave of democratization.[1] The debt crisis of the 1980s gave the Western industrialized countries the leverage to push for economic reforms in many regions of the world, including policies that reduced the role of the state and increased trade and investment, promoting "free markets" to stimulate growth. The so-called Washington Consensus in favor of structural adjustment reforms had the positive effect of reducing inflation in many cases and increasing capital flows, but the negative effect of cutting government spending on social and infrastructure investment, with long-term implications for human security as well as economic competitiveness. Neoliberal reforms also produced an active antiglobalization movement, and the Consensus itself has developed cracks, as is evident, for example, in the harsh criticisms of the International Monetary Fund by former Chief Economist of the World Bank Joseph Stiglitz (2002).

Using the "war on terror" as a rationale, the United States during George W. Bush's administration has promoted "regime change," a process that contrasts starkly with the transitions from authoritarianism that occurred globally from the late 1970s to the late 1990s. These earlier transitions were encouraged by a receptive international environment but were largely driven by internal forces.[2] Since September 11, U.S. unilateralism has undercut multilateral institutions and practices that had been painstakingly constructed over several decades, including a key role for the United Nations in setting international norms, resolving global issues, promoting development, and preventing war.

Globalization and restructuring have imposed disproportionate costs on women, but other aspects of multilateralism have brought positive changes. The worldwide emergence of women's movements, widespread efforts to implement programs to improve women's access to material resources, and the incorporation of women's rights into international law took place during the last three decades in the political space created by the UN Decade for Women (1975–85) and sustained momentum through the Fourth World Conference in Beijing (1995) and beyond. Women's activism influenced UN conferences on issues ranging from human rights, population, and habitat to sustainable development. A reversal of the global trend toward multilateralism will surely undermine these advances. If it continues unchecked, the increasing militarization of international politics could have severe consequences for women's lives and will further divert attention from the pressing issues of improved equity and greater human security.

The U.S. response to the attacks of September 11 includes an argument for increased foreign assistance (on the grounds that poverty is among the "root causes" of terrorism, for example), the U.S.-led invasions of Afghanistan and Iraq and the increasingly controversial efforts to stabilize and democratize them have created a demand for solutions that can be put into place rapidly. Co-optation has been an issue for women in the South who fear that funding from governments and foundations in the North sets their agendas. Co-optation may become a more pressing issue for Northern experts and nongovernmental organizations

(NGOS) as the United States and its allies use the issue of women's rights to buttress its case for intervention, whatever the consequences may be for women in countries where support for traditional gender roles has become a badge of national and religious resistance to Western-style modernization.[3]

These changes in U.S. policies and in the international system pose problems not only for women in Afghanistan and Iraq. The post-9/11 world is a precarious time to do development work. The essays in this volume address the broader issues of women and gender, development and globalization that need rethinking as we move into this uncharted territory. We hope this book will provoke renewed attention to these issues and new energy to seek more effective strategies for the future.

CREATIVE TENSIONS?

The field of women/gender and development has grown rapidly over the last three decades, producing multidisciplinary research and providing the basis for gender-sensitive policies in many public and private institutions, including multilateral and bilateral foreign assistance agencies. Efforts to address women's marginalization have also had to confront persistent bureaucratic resistance. Among the major debates within the field are the conflict between *women in* development (WID) versus *gender and* development (GAD); between those who think poverty is an appropriate focus to reach women and those who find it a "trap"; between gender rhetoric and bureaucratic foot-dragging; and between the theories of researchers and policy analysts and the needs of practitioners. Some are convinced that women can be reached through "mainstreaming" donor projects and programs; others think the focus on "gender" has weakened organizing by and for women.

There is widespread agreement that the market alone does not serve women well, but few have addressed the issue of how to strengthen states to regulate markets or how to confront the corruption that has proven endemic in emerging democracies. There are those who think globalization is inevitable and must be regulated and those who think that the only viable feminist position is to join the antiglobalization movements that have shown their ability to organize effective demonstrations in Seattle, Genoa, Cancun, and elsewhere (see Mohanty 2003).

Postcolonial writers have challenged the assumptions of development theory and practice in ways that are relevant to women, fueling conflicts between universalism and pluralism and producing a new focus on transnational identities.

Some see the rise of civil societies, both local and global, as promising arenas of women's empowerment, yet others insist that a strong and capable state remains critical to women's concerns. The rise of women's grassroots movements during the past few decades is unprecedented. Yet some fear that NGOs may not be sufficiently democratic, representative, or autonomous to represent women's interests and argue that decentralization can reinforce local power hierarchies rather than challenge them. There are contradictions between the promises of neoliberal reform and the realities of most people's lives, often seen in the impatience of voters who can now express their frustrations through the ballot box. These stresses can be mapped onto the increasingly visible tension between development models that focus on economic growth and those that emphasize human capabilities and human security. Meanwhile, gender analysis from different interventions—for example, in forestry, information technology, and the privatization of state assets, to name three included in this volume—are rarely connected to one another or systematically linked to broader trends and policy goals.

There has been surprisingly little discussion of how to approach gender and development in increasingly violent, culturally politicized environments. We would argue that since September 11 and the invasion of Iraq, human security has become even more important as an alternative approach to development. In contrast to the traditional emphasis on military security, the concerns of human security center on health, livelihood, housing and land, environment, and freedom from violence within the home and community.[4]

These debates are engaged by many of the essays in this book. We hope that they will help spur new thinking and action.

ORGANIZATION OF THE BOOK

The book is divided into three sections reflecting the three main themes of the volume: institutions, resources, and mobilization.

Institutions: Opportunities and Barriers

The essays in the first section focus on institutional issues.[5] Jane Jaquette and Kathleen Staudt begin with a historical overview of the evolution of the field beginning with their own experience as policy analysts at the U.S. Agency for International Development (USAID) in the late 1970s. They discuss the rise of WID and the emergence of GAD, showing how each responded to major shifts in the international system, from the North-South dialogue of the 1970s, to the renewed Cold War and Washington Consensus of the 1980s, the post–Cold War 1990s, and U.S. unilateralism since 9/11. Noting that GAD "fatigue" may be setting in, they call for new ideas and alliances and suggest these will have to begin by stepping back from earlier debates and rethinking women's relations to markets, civil society, and the state.

Elisabeth Prügl and Audrey Lustgarten take up the issue of mainstreaming, a GAD initiative introduced to induce bureaucracies to take up the issue of women across the board. Noting that gender mainstreaming has been adopted by governments and donor agencies all over the world, they discuss how several UN agencies defined and tried to implement mainstreaming. In their view, mainstreaming has largely been co-opted, and efforts to implement the concept "turned a radical movement idea into a strategy of public management" by emphasizing processes rather than outcomes. They observe that evaluations still uncover the kinds of problems that mainstreaming was supposed to overcome.

David Hirschmann focuses on the difficulties of translating gender rhetoric, which is widely accepted by donors, into gender equity in practice. A consultant to USAID, the World Bank, and other donor agencies, Hirschmann recounts how things change but remain the same. In the 1980s, when he visited projects to assess their gender impact, he was directed to the "home economics" people. By the 1990s, he was told to go talk to "the sociologists," although it was clear that the economists had the power. Hirschmann concludes that the macroeconomic priorities of foreign assistance agencies such as USAID and the World Bank make it very difficult to raise concerns about women and other marginalized groups.

Sylvia Chant examines how a gender perspective can inform an analysis of poverty, which remains a priority for foreign assistance agencies. Cecile Jackson (1998) and others have argued that poverty is a "trap" on the grounds that it takes women-headed households as a proxy for poor women. But women may be just as poor in intact households if they do not control their own incomes and, on the other side, many women-headed households are doing well economically. Reviewing early women in development approaches, neoliberal restructuring, and women's "empowerment" efforts, Chant argues that research indicates that women's capacity to *command* and *allocate* resources is equally or perhaps more important than women's power to *obtain* resources. Women may actually choose to give up material resources in order to gain control of their own lives. Women invest more in their children, and data on younger generations in female-headed households "frequently reveal comparable, if not greater (and less gender-biased) levels of nutrition, health and education." Although not arguing against marriage, Chant notes that women who go it alone may be in a better position to "challenge the diverse factors that make them poor." Women's empowerment cannot be measured by using indicators that ignore women's felt experiences.

Finally, Maruja Barrig looks at gender equity from the standpoint of a feminist consultant to programs carried out by local NGOs funded by European donors in the southern Andean region of Peru. She documents how the effort to implement gender guidelines has run up against the principle of support for indigenous cultures. Anthropologists committed to preserving Andean values contrast the moral purity of rural village life to the capitalist corruption of Peru's cities, to which many Indians are forced to migrate by the lack of economic opportunities in the highlands.

Barrig's interviews with several staff members show that local NGOs may accept gender guidelines (which are required by donors) but that they justify their failure to implement them on the grounds that the Western model of gender equality does not fit the Andean ideal of gender complementarity. The evidence of discrimination against Andean women is very clear (they lack the education, knowledge of Spanish, and spatial mobility that the men of the villages enjoy), but Barrig also asks how, given all the constraints, Andean women themselves can be given their voice.

Control of Resources and Livelihood

Both WID and GAD approaches have addressed women's access to and control over resources that could increase their productivity and intrahousehold bargaining power. Practitioners have organized women to learn about their rights and to claim shares in countries where state holdings of land and other assets are being turned over to private ownership. The wave of privatizations in the 1990s, especially in former socialist economies, raised new issues about ownership and use rights. Do women in rural areas have property rights in land? How can urban and rural women retain ownership of their houses, which are an important form of capital and often a source of income? Inheritance of land and house is a particularly pressing issue in Africa, where conflicts between customary, religious, and civil law tend to favor men and impoverish women. Property rights are an integral and frequently overlooked component of human security, and the work that has been done on human security does not take gender sufficiently into account.

Gale Summerfield looks at the case of China, where incremental processes of

land privatization are having more complex gendered effects than previously recognized. As families reassert control over rural land that was collectivized after
the revolution, some have argued that this reform seems to represent a return
to the virilocal prerevolutionary pattern. Summerfield argues that this is not so
obviously the case because, despite serious problems, new laws and greater opportunities for rural employment, migration, and sideline production give women
options they did not have in the earlier period. At the same time, male migration is
feminizing subsistence agriculture. Because rural housing was not collectivized,
rural families invest more in their houses than in their land, which was generally allocated for a relatively short time and periodically reallocated, for example,
when women left their natal village to live with their husband's family. New laws
provide longer tenure and thus encourage investment, but ending periodic reallocations will have potentially harmful implications for women.

Diana Lee-Smith and Catalina Hinchey Trujillo show how cooperation
among different groups concerned about women's access to property had an impact on the Fourth World Conference on Women in Beijing in 1995 and helped
shape the UN-HABITAT's Program of 2000–2001. In rural areas, where women
traditionally had use rights to land and house, the growth of the cash economy
has made it increasingly necessary for women to convert use rights into formal
ownership. Few privatization programs have considered the impact of their programs on women, especially single women. Using Uganda as a case study, the
authors argue that the issue is not only to make the laws more equitable but to
enforce the laws already on the books. Studies must be done to address how property systems are gendered and also to challenge the cultural traditions that make
it difficult for women to assert their legal rights.

Faranak Miraftab's chapter looks at a project undertaken by the UN Center for
Human Settlements (UN-HABITAT). The study examined gender patterns in the
access to professional knowledge and administrative power in the area of housing.
Perhaps not surprisingly, the HABITAT team found that women were less well
represented than men in the fields of planning and that there is an inverse relation between the number of women and the level of authority in most housing-
related ministries. Because role differences are so ingrained, the team found that
gender discrimination often went unobserved. The idea, for example, that an
agency would give women maternity leave and time to breastfeed their children
was taken by female employees as evidence that the agency was not discriminating against women, whether or not its policies took gender sufficiently into

account. Miraftab concludes that women were rarely in a position to have *final* say on housing issues in ways that could improve their secure access to housing, thus making the case (as the larger study does) for increased involvement of women in the process of making and implementing housing policy at all levels.

All three of these essays show that the relatively neglected issue of women's control over land and housing is critically important. They show how a combination of factors—ranging from women's organizations, privatization, international norms, domestic laws, and cultural practices—shape the conditions under which women's property ownership and use rights are being raised, formulated into specific demands on relevant agencies, and translated into policies that can be implemented. As economies are increasingly marketized, this issue is becoming more significant for women.

Louise Fortmann addresses another consequence of gendered ownership when she looks at how women and men manage forest resources. Modern patterns of ownership are changing the conditions of land use. As private ownership displaces traditional use rights, women may lose access to tree products, for example, yet the prevalence of traditional values concerning women's ownership may make it difficult for them to claim rights, even to the land they legally own. Using data from Zimbabwe, Fortmann shows that the fact that women were half as likely as men to plant trees on their homestead land could not be explained by differences in wealth or the kind of labor needed to manage the trees. Instead it was because women did not own the land and were much less certain than men that they would reap the products of their investment. Drawing on her work comparing forest management projects in the United States and in developing countries, Fortmann concludes that the tendency to see problems of community forestry management in the South as quite different from those in the North is misguided. Resource-dependent communities in both North and South share similar macrolevel constraints and benefit from thinking cooperatively about how to confront them. At the same time, "situated knowledges" are essential to effective interventions that will meet women's needs.

Kirk Smith examines the serious environmental problem of indoor pollution. Cooking fuels that emit smoke and toxic fumes are common in poor households in many developing countries, and women and children are more exposed because they typically spend more hours in the house than men and do most of the cooking. Smith points out that acute lower respiratory infection (ALRI), which commonly leads to pneumonia that kills within a few hours, is one of the leading causes of death of children under five in developing countries. There is a probable link between indoor pollution and ALRI, and many of the deaths could be prevented with proper ventilation and treatment, but adequate health care and research funds have not been allocated to the problem because it is not a headline-grabbing issue, unlike severe acute respiratory syndrome, which threatened to become an international epidemic in 2003. Smith's chapter is based on his experience as a researcher in this field and on a project currently being carried out in Guatemala. He argues that a strategy of *prevention* (the installation of new, well-ventilated stoves) is effective and should complement the current strategy of *intervention*, treating respiratory infections after children have become ill.

Women's Mobilizations and Power

How women's mobilizations intersect with larger trends, such as globalization and the increasing impact of new communications technologies, is the focus that unites the chapters in the third section. In the first essay, Amara Pongsapich traces the impact of women's movements on the international environmental agenda, through the Decade for Women and Beijing and the UN environmental conferences. She then turns to her own country to assess how environmental issues have been addressed under conditions of globalization in Thailand. Although the Thai economic crisis was very hard on women workers, civil society movements have consolidated and expanded. Pongsapich provides several case studies of women-led local efforts to halt development projects that would have had detrimental environmental effects.

Pongsapich sees these women-led efforts as consistent with a global trend of "new social movements," which are less committed to material ends and more oriented toward the quality of life. In her view, the "modernist paradigm" has emphasized industrialization and economic development, but grass-roots people want a human-centered development paradigm that is respectful of nature. Donor agencies have recently put the emphasis on poverty, but fail to make the connection between women, poverty, and the environment. In an essay that is highly critical of globalization, Pongsapich concludes that women are turning their attention from issues of gender equity to issues of trade and investment.

Doe Mayer, Barbara Pillsbury, and Muadi Mukenge document the lessons of a five-year project funded by the Gates Foundation to provide women's organizations access to information communication technology (ICT; in this case, the Internet and e-mail) and to train them in how to develop effective communications strategies. Pillsbury and Meyer worked with 30 NGOs in Zambia, Zimbabwe, and Uganda that had been identified through projects funded by the Global Fund for Women. Mukenge evaluated the project.

The project found that the successful use of information technology depended on several factors, including the hierarchy of the organization and the degree to which ICT could make a noticeable difference in the organization's success, particularly its ability to attract foreign donors. The project also emphasized more traditional forms of communication and the need for NGOs to reach local organizations or networks to be effective at advocacy.

The problems faced by Women Connect! illustrate another theme of this volume. As Barrig emphasized in her discussion of NGOs working in the Andes, relations between Northern donors and Southern NGOs are often conflictive. From the perspective of the Southern NGOs, donor requirements can distort NGO agendas and produce complicated reporting processes that may waste valuable resources or produce a rhetorical agreement that is not reflected in project implementation. Pillsbury and Mayer show how this looks from the Northern perspective: the grant required that this initiative work on women's reproductive health issues, especially HIV/AIDS, but that was rarely the top priority of the local NGOs. The need to meet the donor's conditions affected which NGOs were chosen and how the projects were carried out, with Pillsbury and Mayer in the role of intermediaries.

Global connections have been shown as a reason for the success and survival of local NGOs. But the ties between local groups and their audiences are assumed rather than studied. If NGOs are to be autonomous and responsive, the role of local members and supporters is critical. The chapter by Mayer, Pillsbury, and Mukenge emphasizes the importance of "traditional" outreach strategies to connect groups with local audiences as well as the usefulness of the Internet to link groups transnationally and to access sources of information that can be repackaged for local use.

In the final chapter, Irene Tinker reflects on her experiences over several decades working with individuals, NGOs, scholars, and donors on issues of women in development. Tinker's theme in this chapter is empowerment, not as a theoretical issue or an organizational goal, but as it "happened"—that is, as women's mobilization was the often unintended result of initiatives intended to change the economic but not the gender status quo.

Tinker believes that early efforts to redirect economic resources helped women's organizations to get started, and she recounts the effects of the UN Decade and Beijing (1995) on the growth and increasing power of women's organizations. She looks at the current status of the broad range of issues in which she has engaged, from promoting Ester Boserup's work and the Percy Amendment, which drew attention to the issues of women and development, to exploring the relationship between women, technology and the environment, street foods, and housing and land. She takes a close look at the relative effects of different microcredit programs. Returning to her original field of political science, Tinker discusses how different kinds of electoral systems, including gender quotas, are producing changes in political leadership in many countries, a process that works best, she argues, when government "insiders" are closely engaged with independent women's movements and with activist women leaders on the "outside." Tinker's assessment of women's organizing and its impact on policy is, like Irene Tinker herself, an equal mix of deep intellectual curiosity, constructive critique, and confidence that we can make change happen.[6]

COMMON THEMES AND NEW DIRECTIONS

Several themes emerge from the creative tensions addressed in this volume. Changing institutions, controlling resources, and mobilizing for power are not issues only in developing countries; they are challenges in all countries. A truly interdisciplinary perspective is needed to address the concerns of political participation, economic fundamentals, and the expanded capabilities that stress quality of life as well as material measures of what women value (see C. Graham 2003). The concern to recognize different goals and practices that drives the postcolonialist focus on equity (rather than equality) must be integrated with policy- and action-oriented efforts to improve women's lives (see Benería 2003; Zein-Elabdin and Charusheela 2004). These chapters underline the need to maintain a focus on women while keeping gender power relations in mind.

Crossing borders is also a recurring theme. Globalization and the need to bring lessons from the South to the North suggest the necessity of an approach sensitive to transnational issues. Migration, technology, resource management, employment patterns, and political mobilization are important examples. Yet the permeability of borders and the impressive rise of women's movements do not suggest giving up on the state; on the contrary, state capacity to regulate markets, provide social insurance, and criminalize various forms of trafficking in women remains a critical issue for women.

Another theme is the way globalization appears to be transferring risk to those least able to cope with structural changes and survive the inevitable cycles that occur, even when the growth trend is positive. The human costs of structural adjustment in Africa and the Latin American and Asian currency crises of the 1990s show that we cannot assume that "development" is a smooth or irreversible process, even in those countries that are seen as the most successful cases of reform. In the 1990s, the end of the Cold War led to discussions of human security as a peace dividend (UNDP 1994), but more recent political and economic tensions have prompted WID and GAD advocates to argue for a human security approach as an alternative to militarization. Behind the idea of human security is the need to develop effective policies to prepare women to survive and compete in increasingly marketized economies in an increasingly globalized world. It brings together the discourses of those who stress a rights-based approach to development with those who emphasize cultural pluralism and who argue that all women do not necessarily share the same interests and goals.

Transition, restructuring, and globalization have been accompanied by recurring economic crises that have not been adequately addressed. The neoliberal development model puts overwhelming stress on growth rather than equity and on markets rather than states. Although most who work on global financial and economic models omit gender issues, feminist critics have made some progress in bringing gender into the discussions of the UN's Millennium Development Goals, trade, and global public goods (see Cagatay et al. 1995). Gender budgets, labor policies in free trade zones, and transnational caring labor (such as the U.S. importation of nurses and the employment of immigrant women as household help) are among the issues being addressed (e.g., Ferber and Nelson 2003; see also Kardam 2004).

Another common theme is the role of women's movements. Women's organizations are both local and embedded in cross-national networks that provide support and resources to make local action more effective.[7] Women's growing access to political power, through gender quotas in some cases and through the appointment of women to top administrative positions, is a new resource that could be linked more closely to development programs and negotiate the growing tensions between gender equity and traditional laws and customs.

Persistent inequalities demand continuous reevaluation and daring experiments. The call for gender equity is fundamental and transformative, but the barriers to achieving this goal are formidable, as thirty years of efforts to promote women and gender in development illustrate only too often. Earlier rejection of efforts to "integrate women" met with bureaucratic resistance. The adoption of gender strategies was a victory at the level of policy but less reliably at the level of practices. In the 1990s, private investment greatly outpaced public capital flows, reducing the reach of gender equity policies, which can shape bureaucratic but not market behavior, and making macroeconomic policies the critical focus.

Today, we think the field that addresses women, gender, development, and globalization needs to renew and regroup. Efforts to reform bureaucratic practices and link them to women's self-empowerment must be accompanied by investing more attention in how to modify the regulatory and ideological contexts in which macroeconomic and trade policies are conceived and carried out. This will require new levels of interdisciplinary and cross-national cooperation and a sense of urgency. We think now is the time.

NOTES

1. The term "third wave" of democratization is from Samuel P. Huntington (1991). On the success of economic and political liberalization, see Fernandez-Armesto (2003).
2. For a defense of these policies, see Frum and Perle (2004). For a critique, see Dalder and Lindsay (2003).
3. A striking example is the Bush administration's call for 40 percent representation of women in the new Iraqi parliament. ("Iraqi Council to Debate Plan for Transition" 2004, 1). Women's representation is a means to avoid the potential institutionalization of a regime dominated by clerics and the adoption of sharia law, but it is likely to produce local resentment and may put women leaders in an untenable position; at this writing one American woman who was working on setting up women's centers has died. Cohn, Kinsella, and Gibbings (2004, 138) argue that the Security Council resolution on women's rights in Iraq may be seen as positive support for "women's rightful inclusion," but also a "tool to justify military occupation on behalf of 'liberating' women."
4. On the first, see Molyneux and Razavi (2003). On the capabilities approach, see Amartya Sen (1999) and Martha Nussbaum (2003). On human security, see UNDP 1997 and 1994; Commission on Human Security 2003; and Basch 2004.
5. There is an excellent and growing literature on institutions (see Jaquette and Staudt in this volume).
6. Because Irene Tinker has been so influential in shaping the field of women, gender, and development and because a full list of her publications hasn't appeared elsewhere, we list her complete works at the end of the bibliography.
7. Much has been written on local and global connections, but for a theoretically and empirically rich review, see Brysk (2000).

I. Institutional Opportunities and Barriers

Women, Gender, and Development

Jane S. Jaquette and Kathleen Staudt

By many measures, the field of women/gender and development (WID/GAD) is quite robust.[1] The UN Development Program (UNDP) and other UN agencies have made gender a focus of their development reviews. The World Bank (2001a), long noted for its resistance to gender issues, recently published *Engendering Development Through Gender Equality in Rights, Resources and Voice*, linking development to the broader context of women's rights, the explicit focus of a new volume edited by Maxine Molyneux and Shahra Razavi (2003). Economists Diane Elson (1995a, 2003), and Lourdes Benería (2003) use gender as a fulcrum to better understand and critique economic processes of globalization.

WID and GAD analyses have had an impact on development discourse and on the way aid is administered, but they have been less successful in making a material difference for the vast majority of women in developing countries.[2] Development is not mainly produced by the actions of donor agencies, of course. In the last decade, the direction of economic change has been vastly more affected by private capital flows, currency crises, privatization, and the pressure to adopt open markets and export-oriented growth than by public or private development assistance. Cuts in social spending have increased the burdens on women's labor. Declining incomes and higher male unemployment have pushed women into paid work. Women's labor is the key to export strategies based on free trade zones (FTZS). Market reforms have not generated the growth that the reformers promised. Inequalities are increasing, and the number of people living in poverty, a category disproportionately occupied by women and children, has been growing (see Benería 2003).

Yet donor agencies remain an important arena for addressing development issues and pursuing gender equity. Donors, not markets, engage in policy dialogues, take social criteria into account, and try to implement "participatory development." Bureaucracies are often thought of as resistant to change. In our experience, development agencies and NGOs actively seek new approaches, and advocates for women can take advantage of these openings. Growing discontent with "market fundamentalism" may also provide opportunities that those in the field should be prepared to pursue.

However, the field is divided, and advocates and scholars seem unable to move beyond the debates that were salient over a decade ago. In the thirty years since Ester Boserup published her classic study, *Woman's Role in Economic Development* (1970), two major approaches have dominated the field. The women in development (WID) model challenged the male bias in foreign assistance in the 1970s, and the gender and development (GAD) approach, which emerged in the late 1980s, put women and development in the context of gender power relations.

This essay reviews WID and GAD with two goals in mind. The first is historical. It is clear that both models reflected trends in feminist theory: WID drew on the liberal egalitarianism of "second wave" Northern feminism in the 1970s, and GAD responded to the rise of postcolonial feminism and the impressive growth of Third World women's movements in the 1980s. But the turn from WID to GAD in the late 1980s (and the addition of the "democracy agenda" by the 1990s) were also reactions to major shifts in the international system. In the 1960s and 70s, international development politics operated from Keynesian assumptions, which were being pushed to the left by dependency theory and the North/South dialogue. By the mid-1980s, supply side economics had displaced Keynesianism, and the neoliberal Washington Consensus remains the dominant view twenty years later. Economic "liberalization" was joined by policies to promote political "liberalization"—democracy—in the 1990s, after the fall of the Berlin Wall. Putting WID and GAD in this broader international context makes it possible to move away from seeing these two models as competing "truths" about how to approach women and development to understanding them as successive efforts to respond to—and influence—changing policy environments.

The second rationale for this essay is political. September 11 has changed the dynamics of the international system once again. It is our hope that reframing the WID/GAD debate may provoke creative thinking as the international system enters a new phase of rapid change that may push aside or distort women's agendas.

SHIFTS IN THE INTERNATIONAL SYSTEM: 1975–1990S

Since 1975, when women met in Mexico City for the first conference of what became the UN Decade for Women, the international system has undergone three significant shifts associated with, although not entirely caused by, changes in U.S. foreign policy.

In the 1970s, the United Nations General Assembly, following the logic of dependency theory, was calling for a New International Economic Order (NIEO) that would substantially redistribute resources from the wealthy North to the underdeveloped South. Under President Jimmy Carter (1976–80), the United States, defeated in Vietnam, tried to become a better global citizen. Carter negotiated the Panama Canal treaties, brokered the Camp David agreements, and argued that the United States should accept environmental limits to growth.

The election of Ronald Reagan (1980–88) reversed those trends. Carrying out a "monetarist" revolution that was thirty years in the making, the Reagan administration rejected the Keynesian consensus that had guided U.S. policy since the Depression. With strong support from British Prime Minister Margaret Thatcher, Reagan promoted open markets and opposed statism at home and abroad. Helped by the debt crisis, the neoliberal reformers cut a wide swath. The International Monetary Fund (IMF) began to condition its loans on the adoption of structural adjustment programs (SAPs), which reduced the role of the state, privatized assets, and opened up many of the world's economies to expanded foreign trade and investment (e.g., Kucynski and Williamson 2003; J. Richardson 2001).

In the early 1990s, the disintegration of the Soviet Union, the adoption of market reforms in the former Eastern bloc and their consolidation in China further buttressed the neoliberal model against those who had begun to document its human costs. Democratization created tensions between economic and political reforms. Those who lost jobs, social services, and economic opportunities as a result of government cutbacks and lowered tariff barriers expressed their discontent through the ballot box, but to little avail as presidents elected on platforms to resist IMF reforms often succumbed to international pressures once elected. The end of the Eastern bloc produced a single international finance and trade system, further reinforcing the market model.

The 1990s were also marked by new forms of resistance, including the Zapatista revolt in Chiapas, the rise of such populist leaders as Hugo Chavez in Latin America, the resistance of indigenous movements, and protests in Seattle, Cancun, and elsewhere against the World Trade Organization and other symbols of globalization. Criticism of the way the IMF handled the Asian currency crises indicated that the Consensus might be breaking down.

The United States had preponderant power in the 1990s but used it ambivalently. After the first Gulf war, U.S. interventions in the former Yugoslavia, Haiti, Somalia, and Kosovo were carried out under multilateral mandates but were not popular at home. The events of September 11, 2001, moved the United States from debating the costs and benefits of humanitarian interventions to preventive war. The invasion of Iraq undermined the Western alliance, weakened the United Nations, and likely increased the likelihood of terrorist attacks around the globe.

U.S. policy alone does not determine what happens in the international system. But changes in U.S. leadership have set the tone for international politics since World War II. Recent administrations have remained wedded to an economic model that is not only globalizing but hostile to the state, and there is no alternative in sight. Whether the international opposition to U.S. unilateralism will create space for challenges to U.S. leadership—and to economic orthodoxy—is possible, but not a likely outcome. Yet September 11 and the U.S. invasion of Iraq have unsettled the international system and may offer a new context for the development debate.

INTERNATIONAL WOMEN'S MOVEMENTS
AND THE UN CONFERENCES ON WOMEN

The foregoing brief history of international politics over the last thirty years ignores an important phenomenon: the dramatic rise of women's movements over these same three decades, which has given women greater voice and has increased their access to political power. In this period, women's movements have brought about unprecedented changes in women's roles and status. But the wave of women's empowerment may have reached its peak. It is clear that, without continued efforts to increase women's control over resources, current gains could be lost.

After the establishment of the United Nations at the close of World War II (sex was included among the forms of discrimination banned by its charter), a few women on the UN Commission on the Status of Women (CSW), led by Finnish feminist Helvi Sipila, worked within the UN to raise women's issues. In 1970, the CSW succeeded in getting the General Assembly to pass a resolution encouraging "full integration of women in the total development effort" (Tinker 1990b, 29). In 1972 the General Assembly declared 1975 International Women's Year (IWY), and in 1974 it approved a conference on women, to take place in Mexico City in 1975.[3]

Most CSW efforts had focused on improving women's legal status. But in the 1960s and 70s, the UN General Assembly was gripped by the issue of development. Its deliberations were strongly influenced by dependency theory, the view that the South was not merely undeveloped but had been exploited by the North through decades, even centuries, of unequal trade. Declaring the 1970s the Second Development Decade, the General Assembly called for transfers of capital and technology from North to South and the stabilization of the prices of primary products, which comprised the bulk of Third World exports.

In June 1975, just prior to the Mexico City conference, the American Association for the Advancement of Science brought together 95 women and men from 55 countries to discuss women and development. The seminar focused on the lack of reliable data on women's economic participation. It "naively assumed," as organizer Irene Tinker later wrote, "that correcting the biases of data concerning women's work and exposing the constraints on women's education and credit would automatically solve many [gender] inequalities as planners incorporated the new data and insights into their programming" (Tinker 1990a, 5).

Efforts to put women on the development agenda in the 1970s coincided with the recognition on the part of many donors that their programs had not "trickled down" to the poor. Under the leadership of Robert McNamara (1968–81), the World Bank adopted Basic Human Needs as a priority.[4] Although the Bank remained firmly in the hands of economists, anthropologists and other social scientists joined its and other donor staffs, providing a more sympathetic audience to those concerned about sex discrimination. Private philanthropic institutions like the Ford Foundation (Flora 1982) joined the Rockefeller Foundation (long known for its health and population programs) as significant players in the emerging "development community." Several UN agencies as well as European and Canadian bilateral donors began to give serious attention to poverty and to women's status (as it was then called) as related development issues.

As each delegation presented an analysis of the status of women in their country, pulling together basic demographic data, statistics on women's health, in-

come, labor force participation, education and, where available, political participation, the socialist countries made impressive showings. This reinforced those
who argued—much more persuasively in the 1970s than is remembered today—
that socialist revolution was a prerequisite to making real advances in equality
for women.

The Mexico "Plan of Action" called upon governments, the private sector,
and UN agencies to take specific actions to remedy "sex" disparities. It focused
on women's legal rights and economic disadvantages, but skirted the issue of political representation, which was not surprising given that the majority of the
delegations represented countries under authoritarian rule. The process of preparing for the conference had the unintended effect of raising political awareness
of women's issues in many countries and provided an excuse for women to meet,
sowing the seeds for a subsequent wave of women's organizing.[5] Those from the
North who attended the official meeting and the parallel NGO Tribune in Mexico
City expected to focus on feminist issues. However, the official debates soon revealed deep divisions between North and South. U.S. feminists who attended the
Tribune looked forward to a spirit of global sisterhood, but soon learned that
most Third World women rejected "feminism" as hostile to men and believed
that economic exploitation by the North, not patriarchy, was the major cause of
women's oppression.

After IWY the General Assembly declared 1975–85 the Decade for Women.
Women's movements grew exponentially, organizing to address issues from human rights and the environment to day care, health, and reproductive rights.
Some groups were organized by donor agencies as a means to extend credit and
training more effectively, while local self-help organizations proliferated to provide safety nets for those pushed further into poverty by the economic crises of
the 1980s. Over the Decade (1975–85), as assumptions about international feminist solidarity were questioned, the issue of violence against women emerged as a
shared concern that could bring women together across national, class, and cultural divides.

The Mid-Decade Conference in 1980, hastily switched to Copenhagen from
Teheran after the Iranian revolution in 1979, was highly politicized.[6] By contrast, the End of the Decade meeting in Nairobi in 1985 was relatively harmonious and, at U.S. insistence, the language of the final document was decided by
consensus. Whether the spirit of cooperation in Nairobi was due to the maturity of the international women's movement or to the strong-arm tactics of the

Reagan and Thatcher administrations (which had buried the "North/South dialogue")—or both—is hard to judge. What is clear is that the Decade was a spur to women's organizing and helped create transnational networks of women's groups. Women's organizations used the commitments their governments made in Mexico City, Copenhagen, and Nairobi to lobby for more egalitarian legislation at home. By the 1990s, most of the world's governments (but not the United States) had ratified the 1979 Convention on the Elimination of All Forms of Discrimination Against Women (CEDAW).[7]

THE PERCY AMENDMENT AND THE WID OFFICE IN USAID

After Mexico City, "women in development" was quickly adopted as a goal by many national governments and foreign assistance agencies. As Lucille Mair, secretary-general of the 1980 Mid-Decade conference, put it, women came to be seen as "a missing link in development . . . half of a nation's resources that could no longer be wasted" (quoted in Tinker 1990b, 31). In the United States, Congress had passed an amendment to the Foreign Assistance Act in 1973 calling for the establishment of an Office of Women in Development in the U.S. Agency for International Development (USAID), and encouraged other donors to "give specific attention" to women (Kardam 1997a; Staudt 1985). The timing was important. The Percy Amendment (named after the senator who carried the bill in Congress) passed at the height of a wave of feminist legislative reform in the United States, the year the Supreme Court legalized abortion. Antifeminist backlash soon followed (e.g., Faludi 1991), which succeeded in preventing the ratification of the Equal Rights Amendment (ERA) and, some have argued, created a constituency of "angry white men" that is still having an impact on U.S. politics three decades later.

But the mood in 1976 was progressive. Jimmy Carter was elected in the wake of the Watergate scandal that had forced President Nixon out of office. Carter's campaign took the moral high road, suggesting that the United States was now willing to accept some responsibility for the mistakes of the Vietnam War and to stop giving unquestioned support to anticommunist dictators. President Carter became actively engaged in the North/South dialogue and issued a report recognizing environmental limits to growth. He gave Pat Derian, the female head of the State Department's new human rights office, substantial leeway to criticize human rights violations in countries such as Argentina and Chile, which had been staunch Cold War allies of the United States.

Carter appointed Arvonne Fraser to head the WID Office at USAID (AID/ WID).[8] Fraser, who had chaired Carter's Midwestern campaign, hired an activist-academic as her deputy, incorporated academic researchers into her policy team, and commissioned research that could be translated into WID initiatives. Her connections with grassroots women's groups and her political network in Washington helped her move WID higher up on USAID's agenda. The Percy Amendment lacked specific guidance on how its mandate should be carried out. Many in USAID were sympathetic to doing "something" about women, but others resisted, ridiculing advocates as "women's libbers" and labeling WID a "culturally inappropriate" policy that would damage USAID's credibility.[9] Many men, perhaps uncomfortable with the changes feminists were calling for at home, resisted thinking about development abroad in gender terms (Staudt 1985).

In this environment, a simplified version of Ester Boserup's thesis in *Woman's Role in Economic Development* became a useful tool for WID advocates. In the 1970s, fearing the "population bomb" and the possibility of famine, USAID was oriented toward agricultural development. Boserup's view that African agriculture was based on a "female farming system" drew attention to women's roles in agricultural production. It soon became clear that the methods used by governments and the United Nations to measure women's labor force participation, particularly in agriculture, were woefully inadequate. Women were seen as wives and mothers, but not farmers.

Boserup's analysis of the gendered impact of colonialism in Africa—that cash cropping and technology transfer to men had disturbed earlier patterns of male/ female complementarity in food production and household management—made it possible to argue that colonialism, not African tradition or inexorable market forces, had disadvantaged women. In the West, and in the minds of most men working at USAID, progress meant increasing the "family wage" of the male household head, who was supposed to take care of his dependent wife (or wives) and children.[10] In many parts of Africa, however, women remained obliged to meet specific household expenses, including children's schooling, but those responsibilities were not taken into account in programs designed to increase agricultural production. Armed with Boserup's thesis, WID advocates could argue that programs that directed resources to women, including training and agricultural inputs, would improve food production, family welfare, and women's equity—without violating cultural norms.[11] The WID Office also looked at urban women and the problem of women-headed households (Buvinic and Youssef

1978), estimated to be as many as one-third of households worldwide. Income generation projects were developed to increase women's economic independence and ameliorate poverty.

By 1980, the WID Office could show some successes (see Staudt 1985), but the WID approach was beginning to draw serious criticism. Lourdes Benería and Gita Sen (1981) criticized WID as a Band-aid treating the symptom (women's poverty) but not the illness (capitalist development). Dependency theorists focused on the lack of attention to women's unpaid labor (e.g., Kabeer 1994, 49), which was often increased by development projects that seemed to assume women had free time. Canadian scholar Adele Mueller argued that WID turned women into "clients," removing them "from active and authentic participation in public life." In her view, WID supported a development discourse that amounted to a "strategy for producing and maintaining First World dominance in the capitalist world order,"[12] although Mueller conceded that feminist reform within aid bureaucracies was the only way for women to gain access to "even a small portion of the millions of dollars which circulate from the First to the Third World" (1986, 36, 38).

WID did open up a new debate over how resources should be allocated at a time when foreign assistance played a greater role in international capital flows than is the case today. The development model of the 1970s was still based on Keynesian assumptions and concerned about "growth with equity." Many, including many women in developing countries, saw socialism as a viable alternative development model, so it is not surprising that WID advocates were faulted for failing to question capitalism. But in hindsight this seems quixotic; if those who worked in donor agencies had frontally attacked the "capitalist model," WID would have failed before it was tried. In the 1970s, the debate was between Keynesian "liberals" and Marxist and dependency "radicals." Few imagined that the paradigm would shift so radically, and that those concerned with women and development would soon become absorbed by efforts to cushion the effects of structural adjustment on the poor and marginalized, especially women and children.[13]

As Marxist revolutionary rhetoric receded over the course of the 1980s, critics of WID turned to postmodernism to frame their concerns (e.g., Marchand and Parpart 1995). As Lucille Mair put it, although "Women and Development" had become "the Decade's overnight catchphrase," it evaded "the question of what kind of development women were to be drawn into" (quoted in Tinker 1990b, 31).

THE 1980S: REAGAN, THATCHER, AND THE
"SUPPLY SIDE" APPROACH TO DEVELOPMENT

The U.S. elections in 1980 were a stunning defeat for Jimmy Carter who, in the view of the victorious Reagan administration, had "lost" Afghanistan, Iran, and Nicaragua to a Soviet bloc bent on expansion. President Reagan was convinced the United States should reassert its strategic power. He found a ready ally in Britain's Margaret Thatcher.

The Reagan administration's foreign policy was also influenced by those in the United States who were hostile to the United Nations, skeptical of the NIEO, and critical of arguments for "concessions" to the South. The rapid expansion of UN membership to include the "newly emerging nations" had produced vocal Third World caucuses in the General Assembly, including the Group of 77 and the Non-Aligned Movement. With the cooperation of the Eastern bloc, and with the countries of western Europe often abstaining, the United States was increasingly isolated (Jaquette 1995).

In response, the United States withdrew from UNESCO and stopped fully paying its UN dues. Recounting his experiences at the United Nations, Daniel Patrick Moynihan, a Democrat who served as U.S. Ambassador to the United Nations in the 1970s, argued that underdevelopment should be blamed on the misguided, "Fabian socialist" policies of Third World leaders (Moynihan 1975a). Reagan was elected by a large margin in 1980 and felt he had a mandate to change foreign policy. His administration got tough with the Soviets, denied that the North was responsible in any way for the economic weakness of the economies of the South, and dismissed Carter's concern for environmental limits to growth as too pessimistic. Responding to the religious right, which had mobilized against the legalization of abortion and to defeat the ERA, Reagan stopped U.S. funding for international population programs. The United States, which had earlier pushed population control without attending to women's choices, now attacked China for its "coercive" one child policy.

In this changed environment, the WID Office in USAID took a much lower profile and concentrated on internal training and supported microenterprise projects, in keeping with the new emphasis on market-based development. Leadership on WID issues began to shift to other institutions, including the Canadian and Northern European bilateral aid agencies, UN agencies, private foundations, and NGOs.

The debt crisis and the emerging Washington Consensus provided the opening for international financial institutions to impose structural adjustment reforms. In conventional economic terms, SAPs were justifiable. Government regulations, inefficient state ownership of enterprises, high external deficits, and runaway inflation had distorted investment decisions and, along with high tariffs and opportunities for rent-seeking provided by the state's overinvolvement in the economy, could plausibly be cited as causes of low growth and high prices to consumers. The structural adjustment "cure" called for cutting tariffs and lowering barriers to foreign capital, controlling inflation by reducing government spending, and privatizing state-owned enterprises. High growth rates in the export-promoting Asian "tigers" (Taiwan, South Korea, Hong Kong, and Singapore) and Chile's adoption of an open, market-based economy under Augusto Pinochet were cited to prove that the model worked.

In many countries, however, the implementation of structural adjustment policies had devastating social consequences, hitting the middle class and the poor (e.g., Bakker 1994) as well as small and medium local enterprises, which were unable to compete. Unemployment rose, government services were severely cut back, and price controls, which many governments had used to keep down the cost of basic goods and services, were phased out. In Latin America, where SAPs were widely adopted, incomes fell for most of the "Lost Decade" of the 1980s. But these reforms did not produce sustained growth, and the gap between rich and poor world wide grew larger.

As Lourdes Benería pointed out, women were the first to feel the effects of these policies and women's organizations were the first to "make the connections between global development and everyday life"(quoted in Lind 1997, 1206). In Latin America, women were increasingly pushed into the labor force, often taking part-time and marginal jobs and in some cases driving even lower class, less skilled men further down the employment ladder or into joblessness. Women (and men) moved into the informal sector and into homework, that is, industrial piecework done at home. In some countries, women organized neighborhood self-help organizations, including communal kitchens and consumer boycott groups (Lind 1997; Jaquette 1989). Although donors began to provide safety nets to counteract the social costs of structural adjustment (Elson 1995a; Aslanbeigui et al. 1994; Cagatay et al. 1995; Datta and Kornberg 2002), the earlier notion of assisting women in development was replaced by fears of the feminization of poverty. The fact that structural adjustment took place in a strongly pro-market, antistate environment was critical, postponing needed reforms in state capacity and preempting all arguments for redistributional policies (Jaquette 2003). The positive role of the state in the Asian development experience was ignored. Government spending cuts, which were justified to reduce the state's role in economic production, to reduce the opportunities for corruption, and to control inflation, required disinvesting in education and health, with long-term implications for income distribution, competitiveness, and the quality of life.[14]

THE GAD CRITIQUE AND THE EMERGENCE OF A NEW MODEL

At the end of the 1980s, a new "gender and development" (GAD) model emerged. Arguing that WID had been ineffective in improving women's material conditions and that it was insensitive to the differences among women, GAD advocates suggested an innovative approach that would take account of women's diversity (Prügl and Meyer 1999, 6) and confront the gender power relations that were holding women back.

Carolyn Moser's "Gender Planning in the Third World" (1988? and 1989a) is widely cited as foundational to the GAD approach. Moser acknowledged that WID had brought about a progressive shift in development thinking, which no longer viewed women solely as mothers. But, she noted, under WID, AID had treated women as an untapped resource in development, ignoring their triple burden of reproductive, productive, and community work. Moser called for a deeper analysis based on gender, that is, on an understanding that women's and men's roles are socially constructed, not biologically determined. Because gender constructions vary by culture, GAD would be able to respond to the differences among women rather than seeing them as a homogeneous group.

Moser cited Mayra Buvinic's observation that donor policies had moved from an emphasis on growth (from which women had been largely excluded), to equity (following Boserup's implicit "affirmative action" argument), to antipoverty as SAPs took hold. In Buvinic's view, however, donors had never given more than lip service to equality; she believed antipoverty projects were more readily adopted because they were less threatening (see Kabeer 1994, 7; Jackson 1998). Moser suggested that bureaucratic resistance had kept women's projects small and focused on training in "activities traditionally undertaken by women"(1988, 28–29). Labeling WID's emphasis "home economics," she argued that it did not recognize "women's productive role" or their "practical gender need" to earn an income (13).[15]

Moser then outlined a new GAD approach intended to challenge gender roles in several ways: by training women in "male" skills, changing zoning regulations to allow household enterprises, ensuring women's ownership rights to land and housing, and providing child care and transport facilities suited to the demands made on women. On macroeconomic issues, Moser questioned UNICEF's claim to be doing "structural adjustment with a human face" by asking whether any international agency in the neoliberal environment could possibly implement policies that would "increase the independence of women" (33).

As the GAD critique gained adherents, its proponents increasingly treated WID as the problem. The WID model was dismissed as too women-specific and welfarist to make a difference. Negative assessments of WID became common in the mainstream development literature. To cite two typical examples, John Brohman's text *Popular Development* labels WID efforts as "Western-style reformist measures that obviated the need for more radical structural change" (1996, 283), and a recent study of women in Latin America and Asia concludes that GAD was an improvement over WID because it went beyond "document[ing] the negative impacts of economic development on women" to addressing "the dynamics and structures of gender relations" (Smith, Hünefeldt et al. 2004).

But this binary comparison distorts the WID model and exaggerates the possibilities for radical feminist and anticapitalist outcomes. Like GAD, WID made women's economic empowerment a priority and was not convinced by those who argued that WID was unnecessary because existing health, education, and population programs were already reaching women. WID advocates maintained that health and population programs did not look at the consequences of women's *economic* marginalization (e.g., Blumberg 1995). Boserup did not construct women as "hapless victims," as some have argued (e.g., Parpart 1995), but portrayed them as independent economic actors within a decaying but once viable system of complementarity, and she emphasized their capacity to enter into market activities. When GAD advocates attacked population programs as "the WID approach," they ignored the fact that WID advocates in USAID and elsewhere were highly critical of existing population programs for manipulating women's choices and for ignoring the many economic, social, and political factors that made it difficult for women to control their own fertility (e.g., Jaquette and Staudt 1985; Helzner and Shepard 1997).[16]

In the late 1970s, the WID Office fought for sex-disaggregated data at the micro and macro levels, funding an analysis of national censuses to track changes in women's status since the 1950s and calling for project evaluations that would distinguish their differential impacts on men and women.[17] The statistical office at the UN eventually developed more sophisticated measures of gender differences (the GDI and GEM indexes) that directly measure male/female differentials, but the intent to draw attention to gender inequities in order to influence policy was behind both efforts.[18] Despite the current tendency among critics of development to dismiss quantitative data as part of a larger, modernist hegemony in development studies (e.g., Brohman 1996; Escobar 1995), we firmly believe that such indexes and sex -differentiated project data remain critical policy tools.

The WID Office also sponsored a series of "country studies," using household time budgets and anthropological methods to get a fuller picture of women's lives. These showed that women worked longer hours than men, often spending a substantial part of their workday gathering firewood and carrying water. This led to projects to introduce intermediate technologies, such as more efficient cookstoves and water pumps, which did not directly challenge definitions of women's work but, when successful, did increase women's access to an important resource: time.

In the 1970s, AID/WID consciously tried to come in below the radar, offering programs that provided economic benefits for women without setting off a cultural backlash in the host country. The WID Office did not fund projects that emphasized "consciousness-raising" in order to avoid the charge that it was promoting Western-style feminism. Its emphasis on economic rather than political participation made sense in the 1970s and early 1980s when a majority of the world's states were controlled by authoritarian governments. New opportunities presented themselves as local women's movements grew in numbers and visibility and came to be perceived as an important component of civil societies resisting authoritarianism during the 1980s.

The WID approach had been conceived in terms of reaching women who lived in households and were constrained by cultural norms and responsibilities. The rapid growth of women's grassroots organizations during the 1980s made it possible to reach women through women's groups and to call openly for empowerment, allowing GAD to build on a growing organizational capacity among Third World women. This suggested new possibilities for dialogue and partnering. Moser cited a statement by DAWN (Development Alternatives With Women for a New Era), a transnational group of Southern activists and researchers organized prior to the Nairobi conference, as setting the goal for future cooperation:

"We want a world where basic needs become basic rights and where poverty and all forms of violence are eliminated. . . . Meeting the basic rights of the poor and transforming the institutions that subordinate women are inextricably linked" and can be "achieved through the self-empowerment of women."[19]

GAD pushed to broaden WID's horizons while pressing for greater bureaucratic leverage. Because women's projects had been "ghettoized" in specialized WID offices, GAD advocates called for "mainstreaming" to integrate gender into all development projects and programs.[20] Ironically, given GAD's emphasis on gender structures of power, Moser argued that GAD would provoke *less* resistance among bureaucrats in donor agencies.[21] Using Maxine Molyneux's (1985) conceptual distinction between strategic and practical gender interests (that *strategic* needs arise from "an analysis of women's subordination to men" whereas *practical* gender needs are those derived "from the concrete conditions women experience"), Moser observed that it was not necessary for all projects to address "strategic" issues. GAD could thus "diffuse" the "hostile and negative" reactions to feminism (1988, 10) that WID's demands for equality had provoked among women as well as men in donor bureaucracies. GAD's participatory "empowerment" approach meant that Third World women themselves would choose whether and how to make their "practical" needs "strategic."[22]

GAD built on WID's successes and learned from WID's failures. Mainstreaming could be tried because WID had been the entering wedge into bureaucratic discourses and practices. Mainstreaming might dismiss women-specific projects as too narrowly conceived but, in the end, GAD needed women-only programs for the same reasons WID did: because women often could not attend meetings where men were present, because women have different work schedules from men, or because women's leadership is more readily nurtured in women-specific projects than in mixed groups. A recent review of mainstreaming argues that women-only projects are "still widely and profoundly, if not universally, necessary"(Chant and Guttman 2000, 43).

If GAD was not that different from WID in practice, why did GAD supporters insist so passionately that it was? One explanation is the way bureaucracies work. By portraying GAD as a new, coherent alternative that could correct the defects of WID, GAD supporters could gain traction in bureaucracies suffering from "WID fatigue." GAD advocates were sought after by donor agencies. Moser took a position in the World Bank, and Eva Rathgaber, a fellow architect of GAD, was named head of the Gender Section of the Canadian International Development Agency

(CIDA) and then of its regional office in Africa. GAD gave non-U.S. donors the opportunity to move into the space left by a now cautious AID/WID and allowed them (and Southern project recipients) to distance themselves from USAID.

GAD's emphasis on "bringing men back in" provided not only a bureaucratic strategy but a new analytical focus. Instead of talking just about women as a uniform category, GAD emphasized the differences among women and drew attention to gender conflict. As issues of violence against women became more salient for women's movements worldwide, for example, GAD advocates pointed out that improving women's access to resources in an environment where men are losing jobs and status creates male resentment and, in some cases, violence. Some projects tried to address this by increasing women's and men's productivity in tandem.[23]

THE 1990S: THE NEW INTERNATIONAL CONTEXT

The 1990s created an unanticipated unipolar world. The first President Bush (1988–92) organized a broad coalition, under the auspices of the United Nations, to force Saddam Hussein to relinquish Kuwait. Victory in Iraq did not guarantee his reelection, however. Bill Clinton tried to position himself as part of a "Third Way," joining Tony Blair and Gerhard Schroeder as a group of young leaders seeking a more socially responsible capitalism (J. Richardson 2001, 192–200). Despite his doubts, Clinton eventually supported the North American Free Trade Agreement (NAFTA) and worked with the UN and NATO, engaging in "humanitarian" interventions in the former Yugoslavia, Haiti, Somalia, and Kosovo, although not Rwanda (Halberstam 2001). He restored funding to international family planning programs.

The global context of foreign assistance was also shifting once again. As GAD advocates worked to "get the institutions right," as Anne Marie Goetz (1997a) put it, the international system was moving further away from state-led development. Public capital flows were strongly outpaced by private capital, except for the poorest countries. Short-term private investment flows into emerging markets in Eastern Europe, Russia, Latin America, and Southeast Asia produced a new round of crises due to capital volatility. Democratization gave some donors, including USAID, new direction, shifting resources from economic growth to political institution-building and support for civil society (Carothers 1999; Lewis and Wallace 2000).

In the 1990s, women's international networks showed they could effectively influence the outcomes of UN conferences. The environment became the organizational focus of NGOs like WEDO (Women's Environment and Development Organization) which helped coordinate NGO strategies at the Earth Summit in Rio in 1992 and the UN International Conference on Population and Development ICPD in Cairo in 1994 (Higer 1999, 134). In Cairo, the international women's health movement—which had been in the making since the 1960s when heavy-handed U.S. population control policies had provoked feminist as well as nationalist resistance—came into its own, the result of an effective women's caucus, greater feminist representation on national delegations, and more lenient accreditation rules for NGOs attending UN meetings. Cairo dealt with controversial issues such as abortion, female circumcision, and violence against women (Higer 1999, 136–38; Stienstra 2000) and put women's fertility choices in a larger context, including women's access to education and credit.

Women also made important gains at the 1993 UN Conference on Human Rights in Vienna. The conflict in Bosnia made it easier for the international community to accept that rape was a "weapon of war" and toward accepting the view that "women's rights are human rights." In 1993, the General Assembly adopted a Declaration against Violence Against Women by a unanimous vote. UNIFEM, which had resisted adding women's rights to its programs throughout the 1980s, began to treat violence against women as a development issue (Joachim 1999, 152–57).

The conferences on environment, human rights, and population were major advances in progressive international norm-setting and proved that women's movements could work cross-nationally within the UN context (Meyer and Prügl 1999). But there were signs that the progressive phase of women's international organizing might have peaked; successes in Vienna and Cairo came under attack from the left and the right. Amy Higer points out that the victories of the "pragmatists" in Cairo (who succeeded in getting their feminist approach to reproductive health adopted) deepened divisions between them and the "outsiders" who wanted to put the population issue in a different global frame: "By not pushing on debt relief issues . . . they risked having alienated the very movement they claimed to represent" (Higer 1999, 139). Among human rights activists there was a similar split between those who saw human rights in individual and political terms and those who believed that human rights should include economic and social rights.

More ominously, in Cairo there were early signs of a growing conservative backlash that gained greater strength at the Fourth World Conference on

Women in Beijing in 1995. The Vatican, backed by some Middle Eastern and Latin American countries, contested the word "gender" everywhere it appeared in the Beijing Platform of Action. Conservatives challenged the idea that sex roles are "constructed," calling the concept of "gender" an attack on traditional, heterosexual definitions of the family. Feeling they had lost the battle in Cairo, conservative groups came better prepared to Beijing, claiming that feminist NGOs had distorted the draft platform, that heterosexuality was determined by nature and supported by religious belief, and that feminism was an "ideology" that most women did not share, even in the West. After Beijing, many feared that future global conferences might reverse the feminist advances already made (e.g., Eccher 1999). Concerns about backlash affected planning for Beijing+5 and Beijing+10 activities.

In this more conservative environment, many felt GAD offered a way to extend the life of the dependency and socialist critiques of capitalism that had become difficult to sustain in the neoliberal policy climate. But GAD advocates did not push an anticapitalist agenda for the same reasons that WID advocates had not done so. Like WID, GAD was funded by donor agencies in states committed to liberal capitalism. During the 1990s, as persistently low growth rates and increasing inequalities made the promises of neoliberalism appear to ring hollow, GAD was no better equipped than WID to counter the neoliberal agenda. Increasingly anticapitalist critics, male and female, found a platform in antiglobalization movements. Grassroots women are taking significant roles on the local level in these movements (see "Women's Movements in the Globalizing World" in this book), but women's issues have been marginalized and women's movements are not seen as important social actors in the push for radical change (see Eschle 2003).

The emphasis on participation and empowerment brought out the conflicts between multiculturalism and projects promoting gender equality. Some theorists have defended universal norms (e.g., Nussbaum 1999; Ackerley and Okin 1999; Phillips 2002) against the view that they represent Western cultural hegemony. Ironically, GAD's postmodern embrace of "difference" may have weakened its ability to rebut cultural defenses of gender discrimination. As Elisabeth Prügl and Mary K. Meyer point out, "gender" has resulted in "a proliferation of descriptions of women's local experiences" and "gender feminisms in diverse contexts," bringing about a "retreat from claims to commonality, including those of common oppression . . ." (1999, 6).

In the 1990s, feminist international relations theorists challenged IR realist orthodoxy (e.g., Sylvester 1998; Zalewski 1993). One approach broadened the narrow military definition of security to include issues like environmental and economic security and security against torture and gender violence (e.g., Tickner 1992). Amartya Sen and Martha Nussbaum put women at the center of their "capabilities" approach to development, drawing attention to the devastating impact of inequalities on the life chances of individuals (Nussbaum 2000; A. Sen 1992, 1999). DAWN continued to contest top-down development while feminist economists critiqued the masculinist assumptions of neoclassical economics (e.g., Folbre 2001a) and structural adjustment (Cagatay et al. 2000). Others documented the continuing exploitation of, and resistance by, women workers in export production and in the international trafficking of prostitutes and domestic workers (e.g., V. Peterson and Runyan 1999; Rowbotham and Mittner 1994; Marchand and Runyan 2000; Enloe 2000; Ehrenreich and Hochschild 2003). Social development advocates promoted "development with a human face" (see Green 2002). "Fair trade" advocates contested the value of "free" trade.

But for many, GAD, like WID before it, has become part of the policy status quo. And sadly, women's organizations (and other groups in "civil society") have been criticized as enablers of neoliberal policies, for example by providing social services that reduce the state's responsibility and make it more "efficient." Whatever their achievements, critics claim, women are deluding themselves into thinking they are empowered when in fact they are co-opted.

DEMOCRATIZATION, CIVIL SOCIETY, AND GLOBALIZATION

As more countries made the transition from authoritarianism to democracy, the United States and other donors put greater emphasis on electoral assistance, legal reform, and strengthening civil society. Women's organizations were an integral part of this strategy (see Carothers 1999). UN agencies were also deeply involved in democratization efforts, particularly in postconflict situations ranging from Guatemala and El Salvador to Bosnia and Cambodia. The rise of women's organizations in authoritarian states showed that civil society could emerge in hostile settings in ways that appeared to reinforce progressive ideals: women's organizations were participatory, lacking internal hierarchies, with commitments to goals beyond the narrow economic concerns ascribed to interest groups in capitalist democracies.

Democratization provided a new rationale for directing resources to women: women's groups could help promote political development by their active participation, making political parties more representative and governments more accountable. Women's organizations also gained international recognition as civil peacemakers, although they were rarely given a place at the table when it came time to negotiate. In Africa, research suggested that, in some cases, women's groups had succeeded in working around the dysfunctional politics of ethnic patronage that had crippled many African states (e.g., Tripp 2000a).

Not all donors and lenders equated "good governance" with deepening democracy, however. For the World Bank and International Monetary Fund, good governance meant limited social spending and reduced regulations on private capital, whether internal or foreign, policies many democratic electorates have balked at (e.g., Chua 2003). On the other side, not all civil society movements have been willing to work within the neoliberal frame. On January 1, 1994, the NAFTA agreement came into force, and on the same day, the Zapatista rebellion began in Chiapas. The Zapatistas attacked the neoliberal rationale for NAFTA, which required privatizing communally held *ejido* lands in order to marketize agricultural production. The plight of the people of Chiapas provided a dramatic illustration of the injustices—material and cultural—of unfettered capitalism.

In 1999, in Seattle, groups from around the world came together to protest globalization, including the growing power of multinational corporations, sweatshop labor, the loss of the local (jobs and indigenous traditions), large-scale infrastructure projects, disregard for the environment, and the damage caused by unregulated international capital flows. Although the protests in Seattle, Genoa, Cancun, and elsewhere could not have happened without another form of globalization—the Internet—and although the protesters did not agree on what the problems were or what their goals should be, the movement attracted those who saw antiglobalization as the most promising path of resistance to policies that had been set in Northern and Southern capitals but that were rejected by most of the people affected by them.

The 1990s also brought a new generation of development critics. Arturo Escobar (1995) labeled the antipoverty perspective a "sociological invention" that made it easier for the Northern donor bureaucracies to expand their grip (32). He criticized the sustainability discourse, arguing that behind the "we" of sustainability were the "Western scientist[s] and manager[s]" who had predicted environmental catastrophe in the 1970s (193). John Brohman criticized development for its "grand theories and ethnocentric biases" and called for multidisciplinary approaches with more attention to the "subjective realm" and less to quantitative data (1996, 324–27). In Brohman's view, aid must be "uncoupled" from the foreign policies of donor states (254).

Jude Howell and Jenny Pearce directly criticized the policy of "developing" civil society, noting that the rubric was convenient for donors because it seemed to address problems of development "outside the state" (thus fitting neoliberalism's antistate bias) while suggesting activities that could be "fashion[ed] into fundable programs" (2001, 6). Howell and Pearce were particularly impatient with the U.S. democracy agenda for taking a narrow, "Toquevillean" approach that defined civil society and markets as "similar realms of individual freedom" and allowed the United States to tie its funding for civil society groups to their support for the U.S. economic agenda. Like Escobar and Brohman, Howell and Pearce prescribe "popular development" and conclude that NGOs "need support in developing their own agendas" and not "in implementing those of external donors"(223).

BEYOND GAD?

The international context matters. During the course of the last thirty years, shifts in the international system opened new opportunities and created new challenges to addressing the strategic and practical interests of women. Liberal egalitarian feminism and a generally Keynesian developmental model opened the door to WID in the 1970s; the debt crisis and the conservative revolution of the 1980s produced SAPs, but also antifeminist backlash. Multiculturalism and the rise of women's organizations shaped a more culturally sensitive, participatory approach to foreign assistance but have made it difficult to make claims for women as a whole. Democratization expanded the development agenda and increased support for women's organizations, but civil society groups feared co-optation and were unable to mount a significant challenge to neoliberalism.

The international context is important, but feminist thinking matters as well. Over the past two decades, significant differences have emerged among feminists that have implications for development policies. Feminists are divided between egalitarian and "difference" feminists; between those who see substantial grounds for unity among women and those who think that cultural differences should outweigh any universal claims; between those who insist on autonomy and those who think that change will require working with and within the state; between those who support "radical change" and those who are working to "get the institutions right." Socialist feminists have assumed a low profile, and critique is privileged over action among postmodern feminists. Many feminists reject globalization on the grounds that it is attacking national and local economies that are otherwise viable; others see it as a process that must be managed because it cannot be derailed.[24]

As the new century began, there were signs that GAD was losing momentum. Mainstreaming had not redirected a significantly greater proportion of development assistance to women, and GAD criteria were not fully internalized by donor agency management and staff.[25] Empowerment did not have the radicalizing effects its advocates had hoped for. As Jane Parpart recently pointed out, "when people talk about women's empowerment, they use the word *power* in a nonthreatening, almost romantic way," and almost always in local, not global terms (Staudt et al. 2001, 1253). The location and scale of GAD empowerment initiatives diffused their impact while allowing advocates to avoid potentially divisive debates within donor bureaucracies. Donors (and scholars) often simply substituted the word "gender" for "women." Sometimes gendered approaches actually redistributed resources from women to men, despite the paltry spending on women. Finally, the shift from what Nancy Fraser (1998) called the "politics of redistribution" to the "politics of recognition" depoliticized economic disparities.

Some see deepening GAD as the solution. On one hand, Andrea Cornwall (2002) makes the troubling point that although scholars may make important distinctions as they try to grapple with gender and development, these are often lost in development practice, where "operational frameworks tend to treat women and men as if they constituted immediately identifiable groups" with conflicting interests. Men are generalized about as "powerful, shadowy figures who need to be contained," while women "are invariably the weaker party" (2002, 202–3). On the other hand, Deniz Kandiyoti (1998) calls the tendency to slip back into using the word "women" rather than "gender" evidence of a "tactical essentialism" and a form of "identity politics" that fails to "reveal how all forms of social hierarchy are ultimately gendered" (145–46).

Not all groups are pleased with the change from "women" to "gender." Rounaq Jahan (1995) observes that the term is not translatable into most languages (and we note that it did not have its present meaning in English until the 1980s). In Jahan's view, gender obscures rather than highlights the power disparities between men and women. An account of debates about gender at the Fourth Women's Conference in Beijing reported that some Third World women felt that

GAD emphasized "processes rather than results" and that gender was being used "to deny the very existence of women-specific disadvantage" (Baden and Goetz 1998, 38–39).

UNIFEM's *Beijing and Beyond* (1996), an institutional public relations report, painted a picture of progress on gender equity in the 1990s. It identified successful projects from women's banking and microcredit to women's rights, women refugees, women's health, and women's growing roles in political leadership; gave space to Third World voices, from DAWN to the Asian Indigenous Women's Network; and featured the views of women in leadership positions in UN agencies. But another UNIFEM report (Heyzer 1995), directed toward a narrower audience knowledgeable about the field, offered a more critical assessment of progress, emphasizing the negative effects on women of the globalization of trade and increases in intrastate conflict. An acerbic essay on mainstreaming in this collection (Longwe 1995) suggests that male bureaucratic resistance to integrating gender into development planning has not changed much from the early days of WID.

September 11 marks another shift in the international system. Although we do not yet know what the long-term implications of the "war on terror" will be, it seems clear that military power is again at the center of international politics, and this "war" is likely to have profound effects on domestic and international issues from civil liberties to migration. U.S. unilateralism has brought the future of multilateral institutions into question and is testing the limits of international law. The second Bush administration treats women's rights instrumentally, using accounts of women's oppression to demonize its enemies and portraying its desire to "liberate" women as evidence of its good intentions.

Perhaps the rift between the United States and most of its traditional Western allies will create a new opportunity to press for change as the "rest of the West" tries to distance itself from American policy. Howell and Pearce look to Europe for examples of strong states with strong civil societies, evidenced by the fact that Europeans are more committed than Americans to public goods and more tolerant of the taxes to pay for them. To date, however, these differences have not meant that European governments are ready to challenge the neoliberal model of development. We may need to look to the South to find alternative approaches.

If conflict is a prerequisite to change, the current turmoil in the international system could provide the impetus to link new ways of thinking about international politics to new ways of thinking about women and about development. Both WID and GAD succeeded in turning complex intellectual critiques into effective arguments for changing bureaucratic priorities and practices within donor agencies; both contributed to bringing women into development discourse and to shaping new international norms. This suggests that theory can affect practice.

Our essay does not develop new theory. But in what follows we try to sort out some of the elements that would be necessary to begin thinking systematically about how to regain momentum.

TOWARD A NEW DEVELOPMENT STRATEGY FOR WOMEN: ARENAS OF POWER

We identify four arenas of power that must be taken into account in any revitalized effort to address women's practical and strategic interests: bureaucracies (both donor and knowledge generating), markets, states, and civil societies. Cultures and families are also critical to how institutions function and how normative regimes are translated into daily life. We considered giving them separate attention, but opted instead to view them as permeating all other arenas. We do think, contrary to assumptions often made about them, that families and cultures are dynamic factors rather than "givens," capable of acting as agents, not merely objects, of change.

Bureaucracies

The WID and GAD models were largely designed to influence the behavior of public and private donor bureaucracies and UN agencies. Any new effort to work from within donor agencies to bring about change must first be institutionalized within those agencies. There are several excellent books on how donor institutions can be rethought and reformed, and it is not our intent to summarize them here (e.g., Goetz 1998; Staudt 1997, 1998; Miller and Razavi 1998b; Parpart et al. 2000; Rai 2003; Rao et al. 1999; Cockburn 1991). Insider analyses of rule making in the less transparent organizations of global economic governance are harder to come by but critical to forging a new approach.

We emphasize a few key issues. First, mainstreaming cannot fulfill its promise if it is not backed by real resources and incentives. GAD, like WID, was forced to rely on a combination of moral suasion and arguments based on economic efficiency, retreating to welfarist appeals when macroeconomic policies set women back and always underfunded. As Buvinic observed nearly twenty years ago, donor institutions easily brush aside demands for equity. Some development practitioners may make women and gender an ongoing part of their work because they have a personal stake (Goetz 2001, 9), but individual commitment does not add up to institutional change. Recent assessments (e.g., Chant and Gutmann 2000; Jahan 1995; Staudt 1998; see also "From 'Home Economics' to 'Micro-finance'" in this book) suggest that mainstreaming has been only halfheartedly implemented and that gender issues are still assigned low priority by most donor institutions. We believe that incentives—that is, promotions, salaries, and re-spect—are the only way to ensure that bureaucrats implement mainstreaming rather than merely giving it lip service. Mainstreaming should not become an excuse for eliminating WID or GAD focal points (Anderson 1991) that can moni-tor, train, apply research findings, and perform other necessary roles that are often lost in mainstreamed projects; mainstreaming that reinserts male prefer-ence undermines several decades of effort. For example, the Dutch government recently used mainstreaming as a rationale to cut off its funding to UNIFEM.

Bureaucracies are arenas in which to generate paper trails and reports, useful leverage to maintain pressure on recalcitrant institutions. For example, the UNDP regularly reports on the eight Millennium Development Goals and their progress toward achievement in its annual *Human Development Reports*. The third Millen-nium goal is "Promoting Gender Equality and Empowering Women" and UNDP reports are replete with gender-disaggregated data, charts, and figures (2002b, 16–33) that show where progress has been made and where more effort is needed.

WID and GAD largely succeeded through small-scale programs carried out by women's organizations and through microcredit projects. Many thought the em-phasis on participatory development would increase women's leverage. But, as Goetz observes, local participation does not necessarily support gender equity. In mixed groups, which are preferred under the mainstreaming model, women are involved in development programs "on male sufferance" (1997a, 189). Par-ticipatory development may actually silence women's voices, in part because of the way fieldworkers frame what they see, according to Cornwall (2002; see also White 1996).

Just as GAD tried to enlarge the scope of WID, going from women-specific projects to mainstreaming, we believe a new strategy must set its sights on larger issues. Even a "poverty" focus is too narrow, Maia Green argues, because an em-phasis on "narrow social categories" denies advocates access to the "central insti-tutional space" where policy is made (2002, 57). Strong ties between donors and women's organizations have meant working with women's groups at the project level rather than thinking systematically about what kinds of sectoral interventions might be worthwhile. In the late 1980s, the World Bank funded studies on gender differentials in primary and secondary education. These showed that a year of additional schooling for girls produced more support for the family than an additional year for boys at the same level—a finding that challenged the conventional wisdom not only of educators but of families making decisions about investing in their daughters (Herz and Sperling, 2004).

Whatever criticisms can be made on the implementation side (including the failure of international institutions to give adequate support to education while they were insisting that governments cut their budgets, and the lack of attention to gender biases in educational curricula), increased education for girls arguably empowered many more women than hundreds of individual projects.

Today, policies on trade and debt may matter more than those on aid, yet feminist analysts and activists have rarely taken them on (Liebowtiz 2002). Exceptions are those feminist economists who have challenged mainstream orthodoxy. But macroeconomic analysis cannot deal with the complexities of differences among women and the lack of sex-disaggregated data. Asking about the gender consequences of a given policy may raise consciousness but does not provide specific proposals for action. Feminists will need to engage in provocative thinking. One example is the suggestion of the "Tobin Tax" on currency transactions that can devastate nations overnight, and another the newer notion of the "Maria Tax" (Baxi 2004), which has an explicit gender agenda. If such taxes are authorized, who will administer their fruits? How likely is it that resources will trickle down to those who deserve them, men or women?

Designing ways to improve the conditions under which women work in FTZs, while avoiding using "labor standards" or bans on child labor as excuses for Northern protectionism, suggests one area worthy of a more focused attention, along with the criminal bases of human trafficking. Feminist revisions of macroeconomic models deserve a wider discussion. All such efforts should take advantage of the increasing number of women in political office in many countries, which might suggest alliances that could support greater independence from Northern donors and help groups improve local bureaucratic performance (Jaquette 1997; Krook 2003).

Universities are also bureaucracies of a specific kind: they are arenas for the generation of knowledge. Women and gender studies units have proliferated over the last three decades. But even with a female majority in U.S. universities, women and gender studies programs struggle with inadequate budgets and far-from-perfect mainstreaming (Wiegman 2002). The issues universities identify will affect the way development problems are framed, the expertise available to address them, and the energies and commitment of those who are engaged in them. Universities are important foci of any strategy for change, because they help shape the intellectual and action coalitions that can emerge in civil societies, both national and transnational. Scholarly work on globalization should automatically include gender, but this is still rarely the case.

Civil Societies

Civil society organizations have power to set agendas and create new expectations. Organizations do not have to change "the system" to change the world. Howell and Pearce compare civil societies that take a "problem solving approach" to produce "socially responsible capitalism" with those that are "critical of the global economy." They ask whether "the pursuit of commercial interest and gain is compatible with social and ethical responsibility to the wider society" (2001, 17). But we think pitting civil society against globalization and commercial interest against social responsibility misses the range of ways in which civil society can relate to the state and to markets. It implies that civil society cannot be both critical *and* constructive.

Civil society recipients of foreign assistance have been concerned about dependency and co-optation, and rightly so. But it is unrealistic to think that either private or public donors will begin to give away money with no strings attached, as Brohman, Escobar, and Howell and Pearce propose. GAD advocates should expand their interest in cultural construction to include politics, and draw attention to the many patterns of state and civil society interaction that exist in the world today. For example, what would be seen as "co-optation" by some women's groups in Latin America is viewed as "access" and even empowerment in various East Asian contexts, with important implications for NGO strategies and effectiveness.

More awareness of these differences might also make it easier to encompass those who work "inside" bureaucracies and political parties and those who remain "outside" within a single worldview, allowing women's organizations to be both independent and influential and to make governments more effective and accountable. In the end, the *self*-empowerment DAWN championed in the 1980s is the only real road to full autonomy for civil society organizations, but lack of local traditions of philanthropy, low rates of growth, and persistent class differences make it unlikely that we will see influential civil society organizations in the South that are fully independent. The process of "NGO-ization" (Alvarez 1999) is likely to continue, as organizations professionalize yet remain dependent on external or government funding.

Feminist attention needs to be paid to how to "thicken" civil society and how to more closely balance the negotiating power of NGOs and grassroots organizations with that of governments and other donors. Thickening may involve coalition building with partners that feminists might have once deemed hopeless. Whether at national or transnational levels, for example, labor unions not only look more to women in their recruitment pools but also have their own advocacy units within that have strategically placed feminists and resources. Women's advocates may need to work with the Catholic Church on issues of poverty, even as they oppose the Church's stance on reproductive rights.

States

The other half of the state and civil society relationship is the state.[26] In the United States, neoliberal critiques of "statism" have been joined to politically popular campaigns against the redistributional state. This is reflected in the tax revolts that have repeatedly occurred in the United States since the late 1970s, despite the benefits middle class and even wealthy voters gain from public goods, and the almost inexplicable lack of state-based responses to the threat of terrorism within the United States, which is relying on the self-interest of companies in sensitive areas like chemicals and transportation to spend the money to protect themselves (Flynn 2004). U.S. public opinion on these domestic matters affects U.S. foreign policy.

Howell's and Pearce's European model of a "strong state and a strong public" sounds desirable. But Howell and Pearce do not recognize the antistate bias of their own position, which draws on feminist and Marxist views of the state as patriarchal and an instrument of capitalist exploitation. They seem to assume that popular movements are progressive and democratic, when they may be neither. Strong states and strong civil societies do go together. Those who claim to represent women's interests should be wary of delegitimizing the state. States are critical to implementing norms, disciplining markets, and making investments in public goods. They can promote better access to markets for those who are marginalized (a category that fits most women and not just those who are poor) and rescue those who fall between the cracks. States give concrete meaning to citizenship and, when functioning well, energize people to seek ends beyond material gain and above partisanship. As John Ackerman argues, we may need to move beyond notions that "envision and defend an arm's-length relationship between state and society" (2004, 6). "Co-governance," such as participatory budgeting in Porto Alegre, Brazil, offers a model with gender-inclusive implications and opportune spaces to alter power relations.

Of course, not all state activity is productive. And when states regulate markets, redistribute wealth, or provide public goods, there is always the danger of corruption, which is perhaps the greatest barrier to increasing state capacity today as "democratizing" publics become increasingly cynical about their political leadership. Yet, as long as women take most of the responsibility for social reproduction, doing the unpaid labor of child care and elder care, they will need states strong enough to discipline markets and underwrite social services. Women's organizations can be particularly effective in promoting transparency and demanding better performance from politicians and civil servants, reforms that are needed to restore confidence in the state, deepen the rule of law, and build state capacity.

Empowerment strategies look to the local as well as the global, often with the vision of "going around" or even substituting for the state (Elliott 2003). Lappe and Lappe offer many examples of women challenging global capitalism (2002), and many have argued that decentralization is positive for women. But there is also evidence that the devolution of power to local governments can simply reinforce local hierarchies (e.g., G. Sen and Grown 1985). Creating "viable alternative organizations" in local communities requires a commitment of time and money that goes beyond what most donors are willing to provide (Meinzen-Dick et al. 1997, 1312). Further, the emphasis on participation and decentralization often ignores the "increased burden upon poor households and poor women in particular" (Lind 1997, 1218). More attention to local political contexts and how to empower women within them could be an important direction for future research and a critical issue as "traditional" cultural values are locally reasserted and enforced, often with negative implications for gender equality (e.g., K. B. Warren and Jackson 2002, 29; Braidotti 1997).

Howell and Pearce argue that the relations between the state and civil society should not be too "partnered." But the stance of civil society toward the state should not be too destructive, either. Strategies of resistance are seductive, but they do not solve problems and implement solutions. Popular mobilization strategies often succeed by offering a radical alternative, but the likely radical alternative to liberal capitalism today is a theocratic, not a socialist, state.

Promoting an effective state requires progressive political involvement. We think that what has gone "wrong" in the United States is not its Tocquevillean model of civil society, as Howell and Pearce suggest, but the dramatic political shift to the right over the last thirty years. (We forget, for example, that Republican President Richard Nixon proposed universal health care.) There is evidence that U.S. values are diverging from those held elsewhere in the industrialized West on critical dimensions ranging from religiosity to the death penalty and gay marriage. Given the direction of these trends, the United States government cannot be relied upon to support progressive policies in international forums.

Many U.S. feminists and their organizations develop only a narrow and selective interest beyond U.S. boundaries, as perusal of Web sites quickly shows for the National Organization for Women (NOW) and the Feminist Majority, among others. As Liebowitz underscores, U.S. women's national and transnational organizing around gender and trade has been limited (2002, 176). Perhaps U.S. women's organizations are too deeply engaged in trying to hold onto gains at home to engage in a serious discussion of international development. We need a new generation to go beyond GAD the way GAD reinvented WID, but there is little sign that this thinking will come out of antiglobalization movements with their multiple agendas and lack of interest in women's issues.

Markets

Markets are an arena to which women need access, but on their terms. In general, it is easier for women to affect the governmental policies that shape markets rather intervene in markets directly, although boycotts and protests against corporate practices can be effective. As Lourdes Benería urges, feminists should be supporting the rights of women to organize in labor unions (2003), and they should be pressing harder for action against human trafficking.

The WID view was that women were excluded from or discriminated against in markets and that they would act entrepreneurially if they had even minimal resources to do so. The democracy agenda and GAD's focus on gender power relations broadened the arenas of empowerment, but also diverted attention from the core issue of improving women's incomes. Feminist economists have tried to convince their mainstream colleagues to address gender by pointing out that discrimination distorts markets and therefore reduces the optimal production of goods and services (e.g., Elson 1998 and 2002). But affirmative action in employment has not been a priority for most Third World women, and discriminatory hiring practices are still widespread for those who work in the formal sector. Women will continue to enter the market at a substantial disadvantage, even where they are allowed public mobility and can gain access to education and other resources. Class and race discrimination are often most keenly felt by poor women.

Some have criticized microcredit projects by arguing that women turn the money over to men or use it to serve their status and kinship needs rather than invest it. There are data showing that women are significantly less likely than men to "grow" their microenterprises (e.g., Gold 1991) or move out of the informal sector. But a feminist analysis should defend women's use of these resources, pointing for example to the evidence that microcredit has given women greater leverage in their families and communities, even if the accounting is not strictly economic (Tinker 1995a). Following earlier analysis by Boserup, Tinker (1997b) has observed that microcredit projects are successful for women because they are not fully marketized, and therefore are compatible with women's needs to fit entrepreneurial activities into schedules largely determined by unpaid care work (see Kittay 1999; Nussbaum 2003). Poor women are likely to benefit more from programs that are not evaluated on economic grounds alone, yet the failure to understand this may lead to misguided reductions in microcredit funding.[27]

Some argue that feminism and economic analysis are simply incompatible.[28] But others have tried to change the field from within. Nancy Folbre (2001b) maintains that neoclassical economics takes too narrow a view of human beings, excluding all human characteristics except those relevant to profit maximizing (see also C. Scott 1995). Diane Elson and Lourdes Benería have called mainstream economists to task for tolerating gender distortions that their theories do not allow; they have looked for ways to measure the economic costs of implementing the neoliberal model. Women's organizations (like Wages for Housework) have insisted that national economic statistics recognize the value of women's unpaid labor.[29]

Folbre's view that economics is biased toward the competitive and selfish male personality may be correct. But it may also be the case that, if we want more of the goods and services that (women's) unpaid labor provides and we want to reward the women (and men) who provide those goods and services, then their production will have to be more, not less, marketized. What we want from markets (greater production of goods and services at the lowest possible cost) may require the kind of behavior that the market rewards. That does not mean that markets can be left to operate on their own, generating or reinforcing inequalities. But changing the current paradigm that emphasizes supply over demand and maximizes short-term gains over long-term sustainability will require a more concerted effort than has been mounted thus far. More initiatives are needed to engage scholars across disciplines (see Jackson 2002), another place where universities can play a key role.

Women's organizations can affect markets directly through boycotts, via the accumulation of millions of changes in consumer choices, and by lobbying corporations or protesting their policies. These efforts should not be minimized. But using political power to tame markets and counter globalization may be more costly in the long run than activists admit. For example, it seems likely that resistance to the privatization of water markets in Latin America and Africa will keep water free as governments continue to own water companies rather than sell them to international companies who will charge more but invest in infrastructure. Political resistance can prevent privatization in the short run but make affordable potable water scarce in the long term. Ultimately, people must engage over whether water is a social and public good (while recognizing it is not a free good) in democratic forums. To take another example, boycotts of products produced by child labor assume that children are working rather than going to school, but children may have no schools to go to and their work may be essential to their dignity as well as to family survival.

For decades, transnational activists have struggled over standards of conduct practiced in global corporations and the social accountability of corporations to their local contexts, including the recent UN Global Compact. These are presented as "Third Way," as public-private partnerships that can "give a human face to the global market" (Elson 2004, 46). But as Elson points out, there are numerous problems in implementation, including transparency and coverage. Critics worry about excessively close and compromised relationships between the United Nations and global corporations. The expense of international conferences and the need to fund-raise from the very corporations that may be part of the problem taint possible solutions.

Direct political action against marketization is too blunt an instrument to make markets work for the greatest number; states and international bodies must take a more active role (see, for example, Held and Koenig-Archigugi 2003). Radical visions of a future in which increases in material production are not highly valued seem utopian. By contrast, a fairer redistribution of wealth is justifiable on both moral and economic grounds and can build on the strengths of liberal capitalism rather than trying to resist on the hope that, if we just had the political will, we could have an economic system that is radically different. Global trends in economic growth, if anemic and unreliable, are positive enough to avoid a full-scale rejection of the neoliberal model. This suggests the need to seek ways to reshape it rather than hoping it will self-destruct.

Markets do not recognize much of the work that women already do. Many feminists argue that care is real work that needs to be recognized and properly valued, and we agree. The question is how to do so. Individuals and families can decide to reward care more (an outcome more likely to occur when there is feminist awareness, and women can negotiate rather than obligingly produce free goods). Or states can intervene with policies that support child care or tax credits for elder care, for example, which admit the social value of domestic labor. Or men could be pushed by law and social control to reward unpaid labor within households, a desirable goal, but one likely to be implemented at the cost of identifying women too closely with the home and with men deciding at their own discretion how such work will be materially recognized. Working on markets from the standpoint of care may increase the value of "women's work" but will inevitably blur the line between marketized and nonmarketized, selfish and altruistic labor.

CONCLUSIONS

U.S. unilateralism and the remilitarization of international politics are edging out the more layered approaches to women's issues that were emerging during the 1990s, which incorporated issues of gender, the environment, justice, and human rights in a transnational framework. Even before September 11 there were indications that the period of feminist norm setting may have reached its peak. "Gender" became a contested term in Cairo and Beijing, and the UN moved to limit NGO access to international conferences. Beijing, Beijing+5, and Beijing+10 are signals that backlash could halt what had appeared to be an almost irreversible trend toward increasing women's rights and voice.

Together, GAD fatigue and U.S. overreach may offer new opportunities to rethink both aid and macroeconomic policies, taking advantage of broader economic and ideological shifts. The history of WID and GAD suggests that clear and well-articulated models can make a difference in donor policies. It is time to refocus attention on women and on development and to reconnect analysis and practice. This effort will require cooperation between North and South and among scholars, advocates, and practitioners. It will depend on the active involvement of women themselves as agents of change and protectors of the traditions they value. It will need to recognize that although radicalism can inspire reform, neither capitalism nor patriarchy is going to be swept away by revolutionary fiat. We have to begin where we are.

NOTES

1. E.g., Goetz (1997a); Momsen (2004); Jackson and Pearson (1998); Miller and Razavi (1998b); Razavi (2002); Rao et al. (1999); Connelly et al. (2000).
2. Apodaca (2000) has argued, based on a GAO study of U.S. WID aid, that "foreign aid programs hinder women's realization of their economic and social rights" (6) because aid programs are negatively correlated with improvements in women's status. Foreign assistance plays a very small role in the global processes affecting "women's status," and very little foreign assistance goes to women, but her thesis does show how difficult it is to justify WID/GAD programs on the grounds of effectiveness alone. The data in *Engendering Development* (World Bank 2001a) suggest that, in general, as equality of rights and income for women improve, other gender indicators also improve (233).
3. Tinker notes that the UN General Assembly approved the conference but did not authorize UN funding (Tinker 1990b, 28–29; see also West 1999).
4. See Kardam (1997b). The Bank's Basic Human Needs approach was adopted when Marxist insurgencies were on the rise, and Vatican II and liberation theology had moved the Catholic church to the left. The growing number of Third World states in the United Nations shifted the power balance in favor of the South in the General Assembly, which played a central role because of the Cold War standoff in the Security Council.
5. This point is made in Tinker and Jaquette (1987) but has been reinforced by subsequent research in several regions. There were "women's emancipation" movements in many countries during the first decades of the twentieth century, organized to achieve the vote and other legal rights for women. International women's groups that were still active in the 1970s include the Women's International League for Peace and Freedom, Zonta International, the Soroptimists, and the YWCA, founded in 1864.
6. Australia, Canada, and Israel joined the United States in voting against the Program of Action for language equating Zionism with racism. The vote was 94 to 4 with 22 abstentions, including most western European countries (Jaquette 1995, 56).
7. As of 2004, over 180 countries had ratified the convention. On the history of CEDAW, see A. Fraser (1995); on women's movements and international norm-setting, see Keck and Sikkink (1995) and Meyer and Prügl (1999).
8. This essay starts from an AID/WID standpoint, where the authors worked as policy analysts in the AID/WID Office in 1979 (Staudt) and 1979–80 (Jaquette). WID was adopted by a range of agencies (see Kardam 1997b; Marks 2001; and M. Snyder and Tadesse 1995), but many critiques of WID have focused on how WID was implemented by USAID.
9. Similar arguments were encountered in other agencies; see Kardam (1997b), essays in Staudt (1985 and 1997), Longwe (1995); see also "From 'Home Economics' to 'Microfinance'" in this book
10. Intrahousehold gender dynamics have received attention only in the past twenty years or

so, e.g., Dwyer and Bruce (1988); A. Sen (1990); Kabeer (1994). Labor unions, historically male dominated, have been strong supporters of the "family wage" (e.g., Tinsman 2002), and it appears in the UN Declaration of Human Rights.

11. Suellen Huntington (1975) rejected Boserup's characterization of female farming systems as complementary but equal, arguing that women had been oppressed in traditional systems. But the image of "female farming systems" resonated with the feminist search for matriarchal societies, particularly in Africa. The idea of a female farming system applied less well to women's roles in Asian and Latin American agriculture, although women's contribution to agricultural production was grossly underestimated in both regions. Boserup portrayed women as "rational actors," but her discussion of precolonial gender complementarity is compatible with difference feminism. She rejected the assumption that modernization was good for women and emphasized the heterogeneity of premodern societies.

12. Mueller drew on Kathy Ferguson (1984) whose "feminist case against bureaucracy" drew on Foucault, Habermas, and Gramsci.

13. Razavi (1997, 1111) notes the importance of the shift from Keynesianism to neoliberalism. She argues that instrumental ("efficiency") arguments arose under neoliberalism, but we observe that efficiency arguments were already widely used in the late 1970s and that equity arguments (as Buvinic and Moser note below) were resisted. On the implications of equity, welfare, and efficiency arguments for WID, see Jaquette (1990); for discussion see Tinker (1990b), Kabeer (1994), and Staudt (1997).

14. See, for example, Anastasakos (2002). In Elson's critique, SAPs "privatize the costs of social reproduction"(1995a, 1852), with women "filling the gaps"; they diminish future growth by cutting investment in public health and education. Countering those who were arguing that there were women among the "winners" as well as the "losers" from neoliberal policies, Elson argued that SAPs destroy "alternative remunerative job opportunities" for women, and for their "fathers, brothers and husbands." Female employment in export zones is just a new kind of "women's work" (1853). Elson concludes that the weaknesses of SAPs have not been sufficiently acknowledged by mainstream economists: SAPs assume supportive relations between the state and the private sector that their implementation undermines: they ignore the effects of weak demand as a constraint on investment and growth, fail to register the value of social goods outside the monetized economy, and do not take into account how the gender dynamics of household decision making affect policy outcomes (1854–58). See Morvaridi (1995) and Engle (1995) for the implications of SAPs for gender dynamics in the family.

15. WID project heads were often trained in home economics, not because the WID model called for this, but because of bureaucratic realities. USAID projects were usually put together by university teams drawn from consortia of U.S. agricultural universities and, given sex discrimination on campuses, the women faculty who were interested in development were concentrated in home economics or human ecology departments.

16. In a recent discussion of whether the World Bank's Poverty Reduction Strategy Papers (PRSPs) address gender, Elaine Zuckerman and Ashley Garrett (2003) criticize eight such country plans for "spottily apply[ing] an outdated Women in Development approach," because they define gender issues as "reproductive health" and "girls' education." But, reproductive health advocates have moved much closer to the WID/GAD position analyzing women's reproductive choices in the broader context of women's empowerment. On the centrality of economic power to other forms of power for women, see Blumberg (1995).

17. The debate over the role of empiricism in development is discussed at length in Escobar (1995) and Brohman (1996); Mosesdottir (1995) labels quantitative methods "patriarchal."

18. Tisdell, Roy, and Ghose (2001) critique the GEM and GDI indexes, largely on the grounds that they are not fine grained enough to identify subgroups effectively and that they cannot assess nonmarket exchanges. See also Bardahn and Klasen (1999).

19. GAD favored participatory development, but DAWN's use of the term *self*-empowerment suggests a concern about the strings attached to foreign aid as well as the fear of external vulnerability under neoliberalism.

20. For reviews of mainstreaming, see "Mainstreaming Gender in International Organizations" in this book; Chant and Gutmann (2000); Jahan (1995); Rai (2003). Chant and Gutmann argue that "while the short-term goals of GAD are often decidedly similar in character to those of WID (for example, improved education, access to credit, and legal rights for women), these are nominally conceived as stepping stones toward long-term goals" to empower women by "collective action," and "encouraging [them] to challenge gender ideologies and institutions that subordinate women" (2000, 9).

21. Moser's desire to avoid contentious confrontations over gender power relations within donor bureaucracies is also visible in her substitution of gender "needs" for Molyneux's more provocative gender "interests." Although Nancy Hartsock (1981) criticizes interests as too conventionally liberal, Sapiro (1981) and Jonasdottir (1988) defend the idea of women's interests as feminist.

22. Jennifer Schirmer (1993) and others attacked the "strategic/practical" distinction as elitist, noting that women organized for practical goals often raised strategic issues. For her response to such critics, see Molyneux (1998).

23. Thanks to Deborah Mindry for this point.

24. Contrast articles in Jackson and Pearson (1998) with C. Scott (1995) and V. Peterson (2002); see also Jaquette (2001, 2003). Elson and Escobar seem to share with radical dependency theory a zero-sum view of capitalism. Ecofeminists like Vandana Shiva are also antidevelopment; they imply that the productive capacity already in place would be adequate if capitalism did not encourage the profit motive. By contrast Pearson and Jackson reject "green fundamentalism," (1998, 9) and argue that "markets are not necessarily against women's interests" (9–10). See Bergeron (2001) for a critique of reshaping capitalism and Mohanty's (2003) call for new strategic alliances against capitalist globalization. But Jacqui True (2003a), studying eastern Europe, sees globalization as a dialogic process, and Valentine Moghadam (1998) suggests the need to regulate rather than reject globalization. Eschle (2003) cautions that women and women's issues are largely excluded from antiglobalization movements.

25. Chant and Gutmann (2000); Longwe (1995); essays in Staudt (1998) and Razavi (2002); see "What Is Justice?" in this book.

26. For useful discussions of gender and the state, see Randall (1998) and Charlton et al. (1989).

27. P. Richardson and Langdon (2000, 179) note that few NGO staff are trained in entrepreneurial skills, and they often have values that are antientrepreneurial.

28. For example, J. K. Gibson-Graham sees globalization as a triumph of masculine rhetoric and suggests "replacing the rational, abstract and dominating masculine order with the emotional, connected, peace-loving and egalitarian one" (quoted in Bergeron 2001, 997). Janet Gabriel Townsend (1999) emphasizes a feminist preference for "networks" over "institutions."

29. See Chant and Gutmann (2000) for a recent review.

Mainstreaming Gender in International Organizations

Elisabeth Prügl and Audrey Lustgarten

Gender mainstreaming has become the primary tool to advance gender equality in international organizations. The United Nations and its specialized agencies, the Organization for Economic Cooperation and Development (OECD), the European Union, Organization of American States (OAS), and Asia Pacific Economic Cooperation (APEC) all have adopted gender mainstreaming, and governments around the world have followed their lead (True and Mintrom 2001; True 2003b). Despite the widespread acceptance of the strategy, there is considerable debate about what exactly gender mainstreaming means and how it should be implemented. Angela King, the special advisor to the UN secretary-general on gender matters, has listed conceptual confusion among the major constraints inhibiting gender mainstreaming (United Nations 2002, vi). In the European context, gender experts have bemoaned the difficulty of translating the term from English and have described the shifting meanings it has taken in different contexts in the European Union (Council of Europe 1998, 18; Wank 2003).

This essay is an effort to contribute to conceptual clarification. Although we draw on the extensive work of gender experts and consultants involved in the implementation of gender mainstreaming, we write from an academic location that puts us outside these organizational contexts. We are less interested in providing better definitions or tools than in providing an assessment of what gender mainstreaming has come to mean in practical contexts. Our approach is not a policy analysis, that is, it does not treat gender mainstreaming as an organizational tool whose successes and failures need to be measured. Instead, we attempt a political science analysis of gender mainstreaming as a site around which global gender politics operate. Accordingly, we postulate that gender mainstreaming cannot be defined a priori but takes on meaning through organizational processes and politics. The implementation of gender mainstreaming is itself part of global gender politics.

In the Weberian approach governmental organizations have been described as rationalized bureaucracies that implement policies through the methodical application of tools. Indeed, entrusting the implementation of gender mainstreaming to bureaucracies implies a trust that these bureaucracies will realize the mandate to create gender equality in an objective manner. However, organizations also are social organisms with cultures and value commitments. These commitments circumscribe the ways in which policies are implemented. Organizational cultures and value commitments both enable and constrain change, producing distinct organizational pathways of implementation. Furthermore, organizations are sites of power defining identities and exclusions, rights and obligations, and employing categorical differences to place people in a hierarchical power structure. In other words, organizations engage in politics. They do not stand outside the global gender regime as its managers and guardians but are participants reproducing gendered rules and power relations through their practices.

In this essay we explore the distinctive paths that the implementation of gender mainstreaming has taken in three international organizations: the United Nations Development Program (UNDP), the World Bank, and the International Labor Organization (ILO). We show that these institutions have taken mainstreaming to mean very different things once they subsume the strategy under their institutional agendas. We also seek to gauge how power is renegotiated in these organizations through the implementation of gender mainstreaming. Our purpose is to elucidate the politics of gender mainstreaming in different institutional contexts and to provide an assessment of its limits and possibilities as a strategy.

WHAT IS GENDER MAINSTREAMING?

The Beijing Platform for Action, the document negotiated at the UN Women's Conference in 1995, provided the original mandate to the UN system to pursue gender mainstreaming. Its call for "mainstreaming a gender perspective in all policies and programmes" (paragraphs 202 and 292) represented a victory for feminists, mostly from the South, who had called for such an approach.[1] The concept emerged from the gender and development (GAD) approach that had replaced early efforts to integrate women into development policies and programs. Advocates of GAD had criticized development interventions that had targeted only women and had focused on their participation in equal numbers, suggesting that these approaches had not attacked patriarchal power relations. They argued that gender oppression is structurally embedded and suggested that the goal of equality required an approach that addressed the power relationship between women and men. GAD rhetoric (if not always substance) has become orthodoxy among development institutions, and gender mainstreaming has become the primary tool for attacking gendered power relations. Only by focusing on the rules of the game in all issue areas could gendered rules be identified and modified and the pernicious effects of structural power be counteracted (Wichterich 2001).

The adoption of gender mainstreaming by the United Nations turned a radical movement idea into a strategy of public management. In a 1997 conclusion, the UN Economic and Social Council (ECOSOC) offered a much-quoted definition of gender mainstreaming, describing it as "the process of assessing the implication for women and men of any planned action, including legislation, policies or programmes, in any area and at all levels. It is a strategy for making the concerns and experiences of women as well as of men an integral part of the design, implementation, monitoring and evaluation of policies and programmes in all political, economic and societal spheres, so that women and men benefit equally, and inequality is not perpetuated." ECOSOC elaborated by specifying that "the ultimate goal of mainstreaming is to achieve gender equality" (quoted in UNIFEM 2000, 34). Program and project cycles, management processes, and tools now became the object of gender mainstreaming.

The ECOSOC definition is not the only definition of gender mainstreaming. Others typically resemble it in its focus on public administration, but sometimes differ in emphasis. Some focus on specific tools (such as gender analysis) or levels of women's participation, others on the incorporation of gender issues in all functional issue areas and thus within the "mainstream" of policy making. Some treat equality as a measurable outcome, some as an ongoing struggle (Council of Europe 1998, 18). Although suggestive of different understandings, it is difficult to infer political agendas from these definitions without embedding them in institutional and organizational contexts. It is in these contexts that those charged with implementing gender mainstreaming negotiate its meanings and the conditions for its successes and failures. This includes defining what is meant by a "gender perspective" and by "the concerns and experiences of women and men." It also includes negotiating the focus of activity, the style of intervention, resources, and criteria for evaluation.

There are three distinctive aspects of mainstreaming in the ECOSOC definition. First, it describes mainstreaming as infusing gender considerations into *organizational processes*. Second, it calls for integrating concerns of women and men into policies and programs, that is, in the *output* of organizations. Third, it specifies that the *goal* of mainstreaming is equality between women and men. Jahan's (1995) operationalization of gender mainstreaming as composed of institutional strategies, operational strategies, and policy objectives parallels these distinctions. Her first category, institutional strategies, encompasses the assignment of responsibilities for gender mainstreaming, systems of accountability, coordination, monitoring, evaluation, and personnel practices. Her second category includes approaches that the institutions have defined and the guidelines, knowledge, analytical tools, policies, projects, and programs that they have developed in carrying out their operations. Her third category includes the definition of objectives that organizations have arrived at. In this analysis, we borrow from Jahan to describe gender mainstreaming at UNDP, the ILO, and the World Bank. In line with our embedding of this research in organizational theory, we rename her first category "organizational processes" and her second category "organizational outputs." We relate her "policy objectives" category to the objective of gender equality set out in the ECOSOC definition. The international organizations analyzed here emphasize process, outputs, and the definition of policy objectives to different degrees, a reflection of their organizational cultures, worldviews, and core values.

UNITED NATIONS DEVELOPMENT PROGRAM: THE PRIMACY OF PROCESS

Of the three organizations reviewed, UNDP most extensively focuses on the process aspect of mainstreaming, a result undoubtedly of its highly decentralized structure and an organizational philosophy that stresses client countries' ownership in the development process (Kardam 1991; Miller 1998). UNDP made WID one of four major themes in 1986 and created the Division of Women and Development within the Bureau for Program and Policy Evaluation to ensure that women would play a larger role within the organization, both as participants and as beneficiaries. While not yet employing the language of mainstreaming, the function of the division amounted to a mainstreaming of processes: it was to oversee the UNDP committee in charge of project approval to make sure that women's interests were integrated into all projects. As was typical of women's machineries, the WID division suffered from resource shortages that undermined its ability to carry out its tasks. There was also a tendency for WID and gender goals to be subverted at the programming level (Miller 1998, 154–57).

UNDP now formally endorses mainstreaming as the primary method of achieving gender equality. While its policy accepts both the process and output aspects of ECOSOC's definition of gender mainstreaming (UNDP, 2000b, 1), in practice the organization has almost exclusively focused on issues of organizational process (compare Jahan 1995, 24). In 1992 the Gender in Development Program (GIDP) replaced the WID division in an effort to decentralize responsibility for WID to the state level. This included the establishment of a system of "gender focal points" throughout the organization. Within each of UNDP's 134 country offices, a program staff person and a member of senior management are designated as a focal point to oversee the implementation of mainstreaming. A Gender Programme Team facilitates a "global knowledge network" made up of these focal points, UN volunteers, and UNIFEM regional program directors. The team provides guidance on policies and programs and promotes the objective of gender equality throughout the organization (UNDP 2000a, 1–2; UNDP 2002a, 16).

The centrality of process in UNDP's approach to mainstreaming is evident in its focus on capacity building. In a 2002 "practice note" on gender equality, capacity building appears as one of three main approaches, next to providing policy advice and supporting stand-alone gender projects and programs (UNDP 2002a, 8). Capacity building will lead to the creation of a new, less masculinized UNDP. In the words of one participant in UNDP gender training, "Gender is not just about programmes, policies, and personnel balance, but also about institutional culture. It is about caring, flexibility and empowerment, which affects behaviour, rules, programmes, and impacts" (UNDP 2000b, 2). However, unlike in the World Bank and the ILO, there is little concern in UNDP for developing a policy statement that analyzes causes and correlates of gender inequality, provides a rationale for UNDP intervention, and specifies the impacts desired. Indeed, the lack of substantive content was identified as a problem in UNDP exercises to build gender capacity in the 1990s (Schalkwyk 1998, 32). Likewise, the 2000 annual report of the UNDP administrator identified a need to "focus . . . on policy and planning as well as capacity building" (UNDP and UNPF Executive Board, 2001, 29, 32). More recent documents have addressed these concerns by illustrating ways in which gender matters in the UNDP's six "practices areas," that is, democratic governance, poverty reduction, crisis prevention and recovery, energy and environment, information and communications technology, and HIV/AIDS (UNDP 2002a, 2003). The content of gender mainstreaming here emerges in the recounting of best practices at the national level.

Given the UNDP's decentralized structure, its process-focused approach to mainstreaming is a gargantuan task. Indeed, a 1998 review identified a series of organizational constraints to the success of capacity building—many reminiscent of issues identified ten years earlier, constraints that mainstreaming was supposed to overcome. These constraints included among others the isolation of focal points and their lack of information about management priorities; attitudes and priorities of resident representatives that did not necessarily include gender mainstreaming; the continued compartmentalization of gender issues into a separate area not considered relevant to other priority themes; a hierarchical organizational culture that did not encourage the participation of the junior staff who often served as focal points; and the lack of recognition women often faced from professional colleagues (Schalkwyk 1998, 35–37). The UNDP administrator's 2000 annual report, while finding progress in particular in the development of linkages and coherence in country-level activities focused on gender equality, also bemoaned the relatively limited reporting on gender under goals other than gender equality, indicating a limited degree of mainstreaming (UNDP and UNPF Executive Board 2001, 29). A review of UNDP supported activities in sub-Saharan Africa found that gender mainstreaming was lagging considerably. In the area of poverty eradication, fewer than half of the projects reviewed included some gender analysis, and only 33 percent employed a gender specialist. The picture was even more dismal in the area of governance. Here only 6 of 59 initiatives were based on a gender analysis, though 18 employed a gender specialist (*Assessment of Gender Mainstreaming in Sub-Saharan Africa* 2000, 4–5).

The results-oriented 2000–2001 annual reports showed similar results. On one hand country reports reflected an increase in gender activity; on the other, financial allocations for gender amounted to a mere 1 percent (excluding programs where gender was mainstreamed), and there were significantly fewer progress statements on accomplishing the goal of gender equality than on other goals

(UNDP 2002a, 6–7). A recent review of gender mainstreaming in UNDP, spear-headed by the Gender Programme Team, reiterates many of these critiques: there is a considerable lack of gender expertise, and the goal of building capacity has been especially elusive at the national level; gender focal points lack resources and are marginalized; and—in a new twist—making gender a cross-cutting issue threatens to render the issue institutionally homeless: "By making gender main-streaming everybody's job, it can easily become nobody's job. The budget im-plications are significant: cross-cutting issues seldom sit atop dedicated pots of money" (UNDP 2003, 7).

The slowness of change at UNDP illustrates how difficult it is to move organiza-tional cultures but does not in itself invalidate the strategic focus on processes. In-deed, UNDP—often via UNIFEM—has helped pioneer many creative innovations in gendering organizational processes, from gender indices and scoreboards to gender-responsive budgeting. And, of the organizations reviewed, UNDP has the highest percentage of women in professional positions, increasing from 20.6 per-cent in the mid-1970s to 41 percent in mid-2002 (UNDP 2002a, 1998; Jahan 1995). Furthermore, in response to the Gender Programme Team's critique, UNDP man-agement has strengthened strategic programming and accountability by main-streaming gender into work on the UN's Millennium Development Goals and by using gender-responsive budgeting in building economic governance programs. It also has strengthened reporting requirements and stepped up compulsory training and capacity building (UNDP and UNPF Executive Board 2004). There seems to be a commitment to carry gender mainstreaming to its logical conclu-sion and make organizations dedicated to women's empowerment superfluous.

But what may get lost in the process is precisely the focus on women's em-powerment. Feminists within UNDP have come to emphasize the need for a double-pronged approach that encompasses both gender mainstreaming and em-powerment (UNDP 2003, 8). Treating gender as a cross-cutting issue has be-come a threat to organizational spaces that have made women's empowerment their primary goal. There is a movement toward increasingly implicating UNIFEM in gender mainstreaming within UNDP. UNIFEM subregional offices are being merged with UNDP regional centers, and there is a stated intent to integrate UNIFEM's work into UNDP programs; to form joint UNIFEM/UNDP teams to ana-lyze UNDP policies, programs, and resource allocations; and to significantly in-crease UNIFEM support for gender mainstreaming in UNDP (UNDP and UNPF Ex-ecutive Board 2004). The fact that this cooperation is intended to address the lack of UNDP resources for gender mainstreaming may not bode well for independent UNIFEM programming.

The UNDP experience illustrates co-optation of feminist agendas into broader organizational priorities. Mainstreaming gender into the UNDP subsumes gender equality under UNDP's commitment to sustainable human development—equality between women and men is desirable because "gender discrimination is the source of endemic poverty, of inequitable and low economic growth, of high HIV prevalence, and of inadequate governance" (UNDP 2002a, iv). The key to sustainability, for the UNDP, is participatory development and decentralization. Within this approach, a lack of national "capacity" has hampered UNDP efforts to promote gender equality. In a context of scarce resources, it is drawing on UNIFEM to support its gender mainstreaming efforts—both locally and at headquarters, potentially weakening the key feminist organization within the UN system with dedicated resources to the advancement of women.

THE WORLD BANK: FITTING GENDER INTO A POLICY FRAMEWORK

The issue of gender mainstreaming came into focus at the World Bank at about the same time as it did at UNDP. In 1985 a new WID advisor was appointed at the Bank. In stark contrast to UNDP, her duties were to focus on policy. She was to "demonstrate how attention to Women in Development contributed to development objectives in a language that was acceptable to economists and to provide clear operational guidelines" (Miller 1998, 152). In 1987 WID became one of four areas of special emphasis at the Bank. This was followed in 1988 by a new system in which all projects proposed by the Bank were to be analyzed for attention to WID during the approval stage. During this time the staff and budget of the WID sector increased dramatically, from $80,000 to $620,000 between 1986 and 1988 (152).

In the early 1990s, management became concerned that gender was not being sufficiently integrated into World Bank projects and shifted attention to mainstreaming gender into organizational processes. The WID division was closed down and replaced with a Gender Analysis and Policy thematic group in an attempt to improve system-wide attention to gender issues via decentralization. This new group was process-oriented and was charged with the task of overseeing mainstreaming through education, both in training bank staff and aiding interested member states in devising appropriate strategies. The overseeing of policy previously performed by the WID division was not transferred to the thematic group but rather to a monitoring team responsible for both gender and poverty (Miller 1998, 155–56; Jahan 1995, 62).

In yet another major reorganization in 1997, attention to gender became institutionally subsumed under the Poverty Reduction and Economic Management (PREM) technical network, one of four major networks set up to support country-level operations (World Bank 2003a 1–2). Within PREM there is now a Gender and Development Board consisting of representatives from each of the six Bank regions, from each of the four major networks, and from other key units. The Board is charged with developing a rationale for Bank work on gender issues, research and learning on gender issues, training and outreach on gender issues, and the integration of gender into the Country Assistance Strategy process and private sector development activities, as well as the ongoing monitoring and evaluation of gender issues (World Bank 2003a:1). To assist the Board with implementing the work programs it devises, there is also a Gender and Development Group within PREM which provides support to the Board (1). This institutionalization of gender issues within one of the Bank's new core policy areas has been widely considered an important mainstreaming event (O'Brien et al. 2000, 44; World Bank 2001a). It also has entailed a shift back to considering gender mainstreaming not only a matter of process but also a matter of policy and programs.

Even though advocates welcomed the move of gender issues under the PREM network, they pointed out that there continued to be few incentives to encourage Bank staff to consider gender issues and that the demand-driven system, under which the new gender unit operated, left it in a position where it had to "sell" its services in an inhospitable ideological environment focused on neoliberal economics (O'Brien et al. 2000, 44–45). Further, there seemed to be few resources dedicated to mainstreaming gender in organizational processes under PREM. Indeed, a 1997 evaluation of World Bank activities on mainstreaming (Murphy 1997) focuses almost exclusively on organizational outputs, primarily projects but also country assistance strategies and economic and sector work. Process elements specified did include the commitment of senior management to gender mainstreaming and the establishment of focal points. However, the work of focal points often is in addition to existing assignments and funding for regional teams has been low and insecure. For example, the Africa regional gender team was reduced to two members after funding sources dried up. Furthermore, gender training of staff, a key effort at UNDP and ILO, plays a relatively small role at the World Bank. Apparently, "a high level of gender expertise can be found among task managers who have never worked as gender specialists," and training tool kits have been developed mostly to sensitize borrower counterparts (15, 45).

In terms of formulating a policy, the Bank has stated its commitment to assisting its member states in designing "gender-sensitive policies and programs to ensure that overall development efforts are directed to attain impacts that are equitably beneficial for both men and women" (World Bank 1999, 1). It has issued a handbook on mainstreaming gender into social assignments, which offers suggestions for Bank staff to integrate gender into projects. This includes everything from gender-disaggregating data collection and analysis to scheduling meetings at times appropriate for both men and women (Moser et al. 1998, 1–3). However, despite the strong focus on outputs, there has been confusion over what the Bank's policy is on gender and how it should be carried out in practice. A 1999 review found that the Bank lacked a common "gender rationale and language, as well as tools and training for mainstreaming gender and development" (Moser et al. 1999, 5).

In recent years the World Bank has made significant progress both in developing an overarching policy rationale for the Bank's activities on gender and in devising a strategy for enhancing and improving its mainstreaming efforts. In particular, the 2001 World Bank policy report *Engendering Development Through Gender Equality in Rights, Resources and Voice* links gender equality with economic growth, poverty reduction, and good governance. Based on the extensive data reviewed, the report calls for institutional reform "to establish equal rights and opportunities for women and men," "economic development to strengthen incentives for more equal resources and participation," and for "measures to redress persistent disparities in command over resources and political voice," legitimizing the integration of gender concerns in World Bank policies and projects, and making gender fit into the language of economists (World Bank 2001b, 1–2).

The 2002 report *Integrating Gender into the World Bank's Work: A Strategy for Action* also constitutes a significant step forward in mainstreaming gender in the World Bank. The report builds on the policy framework established in 2001, focusing on outlining strategies for action. The report identifies three major goals for mainstreaming gender: (1) make Bank interventions responsive to country conditions and commitments, that is, make gender-related efforts "country led and country specific"; (2) make interventions more strategic and in line with the Bank's mission by focusing on gender issues that are "particularly important for poverty reduction, economic growth, and well-being"; and (3) improve the alignment of Bank policies, processes, and resources to support strategic gender mainstreaming (World Bank 2002b, 15–17). However, what really makes the 2002 report such a significant step forward for the Bank is that it operationalizes these general goals into a concrete, three-step process accompanied with a detailed timetable for implementation at all levels and a significant budgetary commitment. The process entails the preparation of a periodic Country Gender Assessment (CGA) for each country with an active lending program; the development of a priority policy and operational interventions which respond to the CGA; and ongoing monitoring of the implementation and results of the policy and operational initiatives (World Bank 2002b, 18). While the focus is on process, it puts in the center policies and operational interventions. Unlike in UNDP, the process is a means to a defined policy end.

A review of progress of 2003 fiscal year activities (World Bank 2004) found that 22 percent of active client countries had completed a CGA and that there was increased attention to gender issues in core diagnostic economic and sector work and in country assistance strategies. Thirty-three poverty reduction strategy papers included an extensive diagnosis of gender inequalities, an increase over the previous year but still a low percentage given the fact that women make up a disproportionate number of the poor. Furthermore, there was demonstrably greater attention to gender issues in project design and supervision. The review identifies as challenges for the future the need to go from gender analysis to gender-responsive actions and the need to pay attention to gender issues in sectors other than health and education. It furthermore recognizes the need for more extensive "client and staff capacity building."

Not surprisingly, the Bank's focus on policy content has led to charges that it has co-opted radical agendas for institutional purposes. In particular, the 2001 report's linking of gender equality to free markets and economic growth raised consternation in the Bank's External Consultative Group on Gender, a civil society advisory group formed after the Beijing conference in order to establish a dialogue with feminists outside the Bank (World Bank 1999, 20). Aligning itself with World Bank rhetoric, the report celebrates economic growth as a means to gender equality. Far from subverting capitalist (and, some say, therefore patriarchal) agendas, it actually supports them. In addition, the institutionalist economic approach visible in the report has allowed the Bank to tame feminist critiques of liberal economics by defining economic and social issues as inhabiting separate spheres. Gender inequality becomes a social issue needing social interventions (Bergeron 2003), and gender mainstreaming in World Bank practice has concentrated on social issues like health and education. In this way, the Bank has adjusted feminist arguments to the logics of liberal economics, isolating gender analysis from finance and macroeconomic interventions, the Bank's bread and butter issues.

INTERNATIONAL LABOUR ORGANIZATION:
FROM WOMEN'S RIGHTS TO GENDER MAINSTREAMING

The ILO's concern with questions pertaining to women workers goes back to the first wave of the women's movement and the creation in 1926 within the office of a section responsible for women and children (Lubin and Winslow 1990, 209). Because of its long history of engaging with questions of social justice for women, the ILO has most firmly institutionalized policies in the area, formulated as international labor standards (conventions, recommendations, and declarations) and adopted by the International Labor Conference. Where UNDP has focused on organizational processes and the World Bank on fitting gender into its projects and programs, the ILO has participated in defining gender equality through an arsenal of conventions and recommendations. They include most importantly the equal pay convention (1951), the convention against discrimination in employment and occupation (1958), the convention on workers with family responsibilities (1981), and the maternity protection convention (last revised in 2000). These instruments emerge from an institutional mandate of promoting human rights and social justice and from a philosophy that considers government action and the institutionalization of tripartism as key sources of change. This is in contrast to the participatory and client-focused approach of UNDP and of the World Bank's technocratic advocacy of market reforms.

Two documents emerged from the ILO during the UN Women's Decade: the 1985 resolution on equal opportunities and treatment for men and women in employment and a 1987 plan of action that outlines the major areas of ILO activity toward the ends specified in the resolution. Means to accomplish these objectives included advising governments, training constituents, creating new standards, research, and technical cooperation activities. The language of mainstreaming does not appear in the documents, but one of the objectives listed in the plan is "to integrate women workers' questions fully into the overall programme of the ILO and ensure that women's issues feature adequately in research, information dissemination and technical cooperation activities" (ILO 1994, 132).

Perhaps because of its extensive record of formulating rights for women joined with a reliance on legislative strategies and on the social partners as change agents, the ILO was slow to take up mainstreaming as a matter of changing organizational processes. It created a WID coordinator position in 1986 whose mandate it was to integrate women's issues into the ILO's technical cooperation programs (Miller 1998, 152–53). A systematic integration of gender perspectives into a standard setting became an issue only in 1989 when the ILO created the position of Special Adviser on Women Workers' Questions. Efforts at decentralization and mainstreaming included interdepartmental committees and projects, the creation of focal points, the appointment of Regional Advisors for Women Worker's Questions to the four ILO regional headquarters, and finally the implementation of an institution-wide staff training program on gender in 1995 (156–57). Overall, ILO efforts suffered from the typical resource shortages. As at UNDP, many of the ILO personnel designated to address WID were expected to do so in addition to their prior responsibilities, an often impossible task (152–53). A 1998 UNRISD report on the ILO's gender focal point system found weaknesses due to a lack of senior management commitment, a lack of clarity of the role of the special advisor, the lack of an integrated institutional approach, and a shortage of human resources for gender mainstreaming (summarized in U. Murray 2001).

The advent of a new director-general, Juan Somavia, in March of 1999 meant a leap forward in the ILO's efforts to mainstream gender. Making gender mainstreaming a "high priority," Somavia changed the Office of the Special Advisor into the Bureau for Gender Equality, giving it a direct reporting line to the director-general and increasing its human and financial resources in an era of zero-budget growth. Anticipating an opportunity for change, the special advisor had already initiated a research and team-building process in 1998 that created the basis for a new action plan and a policy statement. Senior management adopted the action plan, and the director-general issued a circular on gender equality and gender mainstreaming in December 1999. Both documents placed a strong emphasis on process issues, addressing both the structure of the organization and numbers of women in professional staff in addition to mainstreaming gender into technical and operational work. Four main areas of focus have emerged in practice: structural arrangements in the office, capacity building, an accountability system with adequate resources, and a gender-sensitive human resource policy. There are now gender teams in each technical sector under the guidance of their executive directors to influence programming and capacity building. At the technical and operational level there was a 156 percent increase in resources allocated to gender mainstreaming from the 1998–99 to the 2000–2001 biennium (J. Zhang 2000; ILO, Governing Body 2000; ILO, Director-General's Announcements, 1999).

Capacity building played a key role in the early ILO efforts to mainstream. In 1999, the organization spent $158,000 to conduct eighteen workshops to train staff on gender issues. These efforts moved from general awareness-raising to more specific issues (e.g., gender in social security, poverty eradication, etc.). Various departments, including those not typically focused on gender (e.g., standards, social protection, social dialogue), completed assessments on the degree to which gender has been considered in their work and have participated in workshops to build capacity. Beginning in 2001, the ILO introduced gender audits, a participatory methodology of self-assessment in which facilitators guided fifteen units to review the significance of gender in their work area together with successes and shortcomings. The audits served the purpose of organizational learning paired with a review of effectiveness. The gender bureau plans to institutionalize the audit in future budget cycles. Findings from the first audit are instructive on the progress of gender mainstreaming within the ILO (*ILO Gender Audit 2001–02* 2002).

There has been considerable progress in mainstreaming gender into organizational processes. Although there are still shortcomings in implementation, the gender bureau is focusing on the development of improved indicators, monitoring and accountability systems, and tracking of expenditures to improve implementation. There is also an effort to define the roles and responsibilities of the gender focal points as catalysts while insisting that gender mainstreaming is the responsibility of all staff, including primarily senior management. Discussions in the human resources sector to define "core-competences" of all ILO staff now include a competence on gender matters. Furthermore, there has been progress in moving more women into professional positions; 37.6 percent of staff at the professional level and higher were women in 2003, up from 14.1 percent in the mid-1970s (phone interview of Elisabeth Prügl with Jane Youyun Zhang, 10 July 2001; U. Murray 2001; ILO Governing Body 2001, table 3; ILO 2004, table 4).

Interestingly, the audit found deficiencies in the area of policy. Under Somavia's leadership, the ILO has focused on creating "decent work" in a globalizing economy. Decent work is "work that is productive and delivers a fair income, security in the workplace and social protection for families, better prospects for personal development and social integration, freedom for people to express their concerns, organize and participate in the decisions that affect their lives and equality of opportunity and treatment for all women and men" (ILO Governing Body 2001). Despite the inclusion of gender equality in this definition, the gender audit identified a need to "define and deepen the understanding of gender equality concepts such as gender equity, empowerment of women, men and masculinities" as well as to "clarify what the gender equality issues are in the Decent Work agenda and define objectives" (ILO Gender Audit 2001–02 2002, 14). Gender mainstreaming pushes the ILO beyond the equality policies formulated in existing standards and recommendations. Key among the issues to be addressed is the position of women in the global economy, their disproportionate representation in the informal sector, and the unique policy issues that arise from women's disproportionate work in the unpaid care economy.

Given its institutional commitments, such policy issues may be difficult for the ILO to tackle. One of its key commitments is tripartism, that is, social dialogue between unions, employer organizations, and governments as a means toward establishing social justice. With women vastly underrepresented in unions and employer organizations, tripartism constitutes a significant challenge for the ILO's organizational process strategy. For example, at the 2001 International Labor Conference, women made up only 20 percent of all delegates, down from 21 percent the previous year. Only 14.5 percent of the worker representatives were female, and only 13.7 percent of the employer representatives. Moreover, of 410 speakers in the plenary only 12 percent were women (phone interview of Elisabeth Prügl with Jane Youyun Zhang, 10 July 2001; ILO Gender Audit 2001–02 2002, 65). The difficulty that unions and employer organizations have had in including women, together with a reluctance to include women's NGOs and women's machineries in tripartite social dialogues, is a measure of the challenge the ILO faces in its efforts to feminize the institution.

Aside from having limited the participation of women, tripartism also has limited what is possible in terms of output. For example, although the 1996 homework convention applied mostly to women who did not easily fit into an employer-employee dichotomy, the convention, applying a tripartite logic, forced the issue into this class-based distinction, excluding the self-employed from protection although they are often dependent economically. Arguably the disadvantaged position of home-based workers cannot be captured by a narrow class-perspective but arises as much from their subordinate gender status (Prügl

1999). A similar difficulty has emerged in current discussions of contract labor, which ran into severe conceptual and political problems at the 1997 International Labor Conference. Like home-based workers and the self-employed, contract workers do not fit neatly into the employer-employee dichotomy (Vosko 2001). The ILO also has had difficulty in dealing with the issue of women's unpaid housework and caring work. It has touched neither of these areas, although the disproportionate burden of unpaid work that women carry is one of the most important determinants of their subordination (Delphy and Leonard 1992).

The ILO's focus on tripartite social dialogue constitutes the equivalent of the World Bank's commitment to market forces and the UNDP's focus on participatory development. The foci constitute core commitments of these organizations that are difficult to change without challenging the very existence of the organization. They demand, from the organization's perspective, a co-optation of feminist purposes (Lotherington and Flemmen 1991). Mainstreaming is unlikely to change such core organizational values; whether this necessarily undermines the goal of gender equality is a matter of debate.

CONCLUSION

Multilateral institutions, at least those studied here, have responded to feminist demands to mainstream gender. To a surprising degree they have incorporated mainstreaming into their practices. They have done so on their own terms, fitting feminist demands to organizational purposes in different ways. For UNDP this has entailed subsuming the goal of gender equality to participatory sustainable development, for the World Bank to the rules of the market, and for the ILO to tripartism and social dialogue. Institutional purposes have allowed for different ways to mainstream. For UNDP, the emphasis on participation precluded writing a gender policy and put the focus on creating national and international capacities and a more accountable, feminine and democratic UNDP. For the World Bank, free market commitments precluded infusing gender into policies and shifted advocates' attention away from process in the early 1990s. However, a tempering of free market dogmatism has opened conceptual space for a gender policy that focuses on the institutions of the market at the turn of the century. For the ILO, a long-standing concern for women workers in its policies led to complacency regarding gender mainstreaming in the organization itself, an issue that is now being rectified. Mainstreaming gender in the ILO poses a challenge to the core value of a class-based tripartism.

Given the different meanings of mainstreaming that organizational pathways have yielded, it is difficult to know what success in mainstreaming would mean. Feminist agendas have been subsumed under organizational agendas in all three organizations. Co-optation is evident particularly in the case of the World Bank, the one organization that actually has spelled out its logic for addressing gender inequality. But all multilaterals have agendas in which gender equality is just one element. Does this mean that organizational strategies toward advancing gender equality are necessarily bound to fail?

Organizations are not social movements; they rarely engage in the single-minded contentious agitations typical of social movements and central to undermining structures of power. Organizational strategies thus are no substitute for movement strategies, and gender mainstreaming will be successful from a feminist perspective only if the movement remains involved in the process. Indeed, feminist activists have recognized the need for movement action to ensure that organizations are held accountable, not on the basis of their own priorities but on the basis of movement goals. Various efforts are underway to accomplish this. The "Women's Eyes on the World Bank" campaign seeks to hold the Bank accountable, and the Consultative Group on Gender has reminded the World Bank of the need to integrate gender issues in the areas of finance and economics (World Bank 2002). At the Security Council, resolution 1325 has provided an important opening, and feminists are now using the resolution to demand meaningful gender mainstreaming in peacekeeping operations (Cohn et al. 2004). In addition to this type of feminist activism, there is room for considerably more work on the part of feminist scholars. A beginning has been made by the Boston Consortium on Gender, Security and Human Rights, which seeks to link feminist academics with feminists in the UN.

The gender and development approach that has informed mainstreaming strategies started from the premise that gender inequality is structurally embedded. Thus, rectifying inequality requires a focus on institutions. Mainstreaming enables systematic attention to the differential impacts of policies and programs on women and men in organizational processes and outcomes and in this way addresses the structural embeddedness of gender inequality. At the same time, the experience reviewed here confirms that processes of co-optation are taking place and supports critics who have long warned of this danger associated with mainstreaming. It cautions feminists not to see gender mainstreaming as the be-all and end-all but to complement institutional with movement strategies. Movement agitation and critical research can take advantage of the knowledge produced by feminists inside international organizations and offer critique from a distance. In this way, movement activists and scholars can be an important source of support to femocrats inside organizations, providing ammunition and legitimacy while holding organizations accountable.

NOTES

1. Some donor agencies had adopted gender mainstreaming even before 1995 (Jahan 1995), Northern European agencies prominently among them (Council of Europe 1998, 17).

From "Home Economics" to "Microfinance": Gender Rhetoric and Bureaucratic Resistance

David Hirschmann

This essay begins by tracing changes in both the context of and progress in mainstreaming gender in foreign assistance. (Gender is used here as a shorthand for both gender awareness and analysis and an affirmative focus on women.) Although gender has become an ascendant, often uncontested rhetoric, the essay outlines a series of episodes (beginning with one in the early eighties and ending with another at the start of the new century) that illustrate strategies of bureaucratic resistance to gender. They illustrate changes in the character of that resistance, notably that it has become more professional, conceptual, and reliant on gender-exclusive models, more recently and most powerfully on the precepts of neoclassical economics. These two interconnected and contradictory themes—ascendant rhetoric and ongoing but modified resistance—anticipate the third and concluding section, which observes that implementation lags far behind rhetoric and seeks to explain how the economics and gender divide seriously limits the impact of gender on foreign assistance programs and policies.

My intent is to draw on the literature and record of WID and GAD in donor agencies and to adapt, update, and contribute to the ongoing history of WID, especially in the U.S. Agency for International Development (USAID). While the chapter's primary purpose is not to apply theory to practice, it is nevertheless informed by certain approaches. For a start, it accepts the notion that patriarchy is a prevailing institutional ideology of personnel in both donor and recipient agencies and that patriarchal biases create misperceptions of the roles of men and women in developing countries (Tinker 1990c, 3, 37, 40). But one of its main purposes is to demonstrate changes in the character and representation of those patriarchal attitudes. Through "engagement" and "entryism" (Miller and Razavi 1998a, 6) institutions can adapt to new thinking, but this may not amount to a meaningful acceptance of those ideas. In focusing on the byzantine realm of bureaucratic politics (Staudt 1997; Kardam 1991, 1997b; Tinker 1997b, 7) the essay finds much to learn from the established critiques of large bureaucracies, including goal displacement, reduction of uncertainty, routinizing of interactions, and rationing services (Chandler and Plano 1982, 173–74; Goetz 1998, 45). In observing changes in donor-recipient relationships it draws from literature on aid dependence (Brautigam 2000; Lensink and White 1997; Tsikata 2001), which is often applied to economic and policy change but seldom to gender. Finally, James Scott's writing on resistance of the weak and their hidden transcripts is helpful too, although it will be used here to describe strategies of the not-so-weak and even the reasonably strong. When Scott writes of "routines of deference and compliance" that if "not entirely cynical are certainly calculating" (1990, 278), his observations resonate closely with the responses of bureaucrats described here.

The essay relies to a great extent on participant observation over twenty years of work with aid agencies (mostly but not only AID), national bureaucracies, and sometimes NGOs, where I have had the formal role of researcher or consultant and the informal role of advocate for enhanced incorporation of gender as well as other social categories and issues.

AN ASCENDANT RHETORIC

When this story begins, in 1984, the literature on "dependencia" was more fashionable than today's "aid dependence," and I continue to find validity in much of that earlier literature. Looking at the narrower set of relationships involved in foreign aid, however, the literature on aid dependence is quite helpful, in particular the notion that apparently endless flows of resources, advice, and conditions have fashioned a relationship of asymmetric interdependence between donors and recipients. Aid limits recipients' room for maneuver, creating distorted incentives that encourage further dependency (rather than self-reliance), and leads to ever more duplicitous language in the negotiation and implementation of aid agreements.

In the eighties, the foreign assistance context was dominated by donors. The nature of that dominance has changed, however, as poor governments, seriously in debt, desperately short of resources and increasingly unable to pay even the recurrent costs of basic services, submit to whatever they are told. More significantly, the economic status of the educated mid- to senior-level bureaucrats who are the local counterparts of aid donors has changed. The value of their salaries has dropped precipitously and their tenure is uncertain. Conditions have deteriorated to such an extent that their privileged status as members of the middle or upper middle class is now symbolic rather than substantive. The world poverty line is set at $2 a day or $60 a month. There are many mid-level members of African civil services with university degrees, for example, who do not earn much more.

Humiliated, poor, and seeing little opportunity for government to pay improved salaries, many of the more innovative among them have become personally dependent on foreign donors for their survival. They may achieve access to this flow of funds by having their salaries topped up by donors. Or they may leave the civil service either to work for donor agencies or donor projects or international or national NGOs supported by donors. They are not only dependent but also thoroughly socialized in the ways of donors. There has been a continuous education process with attached incentives: international, regional, and local conferences, fellowships, study tours, workshops and more workshops, one on one relationships with donors, consultancies, and so forth. Donors' requirements are laid down through the conditions placed on grants and through responses to proposals or bids and job descriptions; donor interests are further reinforced through employment of local staff. One way or another, donors make it clear what they want and who they will reward (Hirschmann 2002).

In order to keep the resources flowing to their organizations and themselves, recipients have come to accept and apply these requirements. They keep their ears close to the ground, listening carefully for changes in donor direction, nuance, and jargon. They have learned to say and do the right things, often initiating the very proposals that donors might have made for them in the past. This doubly pleases donors because such proposals not only accord with their policies but appear to come directly from the recipients themselves and reflect their ownership. This has been observed in several sectors, including economic policy reform, privatization, civil society, the promotion of a multiparty electoral system, decentralization, and HIV/AIDS, among others.

So too with gender. Over the years donors have made gender analysis almost a condition (sometimes formal and sometimes substantive) of project assistance. Whatever male bureaucrats in recipient governments or NGOs may actually believe about women's roles, there will be a calculated compliance with the gender component of the program. Out of necessity or conviction, far more recipient agencies today are ready to listen. Both Miller and Razavi (1998a, 13) and Goetz (1998, 43) have taken note of this donor-driven WID or GAD agenda, noting that it is accepted out of financial need and expressing concerns about the degree of local ownership of such programs. Local bureaucrats have also come under pressure from local advocates, usually women in NGOs, in government ministries, in the local missions of donors and, in a few cases, women politicians. These can add up to a fairly effective alliance making the case for gender.

Donor agencies have also changed. In 1984 the pressure to implement WID programs was relatively new and weak, and there were few effective threats or incentives attached. WID policy proposals were not yet backed by solid research findings, and research on women and development had not yet been translated into effective and persuasive user-friendly materials. Today gender is an ascendant and accepted rhetoric; the gender transcript is overt and comes from the mouths of the powerful. Jahan (1995, 2) notes that these advances in understanding and awareness of gender issues have been translated into mandates and policies. There is no leader in a multilateral or bilateral or international NGO who does not express support for gender (ACFVA 2000, 8; United Nations 2001; World Bank 2002b, 1).

Those who argue the case have far more experience in persuasion than they did twenty years ago. An influential constituency of Western activists and scholars who favor enhanced attention to women observes foreign aid policies closely. Impressive academic and applied research findings and publications back up their arguments. Donors also keep an eye on each other. There are more women at senior- and middle-level management than there used to be and, although not all of them are strong advocates of gender, research shows that a higher proportion of women than men usually are (Miller 1998, 154). Many men who belonged to an earlier, more recalcitrant generation have left the service, and the newer generation is much more comfortable with the ideals of gender equality at home, in the office, and as a condition of foreign assistance. Even if they wanted to, they would find it hard to disagree openly because of the powerful pressures of political correctness, the incentive structure in their jobs, and because of the validity and power of the argument.

Gender-awareness is also bolstered by reporting and measurement requirements. There is a wide range of training tools and exemplary success stories backed by convincing evidence, such as women's capacity to associate constructively, women's reliability in microloan repayment, and the positive impacts of girls' secondary education. A "business case" has been made for the causal links between gender-aware practices and improved project and economic performance and governance (World Bank 2000, 8, 9, 11). A recent assessment found that most USAID employees have a "growing general commitment to addressing gender equality." According to one USAID official: "The light-bulb has gone on at USAID; we buy gender equality" (ACVFA 2000, 16–17).

My recent work on a USAID-sponsored program on advocacy in a southern African country provided evidence of the clear influence of gender rhetoric on both donor and recipient. Eleven elements of advocacy were suggested to the NGO grantees to serve as management, measurement, and reporting tools. These elements included consultation with members, steps taken to influence legislators, and so forth; one required a gender analysis of policies. In a spirit of meaningful partnership and local ownership, grantees were encouraged to question and challenge any of these elements with one exception: gender. As it turned out the only element that was questioned (by a minority less experienced in working with USAID) was the gender element. Representatives said simply that this was not a priority in the policies that they were seeking to change. But gender trumped participation. Grantees were told this was not negotiable. In addition there were women's NGO grantees who vocally supported the gender requirement. In the end, the grantees got the message and with help "discovered" and worked on the gender elements of their program.

THE CHANGING FORM OF BUREAUCRATIC RESISTANCE

In response to the rise in gender rhetoric, the face (and voice) of patriarchy in aid and recipient agencies has modified. It is not as thoughtless or arrogant or confident or blatant or overt as it used to be. Professionals have been educated by the arguments in favor of gender, probably acknowledge the good sense of some of them, and know the need to incorporate the language of gender. The following four episodes, drawn from the author's own experiences, are intended to trace the changes in bureaucratic resistance as it has responded to the evolution of gender analysis and pressure for enhanced attention to women's roles in foreign assistance.[1]

Gender and Agriculture in the Mid-1980s:
"Go See the Home Economics People"

In the mid-1980s I carried out research on behalf of the Economic Commission for Africa into women and policy making in Malawi. Part of that process involved interviewing civil servants (overwhelmingly men) about their attitudes toward women in development and women in planning. So began my long (although interrupted) conversation with bureaucrats about women and gender.

Initially, I observed the strange body language of the men as they exhibited discomfort and distancing, and I learned to listen to the language of bureaucratic resistance to the inclusion of women in development. Sometimes it was a wink of anticipated male solidarity implying that I should and did really know better; sometimes it was a look at a wristwatch to indicate that this was not very important and was not going to get very much time; often it was a look of surprise at why I had come to see them or a joke in the bar in the evening after a day in a workshop. At meetings it was the reading or shuffling of papers as women (at that stage, junior and in the minority) sought to make contributions to male-dominated meetings.

To explain male superiority in the civil service and in policy making, in those days Malawi civil servants (and donor officers too) often used phrases such as "customary," "how it has always been," "women's own consciousness," "cultural," and even "Christian." The terms "natural" and "'naturally" also cropped up frequently and in a wide variety of contexts: "Naturally women become nurses/ secretaries and men become doctors/bosses." "Naturally girls don't want to be plumbers." "Naturally women's fingers are more flexible than men's (and that is why they are better tea pickers)." "Naturally more women than men are illiterate." The terms "traditional" and "customary" were used in combination on many occasions, and they could refer to African or Western traditions. "Our custom is that women should be subordinate to men." Many stressed and glorified the role of women in the home (Hirschmann 1990, 170–71).

In the Ministry of Agriculture, custom and subordination were expressed by the emphasis on home economics for women, especially in agricultural training. The model was that women naturally belonged in the home and that their role there should be enhanced. Therefore, the only appropriate vocational training for girls at high schools and training for women at agricultural schools and colleges was home economics. The fact that women were at the time responsible for most of the farming was of little consequence in light of these ideological convictions. I recall the looks of surprise when I began to ask about women in agriculture at the policy level or in technical departments such as crops or livestock. It was suggested in a perfectly friendly but final way that I was in the wrong department and should go and talk with the home economics people.

This is history, but it is useful to recall because the idea that women exclusively operated in the home was both Victorian and colonial. Although much else colonial was rejected after independence, especially when it did not square with African reality, this myth was retained because it conveniently and effectively supported patriarchal notions of hierarchy in production, in cash incomes, and in the ministry's jobs. It was also very much part of rural development ideology and agricultural extension thinking of donors at the time, as women's roles in the agricultural colleges were also largely confined to home economics. The emphasis on home economics, despite its obvious benefits in terms of issues like hygiene and household management, helped men retain control of the core activity of the ministry and focus its core services on male farmers.

Implementing Gender Policy Reform in the Early 1990s:
"That's Micro-management"

In the early 1990s I worked in a southern African country as a member of a five-person evaluation and design team looking at a USAID program that was about two years into its implementation. By the end of the eighties, the World Bank and USAID recognized that they would need to make explicit efforts to address the rigidities and inequities built into the country's agricultural sector. Since the returns to burley tobacco were estimated to be seven to nine times higher than the returns to a similar area of hybrid maize and even more than that of cotton, the donors pressed two reluctant and powerful economic and political establishments, namely the tobacco industry and the government, to open up access to the benefits of burley to peasant farmers. The primary purpose of the program therefore was to deregulate a highly controlled economy, using burley tobacco as a test case, while targeting certain categories of beneficiaries. The tension arose essentially from the fact that although this was primarily a policy initiative, it was also a poverty alleviation program aimed at certain disadvantaged groups.

In terms of targeting, the program was intended to reach smallholders with less than 1.5 ha (3.7 ac) of land and women farmers. The innovation succeeded insofar as a growing number of smallholders began cultivating this very profitable crop. It was unclear, however, if the intended target group, those with less than 1.5 ha (3.7 ac) and women, were benefiting sufficiently. My job was to assess the inclusion of women.

In order to assess the impact on women, it was necessary to learn first what was going on with poorer farmers in general. It soon became apparent, as it has on other occasions, that the "gender person" on the assessment team had become the "people's person," often the only one on the team. This person's responsibility included both gender and equity. In this case, no one on the team opposed this focus in principle. Rather they emphasized the practical difficulties of giving too much attention to small farmers and women. In the second year of the program, women accounted for 12.5 percent of participants. Despite a serious effort, women were at a significant disadvantage for several reasons: the shortage of labor, their caution in the face of risk, their lack of familiarity with tobacco as a cash crop, the size of the credit package, the need to pay someone to build their curing barns, and the requirement that this tobacco be planted pure stand as a monocrop rather than a component of a mixed cropping system with which most of these women were more comfortable.

In a policy environment of economic liberalization, some on the design team made strong arguments for leaving the system to work itself out. In their view, the project was bringing about major changes in tobacco production, the market was being opened up and small farmers—defined as smallholders, a somewhat larger category—were benefiting and stimulating secondary impacts on the rural economy. Furthermore, the limitations on the extension service made effective targeting unrealistic. To challenge this logic and argue for more careful focus on ensuring that farmers with 1.5 ha (3.7 ac) and women farmers were in fact being reached was dismissed as micromanagement. I was given two days to interview women farmers to find out what their problems were, and the burden was placed on me to find incentives, arrangements, and procedures to ensure that the intended beneficiaries actually profited.

This was a new stage in the evolution of gender analysis among donors, including USAID. This was no longer a negative environment; it was pro-poor, a pro-women program and I was working with a gender-aware, pro-women team and mission. Yet neither was concerned enough to confront the details of the challenge. Policy reform was transcendent, and project management became the "orphan." The years of effort that had gone into economic policy reform explain some of the lack of interest in dealing with people and therefore with women at the project level. The emphasis on policy generated a hands-off attitude, which asserted that the donor was not in the business, nor should it be, nor did it have the staff to micromanage development programs. Intellectually and operationally, the focus on the macrolevel issues for a period of a decade or more had taken the Agency away from a focus on people and from attention to participation. Without a project- and people-oriented approach, WID became far more difficult to justify and less persuasive to those who needed to be convinced. This created a heavy burden on the WID advocate who was forced not only to argue for a difficult cause but also to argue for the poorest beneficiaries and be marginalized as an advocate of "micromanagement" (Hirschmann 1995b).

Gender and Democracy in the 1990s: Shut Out of the Model

In December 1990, USAID called for a program to promote democracy. In April 1992, the WID Office of USAID asked me to work on the gender aspects of this new initiative. WID was by then a well-established notion but not yet well institutionalized in the Agency. After a decade and a half of pressure to include women in projects and planning, there was a feeling of "WID fatigue" at USAID. In addition, a serious impediment to the inclusion of gender analysis and women's participation in the democratization initiative was the assumption that since democracy was good for everyone, special attention to gender concerns would not be needed (Hirschmann 1995a).

But the more complex challenge related to conceptual exclusion. During the process of introducing a new direction in USAID, theory and conceptualization are taken seriously. Consultants and experts are brought in to provide intellectual frameworks, and the policy and intellectual leadership of the Agency then engages in debates over these various approaches and their implications. The outcomes of these debates have important policy and expenditure implications.

In this instance the concept papers focused on theories, institutions, systems and processes of democracy, and sometimes the role of the economic environment in making democracy likely to succeed. All these approaches have validity, but all fail to focus on society and people. In assuming that "people" are homogeneous these approaches gloss over the fact that there are different categories of people who will inevitably be affected by, and participate in, democratic change in very different ways. As with economic policy, an institutional approach to democracy that does not look at people makes it much more difficult to attend to gender analysis or women. One serious oversight was the failure of the models to connect the political dynamics of democratization to the private domain. Because they overlooked the fact that many restrictions on women's legal and political capacity derive from limitations established within the household, they were unable to comprehend the predicament of women in the transition to democracy.

Once models harden into policy they become resistant to further challenge or reassessment (or, to put it differently, the bureaucrats in charge may rely on them to resist the challenges). If an issue cannot be fit into the main model, the case for it loses conceptual respect and is excluded from the mainstream efforts under the initiative (Kardam 1991, 7). It is forced into the unenviable position that WID is always fighting to avoid: to be no more than an add-on or part of a list of "check-offs" or requests.

The fate of "civil society" in the democracy initiative provides a telling example. Women's participation was almost excluded from consideration, not because of local laws or constitutional provisions but as a result of the donor's definition of the term, in particular, the donor's view of the relationship between civil society and the state. If civil society is defined as that part of society that interacts with the state in an effort to influence policy, many civil society organizations may be excluded. USAID officials appeared to see advantages in limiting the definition in this way to reduce the complexity of targeting their assistance and simplify the evaluation of the impact of their work.

However, as my own research and that of others (e.g., Tripp 1994) shows, women are active in a far broader ambit. Much of women's associational activity takes place in the social, nonstate-focused sphere. The state-oriented definition not only excluded much of women's activity (and that of other nonelite groups), it missed the essential and dynamic overlap between the private and public spheres and tended to limit USAID support only to the sorts of NGOs, such as think tanks, advocacy groups, lobby organizations, interest groups, and professional and social associations, that fit readily with Western (and elitist) notions of civil society.

Poor people and women mobilize around practical and concrete concerns—this is what makes them appropriate, sustainable, and self-reliant. If civil society is to be meaningful for poor people, it is these sorts of organizations that are most likely to make it so. Too many webs of activity link the public to the private, the social to the political, the nonstate- to the state-focused, and the strategic to the practical to draw neat lines of demarcation. Doing so excludes not only the challenges women face in political participation but also ignores much of women's distinctive and positive contributions to the political, economic, and social dynamics of democratization (Hirschmann 1998).

This argument was made to USAID. It would be claiming too much to suggest that the Agency listened, but it did change its wording slightly—directing its funds to what it now termed "politically active civil society." This did not alter or broaden the Agency's focus, but at least it acknowledged that "civil society" might be a more inclusive concept, and it made transparent what kinds of organizations its missions were likely to support.

Macroeconomics and Gender in 2000:
"Go See the Microfinance People"

More recently I was asked to work in a large USAID mission on strategic planning and performance measurement. The task this time was to ensure that the issues of poverty and gender were incorporated in all performance measurements. The mission was resorting to a typical practice of getting a consultant team of outsiders to do something they did not feel they could do themselves, a tactic that left them with a scapegoat if things did not go well. In this case the major challenge was not so much to incorporate gender in projects—there had been some progress in this regard—but in the area of economic policy.

As one does on these assignments, I visited the contracts office and got agreement to incorporate gender in all future contracts (required in principle since the Percy Amendment of 1973, and by USAID's Gender Action Plan of 1996 [ACVFA 2000, 12]). I got the support from the director and, having conferred with various departments, found ways to ensure a gender (and a poverty) measurement were included in the mission's assessment plan. But, as an outsider, on site for no more than three weeks, my impact was likely to be minimal and even further reduced by the fact that a major transfer of most of the senior personnel was about to take place.

However, the most daunting challenge was to gain the cooperation of the economic policy office. In this mission, the WID Office and the economic policy office were in two different buildings, but in terms of meaningful technical communication, they might have been in different countries. They needed someone to communicate between them. When I went, somewhat tentatively, to visit the economists, they suggested I should talk with the microfinance people, since "they dealt with women." There was an all too clear echo of the agriculture officer telling me to "go and see the home economics people"—déjà vu all over again.

The challenge was even more difficult in this case, however. The inertial patriarchal hierarchy of the bureaucracy was now reinforced by the supposedly gender-neutral convictions of a professional discipline. Economists in the mission were uncomfortable and appeared not to know, or were not going to be helpful if they did know, how to move their analysis from the national level to more disaggregated projections and assessments of policy impacts in any way, including by gender. They said it was not possible to tease out the effects in this way. Since their professional training had not prepared them to do this, such an analysis was not economics to them. It would certainly complicate their work.

Microfinance was therefore convenient. Economists are pleased because it enables them to incorporate something relevant to women without complicating their macroanalysis. WID people too are relieved because they can design and evaluate programs without much economic expertise; donors are happy because it presents them with exemplary success stories to justify their programs for women.

And, it must be acknowledged that being directed to the microfinance section of the mission, located in the economic policy office, represents an improvement over being sent to talk to the home economists in the mid-1980s. The microfinance model accepts that women operate outside of the home, that they are agents in the economy, and can save, borrow, sell, produce, and make money. It even acknowledges that they are much more reliable than men in repayment of credit. However, the model does not let them go very far from home and limits them to the "small" if not always truly "micro" level of commerce. It sometimes dismisses women in these programs as "unbusinesslike" because they often use profits for purposes of family nutrition and school fees (Tinker 1990c, 41). But above all, microfinance excludes women's specific constraints and contributions from broader economic policy analysis.

CONCLUSION

Macroeconomics and Gender Analysis: "Check Feminist Beliefs at the Door" or "Go to the Sociology Department."

Using cases from my experiences primarily at USAID, this essay has traced how the gendered component of foreign aid has been enhanced over a period of about twenty years and how bureaucratic resistance has been modified in response to that success.[2] The overall conclusion is that gender has become a relatively ascendant and often unchallenged rhetoric, yet bureaucratic resistance continues, albeit in different forms, and, partly in consequence, the impact of gender has been limited.

Some evidence for lack of impact is found in the December 1993 review by the U.S. General Accounting Office, which found that twenty years after the enactment of the Percy Amendment on women in development, USAID's progress had been disappointing. In their view, "many agency officials view women-in-development as either a narrow special interest issue or as one more directive for an overburdened staff" (U.S. General Accounting Office 1993, 4,5). In 2000 this lack of progress was further confirmed by the Advisory Committee on Voluntary Foreign Aid (ACVFA) assessment of the effectiveness of USAID's Gender Plan of Action (GPA) launched in 1996 with strong support of the Agency's leadership. Yet, four years later, based on over 500 interviews and a field survey of USAID's 71 missions, ACFVA found that less than 5 percent of those interviewed in USAID and the private volunteer organization communities that work closely with AID were even familiar with the GPA. No USAID personnel outside of the WID Office could cite an example of progress made because of GPA. As is usually the case, many reasons were given. These included a proliferation of other priorities, budget cuts, reengineering, a new management system, and lack of resources or clear support (ACVFA 2000, 15–16). Of interest is a 2003 assessment of the World Bank's most recent gender strategy, which came to the same conclusions about lack of progress on gender: "The other very large camp consists of the majority of the Bank staff who are unaware of the Strategy and among whom few promote gender equality objectives" (Zuckerman and Wu 2003, 50).

Yet the ACVFA assessment also found that despite lack of progress on yet one more gender pronouncement, USAID employees believed (or said they believed) that the Agency did have a growing commitment to gender equality (2000, 16–17). Clearly the gap between acceptance of gender awareness and the failure to take responsibility to implement gender policies calls for some explanation. "Gender" appears to have been widely but not deeply accepted in donor culture. It is supported when it is limited in scope and ambition, has its own resources to support it, does not wander too far or fast beyond its accepted confines, and does not complicate or burden life too much for busy professionals. The result is a quiet undermining of the effectiveness of gender analysis and commitment to women through chronically delayed or unimplemented mandates. Gender analysis is not taken as a serious conceptual framework, especially, as illustrated by the last episode described above, by economists. In the current environment, where foreign assistance is specifically tied to economic policy goals, this is bad news for those who want to support programs that have a substantial impact on women's livelihoods and choices.

Some authors have noted that engendering macroeconomics and economic policy is a major challenge (Tinker 1993c, 64; Miller and Razavi 1998a, 7). Budlender (2002, 4), reporting on experiences with gender responsive budgets, confirms that opposition typically comes from economic affairs departments. Gita Sen notes that macroeconomics "carries with it an aura of technical expertise . . . that shrouds its purveyors in a thick veil of mystery" (quoted in Budlender 2002, 39). Miller and Razavi (1998a, 7) observe "how resistant to feminist incursions" macroeconomic decision making has been "dominated by men schooled in gender-blind neo-classical economics." Cloud (1994, 71) notes the challenges of carrying out gendered research relevant to economic policy. "The closer you come to the household the more the complexity becomes visible." Haddad et al. (1995, 893), pointing out how hard it is to measure impact of economic policy at the macro level, explain how much more difficult it is to evaluate impacts at the micro level of the individual and the household, especially when intrahousehold dynamics are taken into account.

Anne Marie Goetz provides a helpful additional perspective on the power of neoclassical economics to exclude gender analysis (2001, 285). She writes of the "commanding presence" of an "authoritative voice" that interprets situations and people's needs. Economics as a form of "knowledge" is based on "distanced and disinterested applications of 'objective' (as opposed to compassionate or empathetic) rules and techniques . . . on 'destruction of ambiguity and the control of difference.' 'Claims to know' which are based on women's experiences have not carried as much weight" (286).

Researching and discussing feminism and economics in the United States, Randy Albelda comes closest to the core of the problem (1997, 4). Although she takes note of improvements of the feminist contribution to economics (in terms of numbers of Ph.D.s, publications, and associations), she concludes that "feminism has had little impact on economic thinking since the 1970s. Economics holds the distinction of being the most male dominated discipline among the social sciences and the humanities in the United States." And within the field, neoclassical economists exercise "hegemonic control over the discipline's methodology and its social and intellectual institutions" (5). Albelda writes: "It is hard to imagine a theory of social economic interactions that is less responsive to modern day feminist methodologies than neoclassical economics" (6). "Any discipline that assiduously avoids modeling or describing power relations among actors," that is built "on a model that is ahistorical and predicated on harmonious relationships among self-interested, self-satisfying individual economic actors . . . operating in a world with no non-market relations," makes it extremely difficult to constructively incorporate feminist methodologies (5, 6).

Using neoclassical economic analysis to set international, national, and sectoral economic policies, donors in various kinds of negotiation with recipient government ministries determine the major directions and resources of foreign assistance. Lacking gender analysis, the pursuant policy outcomes will be gender blind but not of course gender neutral. By that stage all we are left with is "microfinance."

Of course there are feminist economists who can and do engage in the debate and have the professional expertise, the will, and the creativity to do so effectively and persuasively. There are convincing arguments that gender discrimination creates market distortions, allocative deficiencies, and factor market rigidities. These economists have clarified too when the market alone cannot explain or overcome male bias and illustrated the differential gender impacts of subsidies and taxes (Elson 1995b, 164–90; 2002, 23–30; Razavi 1998, 26–32, Miller 1998, 10, 164; Jahan 1995, 710; Budlender et al. 2002). Non-U.S. donors have made greater headway on more gender aware economic policy, and there has been very interesting early progress on gender responsive budgeting (Budlender 2002; Budlender et al. 2002; VeneKlasen 2002; Bartle and Ruben 2002).

The problem for USAID is that this expertise has not become a sustained part of the Agency's operations and certainly not of the country missions. Missions still bring in outsiders to visit the technical offices to persuade, argue, harangue, nudge, remind, and write a report and then leave. And the mission goes on much as before. Partly (and these are all causally interrelated) this is because the WID officer cannot be expected to be a technical expert in every field in which USAID is working, and without technical expertise it is very difficult to "mainstream" the core of any field. Partly it is because USAID appears not to have selected its economists on the basis of gender expertise (or willingness to engage with the concerns raised by social differentiation or gender analysis), nor its WID officers on the basis of their professional credibility as economists. This lack of expertise is a key challenge. Partly it is because USAID and its still small WID office (possibly discouraged by lack of progress) have not chosen to take on macroeconomic issues in their gender strategy. The recent study of the World Bank, referred to above, observes the same weaknesses in engendering macroeconomic policies (Zuckerman and Wu 2003, 52).

Until gender becomes an integral component of economic policy analysis, there may be small advances in gender mainstreaming in particular areas, but the bulk of foreign assistance resources will continue to be assigned with little attention to women, and gender analysis and pro-women advocates will continue to find their concerns sidelined rather than mainstreamed.

NOTES

I want to thank Irene Tinker for sharing her ideas over the years and ensuring that both gender analysis and a women's focus were incorporated in the curriculum of the International Development Program at American University and for listening to my thoughts on this chapter. I also want to thank the editors and Deborah Brautigam for helpful comments and Robyn Yaker for research assistance.

1. In the first three examples I draw at some length on my own work; see Hirschmann 1990, 1995a, 1995b, and 1998.

2. The first quote in the subhead is the title of a chapter in Albelda (1997). The second is from a quote in Penelope Ciancanelli and Bettina Berch, "Gender and GNP," in *Analyzing Gender: A Handbook of Social Science Research*, edited by Beth B. Hess and Myra Marx Ferree, Newbury Park, Calif.: Sage, which was quoted by Albelda 1997, 3. The quote reads: "If you were to ask the average neoclassical economist to explain the economic basis of gender stratification, you would be directed in all likelihood, to the sociology department."

Contributions of a Gender Perspective to the Analysis of Poverty

Sylvia Chant

Although there is no clear consensus on how poverty should be defined and measured, in general terms approaches to poverty have become more holistic over the past twenty-five years. This has encompassed a shift, at least in theory, from a narrow focus on incomes and consumption to recognition of poverty as a multi-dimensional phenomenon. Integral to the move from a quantitative to a more qualitative approach is the need for analyses of poverty to incorporate people's own voices and to embrace subjective criteria. Concepts of power and empowerment have also occupied an increasingly significant role within debates on poverty at both micro and macro levels. At the latter scale, for example, there has been growing acknowledgment of the fact that imposed, "objective," universalizing, and inevitably Eurocentric constructions and classifications of poverty may be disempowering to people in the South.[1] Another major shift in poverty analysis in the last quarter century has been the incorporation of the hitherto invisible dimension of gender. As summed-up by Kabeer:

> Poverty has not always been analysed from a gender perspective. Prior to the feminist contributions to gender analysis, the poor were either seen as composed entirely of men or else women's needs and interests were assumed to be identical to, and hence subsumable under, those of male household heads (1997, 1).

Gender research and advocacy have not only "challenged the gender-blindness of conventional poverty measurement, analysis and policy in a number of different ways" (1997, 1), but have had other impacts too. An essay of this length cannot do justice to all the contributions made by gender research to the analysis of poverty. My aim is to highlight some of the most important elements through a brief review of four interrelated issues. These are first, the ways in which a gender perspective has influenced how poverty is defined and conceptualized; second, the impacts of gender on how poverty is measured; third, the contributions of gendered analyses to understanding the uneven distribution of poverty and poverty-generating processes between women and men; and fourth, what gender and poverty analyses offer in relation to questions surrounding the economic empowerment of women.

In order to contextualize these themes, it is important to highlight the main bodies of feminist literature which have had direct and indirect influences on mainstream poverty analyses.

MAJOR BODIES OF GENDER RESEARCH WITH
IMPLICATIONS FOR POVERTY ANALYSES

Early WID Research

The earliest substantial work on gender with implications for thinking on poverty came with the United Nations Decade for Women (1975–1985). In drawing attention to the invisibility of women in development, the UN Decade spawned unprecedented efforts to discover and expose what women did and to explore how they fared in developmental change in comparison with men. Given the strong interest in women's material well-being and in their productive roles at this time, much research focused on low-income women. This offered several new perspectives on poverty, one of which was to emphasize how women were consistently more affected by poverty than men. Detailed survey work at the micro level generated a considerable body of evidence on gender disparities in earnings and on the processes which gave rise to those disparities such as inequalities in literacy and education, discrimination in labor markets, and unequal gender divisions of work in the home. Research also showed that in directing development projects to male household heads, women either missed out as heads of household in their own right or as members of male-headed units. In the latter case, for example, increasing resources to male household heads did not automatically confer benefits to women and children. This raised questions about the relevance of "the household" as a unitary, altruistic entity, and, *ipso facto*, as an appropriate target of interventions for the promotion of economic development or the alleviation of poverty.

A second set of perspectives on poverty emanating from this early research on women was that it revealed the difficulties of obtaining meaningful data on *any* aspect of women's lives (whether in respect of material privation or otherwise) from macro-level statistics. This called into question how data that were not disaggregated by gender could provide an effective basis for gender-neutral, let alone gender-aware, policy interventions.

A third feature of early research with relevance for poverty was that it highlighted the paradox whereby women's considerable inputs to household survival went unmatched by social recognition, either within the context of their families and communities or in society at large. The frequently silenced and hidden nature of women's lives indicated that there was more than a material dimension to gendered hardship and subordination. This, in turn, was an important element in stimulating more multidimensional analyses of poverty.

Gender and Structural Adjustment

A second wave of gender work with implications for poverty analysis came with the "Lost Decade of the 1980s."[2] A spate of research on the grassroots impacts of structural adjustment programs in different parts of the world demonstrated unequivocally that the burdens of debt crisis and neoliberal reform were being shouldered unequally by women and men (see Elson 1989; Moser 1989b; Safa and Antrobus 1992). While the importance of "unpacking" households to ascertain gendered dimensions of poverty was an important feature of earlier research, the unprecedented evidence for intrahousehold inequality during the 1980s saw definitive rejection of the unitary household model. The findings of empirical studies of structural adjustment were lent conceptual support by broader shifts in theorizing about households associated with new institutional economics and the notion of domestic units as sites of "cooperative conflict" (see A. Sen 1987a, 1990; also Dwyer and Bruce 1988; Young 1992).

During neoliberal restructuring, cutbacks in state services and subsidies (health care, investments in housing and infrastructure, the rising prices of basic foodstuffs, and so on) transferred a swathe of costs onto the private sector, and it was women who largely "footed the bill" (Kanji 1991). The making-up of shortfalls in household income required more effort in domestic provisioning, which gave women heavier burdens of reproductive work in their homes and communities (see Brydon and Legge 1996; González de la Rocha 1988a). This burden was intensified by the increased time women had to spend in income-generating activities. Meanwhile, there was little evidence for a corresponding increase in the range and intensity of men's inputs to household survival (Chant 1994; Langer et al. 1991; Moser 1997; UNICEF 1997). It became clear that it was impossible to analyze the poverty-related corollaries of structural adjustment without acknowledging gender. This, in turn, underlined the integral part that gender awareness should play in wider work on poverty.

Female-Headed Households and the Feminization of Poverty

The need to mainstream gender within poverty analyses was further reinforced by research on growing numbers of women-headed households[3] both during and after the Lost Decade. Much of this research placed emphasis on the disadvantage borne by female-headed units in comparison with their male-headed counterparts. Women-headed households were linked definitively with the concept of a global feminization of poverty and assumed virtually categorical status as the poorest of the poor (see Acosta-Belén and Bose 1995; Bullock 1994; Buvinic 1995, 3; Buvinic and Gupta 1993; Kennedy 1994; Tinker 1990a; UNDAW 1991). In broader work on poverty, and especially in policy circles, the poverty of female-headed households effectively became a proxy for women's poverty, if not poverty in general (see Jackson 1996; Kabeer 1996; also May 2001, 50).

Women-headed households were typecast as the poorest of the poor on grounds of their allegedly greater likelihood of being poor and of experiencing more pronounced degrees of indigence than male-headed units (see, e.g., Bridge 2001; Buvinic and Gupta 1993; González de la Rocha 1994a, 6–7; Moghadam 1997; Paolisso and Gammage 1996). These assumptions intermeshed with the notion that poverty was a major cause of female household headship (through forced labor migration, conjugal breakdown under financial stress, lack of formal marriage, and so on) (Fonseca 1991, 138). In turn, female headship itself was regarded as exacerbating poverty because women were time- and resource-constrained by their triple burdens of employment, housework, and child care; because they were discriminated against in the labor market; and because they lacked the valuable nonmarket work provisioned by "wives" in male-headed units.[4] More recently, an additional factor held to account for the disadvantage of female-headed households, albeit less documented in the South than the North, has been the "gendered ideology of the welfare state and its bureaucracy" (see Bibars 2001). There has also been a remarkably persistent notion that poverty is intergenerationally perpetuated because female heads cannot "properly support their families or ensure their well-being" (Mehta et al. 2000, 7).

Although it is undeniable that women suffer disproportionately from social and economic inequalities, whether these disadvantages translate whole-
sale to women-headed households is less certain. Indeed, an increasing number
of studies from various parts of the South, based on both macro- and micro-
level data, suggest that in terms of income—the most commonly used indicator
of poverty—there is no systematic link between these phenomena (see CEPAL
2001; Chant 1997b; Fuwa 2000; Geldstein 1997; González de la Rocha 1999a,b;
Kennedy 1994, 35–36; Menjívar and Trejos 1992; Moghadam 1997; Moser 1996;
Quisumbing et al. 1995; Wartenburg 1999). Moreover, there would not appear
to be any obvious relationship between levels of poverty at a national or regional scale and proportions of female heads, nor between trends in poverty
and in the incidence of female headship (see Chant 2003; Chant and Craske
2003, chapter 3; Varley 1996, table 2). In fact, as summed up by Arriagada (1998,
91) for Latin America: "The majority of households with a female head are
not poor and are those which have increased most in recent decades." Other
authors have also stressed how women-headed households are just as likely to
be present among middle- or upper-income populations as among low-income
groups (see Hackenberg et al. 1981, 20, on the Philippines; Kumari 1989, 31, on
India; Lewis 1993, 23, on Bangladesh; Weekes-Vagliani 1992, 42, on the Côte
d'Ivoire; Willis 1994, 79, 102, on Mexico). In short, the diversity of female-
headed households in respect of socioeconomic status, age, and relative dependency of (or indeed, financial contributions from) offspring, household composition, and access to resources from beyond the household unit (from absent
fathers, kinship networks, state assistance, and the like), precludes their categorical labeling (see Chant 1997a,b; Feijóo 1999; Whitehead and Lockwood 1999;
Varley 2001).

This growing body of critical analysis on female household headship and
poverty has had major impacts on poverty research more generally. It has been
crucial, for example, in fueling momentum for examining gender differences in
poverty burdens and the processes giving rise to those differences. It has further
highlighted the need to disaggregate households in poverty evaluations, and it
has underlined the need to consider poverty from a broader optic than levels of
earned income (see Cagatay 1998; Fukuda-Parr 1999; Whitehead and Lockwood
1999). Debates on female household headship and poverty have also brought
issues of power and empowerment to the fore, insofar as they have stressed how
capacity to command and allocate resources is as, if not more, important than

the power to obtain resources and that there is no simple, unilinear relationship between access to material resources and female empowerment.

Women's Empowerment

Leading on from the above, a fourth body of gender research has taken to scrutinizing and problematizing the question of women's empowerment, which, since the early 1990s, has become widespread within the gender and development lexicon. Yet while the stated aim of an increasing number of development interventions is to empower women, definitions of empowerment remain contested, as do the implications of empowerment, both for women themselves and for their relationships with others (see Kabeer 1999; Oxaal and Baden 1997; Parpart 2001; Rowlands 1996; Tinker 2004d; UNIFEM 2000). Although there is insufficient space here to elaborate on the complex and wide-ranging discussions that have taken place on female empowerment, some of the issues which have particular relevance for poverty are the idea that empowerment is a process rather than an end state, that empowerment cannot be "given" but has to come "from within," that empowerment comprises different dimensions and works at different scales (the personal, the interpersonal, the collective), and that measuring empowerment requires tools which are sensitive to the perceptions of insiders at the grassroots and to the meanings of empowerment in different cultural contexts (see Kabeer 1999; Rowlands 1996). Analyses (and critiques) of empowerment have evolved during a strongly postcolonial phase within gender and development research, characterized by the rejection of generalized universal models and of the unproblematized use of "standard" criteria in different cultural contexts (see Fonseca 1991; Marchand and Parpart 1995; A. Scott 1994).

Again, the implications for research on poverty are significant. Weight is given to the idea that poverty is not a static, but a dynamic phenomenon; that the alleviation or eradication of poverty cannot be answered by top-down, one-off, nonparticipatory approaches; that WID approaches (which tend to focus on women only, and as a homogeneous constituency) need to be replaced by GAD approaches (which conceptualize gender as a dynamic and diverse social construct, and which encompass men as well as women); and that poverty is unlikely to be addressed effectively by a singular focus on incomes.

The contributions of this and the other bodies of gender research identified above to general analyses of poverty are now explored in relation to the four interrelated issues itemized at the beginning of the chapter.

THE IMPACTS OF GENDER RESEARCH ON POVERTY ANALYSES

Definitions and Conceptualizations of Poverty

Poverty has always meant different things to different people and can never be politically neutral, reflecting as it does the a priori conceptions of who is evaluating poverty and the data used, or available, to measure it. Although income remains prevalent in many macro-level evaluations of poverty, the past two decades have witnessed rising support in academic and policy circles for broadening the criteria used in poverty definitions (see Baden and Milward 1997; Baulch 1996; Chambers 1995; Moser et al. 1996a,b; Razavi 1999; Whitehead and Lockwood 1999; World Bank 2000; Wratten 1995).

Work on gender has played a major role in calls to acknowledge poverty as a dynamic and multidimensional concept on grounds that static profiles of income and consumption present only part of the picture. Key concepts within the evolution of a more holistic approach to poverty include "entitlements" and "capabilities" (A. Sen 1981, 1985, 1987b) and notions of "vulnerability" and "poverty as process" (Chambers 1983, 1989; see also Haddad 1991), many of which have become enfolded in the operational and diagnostic arena of "livelihoods" (see Chambers 1995; Moser 1998; Rakodi 1999). In different ways, these perspectives have stressed how low incomes per se may not be particularly problematic if people reside in adequate shelter, have access to services and medical care, or possess a healthy base of "assets." Assets are not only economic or physical in nature (labor, savings, tools, natural resources, for instance), but encompass, inter alia, "human capital," such as education and skills, and "social capital," such as kin and friendship networks and support from community organizations (Beall 1996; Cagatay 1998; Chambers 1995; Moser 1996, 1998; Moser and McIlwaine 1997; McIlwaine 1997; Wratten 1995). People's stocks of assets and capabilities influence their poverty in the short and long term, including their ability to withstand economic and other shocks (Rakodi 1999). There is also a strong distributional emphasis in these formulations, with González de la Rocha and Grinspun (2001, 59–60) observing that "Analysing vulnerability requires opening up the household so as to assess how resources are generated and used, how they are converted into assets, and how the returns from these assets are distributed among household members."

Where gender research has perhaps made the most significant inroads within this general call to embrace the multidimensionality of poverty is in respect of highlighting issues of power and agency. An important concept here is that of "trade-offs," which rests on the observation that tactical choices may be made between different material, psychological, and symbolic aspects of poverty (see Chant 1997b; Jackson 1996; Kabeer 1997). Empirical evidence from Mexico and Costa Rica, for example, suggests that women who have split up with their spouses may resist men's offers of child support (where this is forthcoming) because this compromises their autonomy. In other words, some women prefer to cope with financial hardship rather than pay the price that maintenance can bring with it, such as having to engage in ongoing sexual relations (see Chant 1997b, 35). Similarly, women who choose to leave their husbands may have to make substantial financial sacrifices in order to do so. This not only means doing without male earnings, but, in cases where women move out of the conjugal home, forfeiting property and other assets such as neighborhood networks in which considerable time, effort, or resources may have been invested. Although these actions may at one level lead to an exacerbation of poverty and the price of women's independence may be high (see Jackson 1996; Molyneux 1996, 38), the benefits in other dimensions of women's lives may be adjudged to outweigh the costs. As argued by Hilary Graham (1987, 59): "Single parenthood can represent not only a different but a preferable kind of poverty for lone mothers" (see also UNDAW 1991, 41).

In Guadalajara, Mexico, for example, González de la Rocha (1994b, 210) asserts that although lone-parent units usually have lower incomes than other households, the women who head them "are not under the same violent oppression and are not as powerless as female heads with partners." In other parts of Mexico, such as Querétaro, León, and Puerto Vallarta, female household heads often talk about how they find it easier to plan their budgets and expenditures when men are gone, even when their own earnings are low or prone to fluctuation. They also claim to experience less stress and to feel better able to cope with material hardship because their lives are freer of emotional vulnerability, dependence, subjection to authority, and fear (Chant 1997a,b).

The critical point here is that even if women are poorer in *income* terms on their own than they are as wives or partners in male-headed households, they may *feel* they are better off and, importantly, less vulnerable (Chant 1997a, 41). These observations underline the general argument that poverty is constituted by more than income. It encompasses strong perceptual dimensions, and is better conceived as a package of assets and entitlements within which the power, inter alia, to manage expenditures, to mobilize labor, and to gain access to social and community support, are vital elements (see Chambers 1983, 1995; Lewis 1993; Lind 1997; Sen 1987a,b).

Measuring Poverty

Leading on from the above, gender research has had three major implications for the measurement of poverty. First, it has assisted in broadening the indicators of poverty used in macro-level assessments. Second, it has brought to bear the importance of disaggregating households which have hitherto been the most common unit of measurement in income-based poverty profiles. Third, it has stressed how poverty can only be meaningfully evaluated if people's own views on their situations are brought into the picture.

As far as quantitative macro-level assessments are concerned, an important step toward more holistic conceptualizations of poverty has been made through the creation of a growing range of composite indices on the part of the UNDP. The first of these was the Human Development Index (HDI), which appeared in 1990 and included income, literacy, and life expectancy (UNDP 1990). The Capability Poverty Measure (CPM) was developed in 1996 and measured human capabilities in respect to health, reproduction, and education (UNDP 1996). In the following year this was refined into the Human Poverty Index (HPI; see UNDP 1997, and Fukuda-Parr 1999). In incorporating different dimensions of longevity, knowledge, and living standards (see UNDP 2000c, 147), both the HDI and HPI constitute an endorsement of the need to conceptualize poverty as a multidimensional and dynamic entity.

In turn, gender dimensions of poverty, such as disparities in income between women and men, have been made visible at international levels through the UNDP's Gender-Related Development Index (GDI) and the Gender Empowerment Measure (GEM) (see Bardhan and Klasen 1999; also Dijkstra and Hanmer 2000). This said, it is important to recognize that despite improvements in accounting for women's incomes over time, these remain difficult to assess when so many women, compared with men, are involved in informal economic activities (see Baden and Milward 1997; Chant 1991, 1994; Leach 1999; Tinker 1997b; UN 2000).[5] The matter is complicated still further in light of women's considerable inputs into household labor and other unpaid activities such as subsistence farming, which play a crucial role in underpinning livelihoods. Indeed, while gender research has stressed the importance of accounting for the value of women's unpaid labor in poverty assessments, the nonmarket work of women remains grossly invisibilized and undervalued. Although there has been some progress toward improving the gender-sensitivity of enumeration in the past two decades, placing a value on women's work arguably represents one of the biggest methodological challenges facing international organizations in the twenty-first century (see Benería 1999; UNDP 1995).[6]

With regard to the second main impact of gender research on poverty measurement—that of the need to disaggregate households—two sets of arguments have been especially persuasive. One is that since aggregate household incomes disregard the matter of size, larger households appear better off than smaller ones. This is particularly pertinent to comparative analyses of male- and female-headed households. While the use of total household incomes makes female-headed households more visible in income statistics (Kabeer 1996, 14), the danger is to gloss over the fact that women in male-headed households suffer poverty too. Although per capita income figures (derived by dividing household incomes by the number of household members) may not say very much about distribution, since they assume equality (Razavi 1999, 412), they at least give a closer approximation of the potential resources individuals have at their disposal (see Baden and Milward 1997; Chant 1985; González de la Rocha 1994a). Indeed, empirically based gender research has shown that differences in per capita incomes are often negligible between male- and female-headed units or may be higher in the latter, precisely because they are smaller and incomes go further (see Chant 1985; Kennedy 1994; Paolisso and Gammage 1996, 21; Shanthi 1994, 23). Having said this, we must remember that the consumption needs of individual household members may vary according to age (Lloyd and Gage-Brandon 1993, 121) and that larger households may benefit from economies of scale in respect of "household establishment costs" such as housing and services (Buvinic 1990, cited in Baden and Milward 1997).[7]

A second and perhaps even more compelling reason to disaggregate households for the purposes of measuring poverty stems from observations concerning inequitable intrahousehold distribution of resources and the phenomenon of "secondary poverty." Empirical work on inequalities in income and consumption within households has fueled a rich conceptual vein of research which has discredited the idea that households are unitary entities operating on altruistic principles and replaced this with the notion that they are arenas of competing claims, rights, power, interests, and resources (see, e.g., Baden and Milward 1997; Cagatay 1998; Kabeer 1994, chapter 5; Lewis 1993; Sen 1987a, 1990). This perspective requires scrutiny of what goes on inside households rather than accepting them as unproblematized, undeconstructed "black boxes" or as naturalistic entities governed by benevolence, consensus, and joint welfare imperatives (see also Beall 1997a, chapter 3; Bradshaw 1996a; Chant 1985; Feijoó 1999; Molyneux 1996, 35). As argued by Muthwa:

> Within the household, there is much exploitation of women by men which goes unnoticed when we use poverty measures which simply treat households as units and ignore intra-household aspects of exploitation. When we measure poverty . . . we need measures which illuminate unequal access to resources between men and women in the household (1993, 8).

Acknowledging the need to avoid essentializing constructions of "female altruism" and "male egoism," studies conducted in various parts of the world show that many male household heads do not contribute all their wage to household needs, but keep varying proportions for discretionary personal expenditure (see Benería and Roldán 1987, 114; Dwyer and Bruce 1988; Kabeer 1994, 104; Young 1992, 14). Men's spending is often on nonmerit goods such as alcohol, tobacco, and extramarital affairs, which not only deprives other household members of income in the short term but can also exact financial, social, and psychological costs down the line (Appleton 1991; Hoddinott and Haddad 1991). For example, where men become ill or are unable to work as a result of prolonged drinking, the burden for upkeep falls on other household members, who may be called upon to provide health care in the home or to pay for pharmaceuticals and medical attention (see Chant 1985, 1997a). While not denying that expenditure on extradomestic pursuits may form a critical element of masculine identities in various parts of the world and may even enhance men's access to the labor market (through social networks and the like), secondary poverty is clearly particularly serious for women and children where incomes are low and livelihoods precarious (Tasies Castro 1996).

As part of the call to look inside households and to consider material privation in conjunction with differential control over and access to resources, participatory assessments have been regarded as crucial to the gendered analysis of poverty (see Kabeer 1996; Moser et al. 1996b, 2).

Participatory poverty assessments (PPAS) have their origin in participatory rural appraisal methodologies (PRAS), which in turn have drawn on disciplinary traditions such as applied anthropology and participatory action research (May

2001, 45). PPA methodology is based on "outsiders" (e.g., NGO personnel) as facilitators, with local people acting not so much as "informants" but "analysts" (ibid.). In principle PPAs promise greater degrees of empowerment and subjectivity, but the question of who participates at the grassroots may well distort the picture. In addition, the tendency to leave PPA data as "raw" rather than "interpreted" can diminish meaning (Razavi 1999, 422) as well as obscure gender differences (Baulch 1996; McIlwaine 2002; Whitehead and Lockwood 1999). Despite these difficulties, PPA has increasingly been used in a range of contexts. One of the largest PPA projects to date has been that of the World Bank's Voices of the Poor study which was undertaken in 60 countries for the 2000/2001 *World Development Report* (see World Bank 2000, 16). "Triangulation," whereby the findings of participatory analyses are "cross-checked" with objective criteria, has been stressed by gender researchers as integral to the refinement of PPA methodologies (see Razavi 1999, 422), as is recourse to standard qualitative gender analysis which considers gendered relations and processes as well as outcomes (see Whitehead and Lockwood 1999, 539).

Gender Differences in Poverty Burdens
and Poverty Generating Processes

Moving on to the question of what gender research has revealed vis-à-vis gender differences in poverty burdens, from the earliest days of the UN Decade for Women, attention has been drawn to income inequality between men and women. This "gender gap" in poverty, described as a "tragic consequence of women's unequal access to economic opportunities" (UNDP 1995, 36), is also argued to have widened over time. At the Fourth World Conference on Women in Beijing, for example, it was claimed that poverty increasingly had a "woman's face," and that around 70 percent of the world's 1.3 billion people in poverty were female. While this seems somewhat paradoxical given dedicated post-1985 development policy to enhance women's equality and empowerment (Longwe 1995, 18), the "persistent and increasing burden of poverty on women" was accorded priority as one of twelve critical areas of concern within the 1995 Global Platform for Action (see DFID 2000, 13).

It is difficult to measure women's incomes with any degree of precision, but some of the processes which place women at an above-average risk of poverty are fairly undisputed. These include women's disadvantage with respect to poverty-reducing entitlements and capabilities (education, skills, and so on), their heavier burdens of reproductive labor, and discrimination in the workplace (see Mogha-dam 1997). While these factors carry considerable weight in their own right, gender research has also stressed the importance of intrahousehold power rela-tions and resource distribution. For example, even where women earn "decent incomes," they may not be able to control their earnings, because of appropria-tion by men. As described by Blanc-Szanton (1990, 93), in Thailand the cultural acceptability for husbands to go gambling and drinking with friends after work and to demand money from their wives in order to do so means that some women choose to remain single to avoid falling into poverty (see also Bradshaw 1996a on Honduras; Fonseca 1991 on Brazil). In turn, women's earnings may not trans-late into greater personal consumption and well-being because it is undercut by men withholding a larger share of their own earnings when women go out to work. In Guadalajara, Mexico, for example, González de la Rocha (1994a, 10) notes that men usually contribute only 50 percent of their salaries to the collec-tive household fund and, while higher in Honduras, the average is still only 68 percent (Bradshaw 1996b).

In the Philippines, the limited contributions of men to household finances means that even if female-headed households have lower per capita incomes than male-headed units, the amount available for collective expenditure is usually greater (Chant and McIlwaine 1995, 283). Since male heads may command a larger share of resources than they actually bring to the household it is clear that female headship may not necessarily be economically punitive (see Folbre 1991, 108; also Baylies 1996, 77). This is reinforced by the fact that financial contribu-tions from men may be so irregular that women are extremely vulnerable, not knowing from one day to the next whether they will be able to provide for their families or be forced into borrowing and indebtedness in order to get by. One of my respondents from Puerto Vallarta, Mexico, for example, recalled repeated desperation when her now deceased husband (formerly the sole worker in the household) would return from his payday drinking sprees stating *"no hay para comer"* ("there's no money for food"; Chant 1997a, 210).

Adding to vulnerability is the fact that men in a variety of cultures are un-willing, for reasons of pride, honor, sexual jealousy, and so on, to let the female members of their households share in the work of generating income. Even in Mexico, where women's labor force participation has increased massively since the years of the debt crisis in the 1980s, a number of men adhere to the "tra-ditional" practice of forbidding not only their wives but also their daughters to work, especially in jobs outside the home (see Benería and Roldán 1987, 146; Chant 1985, 1994; Townsend et al. 1999, 38; Willis 1993, 71). Failure to mobilize the full complement of household labor supply results not only in lower incomes and higher dependency ratios (i.e., greater numbers of nonearners per worker) but also in greater risks of destitution, especially where households are reliant on a single wage. Indeed, while this is not the case with all male-headed households, it is interesting that despite the pervasiveness of the "poorest of the poor" stereotype and the fact that women face so many disadvantages in society and in the labor market, detailed case study work at the grassroots suggests that relative to household size, female-headed households may have more earners (and earnings) than their male-headed counterparts. As such, dependency burdens are often lower and per capita incomes may be higher in female-headed households (Chant 1997b; Selby et al. 1990, 95; Varley 1996, table 5). In turn, in-depth surveys of younger generations within female-headed households frequently reveal comparable, if not greater (and less gender-biased) levels of nutrition, health, and education (see Blumberg 1995; Chant 1997a 1999; Engle 1995; Kennedy 1994; Moore and Vaughan 1994; Oppong 1997). This not only means greater well-being in the short term, but given investments in human capabilities, encompasses potential for greater empowerment in the longer term too.

Household-level research has accordingly demonstrated there is often as much going on within the home as outside it which determines women's poverty, well-being, and power. The research has not only greatly illuminated the nature of poverty-generating processes but has also shown the dangers of allowing gender to "fall into the poverty trap" of assuming that "being female" and "being poor" are synonymous (see Jackson 1996). One of the most significant contributions here is that of revealing how female household headship is often erroneously construed as a risk factor for women themselves and for the poverty of younger generations (see Chant 1999; González de la Rocha and Grinspun 2001, 61). Poverty-generating processes are often seen to reside in women's social and economic position in society and, somewhat ironically perhaps, their relationships with men can worsen this situation. There is little currency to be gained from adopting a counter-stereotypical stance that advocates female household headship as a "panacea for poverty" and/or an "ideal model for female emancipation" (Feijoó 1999, 162; see also Chant 1999), but the evidence suggests that in some cases "going it alone" (Lewis 1993) can place women in a better position to challenge the diverse factors that make them poor.

Women's Economic "Empowerment"

We have already discussed some of the parameters of women's "empowerment" in general terms. But it is critical to recognize that one of the most common meanings or objectives assigned to the term is women's growth in capacity to make choices (see UNDP 1995; UNIFEM 2000). In turn, access to work or income is often seen as a sine qua non in this process. Yet it is important to bear in mind that access to material resources per se, or even the means by which women are better able to secure material resources (such as education and vocational training) are unlikely to have a significant impact on women's empowerment without changes in other social, cultural, and legal structures of gender inequality, both within and beyond the domestic domain. As Kabeer (1999) argues, resources might help women exercise greater choice and are a step in the right direction, but they by no means guarantee that women will gain power. The issue of "choice" is itself a highly problematic part of this equation and needs to be qualified. As pointed out by Kabeer, the ability to make choices is conditioned by the existence of alternatives, and these tend to be very limited for low-income groups in developing societies. Moreover, the consequences of making certain choices may be high in personal terms and not lead to much change in existing social and economic inequalities. As such, indicators of empowerment need to be sensitive to contextual possibilities (ibid.).

In some situations, for example, economic resources can either lead to women exerting more power within conjugal relationships or to establishing their own households, which is especially noted for Latin America and the Caribbean, to a lesser extent in sub-Saharan Africa, and even in parts of Asia such as Bangladesh (see, e.g., Bradshaw 1995b; Chant 1997a; Kabeer 1999; P. Roberts 1989; Safa 1995). Yet as Kabeer (1989, 1999) points out, where households are organized along more corporate lines, women may prefer to maintain marriages or cooperative household arrangements, since these provide them with kinship-based entitlements that may be a prime source of security, status, and survival. Accordingly, women in these contexts may not be particularly empowered by having independent access to resources, especially if these resources are commandeered by male household members or if women's independence is vulnerable to social disapproval. On top of this, the jobs available to low-income women are often so limited, demeaning, and poorly paid that they offer scant possibilities for substantial improvements in their position (see Bibars 2001; McClenaghan 1997).

It should also be noted that although helping individual women overcome poverty is seen as a critical tool in their own personal empowerment, the policy literature emphasizes that the empowerment of women in general is an "essential precondition for the elimination of world poverty" (DFID 2000, 8; also Razavi 1999, 418; UNDAW 2000; UNDP 2001). The World Bank, for example, has stressed how education for girls is the single most effective strategy for tackling poverty. Women's education is argued to produce positive effects on child morbidity and mortality, nutrition, the schooling of sons and daughters, and, in turn, to contribute to reducing poverty (see World Bank 1994; also World Bank 2000). While not disputing these claims nor that arguments of this nature, which emphasize the importance of reducing gender inequalities in the interests of national and international development, can be extremely strategic for allocating resources to women, it is perhaps important to remind ourselves of the need to maintain boundaries between empowerment as a route to development efficiency and empowerment as a goal for women per se.

As identified by Jackson (1996, 490), instrumentalist approaches to poverty alleviation can lead to women simply being used as a means to other ends (see also Razavi 1999, 419; Molyneux 2001, 184). This is echoed by numerous critiques of the ways in which the targeting of women within welfare and efficiency projects leads not to development "working for women" so much as "women working for development" (see Blumberg 1995, 10; Elson 1989, 1991; Kabeer 1994, 8; Moser 1993, 69–73). Transposing this logic to the domain of empowerment, when definitions of women's empowerment are based on the values of outsiders or imposed, the concept may be divested of meaningful personal or feminist content and thereby rendered redundant. As asserted by Kabeer:

> To attempt to predict at the outset of an intervention precisely how it will change women's lives, without some knowledge of "being and doing" which are realisable and valued by women in that context, runs into the danger of prescribing the process of empowerment, and thereby violating its essence, which is to enhance women's capacity for self-determination (1999, 462).

CONCLUSIONS

Although it has not been possible in this chapter to cover all the contributions made by gender research to the analysis of poverty, it is clear that gender has made a major impact on poverty analyses, and these impacts have, in turn, helped to illuminate gendered dimensions of poverty. As summed up by Razavi (1999,

417): "From a gender perspective, broader concepts of poverty are more useful than a focus purely on household income levels because they allow a better grasp of the multi-dimensional aspects of gender disadvantage, such as lack of power to control important decisions that affect one's life." This does not mean, however, that broader conceptualizations have translated readily into the widespread use of tools which are sensitive to the complexities of poverty and its subjective dimensions. For this reason, despite long-standing feminist concerns about intrahousehold resource distribution, it remains "rare to find standard surveys, such as those carried out in the context of [poverty assessments], embarking on a quantitative exploration of intra-household poverty" (Razavi 1999, 412).

A major obstacle here is undoubtedly the fact that it is difficult to incorporate qualitative and subjective criteria within macro-level accounting, not to mention put a value on all the unpaid work that contributes to people's survival. Another barrier, however, conceivably lies in reluctance on the part of policy makers to engage with gender, as opposed to women, when it comes to alleviating poverty. For example, multilateral, international, and regional financial organizations have attempted to incorporate gender in antipoverty strategies by promoting employment and income-generating activities for women and by providing access to basic social services such as education and health care. In some contexts, these initiatives have been accompanied by microcredit programs for women, special assistance for women-headed households, and, in a few cases, support in managing the dual burden of employment and family responsibilities (see Chant 1999; Grosh 1994; Kabeer 1997; Lewis 1993; Mayoux 2002; UNDAW 2000, 3, 9; Yates 1997).

The fact is, however, that these initiatives concentrate on women only. In line with feminization of poverty arguments which have regarded economic privation as a matter mainly confined to female-headed households, the latter have come to constitute "a 'target group' which is less politicized, for development interventions, than intrahousehold 'interference'" (Jackson 1997b, 152). An added factor here may be that because female household headship is commonly ascribed to "family disorganization," the idea that there is nothing wrong with the "intact" family gains currency (Feijoó 1999, 156; see also Chant 1999).[8] Yet aside from the inappropriateness of using standardized models despite considerable heterogeneity among female-headed households (Feijoó 1999; Wartenburg 1999; Whitehead and Lockwood 1999), when there is no attention to men and to gender relations, then it is unlikely that efforts to help women lift themselves out of poverty will get very far (see Chant and Gutmann 2000). Patriarchal structures both within and outside the home assist in explaining, for example, how microcredit programs for women often lead to their accumulating greater debt (because their husbands commandeer the loans), and why the relationship between employment and increased power for women remains a "vexed one" (Moore 1988, 111; see also McClenaghan 1997; Tiano 2001).

In a comparative analysis of women's income-generating projects in Greece, Kenya, and Honduras, for example, it was found that attempts to raise women's access to income in situations where men had difficulty being breadwinners were rarely successful. Men facing pressures of long-term employment insecurity responded to what they regarded as threats posed by improvements in women's economic status by taking over projects, by controlling the income they derived from them, or, as a further backlash, by increasing their authority and control within the home (Safilios-Rothschild 1990). Whether or not these reactions stem in part from men's general anxieties about the fragility of their livelihoods and status, their exclusion from such projects is unlikely to help. Indeed, UNESCO (1997, 6) further suggests that the consequences of men losing economic privileges in the absence of alternatives can make women more vulnerable to violence than might otherwise be the case.

Recalling Kabeer's (1999) cautionary observations on strategies for female empowerment, it is clear that men's responses and reactions are a vital part of the picture. If genuine strides are to be taken toward the combined imperatives of empowering women and alleviating poverty, then this struggle has to be waged on a gender-inclusive rather than a women-only basis.

In addition to more dedicated attention to *who* should be involved in strategies to promote women's empowerment, questions about *how* are also critical. This is a complex area in which examples of best practices to date are limited, but this should not detract from confronting the challenge. As indicated in this chapter, for example, the private sphere of intrahousehold relations is often a major obstacle to women's assertion of power and access to well-being. Yet the household is one of a series of interconnected sites in society at large. States and markets, as much as they are influenced by domestic ideologies, can also effect changes that filter through to households, even if policy makers remain reluctant to interfere with the internal dynamics of households per se (see Kabeer 1994). Policy and legislation can go a long way to creating enabling environments for women, for example, by promoting (and perhaps, more critically, monitoring and enforcing) the elimination of gender discrimination in schools and in the workplace and by introducing initiatives which encourage greater sharing of parental responsibilities and power within the home (or which endorse alternative family structures) (see Chant 2002). Above all, perhaps, governments, NGOs, and international agencies might be best advised to try to bring about change through investing time and resources in supporting bids for empowerment that emerge from women themselves. Genuine collaboration between public organizations and the grassroots seems likely to offer the biggest prospect of addressing the practical obstacles that stand in the way of strategic gains for women and to render these changes sustainable in the longer term.

NOTES

This essay draws on a presentation delivered at the panel "Economic Empowerment," held at the international conference entitled "Mujeres, Pobreza y Derechos Humanos: Con Voz Propia," of the Foro Internacional de la Red Social Latinoamericana y del Caribe ("Propia"). The conference was held in San José, Costa Rica, 22–24 August 2001, and was hosted by the Instituto Mixto de Ayuda Social (IMAS) and Instituto Nacional de las Mujeres (INAMU). Thanks are due to participants at the conference for their helpful feedback, as well as to Cathy McIlwaine and Ramya Subrahmanian for comments and suggestions on an earlier draft.

1. As asserted by Jackson (1997b, 152): "Poverty reduction appears in poststructuralist perspectives as an imperialist narrative, universalizing, essentializing and politically sinister since it justified hegemonic development interventions."

2. The Lost Decade is most often used in relation to Latin America and refers to the fact that the 1980s saw a reversal in many of the achievements in wealth and social welfare that had been achieved by countries in the years leading up to the debt crisis.

3. Although there are several debates in the gender and development literature on the desirability (or otherwise) of generating definitions which might be universally applicable, the most common definition of "household" for developing societies (and that favored by international organizations such as the United Nations) emphasizes co-residence. In short, a household is designated as comprising individuals who live in the same dwelling and who have common arrangements for basic domestic or reproductive activities such as cooking and eating. In turn, a "female-headed household" is classified in most national and international data sources as a unit where an adult woman (usually with children) resides without a male partner. In other words, a head of household is female in the absence of a co-resident legal or common-law spouse, or, in some cases, another adult male such as a father or brother (see Chant 1997a). Although the majority of female-headed households are lone mother households (i.e., units comprising a mother and her children), "female household headship" is a generic term which covers many other subgroups such as grandmother-headed households, female-headed extended arrangements, and lone female units (see Chant 1997a, chapter 1; also Bradshaw 1996a; Folbre 1991; Fonseca 1991). It is also important to stress that a "lone mother" is not necessarily an "unmarried mother," but is equally, if not more, likely, to be a woman who is separated, divorced, and/or widowed (Chant 1997a, chapter 6).

4. I am grateful to Nancy Folbre for drawing my attention to this point, which clearly applies where female-headed households consist only of mothers and children. In many contexts

in the South, however, a substantial proportion of lone mothers head extended households containing female and male relatives who can share labor burdens (see Chant 1997a).

5. Women's disproportionate concentration in informal employment seems to be becoming more marked over time. In Mexico, for example, official documentation connected with the National Women's Programme (*Programa Nacional de la Mujer 1995–2000*) noted that in the context of ongoing increase in women's workforce participation in the 1990s, those in informal income-generating activities (here described as "nonwaged" work), rose from 38 percent to 42 percent of the national female labor force between 1991 and 1995 (Secretaría de Gobernación 1996, 27–8).

6. In 1995, the UNDP estimated that the combined value of the unpaid work of women and men, together with the underpayment of women's work in the market, was in the order of US$16 trillion, or about 70 percent of global output. Of the $16 trillion identified, approximately $11 trillion was constituted by the "non-monetised, invisible contribution of women" (UNDP 1995, 6).

7. Building on a point made earlier in the chapter, it is also important to note that households are not "bounded entities" and may receive injections of income from external sources, such as migrant members and transfer payments from absent fathers or state organizations (see Bibars 2001; Bruce and Lloyd 1992; Chant 1997b, 1999).

8. It should also be noted that, although government assistance for female-headed households is often strongly motivated by concerns to better the position of women and children, another important agenda has been the aim of neoliberal economic policy to effect reduction in public expenditure on universal social programs in favor of targeted schemes for poverty alleviation (see Budowski and Guzmán 1998; Chant 2002).

What Is Justice?
Indigenous Women in Andean Development Projects

Maruja Barrig

As a consultant to development projects for various international cooperation agencies, I have seen the sincere efforts of many NGOs and public and private donors to pursue gender equity. But at the same time I have also observed the barriers that impede progress toward this goal within some of the organizations working in the rural Andean zones of Peru, Ecuador, and Bolivia. I have shared with colleagues in the North and the South the sense of uneasiness and discouragement I feel in discussions with some directors and staff of rural NGOs who resist what they see as the imposition of a Western way of doing things and openly reject what is evident to even the least sensitive observer: the enormous gaps in resources and power between men and women in rural Andean communities.

Saying that this situation is a result of sexism does not really illuminate the underlying issues of a problem that is often seen as a cultural gap. Thirty years ago, those of us who became feminist activists were urban, educated middle-class *Limeñas*. Our silence with respect to the Andean women was full of signifiers. Lima, the capital city, is situated in a narrow desert strip that runs along the Pacific coast of Peru. Proud of its Spanish heritage, it has always looked to the ocean and the many possibilities abroad, rather than looking at the reality and complexity in the tall Andes that rise behind Lima or to the vast Amazonian region beyond.[1]

Thinking about why those working in rural projects often reject the concept of gender aroused my curiosity about the discourses that project officials and urban feminists from the capital have constructed about indigenous women. Those in charge of projects claim the purity of indigenous lives and customs, while the feminists—products of a *criollo* tradition, unable to grasp Andean cultural codes, and not even speaking Quechua or Aymara—have simply evaded the issue.

In 1999, I received a grant to study the social representations of indigenous women from the Latin American Council of Social Sciences (CLACSO) and the Swedish International Development Agency (SIDA). The fellowship allowed me to review a number of essays on "The Indian Problem," including colonial accounts and fictional histories, and to interview a dozen feminist leaders from the 1970s along with eighteen men and women who made up the staffs of four NGOs based in Cuzco. The capital of the Inca Empire until the arrival of the Spanish in the sixteenth century, Cuzco is symbolic because the majority of its inhabitants exhibit a strong loyalty to the region and a pride that comes from considering themselves the direct descendents of the Incas. This essay includes some of the opinions of directors and staff members I interviewed in April 2000.[2]

Since that time, I have tried to deepen my understanding of my original question: why has the idea of using gender analysis been so firmly rejected in rural Andean zones? In July 2001 and March 2002, I had two further opportunities to explore these concerns when I evaluated projects for various NGOs in Cuzco and in the departments of Ayacucho and Huancavelica in the southern Andes. With the help of translators I was also able to talk with some of the rural women who were the focus of their projects. Nevertheless, I should emphasize that this study is based primarily on conversations with NGO staffs and on my analysis of ethnographic studies, that is, not on indigenous women themselves but on those who describe them. Changing the images of Andean women in a way that could make them the protagonists of their own lives is part of a future agenda and a debt that needs to be paid.

I believe that there are at least three areas of tension when gender is introduced into development practice in the Andes. The first is the social representation of "the Andean," which rejects all outside influences. The second is an ongoing debate between indigenous rights, which are conceived of as collective, and individual rights, such as those implied in most human rights discourse. The third is the institutional policies of international development and the relations between donor groups and Southern NGOs.

Even ethnographic studies that do not embody a gender perspective acknowledge the gaps between "the Andean worldview" and concrete practices. The images constructed by those inside and outside peasant communities seem to correspond to what psychologists call social representation: the categorization of circumstances, events, and people to create a set of meanings shared by a certain group. A social representation suggests a subject position, so the same events and relationships can be represented in quite different ways, depending on who is speaking. Some coastal *criollos* revile Andean peasant traditions, considering them an obstacle to modernization, but those working in rural projects often argue that if indigenous communities had not been contaminated by urban habits, there would be gender equity within them.

This view, strongly held by some today in ways that influence the implementation of gender guidelines, can easily be traced back to the first colonial chronicles. Many NGO staff members believe that ethnographic studies support their position that gender equity is natural to indigenous communities but that colonialism beginning in the sixteenth century and capitalism in the nineteenth and twentieth centuries destroyed the perfection of a harmonious Inca world. Anything that mars this idealization they attribute to contamination from the outside, to "invasions" both symbolic and real. Although NGO staffs are committed to human rights, in some cases they use this ecstatic vision of Andean culture to justify failing to implement programs that promote gender equality on the grounds that this "Western" viewpoint ignores the natural complementarity of the Andean couple. When contemporary practices fall short of this ideal, such lapses are seen as the result of the way modern institutions and the penetration of modern communications and trade have distorted the natural equilibrium.

This essay will argue that this social construction is not fully convincing. First, there is evidence that gender inequalities existed before modernizing projects were introduced into the rural Andes. In addition, whatever their source, entitlements and symbols of power are inequitably distributed between men and women today: women are less literate, have less access to public positions, have fewer opportunities to learn Spanish, and do not enjoy freedom of physical and social movement. The unequal treatment of Andean women has been described by some as cultural resistance, just as veiling among Muslim women can be interpreted as a rejection of Westernization. But to call the treatment of Andean women "cultural resistance" when they are monolingual in their native language, censured for using Western clothing, largely illiterate, and confined to their community lest they be "taken advantage of" outside, ignores women's lack of choices and distorts reality.

This is not to argue that the attempt to defend indigenous rights is wrong. There is a kind of violence in the way that indigenous Peruvians are forced to begin the process of acquiring rights and citizenship by fleeing from themselves, because to be an Andean peasant from the highlands is to be relegated to the lowest rung of the social stratification ladder. As Sinesio López points out, indigenous people are seen as citizens only at the cost of their identity. In Peru, this has meant that Indians must transform themselves into *cholos* (*mestizos*), giving up their language, dress, and customs. Citizenship has been constructed through forced homogenization, not by recognizing cultural differences (López 1997, 442).

Collective rights, which were historically denied in the name of national integration, suggest a second tension with regard to women. In peasant communities, customary law is endorsed by the Peruvian constitution, except when it denies the fundamental rights of individuals. But the legal norms that protect women, many recently strengthened due to efforts of urban feminists, are rarely considered in this category. Customary law tends to be used as an excuse to leave untouched a long list of patriarchal practices that restrict women's freedom. When they are confronted with women's inequality, development organizations can argue that they are simply respecting local culture.

A third tension is found in the institutional policies of international development agencies, mostly private, and their relations with Southern NGOs. Most international agencies have specific mandates requiring them to promote gender equality for sustained development. But most local NGOs engage in both open and covert resistance to what they see as the imposition of "external agendas," resistance that may be further deepened by the gender relations both male and female staff experience in their daily lives, in NGO offices as well as in the field.

SOCIAL REPRESENTATION: BETWEEN IMAGE AND REALITY

An important segment of the Peruvian population shares a particular social representation of the Andean world, a perspective reinforced by some ethnographic studies that claim that alien cultural practices have destroyed the harmonic equilibrium between the community and the family and between husband and wife that used to exist in the Andean world. Other researchers have questioned this idealization of Andean life.

The Reinvented Past

Despite the contemporary bias against "Indians," the Inca Empire (which extended from Cuzco in Peru north to Ecuador and parts of Colombia, and south to Bolivia and northern Chile between the fifteenth and sixteenth centuries) is seen by a majority of Peruvians as the period of greatest splendor and glory in Peruvian national history, a Golden Age of harmony, justice, and abundance that ended with the Spanish conquest and that contrasts sharply with the present weakness and poverty of the country. Studies show that many students and professors at the secondary as well as the university level believe the Inca Empire was benevolent, its power legitimized by its concern for the welfare of its subjects (Portocarrero and Oliart 1989; Oboler 1996).

One of the most important sources of this representation is the *Royal Commentaries of the Incas*, written in the seventeenth century by Garcilaso de la Vega, son of a Spanish captain and an Inca princess who lived in Cuzco. When the book was published in Europe in 1607, it offered a novelistic account of the Inca Empire that ignored important local traditions of those who had preceded the Inca and the revolts of those in regions the Inca had conquered. Pre-Inca history was erased, and advances in agriculture and social and political organization were attributed to the Inca, and to their gods. In Garcilaso's portrayal, the Inca did not repress the peoples it conquered but persuaded them to submit. A century after its publication, the *Royal Commentaries* were already being used by the native elites in their efforts to restore their rights and create support for indigenous revolts against the Spanish viceroyalty (Rowe 1976, 25–35; Burga 1988, 299; Spalding 1974, 187–89).

A few years after the publication of the *Royal Commentaries*, around 1612, an indigenous writer, Felipe Guamán Poma de Ayala, produced a chronicle of the abuses and humiliations to which the natives had been subjected. He sent it to the king of Spain, claiming to reveal the truth that had been hidden by the king's representatives in the New World. Guamán Poma feared that "the Indian could vanish" and, as he traveled throughout Peru, he became increasingly upset by the racial mixing he saw among Indians, Spanish, and African slaves, blaming women—i.e., the "worst Indian whores from this kingdom"—for the accelerating miscegenation (Barrig 2001).

For Guamán Poma, the multiplication of *mestizos* and mulattos threatened to ruin any hope of a pre-Hispanic restoration that would be able to return control of their land to the native Peruvians. His answer was that each racial group should live and reign in its own country: "the Spanish in Spain, the Africans in Guinea, and the Peruvians in Peru." But, facing the fact of racial mixing and in need of a more immediate solution, Guamán Poma suggested that the whites, *mestizos*, blacks, and mulattos should stay in the cities and that only the indigenous be allowed to live in the countryside, to maintain their native purity (Guamán Poma de Ayala 1980; Ossio 1973; Vargas Llosa 1996, 245). For Guamán Poma and scores of his later followers, racial mixture was a form of disorder. Order implied a restriction, a limited selection of elements; disorder and the lack of limits meant the destruction of the symbolic configuration of a society. As Douglas argues, sexual contamination is a sign of fear that the clear internal structure of a system cannot be maintained (Douglas 1991, 106, 164–65).

Flores Galindo argues that the timeless ideal of the "Andean man" represents a composite harmony of desired characteristics but not the reality of a very fragmented world. The fragmentation of Peru generated an Andean utopia: the desire to return to an Inca society with the "Andean man" as a solution to the problem of Indian identity. This is how Flores Galindo interprets the fact that, between 1953 and 1972, in various rural towns in the Peruvian Andes, researchers found fifteen versions of the story of "Incarri" (the Inca king). Incarri refers to Tupac Amaru I, the rebel Indian leader beheaded by Viceroy Toledo in 1572. According to these accounts, the buried head of the Inca king is reconstituting itself and reconnecting with the rest of his body. When this process is finished, the Inca will emerge to put an end to the current epoch of confusion (Flores Galindo 1987, 18).

In addition to these older interpretive propositions, pro-Indian intellectual and political currents appeared at the early twentieth century and celebrated the native population of the Andes. These emerged in reaction to the virtual enslavement of the Indian population that had occurred under the hacienda regime of the nineteenth century. The "Indian" of this intellectual movement was an abstraction, timeless and outside any specific social context. Although the intellectuals were themselves *mestizos*, these *indigenista* narrators divided the world between those who were "Indians" and those who weren't, assigning all positive characteristics to the Indians and all negative traits to whites and *mestizos*. In some of the stories and novels, the moral qualities of the characters are attributed ethnically in a way that suggests a kind of racism (Flores Galindo 1992, 18–19; Vargas Llosa 1996, 271–73).

This literature suggested the need to restore the pre-Hispanic rights of the Indians, and Indian women are responsible for maintaining the purity of the indigenous race. They must be chaste and resist men who are not members of their own ethnic group. As one writer asserts, "The impure Indian woman goes to the city to become meat for the whorehouse; one day she will rot in a hospital" (Valcárcel 1970, 84–85).

How do oral traditions, *indigenista* writings, and chronicles written centuries ago help us understand the contemporary views of the people who are carrying out development projects in the Andean rural areas? By helping us locate what Jean Claude Abric describes as the central nucleus of the Andean social representation. A social representation is built around a figurative core that is stable, concrete, and simple and resonates with the values of the individual who uses it. The representation is seen as objective truth; the object represented is converted into reality itself. A social representation restructures reality and provides a unitary vision of the object. Because the subject invests the representation with his or her experiences and system of values, the object so represented must be made consistent with those values (Abric 1994, 12–22; Jodelet 1988, 472–75).

Two sets of complementary ideas are fundamental to the Andean social representation. The first set includes the designation of a physical and symbolic *territory*; in this case the Andean Eden pictured by Garcilaso de la Vega combines with the positive image of the Andean *social system* that all Peruvians learn in school. The second set of ideas interprets anything "bad" in current social practices—anything that departs from the ideal—as the result of external contamination. In this way, the representation closes the cognitive circle and is able to fend off alternative views.

Andean Ethnography and the Issue of External Contamination

Several contemporary ethnographic investigations reinforce the idealized image presented above, helping to keep the "Andean" social representation alive. One example is the seminal and widely read work of Billie Jean Isbell on sexual equality and complementarity in the Andes. Isbell did her fieldwork in the community of Chuschi in the southern Andes at the end of the 1960s. She argued that the Andean worldview is based on a notion of symmetrical duality, the principle of "the essential other half" by which the man and the woman form a whole, each incomplete without the other. In her view, as industrialization and modernization penetrated the Andes, the principle of complementary sexual equality would be lost. "The traditional women of Chuschi will probably lose status, dignity and independence, and their position of power in the procreative process," she warned, "to the degree that Spanish society, dominated by men, continues to displace the Andean order which is basically, dual, complementary and egalitarian" (Isbell 1976, 55). Some years later, Isbell (1997) revised her conclusions, but her initial propositions—that complementarity and sexual equality are equivalent among Andean peasants and that this ideal has eroded as rural communities became more connected to the urban system—have endured as points of reference for other researchers and activists.

A second study that emphasizes "original harmony" and sees departures from that state as the result of "external degradation" is Florence Babb's analysis of the archives of the Vicos project. From 1952 to 1962, scholars from Cornell University, under contract with the Peruvian government, carried out research and modernization interventions at Vicos, a hacienda in the central highlands, introducing new agricultural technologies, eliminating the near-serf status of the peasants under the hacienda system, and developing new leadership. Decades later, drawing on the field notes and interviews of the project anthropologists, Babb analyzed what had happened to the women of Vicos. Although she claimed that she did not want to idealize the past or deny preexisting gender inequalities, Babb concluded that the project had introduced "relatively greater inequalities" for women (Babb 1999, 96).

Before the Cornell project, Babb's study shows, the men of Vicos owned more land and animals than women. Men were recognized as heads of families; the public status of women was less than their status at home; and, in spite of expectations that both spouses would be faithful, men enjoyed greater freedom. Babb describes this initial condition as "a general pattern of mutual respect." The only exception she notes is that alcohol (also an "external" factor?) made men "sexually aggressive." She concludes that women may not have been exactly equal to men, but their public roles were less important than their status within the family, where they were nearly equal (98–99).

Babb identified several reasons why women lost power under the Vicos project. Productivity was increased on lands owned by men, who received training in new agricultural techniques that was not extended to women. The monetarization of the economy marginalized women, and sending children to school reduced their role as the socializers of children. Women resisted these changes. Babb concludes that the capitalist economy devalued the contribution of women to the family economy while the diffusion of the ideology of the dominant class judged women inferior (114). To explain cases of violence against women (evidence that did not fit the idealized social representation), Babb blames external influences, attributing it to *mestizos* or those *vicosinos* who had the most contacts outside the community. In general she notes an "absence of machismo among the men of Vicos." To explain the occurrence of sexual rape, Babb concluded that "as men of Vicos expand their sphere of displacement and bring the manner of acting of the dominant culture to their community, it is probable that women will increasingly suffer the kind of violence that was exercised in the past by men from the class that oppressed them, but now will be exercised by the peasant men themselves" (109-10).

For Babb and other researchers, violence against women is alien to indigenous traditions and therefore must have its source in the degradation of pre-Hispanic customs as a consequence of the violent introduction of European practices and colonial abuses. Similarly, in her analysis of the chronicle of Guamán Poma de Ayala, Irene Silverblatt explains alcoholism and violence against women as evidence of the deterioration of indigenous culture produced by outside factors (Silverblatt 1990, 107). In these interpretations, outsiders—the Spanish conquistadors and later the *mestizos*—introduce violence and pervert the traditional customs of mutual respect between the Andean husband and wife.

Although less widely known than Isbell's theory or Babb's analysis of the Vicos archives, Carol Andreas's monograph of life in the Andes complements this idealized, autarkic vision of the Andean world. For Andreas, "In the Andean mountain regions bordering the Peruvian jungle, the regions least affected by *mestizo* or foreign influence, the balance between men and women in complementary work roles can be seen in its purest form" (Andreas 1985, 173). She acknowledges the existence of sexual violence and abuse, but their causes are alien to the idyllic picture she paints of Andean society: the influence of *mestizos* and the negative effects of market forces. "What does seem to be true is that domestic violence is more common where *mestizo* influence is greatest. Rape, especially, is identified with Spanish-style machismo. . . . Male violence toward women is a product of colonial and present government policy, for it gives men effective power over women by making women economically dependent. . . . Loss of self-esteem among women is produced largely by their weak position in the money economy" (65-67).

In Andreas's view, modernization separates men from women, and the market even affects their health differently: "The diet of Indians has changed with the introduction of a money economy and government subsidies that make available manufactured products such as soda pop, noodles and refined sugar . . . As the consumption of refined products has weakened peasant women physically, their daily work has become harder" (64). Without presenting any data to support her assertion about the effects of noodles and sugar, Andreas goes on to condemn the devastating impact of another product: beer. "Men have taken to drinking more bottled beer than homemade *chicha* . . . The beer men drink regularly comes from the city; it must be bought with money, and it makes them lethargic and sometimes violent" (65).

These brief summaries cannot do justice to the fieldwork and analysis that have gone into the study of Andean life, but they are sufficient to suggest the effects these studies produce. Seeking to preserve an idealized world, these researchers emphasize the dichotomies between the Andean and *mestizo* worlds and suggest that the degradation of Andean society has been caused by modernization, industrialization, and the penetration of capitalist markets. Yet, as I try to suggest below, these studies never question why "external contamination" is bad for women's status and power, but not for men's, or why external contact alters gender power relations in ways that are bad for women but not for men.

The Andean social construction was clearly present in the thinking of the NGO staff members I interviewed in Cuzco in 2000. Although they showed their concern for peasant women and "questions of gender," they were much more prone to discuss how hard life is in the highlands and how adversity maintains the purity of community values. A comment from a Cuzqueñan field technician is illustrative: *There are communities located at the headwaters area* [more than 3,500 m (11,483 ft) above sea level] *that keep the traditions. They are more natural; there everything is pure. A couple in these communities is more innocent, more ingenuous and honest, more responsible because they have not come into contact with urban people. These people go to the city only rarely, but the woman does not go, only the man, because the woman belongs in the house, the wife is not supposed to go out. If she does it is for a special occasion. The women say, "Ay, I am afraid; what will happen? I am happy here." Therefore we are talking about a couple that still maintains the traditions proper to these communities; they live happily as they are: the husband is the messenger, the one who goes to the city and does the talking.*

For this NGO staff member, honesty, ingenuousness, innocence, and responsibility are traits that are possible only in the most remote villages. Women ought to stay home and be happy because they have a man who will speak for them—necessary because these women can only speak Quechua, one of the native languages in Peruvian Andes. They are afraid to venture out: how can they interact with people from outside the family and the local community, or enter into transactions in Spanish in order to sell livestock, if they don't have the skills to do so? The message is, don't disturb this natural harmony; they are happy as they are.

The Symbols of Power

Based on her reading of Guamán Poma, Irene Silverblatt challenges the view that the Inca were benign rulers, concluding that the Inca conquerors used the dualism of pre-Inca social and economic organization to reinforce their power. The way they disguised their imperial domination is also relevant: the myth that the Inca, a warrior male, was the son of a god changed what Silverblatt sees as a pre-Inca power balance between men and women by emphasizing the primacy of the male gods. The empire established a tribute system based on households, which transformed complementary gender relations into gendered hierarchies in the Andean regions that came under Inca control (Silverblatt 1990, xxiii–xxiv).

Silverblatt suggests that gender equality existed in pre-Inca society because the work done by both sexes was equally valued. The contributions of both sexes were indispensable to the maintenance of rural life and to the fulfillment of labor obligations to the Empire; this rather than the customs of the Inca provided the basis for the Andean ideal of gender complementarity. When the colonial regime was established in the sixteenth century, paying tribute and labor service was no longer obligatory for the household, but only for male commoners (not the Inca nobility) from the ages of eighteen to fifty. This further devalued women's work, as women were excused from this obligation. The colonial system of taxation undermined one of the fundamental institutions on which the Inca Empire had extended its power and enriched itself. But, in Silverblatt's opinion, it made women more vulnerable, not only because their work was made invisible, but because the men tried to escape forced labor in the fields and the mines by abandoning their communities and leaving the women responsible for meeting the demands of the Crown. Guamán Poma had observed that rural men were fleeing to the cities, cutting their hair in the Spanish style and using Western clothes to appear *mestizo* in order to evade the virtual slavery they would suffer as natives. Thus, European institutions eroded Andean values and strongly exploited women's labor (101).

Although Silverblatt contests the origins of gender complementarity, she agrees that Western institutions undermine it as the basis of the family, while eroding communal solidarity and devaluing Andean women. If we accept that moral enclaves did exist where complementarity between men and women had cultural as well as instrumental value in reproducing the family economy—that gender complementarity was an integral part of the Andean worldview—why did the men abandon their wives and their kinship groups? And what advantages did men enjoy and women lack that enabled men to abandon their families and their communal responsibilities?

Today it is possible to argue that men have advantages not unlike those that allowed Andean men to leave their rural communities under severe economic and cultural pressure in the colonial era. For example, Olivia Harris shows that men have asymmetrical advantages over women in Andean communities. "The couple" is the unit of analysis that identifies the roles of husband and wife, and it is a normative and organizational element of community life. But the focus on the couple fails to look at the relations between men and women as distinct social groups. If we look at gender relations the way we look at class or race relations, the asymmetries are clear: it is the men who have the power and authority in the community. There is a structural contradiction between the representation of "the couple" as egalitarian and the hierarchical relations between men and women in other social spaces (Harris 1985; J. Anderson 1990, 86).

As noted earlier, citizenship in Peru has been constructed at the cost of loss of identity of the diverse ethnic groups that inhabit it; men and women must adopt customs and Western clothes and use Spanish to be able to exercise their basic rights. The native populations are the victims of what Taylor calls "false recognition." The hegemonic social and political discourse gives them a degrading picture of themselves that is internalized and becomes an instrument of their oppression. Within highland Andean communities, those with more power are those who are "less Indian" because they have access to the urban codes and more physical and social mobility (Taylor 2001; de la Cadena 1992).

The power of men as a social group within rural Andean communities is a reflection of these external symbols of identity. Men practically monopolize the symbols of modernization: speaking Spanish, wearing Western clothing without being criticized for doing so, and taking on active leadership roles. Gender inequality is so evident that those who wish to preserve the "ideal Andean" social representation are forced to argue that modern civil responsibilities have introduced *machismo*, disrupting the gender equilibrium that formerly existed in the Andean zones (Lapiedra 1985, 54; Andreas 1985, 58).

Despite the pressure to idealize, many ethnographic studies provide evidence of gender asymmetries in Andean communities. In community assemblies, for example, male leaders use Spanish to discuss the "important" issues and only use Quechua for "private" or domestic issues. In highland communities, female illiteracy is over 50 percent; in their own language women assert that they are "blind" and "mute" because they do not know how to read or speak Spanish, and therefore they cannot talk or deal with foreigners, much less aspire to community leadership. A Bolivian man, describing his wife who speaks only Aymara, says that when she leaves the village for the city, she is like "a dog," because she doesn't know anything. The evidence suggests that the subjection of women in Andean communities preceded the greater presence of the state, new forms of political and economic organization, and modern communication networks. Some argue that these have not produced the differences that exist between men and women but have simply exacerbated them (de la Cadena 1992, 1997a; Harvey 1989; Ruiz Bravo et al. 1998; Canessa 1997, 242–43).

In my interviews, women staff members of the NGOs based in Cuzco described the constant ridicule women suffer from men when the women want to say something in a community meeting. And even a male expert from one of the NGOs I visited practically denied them the right to speak, commenting that, in the community meetings, *there is a gap in participation, bearing in mind that for hundreds of years educational levels for men and women have been so different. For various reasons there is more illiteracy among women than men, so despite the efforts of the NGOs or the gender requirements of the donors, this gap persists. Although we might think that women should play a role in community assemblies, they do not have the background or capacity to speak or debate.*

Another important social marker is clothing and, in the case of indigenous women, it is directly correlated with geographical and social mobility. When women go to the cities, their traditional dress becomes an unmistakable sign that they belong to a group regarded as inferior and backward. Just as the ability to speak Spanish is a tool that can increase the power of those who have it, Western dress, like other signs of urban life, can represent a sign of upward mobility[3] and recognition within their communities (de la Cadena 1997a, 25).

In Peru, the *pollera* (traditional skirt) is a sign of backwardness, a sign of being "Indian" and therefore "inferior." Corroborating what Penelope Harvey found in the 1980s in her fieldwork in a highland community in Cuzco, the female NGO staff members I interviewed pointed out that women who abandon traditional clothing experience constant social censure. Within the community, and even in a wider scale, there is a marked differentiation between indigenous men, who may adopt *mestizo* clothing and language, and women, who are considered symbols of Indian identity. Radcliffe points out that "Under the cultural politics of the indigenous movement . . . indigenous femininity stands in for indigenous resistance to the urban, national, mestizo nation-state." From the perspective of the indigenous communities, becoming a *mestizo* is a more ambiguous and frightening process for women than for men. In Ecuador, the men of the highlands can adopt cultural markers like blue jeans or short hair without losing their indigenous identity, but women cannot move away from the well-established categories of what is considered "Indian" and "white" without being accused of inappropriate sexual conduct (Radcliffe 1998, 10). A fieldworker from an NGO in Cuzco put this graphically: *The women from the communities migrate to the cities and when they return they are rebellious, starting with wearing different clothes; they have a different approach, a different kind of development. Then men's power begins to decline.*

Social representations can incorporate various readings of the same object, depending on the views and values of the interpreter. Some researchers think Andean women are restrained by an invisible barrier of sarcasm and social sanction—barriers that indigenous men do not face. But others see women's self-restraint as voluntary and positive. Thus, for Florence Babb, wearing the *pollera* is a heroic gesture of cultural resistance. In her opinion, based on her study of the Vicos project, the close linkage between the language people use and the type of clothes they wear explains why "Quechua-speaking women of Vicos [kept] their traditional dress while the Spanish-speaking males adopt[ed] *mestizo* clothing. [As] language and clothing are key indicators of social class in Peru, the women's resistance to speaking Spanish and wearing *mestizo* clothing can be seen as a rejection of the culture of the dominant class" (Babb 1999, 112).

These examples reinforce Sinesio Lopez's understanding of how Peruvian citizenship is formed. Since the beginning of the Republic, Peru has offered its people the illusion of miscegenation and integration, neutralizing the identities of Quechua and Aymara groups inhabiting the Andes to the point that, as some recent studies conclude, today it is difficult to define what typifies indigenous people or what "Andean" actually means. But this does not seem to be the case for women, who seem to be anchored, in spite of themselves, in a rigid identity that is not allowed to change. The situation of women in Andean communities is a further illustration of Amartya Sen's thesis that the restriction of women's entitlements limits their capabilities. In the Peruvian case, the restrictions on freedom of movement for many women in Andean areas have resulted in the limitation of their cultural portfolios, which are broadened when people move from one structural context to another and learn to act appropriately in various settings. This process is enriched by communication and interaction with others (Wolf 1996, 96). The density of an individual's daily life experiences, a product of real or symbolic migrations, creates the capacity to choose between a plurality of identities. Andean peasant women are denied this freedom and this capacity.

IN THE NAME OF CULTURE

The previous section reproduced a dialogue about Andean social representation that has been molded over decades. What follows is a discussion of the views of some researchers and development activists on the cultural practices that govern relations between Andean men and women and that often conflict with international human rights standards as well as national legislation with regard to women's rights. In addition to the ideal of gender complementarity, a basic reason for this conflict is the primacy of collective rights over individual rights in Andean communities, which is intended to ensure their economic and social survival.

Studies of the ideology of pre-Hispanic Andean communities, among them that of Maria Rostworowski, agree on the existence of common principles that have at their apex a concept of duality, in mythology and even in political organization. Dualism is an ordering concept of the Andean worldview: each masculine god has his double, an exact replica who, in the "mirror theory" of Andean cosmology, reproduces itself as a mirror image with characteristics that are both opposite and complementary (Rostworowski 1988).

Several analyses of Andean gender relations have taken this system of organization as their starting point, noting that complementarity in gender roles is necessary to reproduce the family. Both men and women's roles are valued equally when both cooperate in agricultural production, but the intrusion of new production techniques and cultural contact introduce the pattern of male dominance that exists between men and women in the non-Andean world. Other researchers, although they acknowledge the continuing relevance of this representation, have suggested that there is evidence that there is competition and even rivalry within the Andean pair-bond (Ortiz Rescaniere 2001, 162).

Social pressure within Andean communities helps ensure that each person is part of a stable and procreating marriage, linked to a group of productive activities and exchanges that guarantee the continuity of the family and the community. Some studies contrast "Western individualism" with "Andean solidarity and fraternity" made possible by a worldview that emphasizes the complementarity of opposites and reciprocal exchange (PRATEC 2001, 109).

These concepts were reflected in my interviews. One of the Cuzco-based NGOs presents the idea of complementary dualism as follows. In the rural communities, *there is a notion of "incompleteness." Everyone recognizes that he or she is not self-sufficient. The idea of the "individual" does not work in the community; each person is subordinated to the social collective within which the man as well as the woman plays an important role, but only as part of an established couple, which gives each person a level of maturity and completion; the couple comes together and makes a unity. The couple, not the individual, is recognized as a member of the community.* Complementarity understood in this way allows some of the NGOs working in Andean communities to rationalize the fact that men make community decisions and hold title to the land and women do not, because the couple is a unit that is represented by the man.

With the individual subordinated to the social group, collective decisions supersede individual wills, with gendered consequences. Studies on family dynamics in Andean peasant communities recognize the power of parents in choosing partners for their children. "Arranged marriages" are decided largely on economic grounds, and the parents pressure their children, especially their daughters, to accept the partner they have chosen.[4] Such "contracts" are made for several reasons: to broaden relations of reciprocity among families in agricultural tasks, join small parcels of land, or raise a family's social status. Although this tradition is weakening, it is still maintained in the most isolated rural communities, frustrating the aspirations of youth and, on some occasions, precipitating the flight of women from their communities (de la Cadena 1997b; Denegri 2000; Pinzás 2001; R. Valderrama and Escalante 1997).

In addition to arranged marriages, mock abduction is practiced in highland communities in the southern Andes. In this tradition, the relation between the man's initiative and the woman's acquiescence with regard to a union initiated without the parents' permission is less clear. Ethnographic studies in the highlands of Cuzco show that sometimes women are forced into being "stolen"; they are often very young and lose social support if they express their disagreement (Pinzás 2001). Others see mock abduction as part of a ceremonial "battle," which can initiate the *rimanakuy*, the process of negotiation between the families of the two who are about to marry. "In some cases, the abduction initiates the *rimanakuy* . . . [In the case of] rival villages that exchange women, the suitor and his supporters "attack" the relatives of the young woman. . . . The victor, after taking the woman (or having gotten one in the noise of the fight) goes with his parents to the house of the 'aggrieved' and her 'defeated' relatives to begin the visits and conversations appropriate to the *rimanakuy*" (Ortiz 2001, 153).

At the end of the 1990s, one NGO in the southern Peruvian Andes, whose declared mission is to defend human rights, began a pilot project of creating alternative centers for the administration of justice based on customary law and managed by the rural communities. The NGO based its project on the assumption that the law of the state and customary law each represents "a different set of values" and that the view that the constitution should prevail had led to the "criminalization of cultural practices." One of these practices "that creates the most conflict is trial matrimony or '*servinakuy*.' In this tradition the age of marriage for the girl is between fourteen and eighteen years and the usual form of marriage is mock abduction with the hidden complicity of the girl's family. But these practices are illegal under the Penal Code which labels them as rape, seduction, kidnapping and violation of sexual freedom" (IPAZ 2000, 19). This "human rights" NGO was advocating the preservation of this cultural tradition despite the fact that these practices violate national and international norms that protect women's rights.

If scholars and NGO staffs assert, as many do, that the "individual" does not exist in Andean communities, the possibilities for debating these contradictions are closed off. I interviewed the director of a Cuzco-based NGO who is very respectful of local traditions. He insisted that it is impossible to apply Western norms to customary law: *When you recognize the individual as an individual under the constitution, and you respect the state's authority, you can exercise your rights. But in the Andean community, the collective has the authority, because the collective determines each moment of existence of its members.* This position illustrates a point Adam Przeworski makes in his analysis of the relationship between customary law and the new constitution of South Africa: the area of greatest friction between the two systems is related to patriarchy. Cultural practices that allow women to be coerced—abduction, arranged marriages, infant betrothals, and the like—illustrate the conflict between the individual rights consecrated in the constitution and the cultural rights which are entrenched against them (Przeworski 1998, 132).

A further example of tension between cultural practices and the universal claims of human rights is the issue of violence against women. Violence against women occurs everywhere, but there are marked differences between the way it is analyzed and dealt with in various regions. It provides a difficult challenge for those who defend the autonomy and natural goodness of indigenous social structures. There is extensive documentation of such violence in the Andes, both historically and today. An analysis of petitions for divorce or nullification of marriage in two regions of Peru in the seventeenth and eighteenth centuries, for example, found domestic violence the most widespread and well-documented complaint, whatever the social level or ethnic origin of the litigants. The archives of lawsuits in the rural zones of Cuzco during this period suggest that among the indigenous, personal violence was commonplace in daily life. Family abuse and disputes motivated by sex were the principle causes of homicide in three provinces located southeast of Cuzco at the end of the colonial period, even more than cases involving land, taxes, or robberies (Lavallé 1999, 87; Stavig 1996, 14).

Since the enactment of the Law against Family Violence in Peru in 1993, some of the evaluations carried out by human rights and feminist groups in the highland areas have documented that family violence is primarily violence against women. Eighty percent of the rural population believes it is one of the main problems of justice that needs to be addressed (Fernández and Trigoso 2001). To this day, violence against women is allowed and legitimized by recourse to custom. In the Andes, men see women as susceptible to "bad behavior," prone to speak and laugh with men, which offends the husband's honor and justifies his maltreatment, according to a study of six rural communities in the department of Cuzco (Pinzás 2001). In various rural areas men beat their wives frequently, but the wives do not abandon their husbands because the alternatives for women outside marriage are virtually nonexistent; the only real alternative is to leave the community. When abused women seek refuge with their parents, the parents try to send them back to live with the husband because it is so expensive to support a daughter and her children; social norms say that women should resign themselves to mistreatment (Bourque and Warren 1981). Anthropologists Valderrama and Escalante report this admonition of a mother to her daughter who was having problems with her husband: "You brought him, and now don't tell me you can't live with him. No, *senora*, I cannot have a married woman living in my house. Go, *senora*. You need to be behind your husband." (R. Valderrama and Escalante 1997, 169; their translation from Quechua to Spanish).

For battered women, the Andean community provides little recourse. Social expectations are that the wife will view her husband's wishes as her destiny, and any outside efforts to protect women are viewed as meddling in the community's affairs. Such interventions are permitted only when called for by intimates of the couple (such as brothers and sisters, godparents, or communal authorities). They also have their risks, as is shown by a study carried out by Ruiz Bravo in eight communities of Puno, in the southern Peruvian Andes. Because custom and practice accept some forms of violence against women, when a woman who is abused seeks the help of third parties, it is up to her to prove there was no "offense," that the violence was not legitimate in customary terms (Pinzás 2001; Ruiz Bravo et al. 1998).[5] Some argue that differentiated systems for treatment of violence against women in Peru are needed because formal laws are geared to the needs of urban women and require urban institutions to support them. By contrast, highland communities are far from the official centers where a police report can be drawn up and women can be given protection.

Article 149 of the constitution recognizes that "the authorities of peasant and native communities, with the support of peasant patrols,[6] can exercise judicial functions within their areas in accordance with customary law as long as they do not violate people's fundamental rights," which makes it difficult for individuals to claim the protection of the state. In practice the state does not intervene in communities when there are violations of human rights, which gives gender violence a high degree of impunity.[7]

Two of the four Cuzco-based NGOs whose staffs I interviewed in 2000 have institutional guidelines that include informing people about the content of the Law against Family Violence in force in Peru. In spite of this, they assert that some of their efforts at prevention and condemnation have failed because the NGOs did not understand "the perspective of Andean women." A director told me at length of a case of a woman who, tired of being badly treated, had sought refuge in the house of a friend and had filed a complaint with the police with the help of the NGO. But he was very surprised to find that when she returned to her house and found her children and her farm neglected, she decided to go back to her husband: *This has happened to us often, because a woman who is badly abused will make a complaint but then the woman herself will ask that the charge be withdrawn. This shows that women value something more than their individual rights—they value their relation with the land.* For some NGO staff members, these distinct cultural codes inhibit more decisive action in favor of women. As an anthropologist from Cuzco who is responsible for gender issues in her institution put it, *We say, "How can it be that he has beaten you so badly?" But they say: "We have a way of dealing with things; I am with him for my children; we've been together for years." To their mothers who see them being abused, it just seems normal that the husband mistreats his wife. For them it's a way of life, and the women don't want their husbands to be punished. If we file a complaint, we make the problem worse because, as the women say, they can take care of it themselves and it's always been this way. We can't interfere with their lives.*

Twenty-five percent of the women who live in rural zones of Peru are illiterate, and this percentage is greater in the Andean countryside and in some zones of Amazonia where the maternal tongue is not Spanish. There is also a marked difference between urban and rural women in terms of their fertility rates (2.2 in the city and 4.3 in the countryside). One dramatic indicator is maternal mortality, which is one of the highest in Latin America. In 2000, the national rate was 185 maternal deaths for every 10,000 live births, but it could double in the rural areas (Fernández and Trigoso 2001).

Women of the highland communities of the Andes are part of what Nancy Fraser calls "bivalent communities"; they suffer both from an economic and social injustice and also from cultural devaluation. One is not a consequence of the other, and both must be addressed by redistribution and recognition (Fraser 1998). Given the tension between the idea of universal rights and recognition of the specific rights of groups, how far do collective rights extend? Rodolfo Stavenhagen suggests that collective rights that promote the individual rights of the members of a group or community should be considered human rights if they do not violate the rights of individuals (1996, 163). Enrique Mayer responds by asking who defines which collective rights contradict individual rights? Doesn't any selection of such rights by outsiders smack of colonialism and the missionary spirit? He suggests that one way to resolve the conflict is to recognize collective rights as human rights when they can be exercised without coercion (1996, 173).

Without wanting to enter into this debate, I think that even Mayer's alternative fails to provide a clear boundary between the coercive and noncoercive exercise of collective rights, and this is particularly important in the case of Andean women, who have a very narrow margin of choice.

HORIZONTALITY AND RESISTANCE: DONOR AGENCIES AND COUNTERPART NGOS

The third tension in the effort to address gender inequalities in Andean peasant communities is one that has emerged between local NGOs and the donor agencies that fund them. Although both are seeking to promote development, their communication breaks down when it comes to gender.

In 1998 there were 534 officially registered NGOs in Peru. This number may be misleading: many may be inactive, and others may have formed since then. Lima, the capital city, has the largest share of these organizations, but there are a significant number in other regions on the coast and in the Andes, such as Cuzco and Ayacucho. Their activities in rural areas are primarily directed toward improving agricultural production and the provision of basic services. Women's and feminist NGOs are not as common outside the capital as they are in Lima; in the areas in which I carried out interviews, the common pattern is "mixed" NGOs with men and women on staff. In general, they direct their efforts toward working with men; their programs for women include training to improve their skills in family health care and nutrition and small income-generating activities. These NGOs receive funds from various countries and multilateral agencies, and recently they have entered into competitive bidding to do projects in partnership with the state. Still, the majority of their funds come from private international organizations: in 1999, funds provided by such organizations to Peruvian NGOs grew to $153 million (M. Valderrama and Negrón 2001).

The emergence of NGOs, which started in Peru at the beginning of the 1970s, had strong political ties to the popular sectors. These coincided with the agendas of the private donors—fundamentally European and especially Dutch—which were committed to overcoming poverty through support for civil society. In the 1990s, political and economic changes in Peru and in the international system caused these agendas to be modified. The European donors expanded the goals of their interventions to include issues such as the environment and gender, creating a gap between donors and recipients and increasing the likelihood of undesired pressure from Northern NGOs on their counterparts in the South. Partnership has always been a sensitive issue in the relations between donors and local NGOs. Despite the efforts of some donors to build more "horizontal" relationships, including processes of consultation to set institutional priorities, attempts of Southern NGOs to achieve greater autonomy and more balanced relationships with the North are inevitably distorted by the financial dependence of the local NGOs on Northern donors (Baumann 1999).

International cooperation agencies often raise funds from private sources within their home countries, but direct government funding of NGO donors often plays a major role and reflects the official aid policies of governments in the

North. Accepting official support requires international cooperation agencies to achieve high standards of efficiency, causing them to impose a list of conditionalities that are onerous from the standpoint of Southern NGOs. These range from planning, monitoring, and evaluation requirements to insisting that local NGOs take on substantive issues, like the environment and women (M. Valderrama 2001). Over time, it has become increasingly common for gender equity to be specified as a condition for the approval of grant requests. Lack of progress in this area can lead to cutting off support to local NGOs (HIVOS 1996, 1993–98; SNV 1993–98, 1998; NOVIB 1997).

The UN Decade conferences have also reinforced the use of international policy guidelines with regard to women. These are sometimes far-reaching. The Netherlands Ministry of Foreign Affairs, for example, developed a cooperation and development framework for the 1990s that explicitly called for more equity for women at all levels, beginning with their autonomy in four arenas: physical (control of their own sexuality and reproduction); economic (equal access to and control over the means of production); political (the right to participate in decision making); and sociocultural (understood as the right to an independent identity and self-esteem) (Netherlands Ministry of Foreign Affairs 1992).

The WID approach taken by the North in the 1970s and 1980s coincided with concerns in the South about the feminization of poverty and the need to address it. But, as a more layered analysis of women's oppression uncovered root causes, and gender became the relevant framework for development interventions, the previous consensus weakened. Many mixed NGOs now see gender requirements as an "imposition" from the North. A growing resistance on the part of NGOs to having these conditions imposed on them is rapidly closing the opportunity for dialogue and consensus.

This tension is stronger in organizations that work with indigenous populations, because gender inequalities have come to be understood as cultural characteristics that ought to be respected (HIVOS 1993a,b). Generally, as they accept requests for funding, donor agencies use ambiguous language and sometimes run into contradictions as they try to balance their gender equity requirements with their own desire for self-determination and the cultural integrity of the indigenous. On the other hand, although some donors acknowledge the importance of preserving indigenous identity, culture, language, and access to land and other natural resources, stressing a multicultural approach, they are also aware that cultural arguments may violate women's human rights and contribute to maintaining women in a subordinate position. Considered static and immutable, culture can become an instrument that perpetuates and legitimates gender inequalities (HIVOS 1993b, 1995; Netherlands Ministry of Foreign Affairs 1992).

Various male leaders and staff members of NGOs that operate in rural Andean areas think that changing gender relations is forcing Western ideas into the daily lives of Third World women. As the director of a southern Andean NGO declared in 2002, *International Cooperation is promoting an agenda that is designed for other contexts; they cause us to violate practices and structural relations in the societies where we work. Among the staff here there is resistance to the concept of gender; they only accept it because they fear they will lose the funding.* And the head of an NGO in Cuzco was even firmer: *It is a mistake to try to impose Western norms on our country. Reality shows that these things always backfire.*

If we stop to think about it, this resistance follows a gender double standard. Dozens of NGO development plans in the rural Andes have the goals of modernizing agricultural methods, improving livestock production, installing potable water systems, and integrating peasant producers into new markets along with other practices intended to make structural changes in the relationship between the countryside and the city. This "technological Westernization" is not considered offensive to local traditions—on the contrary, it is viewed as necessary.

But talking about changing gender relations is not like talking about improving the production of potatoes. Well-documented experience shows that greater sensitivity to the imbalance between men and women in access to power resources does not emerge from adequate reading matter on gender or impeccable project work plans that include a "focus on gender." Instead, the sensitivity to gender issues arises from the personal and daily life experiences and preconceptions of flesh and blood people who go into development work. The people who go into the field in rural areas are generally men, with technical backgrounds, born and raised in the Andes. Thus, as the head of a Cuzco NGO pointed out: *There is a problem in the team and in the institutional culture. Here everyone will tell you, "Yes, we are all concerned about women." But the perspective of those who carry out projects is that "gender" is just a phrase, not something they have internalized. The majority of our staff come from rural families. They may participate in discussions about the gender approach, but in their own lives they have a very clear idea about the roles of men and women. They can go through the motions of incorporating women in projects and strengthening women's roles and capacities, but in the way they see life, women already have a role, and it is to take care of children and the family, and so forth. These are cultural patterns that are very difficult to change.*

An expert in a Cuzco NGO confessed, in a way that graphically reinforces this point, that his organization has difficulties carrying out activities to promote gender equity. *Obviously, there are slip-ups in the community; it's human. And we make them ourselves. So many times in our conversations about our projects, we say, "But if I in my own house do these things, how can I go to the field and promote something else?"*

A review of the institutional plans of the development organizations in which I did interviews in April 2000 suggests that they have adopted a gender discourse: they acknowledge the indicators that show the oppression of rural women: little or no schooling, health problems, and their contribution to production traditionally hidden as part of their reproductive role. But in almost all cases their efforts at "gender mainstreaming" result in activities directed toward women in their "feminine" roles, such as caring for small animals and household gardens. Despite the investments in economic and human resources made by donor agencies to improve the capacities of their counterpart NGOs to do gender assessments and build capacity, they often meet with passive if not overt resistance. As some of the experts I interviewed in Cuzco suggested: *For a long time, the word gender was like a label we put on what we were doing, which was working with women. We called this gender, and we included in our project papers what we had read about the topic.* This approach was confirmed in an interview with a field expert: *We tried in everything we did, in every project we designed, to introduce a gender approach. Then, when we analyzed it, we asked, "What is this gender focus?" It's not so easy. At times it meant highlighting the fact that women also participate in projects—but women always participate. Then, as it wasn't clear what gender really meant in practice, at times we just wrote it in the report.*

These comments illustrate a broader tension between the international development cooperation agencies and the local NGOs: the former insisting that they are pursuing "horizontal" relations with their counterparts, and the latter resisting attempts to impose conditions. Gender conditionality is sometimes supported by women staff members, but their concerns about what they see in the field do not get support from the top. The view that the gender focus is "just on paper" clearly distorts and depoliticizes the issue.

CONCLUSIONS

When I wrote this essay, I was aware of a fourth tension that has not been articulated. This is "our" role, the position of us Latin American women who are simultaneously inside and outside development practice. We recognize the importance of donor agencies' contributions to the promotion of women's rights.

Yet, at the same time, we are also keenly aware that the policies and initiatives of such donors put at risk the autonomy of NGOs.

Something similar to being inside and outside simultaneously has also happened with regard to Andean women. The testimonies of the peasant women in the southern Andes who had to cope with the violence and destruction originated by the conflict between the terrorist group Sendero Luminoso and the Armed Forces during the 1980s show a determination that is far from passive. However, before and after the conflict, their options remained very limited outside the communal ambit. The need to broaden the horizons of Andean women presupposes not only access to material resources but also greater flexibility in how they are allowed to mark their identities, including their language, dress, and customs. But this would require a reassessment of the social construction of the "Andean community," which is very difficult to pursue while simultaneously supporting indigenous rights.

It is clear that there are unsolved conflicts in the lives of Andean peasant women, for example, their right to health care as it relates to the recognition of their traditions. One of the worst public health problems in Peru is the high level of maternal mortality and the limited institutional assistance available when women give birth. According to recent data, only 24 percent of births in rural areas receive professional attention, and in the rural Andean zones it is even less. There are many reasons for this, ranging from the distance between the community and the nearest health center, the cost of services, the depersonalized and even disparaging care that professionals give to these women, and the differences in environment. The Andean peasant woman gives birth in her home, in a dark and warm place, accompanied by her husband and her mother, who offer her herbs; birth is vertical or squatting; the umbilical cord is cut with a bit of pottery; there is the belief that during birth the body "opens" and is porous and one should not let the cold come in. The difference in using stainless steel to cut the cord and the requirements of gynecological beds, lights, and wall tile, as well as leaving the spouse and mother outside the delivery room, illustrate the conflict between the urgent need to provide Andean women access to the basic right to health care but also to the right to give birth in accord with their customs and in a family setting.

A national feminist organization is experimenting with a pilot project in several Andean provinces to provide "annexes" to health centers where women can come with their husbands and give birth in a vertical position but have a professional nearby in case there are complications. Why do we accept and celebrate this recognition of the value of tradition, but reject cultural practices like mock abduction, arranged marriage, and relying on communal justice in cases of domestic abuse? From what position can we "choose" what practices are to be accepted as "collective" rights and which violate the human rights of individuals if experts on Andean culture, anthropologists, and NGO staff working in these communities say that the notion of the individual does not exist in the Andean world?

Despite the current controversies about universality versus difference, I would argue that international norms of human rights, including the Convention Against all Forms of Discrimination Against Women (CEDAW), represent important values and are a necessary point of reference for the debate that must include the voices of indigenous women.

NOTES

1. Peru is a country with about 25 million inhabitants, 28 percent of whom are considered rural; a similar percentage identifies itself as indigenous or native. There are seventy-two distinct ethnic groups, of which seven live in the Andes and the other sixty-five in the Amazonian region, grouped in fourteen distinct language groups. The census is, however, not fully reliable because it stopped using a race/ethnicity categorization after the 1940 National Census, and constant internal migration from the Andes to the coast has "de-Indianized" the urban population (Fernández and Trigoso 2001).

2. Some of the ideas discussed in this text are an updated version of an essay related to NGO perspectives on indigenous women, *El Mundo al Revés: Imágenes de la Mujer Indígena*, published by the Latin American Council of Social Sciences (CLACSO) and the Swedish International Development Agency (SIDA) in Buenos Aires. The investigation, which was the source of the publication, was carried out with a grant awarded in a regional competition for senior researchers on the topic, "Women in Latin America and the Caribbean: Between Emancipation and Exclusion," sponsored by CLACSO-SIDA in 1999.

3. In an interview in March 2002, when I asked a group of women leaders of the Peasant Women's Federation in Huancavelica (southern Peruvian Andes) about the contrast between traditional and Western clothing, one peasant woman told me that if she stopped wearing her *pollera* (peasant skirt), in her community she would be called a *pituca*, Peruvian slang for a woman who takes on upper-class airs, and she would be criticized.

4. In July 2001, in a group interview with peasant women in the community of Patacancha in Cuzco, at 4000 m (13,123 ft) above sea level, although their ages ranged from 22 to 50 years old, all confirmed that their parents had chosen their husbands. And if they didn't like the men their parents chose, they had to accept the choice anyway. These women were part of a group with whom an NGO was working that had as part of its working principles the empowerment of women and integration of a gender perspective. When the staff was asked about this contradiction between their principles and reality, they responded that "arranged marriages" were issues they could not interfere with.

5. In this context, efforts to educate people about the Law Against Family Violence are viewed with suspicion and even rejected by the men of highland communities. An NGO that operates

in the high Andes carried out training workshops for women which caused conflict between men and women, in the view of the men: *We have had problems. One group of women said that they now knew their rights; they wanted to separate and said that they did not like being beaten. We* [the community leaders] *suggested* [to the NGO] *that they work more harmoniously, because now our wives won't let us touch them. When women know their rights they think of themselves as untouchable.* (Interview by the author in the peasant community of Ccarhuahurán, Huanta, Ayachucho, March 2002.)

6. The so-called peasant patrols are groups of rural men and women who fulfill security functions for their neighbors in the community. Founded on their own initiative, originally to control rustling, in the second half of the 1980s they played an important role in contending against Sendero Luminoso in the Andes.

7. "Pluriculturalidad y Violencia Familiar," *Diario El Comercio*, 20 October 2000.

II. Livelihood and Control of Resources

Gender Equity and Rural Land Reform in China

Gale Summerfield

In China, dramatic changes in land rights have been integral to the market-oriented transition, which is based on policies similar to neoliberal restructuring elsewhere. During the early 1980s, the communes were broken up and use rights to farmland were contracted to families under the Household Responsibility System (HRS), an agrarian reform designed to provide private incentives, improve efficiency, and increase output. Women as well as men received allocations of land as approximately 200 million small, fragmented, household farms were established. Changing demographics of the villages and the need to consolidate the small plots of land have led to frequent redistributions of farmland, but insecure tenure discourages investment in the land. The 1998 Land Management Law and the 2003 Rural Land Contract Law address this problem by extending leases to thirty years and prohibiting redistributions. However, rural women are finding that their land rights have become less secure with the latest reforms that end redistribution.

Although land-titling campaigns are common in restructuring economies, women's changing rights to land and housing are usually overlooked because those distributing titles view the allocation of these resources as a family issue. A few studies have pointed out that women often lose out in the distribution of property rights and that these rights are crucial for human security and development (Tinker and Summerfield 1999b; Razavi 2003). To gender specialists analyzing Chinese reforms, family farming in the HRS resembles the traditional virilocal, patriarchal system that dominated the countryside until the establishment of a socialist state in 1949 (see Aslanbeigui and Summerfield 1989; Croll 1985). There are, however, critical differences. Women have legal rights to land, even though in practice the results are rarely equitable, and nonfarm opportunities are increasing. Still, the incentive to have more children associated with family farming conflicts with the One-Child Policy, which was instituted at the same time, resulting in numerous accounts of discrimination against women and girls. Gender effects of the HRS are more complicated than simply a return to tradition.

This essay examines the gendered control of resources under the rural reforms in terms of income-related opportunities (changes in income from farming, migration options, and work in nonstate industry and agricultural sidelines). It also focuses on problem areas of the HRS in terms of feminization of agriculture, insecure property rights, intrahousehold bargaining power, and interaction with the One-Child Policy.

LAND DISTRIBUTION UNDER THE HRS: LATE 1970S–PRESENT

In 1978, at the Third Plenum of the Eleventh Central Committee of the Chinese Communist Party, officials announced the HRS, which became a uniform national policy in 1983 (Aslanbeigui and Summerfield 1989, 343). Throughout the country, collective farms were divided up, and rights to small plots of land were allocated to families based on the number of individuals in the household. Under the "two-tier system," the village collective (or village cooperative) retained ownership rights to the land and leased use rights to households.[1] Initially the leases were for only a few years. The household provided seed and fertilizer, fulfilled a production quota to be sold to the state at a set price, paid taxes, and contributed to the village public accumulation and welfare funds (Dong 1996, 916). The rest of the crop and other output could be sold at rural markets, along the sides of major roadways, or even in nearby cities. Rural markets had been a traditional institution in China but were suspended during the Cultural Revolution. Since many people had experience trading in these markets before they were disbanded, it was fairly easy to revive them once legal prohibitions were removed. Officials made some effort to negotiate the local market prices rather than allowing them to respond completely to supply and demand, but market prices were almost always higher than state procurement prices, which in turn were higher than they had been in the period before reform.[2]

TABLE 1   Agricultural Land per Household in China, 1986–92

Year	Area per household (hectares/acres)	Number of parcels per household
1986	0.466/1.15	5.85
1990	0.420/1.04	5.52
1992	0.466/1.15	3.16

Source: Zhou 2000

The state relaxed requirements for self-sufficiency in grain production and permitted greater flexibility for farmers to choose which crops to plant. Farms near urban centers quickly switched part of their land to products such as green vegetables and fruit and marketed them in the cities. This produce was usually fresher and of higher quality than that available in state stores, and the markets flourished.

The plots of land initially allocated under the HRS were extremely small—less than one *mu* each (a *mu* is a fifteenth of a hectare). As shown in table 1, each family held, on average, less than half a hectare of land divided among five to ten plots; these were scattered geographically as villages tried to allocate pieces of good, mediocre, and poor land to every family.[3] Although the plots have been consolidated over the years, the average farm for a family is still less than half a hectare (about one and one quarter acres).

With use rights to the land specified by the HRS, farmers acted more like owners, but the insecurity of tenure made them reluctant to invest in improvements to the land and infrastructure. By the late 1980s the length of leases had increased to an average of fifteen years, but land rights remained insecure for several reasons. There were redistributions to consolidate plots and to adjust for births, deaths, and marriages. When someone married, for example, her natal village might take some land from her family and allocate it to someone who had just had a child. The village she moved to would also need to reallocate land to adjust for an additional resident. Some villages redistributed part of their land annually; others waited a few years and adjusted the plots of all residents simultaneously. Eighty percent of villages have redistributed land since introduction of the HRS (Schwarzwalder 2001) giving considerable power to local village officials. The state retains the right to relocate people for projects such as dam construction.

In 1993, the central government began to promote thirty-year leases, but most villages continued to have land redistributions (Prosterman et al. 2000). At the end of 1998, a new Land Management Law decreed that leases be binding for thirty years and that redistributions be avoided during the lease. If a redistribution is deemed necessary, it must be approved by two-thirds of the residents involved. The Land Management Law of 1998 marks a significant change from egalitarian to efficiency-oriented mechanisms and is perhaps a move toward a market in land rights. A 1999 survey indicated that most people still expected additional redistributions, and many villages have indicated that they plan to make one last readjustment before complying with the decree (ibid.). The Rural Land Contract Law of 2003 further strengthened the thirty-year lease regulation and for the first time explicitly mentioned women's equal right to lease land (*People's Daily* 2003).

GENDER ASPECTS OF THE HRS

The HRS reforms produced an initial surge in agricultural output, large-scale migration to urban areas, growth of nonstate industries and sideline businesses, and the feminization of agricultural production. These changes have had mixed gender effects. The vibrant economy has created positive opportunities for both women and men. Growing household incomes can increase the well-being and agency of everyone in the family; better housing benefits everyone; and off-farm opportunities have emerged for women and men. But some of the changes have introduced inequities that have not been fully addressed. Land tenure laws are not clear about women's rights. Patriarchal and virilocal traditions that require a woman to move to her husband's village upon marriage still place women at a disadvantage under the reform policies, and traditional gender biases have resurfaced.

Growth of Agricultural Output and
Income-Earning Opportunities
AGRICULTURAL OUTPUT AND HOUSEHOLD EXPENDITURE

Despite their tiny, dispersed plots of land, Chinese farmers increased their output dramatically in the early 1980s (as shown in table 2). Between 1979 and 1984, grain production increased at an average rate of 4.9 percent per year, and the gross value of agricultural output grew by 7.6 percent annually, in real terms (ZGTJNJ 1989; K. Chen and Brown 2001, 281). In the first half of the 1980s, agricultural growth provided a substantial increase in the standard of living for millions of rural residents. The gains were widely distributed since land was fairly equally divided among residents in any area, but villages near coastal urban centers had

TABLE 2   Production of Major Crops in China, 1980–2000 (Millions of Tons)

Crop	1980	1985	1990	1995	1999	2000
Grains (besides wheat)	320.56	379.11	446.24	466.62	508.39	462.18
Rice	139.91	168.57	189.33	185.23	198.49	187.91
Wheat	55.21	85.81	98.23	102.21	113.88	99.64
Fruit	—	11.64	18.74	42.15	62.38	62.94

Source: National Bureau of Statistics 2000, 370, 387; 2003

large markets for their products and prospered more than those in remote areas. Rural poverty rates fell from an estimated 27 percent in 1980 to around 11 percent by 1988 (World Bank 1992, 4).[4] Per capita income in rural areas increased from 134 yuan in 1978 to 398 yuan by 1985 (State Statistical Bureau 1986, 582). Nominal rural incomes have continued to grow rapidly, reaching 2210 yuan in 1999 (National Bureau of Statistics 2000, 22–23).[5]

The high rates of output growth in agriculture have not been easy to sustain, however, and slowed in the late 1980s and mid-1990s.[6] This slowdown is partly because the base for comparison has increased as overall agricultural output per hectare has grown, but it also reflects structural problems. The downturn in the late 1980s was blamed on low state procurement prices for grain and the expansion of alternative work opportunities for farmers (Sicular 1991, 343). Others note that the lack of a full market in land rights may cause distortions (see Cooper 1991, 336). Agriculture has also had to compete with industry, housing, burial mounds, and roads for available land. Farmland has decreased near cities even though marginal lands are being reclaimed to try to offset the loss (Croll 1994, 101). Overall, there has been a net decrease in cultivable land of about 4 percent (Ho 2001, 395), but some arable lands lie fallow because more lucrative opportunities are available off-farm and agricultural taxes are too high to merit the effort to utilize the land (Dong 1996, 917).

Under the HRS, the initial surge in agricultural output quickly translated into higher income for most rural households, and incomes have remained high despite the slowdown in agricultural growth rates. The purchase of durable consumer goods, such as bicycles, sewing machines, and television sets, has increased dramatically (see table 3). Although these gains are not likely to be equally distributed to all family members, women and men share in the benefits in many ways. Farmers expanded their houses or built new ones. Housing in rural areas had remained private throughout the socialist period; by contrast workers in the cities occupied units provided by state-owned enterprises. Under the HRS, farmers have

TABLE 3 Number of Durable Consumer Goods Owned per 100 Rural Households, at Year End (China, 1978–99)

Goods	1978	1983	1985	1990	1995	1999
Bicycles	30.73	63.41	80.64	118.33	147.02	136.85
Sewing machines	19.80	36.07	43.21	55.19	65.74	67.06
Radios	17.44	56.82	54.19	45.15	31.05	26.97
Color TVs	—	—	—	—	16.92	48.74

Source: State Statistical Bureau 1986, 585; National Bureau of Statistics 2000, 339; 2002, 350

more secure tenure for their houses than for land, so they tend to invest more in expanding and improving their homes. Housing investment accounted for 70.1 percent of total investment in fixed assets in rural areas in 1986 and rose to 87.9 percent in 1988 (ibid.).

Housing size is one area where rural residents have some advantage over urban residents, as shown in table 4; rural per capita living space is more than twice that of urban areas, and urban per capita living space in 1999 was still less than what the average space had been in rural areas in 1985 (14.7 square meters [158.2 square feet]). All family members benefit from better housing, and the gains may be even greater for women because they spend so much of their time in activities in the home and are more likely to work in home-based businesses than men (Tinker and Summerfield 1999b).[7]

RURAL-URBAN MIGRATION UNDER THE HRS

Although rural residents were expected to contribute to public works projects throughout the Maoist period, and small-scale rural industry was promoted during the Cultural Revolution, off-farm opportunities to earn income in rural areas were scarce in the late 1970s, while severe restrictions on migration, tracked through the *hukou* registration system, prevented mass movements to the cities. This protected the cities from the squatter settlements and slums seen in many developing countries and protected urban jobs. Rural residents, however, were deprived of the opportunities and the additional state benefits associated with urban life. Thus, while the overall Gini coefficient measuring inequality was low during the socialist period, there was a large gap in opportunities between rural and urban areas.

Since the HRS reforms, it has been harder for the state to control migration. Migrants can get nonstate jobs or open small businesses instead of depending on jobs in state-owned enterprises or collectives. Before the reforms, ration coupons

TABLE 4 Urban vs. Rural Housing in China, Net Floor Space per Capita,
1985–99 (Square Meters)

Floor space	1985	1990	1995	1999
Urban	5.2	6.7	8.1	9.8
Rural	14.7	17.8	21.0	24.2

Source: National Bureau of Statistics 2000, 28–29

for grain, oil, and cloth were issued to prevent hoarding of these goods. The ration coupons were linked to the registration of the household and discouraged rural-urban migration. The coupons quickly became less of an obstacle to migration in the market-oriented economy because the production of grain, oil seeds, and cotton was plentiful enough that officials no longer needed rationing, and the coupons were discontinued in the mid-1990s. Other regulations such as school registration for children can slow migration, but the state does not seem interested in enforcing migration laws too vigorously because migrants provide cheap labor for construction and high-risk urban jobs. Reforms in 2003 were designed to eliminate most registration requirements (*China Daily*, 8 August 2003), but the process remains incomplete.

Over 100 million people (estimates range up to 150 million) have migrated from rural to urban areas or between smaller and larger cities over the past two decades, and the trend is expected to continue (National Bureau of Statistics 2002). Women have gradually come to comprise about 40 percent of total migration (see Davin 1998). Usually the whole family does not migrate since someone has to remain on the farm to guarantee rights to the land, grow enough crops to pay agricultural taxes, and care for the husband's elderly parents who cannot or will not move to the city. Not surprisingly, usually the wife, young children, and in-laws remain, while the husband and teen-age sons and daughters migrate. Women who do migrate often work as child care providers and housekeepers, waitresses, or assembly-line workers in export-processing plants. Men typically are involved in construction, transportation, and restaurant work. Much of the migration is temporary or cyclical. Family members often return to help out on the farm at peak times such as harvesting. Women, especially, are likely to return to their rural homes unless they marry while in the city. Rural-urban migration has had a significant impact on the growth of income. Although serious problems exist, such as deceptive job offers from those trafficking in women and abandonment by spouses, for many rural residents, the ability to seek employment in the city has given individuals and their families more options and has had a positive impact on the incomes of rural families.[8]

Ties remain between the urban migrants and rural areas, including remittances. The massive migration, however, has not reduced the rural-urban income gap, which instead has grown during most of the reform period. One reason is that migrants to the large cities are generally not the poorest group but rather those better off financially and more educated (Mallee 1998, 222–23; Davin 1998, 230). Opportunities for jobs that pay high wages, such as work in joint ventures and foreign banks, are growing faster in urban areas but tend to go to the better-connected, better-educated urban residents and not to migrants. This widening rural-urban income gap represents growing relative poverty for women and men in rural areas compared to those living in the cities even if absolute poverty is declining in both areas. Because middle-aged, rural women are concentrated in the lowest income-earning sectors in agricultural work, they are particularly threatened by the growing disparities.

SIDELINES AND OFF-FARM JOBS IN TOWNSHIP
AND VILLAGE ENTERPRISES

Since 1978, people who remained in rural areas have had more job opportunities in the nonfarm sector. Diversification of income-earning opportunities for rural residents is apparent in farm-based businesses and nonfarm work. The HRS resulted in higher incomes from farming in the first half of the 1980s, but since then township and village enterprises (TVEs) and other nonfarm work have provided the main stimulus to rural income.

With the HRS in place, women and men began setting up small business ventures at home to complement their farm income. State policy encouraged this through the expansion of private plots and legalization of rural markets (Croll 1994, 24–25). Some argue that only nontraditional work can increase the status of women within the home in rural China (see Entwisle et al. 1995). Initially this seems to be a reasonable assumption because studies have shown that the source as well as the amount of income is likely to influence bargaining power. Yet, the ability to make key decisions about production and sales of goods may have greater influence on women's status in society and bargaining power in the home than whether the good she produces and sells was traditionally produced by women or instead results from work off the farm or in a home-based business (also see Croll 1994). Traditional sideline production is an important source of income and should be included in the study of factors affecting women's agency.

Women are producing traditional sidelines, such as raising animals or preparing food for sale, but the scale of production is larger, the goods are frequently sold on nontraditional export markets, and the economic return is often much larger than it would have been in the traditional setting. Drawing on both traditional sideline production and modern industry, rural women raise chickens and hogs, run home-based doufu and noodle shops, and assemble batteries and radios. They sell their goods in local markets and export them to other countries. Local and central governments have facilitated exports of sideline production by setting up distribution mechanisms, and provincial authorities often arrange contracts directly with foreign businesses (ibid., 25). Sideline production appears to add substantially to women's income and to exert a positive influence on their decision-making power at home. Since husbands often work in cities or off-farm, women are frequently the major decision makers in home-based rural businesses even when they are not the owners, regardless of whether these businesses would be classified as traditional women's work. Their fathers-in-law are usually present on the farm and may retain decision-making authority over both agricultural and sideline production, but this is slowly changing as nuclear families become more common.

Off-farm businesses have flourished in many rural areas. Higher incomes from farming initially provided investment funds for enterprises run by townships and villages. In addition, some villages retained funds from the collective period that they invested in TVES, such as brick-making factories. Provinces near the coast were able to attract substantial foreign investment (much of it from overseas Chinese and Hong Kong) and have diversified and flourished while the hinterlands muddle along. By 1989, nonstate rural industries produced 58 percent of total rural output value (Gao 1994, 85).

Textiles and electronics are common in the coastal TVES and, as in other countries, these industries hire mostly women. On average, women were 35 percent of workers in TVES in the early 1990s, but in some areas, such as Fujian and Jiangsu near the coast, they held almost 50 percent of the jobs (ibid., 85). In 1999, TVES employed about 127 million people, and private enterprises provided work for another million (National Bureau of Statistics 2000, 115). State policy since 1995 has promoted privatization of the TVES, and by 2000, millions of TVES had been sold to managers, employees, and other investors (Dong et al. 2001, 1). Preliminary studies indicate that privatization of the TVES has increased stratification among the workers and that women are disadvantaged in buying shares (ibid., 16). Because women are less likely to get a share in ownership of the companies, they will have less influence on decisions about running the companies and may face other forms of bias that favor shareholders at work.

By allowing greater worker mobility and decision making by farm families, the HRS has contributed to growth of nonfarm employment opportunities and expansion of sidelines that offer ways to earn income that often exceeds that earned from farming. Women are employed in these areas, so the gender disparities in opportunities for rural employment are low, though they vary with age, education, and type of industry. These industries have gender-related problems that are common elsewhere. Men's wages in TVEs are generally higher than women's depending on the type of industry where the worker is employed, with male-intensive work paying higher wages. Although income may be higher in these firms, working conditions are often unhealthy.[9] TVEs favor young women for the typically female-intensive industries such as textiles and electronics, but when they marry and have children, the women workers often return to farming. Available data do not indicate any change in the real size of this gap in recent years (see Rozelle et al. 2002).

Warning Signs and Equity Problem Areas
FEMINIZATION OF AGRICULTURE

As rural men and unmarried youth switch from agriculture to work in TVEs or migrate to the cities for employment, married rural women are increasingly concentrated in agricultural production and simultaneously engage in home-based sidelines and reproductive, caring activities. Women are 60.5 percent of the 320 million workers in agriculture (*Xinhua* 1999). Even where women are somewhat less than half of the workers, the overall increased concentration of women in the sector indicates the feminization of agriculture.[10] The arrangement may reflect optimization of total family availabilities, but it does so at the expense of women's agency. With the feminization of agriculture, women are becoming concentrated in what is usually one of the lowest income sectors of the economy, and this concentration tends to aggravate gender differences in relative poverty (see H. Zhang 1999, 61; Summerfield and Aslanbeigui 1992).

Available national-level data about labor allocation on farms supply little information about gender, but case studies and interviews show important changes. Under collectivization, it was common for groups of women to weed the fields.[11] In many areas, traditions prohibited women from plowing or working in the fields when menstruating. Although the state promoted tractor and truck driving

TABLE 5   Urban vs. Rural Annual per Capita Income in China,
1984–2000 (Yuan)

Income	1985	1990	1995	2000
Urban households	739	1,510	4,283	6,280
Rural residents	398	686	1,578	2,253

Source: National Bureau of Statistics 2000, 22–23; 2002, 321, 343

skills for women, men dominated these jobs. Models of iron-girl teams showed women moving rocks and doing other heavy labor, but women usually received only about three-fourths of the work points of men and were not paid for household duties.

With decollectivization and the feminization of agriculture, women are doing household chores and fieldwork (and often sidelines). Despite the drop in absolute poverty, the growing gap between urban and rural standards of living exacerbates the problems of relative poverty for rural women who find themselves mired in low-end agricultural work. Rural average per capita income is less than half of urban (see table 5).

Although the feminization of agriculture is occurring on most of the farmland in China (with regional variations), a variety of land leases and leasing systems are used under the HRS. Each raises different gender issues. Collective land (*jiti di*) comprises about 93 percent of agricultural land, and the remaining area is allocated as private self-sufficiency plots (*ziliu di*) that provide vegetables and variety crops for family consumption and a place to raise chickens and hogs. Collective land is further divided into three categories: responsibility land (*zeren tian*) with requirements to deliver part of the output as a quota to the state, contract land (*chengbao tian*) leased by the village to farmers for a fee, and some additional subsistence land called ration land (*kouliang tian*) (Rozelle et al. 1998, 5).

Gender statistics are inadequate, but the statements about the feminization of agriculture refer to responsibility land, the main type of agricultural land lease. (Surveys in 1992 and 1995 of more than 270 villages indicate that responsibility land comprises 78 to 85 percent of collective land in almost all of the villages) (Brandt et al. 2002). Women also do most of the work on private plots since they are usually next to the house. A study in Pingdu indicates that women are the main workers on ration land as men seek off-farm work (Chen et al. 1998, 131). What happens on contract land is the most uncertain and least well documented. This type of land is supposed to go to skilled farmers (Zhou 2000). The experience of Vietnam (with some similar land reforms) indicates that contract land is often some of the best quality land in the village and that it is usually leased to men; this has been an overlooked area of gender discrimination (Tinker and Summerfield 1999b).

PROPERTY RIGHTS

In a market-oriented economy, land takes on new meanings in terms of wealth itself, its ability to generate new wealth, and as collateral for credit. A series of laws give Chinese women legal property rights. Since the Land Law of 1950, women have been guaranteed rights to land along with men. China is a signatory of the 1979 Convention on the Elimination of All Forms of Discrimination Against Women (CEDAW), the first international agreement to call for property rights for women (Warren 1999, 165–66). The Marriage Law of 1980 states that property "earned during marriage is jointly owned by husband and wife unless otherwise provided in an agreement" (Duncan and Li 2001, 20). The Marriage Law is not specific about land rights, but the Inheritance Law of 1985 allows rural land rights to be inherited.

An amendment to the Chinese Constitution in 1988 states that women have equal rights with men in "all spheres of life, including economic interests and family life" (ibid., 19). In 1992, the Women's Law was passed, partly in reaction to growing discriminatory practices in hiring and firing women. It specifies that women and men have equal rights to property and explicitly mentions farmland and housing plots; the law further states that women's land rights should be protected if they divorce (Warren 1999; Duncan and Li 2001). The updated Marriage Law in 2001 confirms the land rights for divorced women, and the Rural Land Contract Law implemented in 2003 states that rural women should not lose their land in their birth village when they marry until they receive a new allocation in their husband's village. If a woman is divorced or widowed, the law specifies that she should retain her land rights where she is living (ACWF 2003). These laws strengthen women's status in society and within the home, but women's rights remain much less certain than those of men.

Practice usually falls short of intent. The courts often do not enforce the laws, and local communities frequently refuse to abide by the legislation, especially in cases of divorce or death of the husband (Li 2003). If a woman divorces (by her own choice or that of her spouse), she is expected to return to her parents' village. Usually, however, she has no real land rights there. It is far from clear that the land contract law of 2003 will be successful in maintaining a woman's rights in her husband's village if they divorce. The language about joint ownership used in legal documents is often difficult for the general public to understand without the aid of a lawyer.[12] Land laws are vague about which type of joint ownership applies to family property and whether the lease is granted to the husband or to all family members. The contract—which can be signed by either husband or wife—is typically signed just by the husband, and a single line for the signature on the contract works against having both signatures.[13] The importance of joint ownership has not been fully instilled. Currently, widows do not have the same property rights in practice as widowers. Although a woman can remain on the land if her husband dies, she is expected to relinquish all rights if she remarries, which is not the case if a widower remarries. The 2003 land law gives widows as well as divorced women legal grounds for remaining on the land that was shared with their husbands, but how the courts will enforce the change and how women will negotiate the uncomfortable situation of living in the midst of their husband's relatives if there is a divorce or remarriage remains to be seen.

With the HRS reforms, both women and men were allocated land and counted in the redistributions. The land allocation of a woman marrying into a village added to the holdings of the husband and his parents. This made the woman appear less of a burden to her in-laws. Many studies of land tenure in China focus on how tenure insecurity reduces incentives to invest in and improve the land (see Dong 1996). With the extension of leases to 30 years under the Land Management Law of 1998 and Rural Land Contract Law of 2003, redistributions of land are supposed to end. Long-term tenure security and the ending of redistributions will mark a dramatic change in gender relations regarding land. In the short run, a freeze on redistributions is likely to provide windfall profits for some and losses for others. People with unmarried daughters, for example, currently have land allocated to support them that would have been given up when the women married. Without redistribution families may keep the land when their daughters marry, but their daughters and sons-in-law will not receive the usual allocations in the husband's village. The 2003 law specifies that in this case women will retain the allocation in their birth village, but it is likely that the daughter will be heavily pressured to donate her land to her parents because she will not be living in the village. In the previous cases when women have retained use of land in their natal village because there was no land available in their husband's village, cultivating the land has been cumbersome, requiring time-consuming commuting between villages (Prosterman et al. 2000). Since 1998, complaints by women about loss of access to land have soared (Yang et al. 2004; Li 2003).

In the short run, the rights one brings to the table are likely to have a large impact on outcomes. Gender aspects of land reform have not received much attention in the large surveys that have been carried out so far. With the variations in leases for responsibility plots, ration plots, and contract land, it would be useful to explore whether all types of land have been allocated equitably or whether women's rights are concentrated in certain land types. Disputes over the quality of the plots have rarely appeared in interviews and news reports, indicating that this has not been viewed as a serious problem.[14]

In the long run, a market in land might develop if the policy environment is favorable. The transfer of use rights is already legal, and villages near urban centers have begun to experiment with leasing arrangements. Farmers sometimes lease their land to villagers from a more distant community who want to work in the suburbs of a large city, while the farmer family moves into the city to work. In some areas, wealthy people have leased land from several families and set up larger farms to take advantage of economies of scale. The goal of capturing economies of scale has prompted some researchers to promote privatization. But farmers are aware of the tendency of large farms to displace small owners and, although they want secure tenure of use rights, they do not support privatization (Dong 1996). As land becomes more concentrated, the poor in general, and women in particular, are less likely to control it. Use rights to land are especially important for poor women, not only for food production but also for developing complementary income-earning activities.

Women's rights to housing are closely tied to those for land, but ownership rights for housing are private. The house is generally viewed as the legal property of the husband and his family; the wife has some rights as long as she is part of the family. Changes are occurring slowly with the formation of nuclear families and of small to medium-sized towns that are not clan-based. Laws that grant long-term leases and joint ownership can protect women, but their inclusion as equal partners is not guaranteed.

Using land as collateral for credit is a common practice in a market-oriented economy, but this is still not legal in China.[15] As in other countries, women face barriers to entering the market economy because they lack assets and collateral for loans. Some women benefit from remittances from wealthy relatives in the city or abroad. Microcredit programs in many areas partially fill the gap in financial markets and help women set up sideline businesses, but microcredit will not help with large investments such as rural industries, which are mostly financed by village accumulation funds or private local and foreign investors. If using land as collateral is made legal, women would need fully transferable rights to be able to take advantage of this, but such a change also brings the risk of loss of land rights if the loan is not repaid. Dong (1996) argues that credit might be unavailable even with transferable rights because the average landholdings are so small, and transaction costs for small loans are high. The tendency toward concentration that is usually observed in land markets may eventually influence credit availability (if China moves to a freer market in land), but will benefit those with larger holdings.

HRS AND INTRAHOUSEHOLD BARGAINING POWER

The changing opportunities for members of the family and the socioeconomic policies outside the family influence gender relations within the family. As Amartya Sen (1990) has argued, these are based on cooperation and conflict. Decision making within the family becomes more important under the HRS because the family decides what to produce and how to produce it. Divorce, though increasing, is still rare in rural China and is not the typical fall-back position, especially for women. Yet, substantial leeway remains for negotiating positions within the family structure. Often the family works together to find ways of maximizing well-being, such as investing in a better house. Sometimes the long-run welfare of one family member depends on current sacrifices by others in the family, for example, when current income-earning opportunities are foregone to send the children to school. (Current sacrifices may be compensated by grown children in the form of support for elderly parents, but this is still more likely to be the responsibility of the son than the daughter, who has to take care of her husband's parents.)

Putting farming decisions back into the hands of families alters the allocation of labor within the household. Small, fragmented farms rely more on small tools or machinery and labor inputs compared to large farms. Crops that yield higher returns, such as fruits and vegetables, are attractive, but the small size of plots requires labor-intensive production. Caring for children and in-laws, keeping house in rural areas where prepared goods are less available through the market, and raising chickens and hogs are also labor-intensive activities, and all are performed mainly by women.[16] Any increased load in productive work falls especially heavily on women since they continue to do most of the housework. When more processed products, such as baked bread, shoes, and clothing, become available in rural areas, some of the burden on rural women's time will be reduced through market exchange.

As women take over more farming tasks, they make more decisions about production and often perform tasks formerly done by men. At the same time, the value associated with these tasks is frequently downgraded within the family (see Li 1999; W. Zhang 1998, 199). When men find higher-paid jobs in construction or industry, for example, decisions about which crops to plant or plowing tasks are no longer viewed as critical to the livelihood of the family. The farm is kept going in some areas mainly to retain property rights and pay the agricultural tax. Despite these problems, responsibility for key agricultural decisions can increase women's perceptions of the value of their work.

Decollectivization and the return of the location of women's income-earning opportunities to the home may strengthen "remembered patriarchy" (Tinker and Summerfield 1999a). In some families, the husband's father assigns work tasks each morning, a practice that differs significantly from being assigned work by a team leader. Women, however, are no longer "inside people" who have had no contact with the world. New laws, off-farm work opportunities, nuclear families, and residence outside the village dominated by the husband's clan create cracks in the traditional patriarchal household structure. Jiangsu Province has been setting up a plan to combine its many small villages into fewer towns. This would merge families and open up more land for farming in an area where agricultural land has been absorbed by industry and infrastructure.

The growth of rural nonstate industry and opportunities for at least temporary work in the cities have also expanded women's opportunities and contributed to their intrahousehold bargaining power. Since there is an abundance of estimated surplus labor in agriculture, urban migration can be expected to grow in coming years and become more permanent. Opportunities for young couples to live separately or relocate to earn a living also help transform rural villages and reduce clan dominance. These changes can be expected to increase women's agency in making decisions within the household, and many reports indicate that women are making more important household decisions since the reforms. Li Zongmin (1999), for example, reports that eight of ten men she interviewed in the northern village of Dongyao said that they make decisions jointly with their wives. The report shows that in some ways the market reforms and decollectivization are more effectively breaking up the clans than collectivization did.[17] The return to the patriarchal family setting under the HRS in China remains a threat to the agency of rural women, especially as they get older or if there is a crisis. Yet, they do not face the same patriarchal constraints because they have more alternatives.

INTERACTION OF HRS AND THE ONE-CHILD POLICY

The combination of the HRS and One-Child Policy, which were both initiated in the late 1970s, has worked against women's rights. As a form of family farming embedded in a patrilineal context, the HRS increases son preference and provides incentives to have more sons in order to diversify earnings. This could have led to more rapid population growth rates. In the early 1980s, incentives to reduce family size, such as education and employment opportunities for women, were not strongly countering the incentives associated with the HRS. Initially, education was not increasing for girls in rural areas, and most school dropouts were girls. Employment for women in agriculture did not work against having more children, and off-farm opportunities were limited in the first few years of the reform. So the coercive One-Child Policy was used to control population growth. Even though enforcement varied, and rural families were frequently allowed to have two or sometimes three children without penalties, the enforcement of the policy was usually harsh. The result was a bias against girls and women that showed up in many ways, including at the level of basic survivability, observed in the greatly unbalanced sex-ratio for infants of 118 boys to every 100 girls (National Bureau of Statistics 2002). Female fetuses are often aborted if detected (illegally) through ultrasound, infanticide has reappeared in some rural areas, and abandonment or hiding extra girls occurs frequently, which forecasts a dismal future for the girls who may not receive education, health care, or other basics of human security.

The increase in bias against women that has accompanied the One-Child Policy is a strong blow against gender equity. The emotional damage done to girls is extreme (see Croll 2000, 1999). A boy is also damaged by being put in the unhealthy position of being the favored child. Women who give birth to a daughter may experience inhumane treatment by their relatives.

As income has grown rapidly, education has recovered and increased for girls in most areas, and nonfarm opportunities have proliferated, but the One-Child Policy has not been transformed into a more positive incentive system. Policies that promote the agency of women might have a longer lag time to take effect but if process is considered part of development, such alternatives are worth evaluating.

HUMAN SECURITY AND POLICY SUGGESTIONS

Women's concentration in agriculture tends to offset gains in bargaining rights within the household, especially for married, middle-aged women, who experience relative poverty compared to those with a wider range of income-earning opportunities. There is evidence that relative deprivation has expressed itself in recent years through high suicide rates by rural women. Chinese women make up about one-fifth of the world's women, but they comprise half of the female suicides. Although women attempt suicide in greater numbers than men in many countries, China is the only country where suicide deaths by women outnumber those by men (WHO 2003b; World Bank 2002a, 23; Cabral 1999). Given that rural standards of living are increasing, it is reasonable to believe that the desperation may be related to increased perceptions about opportunities some people have for better lives combined with continuing problems with domestic violence and hopelessness about making change in one's own life. Policies could reduce the hopelessness by supporting gender equity, basic human security, and real alternatives.

Chinese officials have downplayed equity in favor of efficiency and embraced a reduction in government-provided security mechanisms to promote an expansion in choices through the market. Although there are negative consequences for equity and human security, economic democratization has created new choices for many people in China. The exercise of agency through economic incentives has much to offer compared to coercion. Ironically, with the accompanying One-Child Policy, officials have increased the use of coercion to achieve their population goals, at great costs to women and girls. Markets, however, cannot satisfy all social goals. Although land allocation has remained relatively equal through the first two decades of reform, policies stressing cost reduction and material incentives have promoted unequal outcomes, especially apparent between rural and urban areas and between remote, inland provinces and those near the coast. Rural areas where industry and other forms of diversification have blossomed are doing much better than those more dependent on agriculture alone. The clustering of women in sectors with lower returns relative to those dominated by men has increased relative gender poverty.

China's reforms have tied it more closely to the global economy. Its entry into the World Trade Organization in 2001 has potential repercussions on rural women because Chinese agriculture (which is where poorer, working women are clustered) will not be fully competitive in the global, unprotected market, especially in those areas where off-farm work is scarce. Although the negative impact of joining the WTO has been softened by the reforms already put in place, the costs of adjustment are likely to be borne disproportionately by women (Women's Edge 2000) and will be worsened by crises associated with globalization (Aslanbeigui and Summerfield 2001; Summerfield 2001).

The safety net in rural areas is minimal, and women are still expected to fill the gap. Because there are no pensions for the elderly in rural areas, women are expected to care for them. Married women presently provide security for the household as a whole, and males in particular, by staying on the land when men migrate, maintaining land rights and caring for children and in-laws. If unemployment in off-farm work increases during a recession, the farm may be the fall-back position for those who lose their jobs. Women's unpaid labor increases during a crisis to maintain family living standards. This security component is not fully acknowledged or compensated.

China needs to prepare a social safety net that anticipates uneven gender effects. To compete on a more level playing field, rural women need policies that support education, health care, and property rights. Although it is not clear that education and health care are worse for rural girls now than they were during the collective period, the emphasis on efficiency instead of equity is holding back potential gains in these areas. The progress in gender equity through mass education and health care during the collective period caught the world's attention because it was accomplished at very low levels of per capita income. As per capita income has soared under the reforms, serious gender-related issues in these areas have not been addressed.

Chinese women have legal rights to property ownership, but these are limited in practice. Laws on ownership rights, use rights, and joint ownership need clarification. Tenure security is necessary, but the process must pay careful attention to gender biases to avoid exacerbating inequalities. A good step toward equitable property rights would be the promotion of transparent joint leases with the addition of a second signature line to land titles and the requirement that the wife and the husband both sign. Officials must consider whether women have received a fair quantity and quality of land before redistributions are made final. Support institutions for credit and legal redress need to be established. Interactions of policies such as the One-Child Policy, which provides penalties for having more than one child, and the HRS, which provides implicit incentives for having more children, especially boys, should be acknowledged and addressed to eliminate the distorted outcomes of the past two decades.

CONCLUSION

The warning signs at the beginning of the reforms, that rural women would be forced back into the patriarchal household with few alternatives, have been offset by the growth of off-farm employment and self-employment opportunities that have emerged in the past twenty years. Yet, rural women still have had significant costs and limits imposed upon them in this period, although many have shared in the gains. The reforms have not provided equitable control over rural land, one of the most important resources in China. The extension of leases to thirty years at the end of the 1990s has brought women's insecure property rights into focus. These rights are a key component of human security policies in rural China.

Furthermore, a more comprehensive social safety net is necessary in rural as well as urban areas so that global and personal crises do not lead to permanent losses for millions of people, especially for women (see Aslanbeigui and Summerfield 2001). Gender equity is imperative in the design of these policies. Women's lives should not be thread that forms the safety net; the opportunity costs are too high.

NOTES

The author would like to thank Nahid Aslanbeigui, Jane Jaquette, Shahra Razavi, and Deniz Kandioyoti for their comments on an earlier version of this paper.

1. The state owns the land in urban areas, but the collective owns the land in rural areas. In reality, the state still has substantial input into the decisions made by the collective ownership. For example, villages that wanted to retain collective farming during the 1980s were not permitted to do so. The distinction in ownership does make it more difficult for the state to make across-the-board decisions about land policy and explains some of the variation in policies in different areas of China. In some areas the village is the unit of ownership while in others it is the village cooperative or small group. The ambiguity over ownership has resulted in disputes between these groups over the control of the land.

2. In 1993, Chinese officials further liberalized grain markets, but balked at the rapid inflation of prices and tried to reinstate some price controls. Local grain bureau officials, however, blocked this move (Rozelle and Park 1998).

3. Li Zongmin's study (1999) of Dongyao Village, in north China near Tianjin, illustrates a typical pattern of decollectivization. The account demonstrates some of the variability that occurs across rural China by contrasting the process in Dongyao with that of another nearby village (244–45).

4. Some estimates place the poverty rates at higher levels both before and after the HRS was implemented, but these estimates show similar reductions in poverty.

5. The yuan to U.S. dollar exchange rate was 8.28 yuan to $1 in August 2003.

6. The growth of grain output dropped substantially to only 0.9 percent annually between 1985 and 1994 (National Bureau of Statistics 2000).

7. A scholar in Beijing told me how she had tried to help out a teenage girl from her native province by arranging a child care position for her with a family in Beijing. After spending many hours on the needed clearances, she brought the girl to Beijing. A few weeks later, however, the girl begged her to send her back home. The main reason was that housing is in such short supply in the large cities, that families usually just have an efficiency-style apartment, and everyone has to sleep in the same room together. The rural girl had expected better living conditions, not worse, in the city.

8. Reports of abandonment of their wives by men who have migrated to the city are increasingly common. Divorce rates are growing, but even if they do not divorce, some men set up an urban family illegally. Thus, the increment in total availabilities for the original family unit can easily disguise the uneven distribution of the gains, where in cases of abandonment, the husband keeps the gains in income and the change contributes to impoverishment for the wife and any children living with her.

9. In export-processing work in China, as elsewhere, the jobs are tedious and offer low wages with little opportunity for advancement. The wages are often better than in alternative employment that is available, however. The most extreme problems with working conditions have occurred when basic rights are ignored; a company in Southern China with funding from Hong Kong locked its doors to prevent theft by the employees. A fire killed many employees and stirred calls for enforcement of laws protecting workers.

10. The concentration of women in farm work in China occurs because men are leaving agriculture faster than women, not because women are being squeezed out of off-farm work.

11. An intellectual who returned to Beijing to work after years of working in the countryside as one of the youth sent down to learn from the peasants during the Cultural Revolution told me that she was quite popular with the women weeding the fields. She could tell them long stories from Chinese history as they worked together. The women told her that she made the hours pass like minutes.

12. According to the General Principles of Civil Law of 1986, joint property may be either share joint ownership or mutual joint ownership. *Share joint ownership* means that "each joint owner has an interest in the property and is subject to claims of the creditors in proportion to his or her share in the jointly owned property . . . (*Mutual joint ownership*) is defined as an ownership in which all joint owners have joint rights to the property and are jointly liable to the creditor" (Duncan and Li 2001, 23). Share joint owners may transfer their interest in the property if the other joint owners agree, but individual interest under mutual joint ownership may not be transferable.

13. During the land titling program in Laos in the 1990s, women's advocates took action to get two signature lines on the contracts and educate those involved about the significance of having both wife and husband sign (Viravong 1999).

14. The complicated process of dividing the land into five to ten small plots per family and combining them over time, which occurred during the first years of the HRS, may have avoided some of the conflict over land quality.

15. The right to use land as collateral is likely to be legalized as market reforms continue, especially if land ownership is privatized.

16. Increasing intensity of work affects men as well as women. Most adults are taking on added burdens of labor voluntarily because the prospects of gains are high, and hard work is still highly valued in Chinese society. Since there is uncertainty about how long the opportunities will last, people seize them while they are available.

17. Often, however, the consolidation of villages and transfer of land to nonagricultural uses are carried out with unpopular, compulsory relocation or expropriation of land (Croll 1999).

Unequal Rights: Women and Property

Diana Lee-Smith and Catalina Hinchey Trujillo

This chapter describes a process of global learning and activism by a women's movement and shows how it influenced policy at national and international levels. Drafted by the two authors while working with the United Nations Human Settlements Programme (UN-HABITAT) in 2000–2001, it reflects contributions from other members of the staff[1] as well as input from members of the Huairou Commission, a global body comprising women decision makers and six international networks devoted to issues of women, homes, and communities.[2] In a way, it is the story of how the commission grew out of grassroots women's activism and came to influence global action on women's property rights.

The chapter begins with a discussion of the problems faced by women in relation to property, situating these in a historical context[3] and addressing the question of women and immovable property in general, not only women's relationship to land. It represents an understanding that emerged out of an active dialogue between professional and grassroots women. It is based not only on research findings but also on a process that elicited the views of members of women's organizations from different regions. The chapter then reviews recent activism around the issue of women and property.

In the past few years there has been a notable rise in activities promoting action on women's property rights, particularly at the international level. The range and number of organizations involved in this promotion have broadened and the links between many of them strengthened, due to a combination of better electronic networking and a commitment to collective action and sharing among the organizations involved. The account aims at capturing a complex and vibrant push for social change that came from the grassroots but has succeeded in influencing international events.

Finally, the chapter presents a policy prescription, taking a broader approach than the prescriptions that were formulated to guide immediate action in relation to the Commission on Sustainable Development and the follow-up to the Beijing conference in 2000. Various sources have informed the chapter's policy prescriptions, including the Global Campaign for Secure Tenure, initiated by UN-HABITAT in 2000, and the campaigns of the Huairou Commission and its constituent networks.[4] These are set in a theoretical framework that posits entitlements and capabilities as the way to approach human development.

THE SITUATION OF WOMEN AND PROPERTY — PROBLEMS IDENTIFIED

The Historical Roots of Inequality

Current inequalities have arisen in a multiplicity of ways in different societies, based on how wealth is generated and how systems of governance and institutions[5] have evolved. Women's access to and control and management of property and, in particular, land are crucial aspects of sustainable development. As a development resource, land has several dimensions: ecological diversity, productivity for human sustenance, and wealth creation in the economy. Women's relationship to property as described here is based on learning that has emerged from the women's movement in recent years. Although recent changes in the world economy have exacerbated gender inequalities in the way property is controlled and managed, there are many facets to this issue, with deep social roots. These must be addressed in order to ensure that women have equal human rights.

By property we refer to both land and buildings, including housing, using a shorthand term to describe what would more accurately be called immovable property.[6] Fundamentally, women, like men, need property as a home—a secure place to live. They also need it as a means of livelihood—whether for food production or as another type of workplace. Finally, and especially in a globalizing money economy, they use property as a form of wealth or capital. Each of these aspects is addressed in this section.

Women's and men's relation to land and housing has historically differed, based on modes of production and social structures, particularly kinship systems and constructions of gender. Throughout the world, many women and men live in societies that have relied on subsistence economics but are rapidly changing, as are the laws and institutions that govern economic interactions. Economic restructuring programs are only one symptom of a wider historical process that is called globalization, which converts property into an economic good and privatizes property ownership.

In hunting and gathering, pastoralist, and peasant societies, men and women have used land in production systems to meet their subsistence needs. Peasant agricultural production is still widespread but is in transition to cash crop production in many parts of the world. This process has been ongoing for centuries but is gathering speed. Converting land and property to economic goods, whether in private or public control, has significant implications for the way people manage their lives and on who wins out economically and socially.

The privatization of property affects men and women differently because of the different social roles they play. In peasant agricultural systems, women more than men have been responsible for gathering water, fuel, and other wild and forest materials from land not under direct production of crops and livestock. This type of land has more often been converted to state or public control, while land in direct production of crops and livestock is more often converted to private control. As "gatherers," women have lost access to these resources as land is alienated for other uses in the cash economy. Both the land and the women suffer. The land may be eroded and its productivity decline, and the women lose subsistence resources and status. The grassroots women's environmental movements linked to forest preservation are a symptom of this—for example, the Chipko movement of India and the Greenbelt movement in Africa (Agarwal 1994; Mies and Shiva 1993; Lee-Smith and Trujillo 1992; Sarin 1991).

Further, inheritance customs generally mean that land converted to private control ends up in the hands of men and not women. This is because patrilineal kinship systems are the most widespread in agricultural societies, and they allocate land by passing it from fathers to sons. Even matrilineal systems put the power to allocate and control land in male hands. In subsistence production systems, however, land was never formally owned, and both men and women had the right to use it to produce food for their kin. Within such systems women had reliable access to land, and houses were often under women's control. But the establishment of formal ownership and the titling of land meant that the predominant pattern of men controlling the allocation of land and passing this right from father to son became entrenched as legal male ownership. Houses were taken to be male property along with the land on which they stood (Mies and Shiva 1993; Stone 1997; Lee-Smith 1997; Benschop 2002).

Current Evidence of Inequality

Land is a form of capital. Even when people inherit it without making other types of investment of labor or resources, it can generate wealth in many ways. It may contain wealth in the form of rocks and minerals as well as soils and trees. It provides space for all kinds of productive work, including crops and animal production. Its agricultural production capacity may be vulnerable, but it is still viewed as highly valuable, for example, as collateral. But land brings more intangible benefits as well, including status and influence. Recent work in Guatemala, for example, shows women may be excluded from decision making when they lose property rights. Since they own so little of the world's immovable property, women lack the numerous benefits that come with ownership and control of it (UN-HABITAT 2001c).

Urbanization and the rapid growth of unplanned and informal settlements also affect property rights. Poor families living in these settlements have no secure tenure and can easily be evicted. Forced mass evictions of communities from urban informal settlements, a frequent occurrence in developing countries with high urbanization rates, affect women more than men because they have more family responsibilities requiring them to spend time in the home and neighborhood. In addition to what women may experience as members of intact families, the record shows that women are also more likely to be evicted from their homes as widows or single mothers because of their lack of property rights, especially in cases of land shortage (UNHCHR 2001; UN-HABITAT 2001b).

Women's lack of property rights becomes especially severe in situations of conflict and reconstruction, where widows and single women may be extremely disadvantaged. Without husbands, women survivors of wars or disasters may be unable to secure their own place to live. When they cannot inherit either their parents' or their husbands' property, they are condemned to live in refugee camps. This was the case in Rwanda and Burundi in the mid-1990s, for example (UN-HABITAT 1999).

Property also has the power to generate cash income. Because they carry out their income-generating work in or near the home more often than men, women need property as a means of livelihood as well as a place to live. This may be space in the house for productive work or small-scale business, or similar space within the residential neighborhood. Women grow food for the family not only in rural areas and in places where they are resettled in postconflict situations, but also in towns and cities. The majority of people engaged in urban agriculture are often women from households too poor to buy enough food (UN-HABITAT 2001d; Egziabher et al. 1994).

Property title deeds are the main way to secure loans and credit. Without such pieces of paper, women find it harder to get loans, which is why women more than men have resorted to other means of obtaining credit. This also may explain why so many initiatives have to be designed to enable women to get access to credit, including all the forms of microfinance, women's banking, revolving funds, merry-go-rounds, and so on. Women form organizations not only to obtain credit, but also to obtain land as corporate bodies. Certainly women need credit, but collective and microcredit programs must be deconstructed and understood in the context of women's lack of basic property rights as individuals.

Financing and credit are important, but this essay highlights the more fundamental wealth generation role of capital itself, that is, property in both land and housing. In the current world economy, with globalization and the spread of the cash economy to the remotest communities, women are disadvantaged when property in the form of land and housing becomes capital. Women's lack of equal property rights with men constitutes a structural cause of the feminization of poverty. As long as it is common for men but not women to inherit property, it means that men are inheriting capital for free but women are not. As a result, women's productive activity is lowered and poverty ensues (Baden 1999; Marcoux 1997; Williams and Lee-Smith 2000; Sassen 2001).[7]

In many places, there are legal restrictions on women's equal rights to own, control, and inherit property. Even where women have legally recognized rights, social constraints can prevent them from being realized. For example, in East Africa, where it may be socially unacceptable for women to inherit property, they may be legally "allowed" to buy it but unable to do so without offending custom. In such cases, women often try to obtain land as collectives or women's groups. The prevalence of such social practices discriminates against women and causes poverty (Benschop 2002; UN-HABITAT 2001c; Seager 2000; Williams and Lee-Smith 2000; Lee-Smith 1997).

The limited data that exist confirm the inequalities. It is frequently asserted that women own less than 1 percent of the world's property (Women Watch 2000). Although this is based on somewhat thin data, it is difficult to improve the estimate because, despite the best efforts of the United Nations, most countries do not yet collect data on women's and men's ownership or control of property. Data from only twenty countries on the proportion of women owning agricultural land show them in a distinct minority, while gender-disaggregated housing mortgage figures are only available from one or two countries. It is well known that in many countries women living under customary or religious laws do not have the same legal rights as men to own or inherit property. With the possible exception of some highly industrialized countries, there are institutionalized barriers to women's owning, inheriting, or getting mortgages to property in all regions of the world. From recent research and exchange of information in the women's movement, we conclude that socially discriminatory practices are even more widespread than had been thought (UN-HABITAT 2001c; Seager 2000; personal communication from Sissel; Ekaas 2000).

Legal research in three East African countries shows the extent of disenfranchisement there (Benschop 2002). Research has also brought the Southeast Asia situation to international attention, showing how agrarian customs deny women equal rights (Tinker and Summerfield 1999b). Grassroots organizations working with women in postconflict situations brought out the Central American issues, which were also identified by the Women for Peace Network, operating with local groups on the ground in Guatemala to establish women's equal right to land and housing in the aftermath of civil war (Calderon 1998; Worby 1998). Preliminary research in Kosovo reveals a similar situation (Williams and Lee-Smith 2000). These studies show that the problem of unequal property rights for women is essentially the same throughout the world. The social pressures that limit how women are supposed to behave stop women from having and exercising their property rights (UN-HABITAT 2001c, 2001d; Lee-Smith 2001).

COLLECTIVE ACTION ON WOMEN'S PROPERTY RIGHTS

As a result of growing awareness of the extent of gender inequalities, pressure groups and social movements, as well as states and intergovernmental bodies, have taken actions to address them. Interactions between civil society social movements and UN bodies are an important means of bringing about broad-based reform.

Bringing Women's Concerns to the Policy Level

During the 1980s and 90s, pressure for women's equal rights to land and housing came about through a number of grassroots initiatives that succeeded in shaping their concerns into a program of action that could be used for lobbying purposes. Ideas about women's property rights were furthered in this way through the Women and Shelter Network of Habitat International Coalition. Numerous local, regional, and even international meetings held during this period witnessed passionate pleas by grassroots women for an end to unequal property rights. The issues were articulated in debates involving women from organizations based in rural and urban areas and from many countries. Some of the most fervent pleas came from the African region, and campaigns for "housing as a women's right" were waged in Latin America (Mazingira Institute 1992–2003).

The impact of these movements on international debate, policy, and legislation can be traced to some key alliances and specific interventions by the women's movement. In late 1989, members of the women's movement lobbied the UN Centre for Human Settlements, later UN-HABITAT, to set up its Women and Habitat Program. Delegates responding to this lobby pushed through a resolution, endorsed by the UN General Assembly, linking women's networks to formal processes of decision making.[8] During the preparations for the Beijing Conference in 1995, four global women's networks formed a "Super-Coalition on Women, Homes and Community" to lobby on women's issues of homes and communities. The issue of unequal property rights resonated powerfully among women from all regions.

There were two significant events in Beijing. First, the "inheritance clause," which had been introduced by the Super Coalition and publicized by their effective campaigning, was hotly debated and became a major item in the Platform for Action. It was eventually passed in a watered-down form but nevertheless provided an effective base for local and national action. Paragraph 61(b) of the Platform for Action states that governments should "undertake legislative and administrative reforms to give women full and equal access to economic resources, including the right to inheritance and to ownership of land and other property, credit, natural resources and appropriate technologies." Second, the Huairou Commission was formed, combining the grassroots women's networks in a single body with influential women decision makers, researchers, and professionals. The commission was named for the location of the NGO Global Forum held near Beijing in the city of Huairou.

During the Habitat II Conference in Istanbul in 1996, the same coalition of women's networks (now united in the Huairou Commission and involving women influential in the UN system, international development agencies, and politicians) lobbied for the adoption of women's rights to inheritance, ownership, and control of property as part of the Habitat Agenda (UN-HABITAT 1998).

Among the numerous references in the Habitat Agenda, paragraph 40(b) asserts the commitment of participating states to:

> Providing legal security of tenure and equal access to land to all people, including women and those living in poverty; and undertaking legal and administrative reforms to give women full and equal access to economic resources, including the right to inheritance and to ownership of land and other property, credit, natural resources and appropriate technologies.

Policy Action and Interaction

Although many states still had reservations about women's right to inherit property based on their religious and social customs, the wording of the Platform for Action had established the precedent. Since then, members of the network continue to use these clauses and other international instruments to lobby locally. The networking structure helps such groups to understand and access the relevant instruments and bring pressure for change in their countries or cities.

Through its active links to the women's movement, UN-HABITAT has undertaken a number of activities, including research and action in the area of promoting women's access to and control of property. International meetings were organized by HABITAT in 1995 in Gavle, Sweden, and in Kigali, Rwanda, in 1998, together with the United Nations Development Programme (UNDP), the UN Fund for Women (UNIFEM), and the UN High Commission for Refugees (UNHCR) (UN-HABITAT 1999). Since 2000, women's property rights have been integral to UN-HABITAT's Campaign on Secure Tenure.

Governments have likewise taken up the challenge, not only highlighting women's property rights in the various international agreements they make, but also by amending or passing new legislation to strengthen women's property rights. Legislative measures have been undertaken in Asia and Latin America, such as article 6 of the Bolivian constitution and the land law and civil laws of Vietnam in the 1990s (see Tinker and Summerfield 1999b). In Africa no fewer than ten countries have taken recent legislative action, while at least five others have made administrative reforms, proving that commitments made at international conferences are not just empty promises. When governments reviewed the implementation of the 1996 Habitat Agenda at a Special Session of the UN General Assembly in 2001, they made further commitments on women's property rights, specifically their right to enter into contractual agreements (UN-HABITAT 2001a, c). During that same special session of the General Assembly, several UN bodies agreed to collaborate on promoting women's property rights through co-ordinated action. UNDP and UNIFEM proposed to join forces on women's property rights with UN-HABITAT's Secure Tenure Campaign and the UN High Commission on Human Rights (UNHCHR).

International campaigning on housing rights has also highlighted women's property rights. Initially the Women and Shelter Network influenced its parent body, Habitat International Coalition, which in turn influenced the formal processes of the UNHCHR. Through such advocacy links between civil society and international bodies, the Human Rights Commission has recently passed several resolutions on women's property rights. These specify that women must have equal rights to property, including ownership, access, and control, and the right to inherit. Such tools need to be even more widely disseminated than they are at present, so they can have an impact at local levels. The same networks of civil society groups and grassroots women's organizations can now utilize these various resolutions to bring about change (UNHCHR 1997, 1998, 1999, 2000, 2001, 2002, 2003).

Collective action continues on a number of fronts. Since the Kigali meeting in 1998, the concern about women's property rights in situations of conflict has also received heightened attention. The Women for Peace Network set up in 1996 is active in its member countries, from Bosnia to Guatemala to Burundi, carrying out research and advocacy and supporting grassroots organizing. In 2000 the UN Security Council passed a landmark resolution on the impact of conflict on women and girls, with a follow-up action plan that incorporates women's property rights.

In its strategic planning session in 2001, the Huairou Commission outlined a global campaign on women and secure tenure, including public hearings at various levels to increase public awareness. As a result of several advocacy events in 2000 and 2001, a larger NGO Land Caucus was formed around sustainable development and human settlement issues, including women's property rights. And the Women's Rights Division of Human Rights Watch has taken up special initiatives on women's property rights, starting in 2002.

The Case of Uganda

But it is the work within countries that really counts. The case of Uganda deserves attention as one of the most effective efforts so far. Although it is not perfect, the legal framework, which is backed by the constitution, is moving toward recognition and enforcement of women's property rights. This has occurred because there are widespread and active lobby groups that keep this issue, which is highly contentious, in the public mind. There are support programs on the ground with trained paralegals who help resolve disputes, community by community, family by family.

The paralegals are not paid and they have no transport, but they know the constitutional rights of women and they explain them to people. This helps everyone make decisions that they themselves believe to be fair and just. The paralegals are backed up by storefront legal offices in small towns that receive support from a network of NGOs, who in turn get support from international donors to provide items like bicycles and filing cabinets. They are also linked into the system of local government working to decentralize power to the community level (Mazingira, 1992–2003; Benschop 2002).

The majority of cases involve inheritance of property, including land; the majority of cases involve women; and the majority of cases are resolved at the local level through alternative dispute mechanisms. Some cases are referred to higher courts, but the capacity of the legal system in Uganda is limited. Despite the good collaboration between the courts system, government ministries, local government, and civil society organizations, this successful approach has only reached some parts of the country and is not receiving the resources required.

The paralegals, who now operate in 20 percent of Uganda's districts, make it possible for most cases to be resolved at the local level. Over 90 percent of the cases are brought forward by women. At one center in 1998, it was found that 58 percent of cases brought involved land and inheritance, and about 20 percent involved custody and maintenance of children. The remainder dealt with marital conflict, and a small number were about child defilement. Although several NGOs are involved in running these programs, they are not able to cover the total area, even in the districts where they operate. Their activities are vulnerable to the whims of donors who often do not sustain their funding support beyond a year or two (Mazingira Institute, 1992–2003; Benschop 2002).

Within the East African region and beyond, there have been efforts to spread the model and to exchange experiences between Uganda and other countries. Local NGOs have kept this initiative alive for over a decade, taking advantage of larger networks such as the Habitat International Coalition and the Huairou Commission to spread the word and employing now proven techniques for ensuring that women attain rights to property (Mazingira Institute 1992–2003).

RECOMMENDATIONS FOR POLICY AND ACTION

A Theoretical Basis for Policy Recommendations

The global recommendation made in the Kigali Plan of Action of 1998 still holds as a clear statement of policy intention: "Women should have adequate and secure rights to property. These rights must be equal to those of men, and a woman should not be dependent upon a man in order to secure or enjoy those rights" (Peace for Homes 1998). Economic as well as human rights arguments can be put forward to support this, and such rights are becoming more widely recognized in different regions of the world. It is argued that when people are discriminated against in the factor markets (such as those for land, labor, and capital), they cannot effectively engage in business, trade, and commerce. A large proportion of the population—namely women—engaged in food and other agricultural production but lacking entitlements puts a brake on development (Agarwal 1994; Peace for Homes 1998; Tibaijuka 2001; Walker 2002).

Theories of economic development including poverty reduction are broadening from a narrow focus on incomes to encompass human development, which means building human capabilities to achieve well-being and dignity. Women and men in all societies attempt to realize their basic rights and entitlements but may be prevented from doing so by limits that may be social or political in origin and have been described as "endowment failures." Rights and freedoms are not ideas that, once conceived, implement themselves. They must entail the social mechanisms needed to implement them, including economic development (A. Sen 1999; Nussbaum 2000; UNDP 1995; Sassen 2001).

Martha Nussbaum urges us to engage with the "capabilities approach" by adopting the principle of each person as an end and never a means to someone else's ends. It should be obvious that this approach is particularly relevant to achieving women's rights, as women are so often seen as the means to achieve their children's and families' well-being rather than as subjects in their own right. Nussbaum tells us women may indeed be agents of others' well-being, but that these roles are best played out of love and care and with dignity. Women have rights as persons, and all persons themselves deserve to be treated with love, care, and dignity. Equal property rights are but one aspect of the rights framework that needs to be realized for full human—and sustainable and equitable economic—development (Nussbaum 2000; Williams and Lee-Smith 2000).

A Framework for Policy and Action

There are several international policy commitments now in place on women's property rights. What is needed is coordinated action on a broad front to implement them. The statement made at the time of the eighth session of the Commission on Sustainable Development (in the original paper that formed the basis of this chapter) still applies: "Women's movements and public agencies need to further coordinate their efforts in campaigning for women's equal rights to land [and property]. All of these ongoing activities need to be linked with CSD activities, and synergies built up between partners."

The policy analytical work of UN-HABITAT and the Huairou Commission provide pointers to future coordinated action, as do the conclusions of the event organized by Habitat, UNIFEM, and UNDP in 2001. It has become apparent that legal measures by themselves are inadequate to change significantly the actual situation with regard to women's access to and control of property. In any one place, a range of responses may be required, including legislative, programmatic, or persuasive measures, used separately or in combination.

In each context strategies can be developed to achieve greater political power for women in society through their access to and control of property. Strategies should aim to deepen both individual and collective awareness of the need for social and legal change, putting the appropriate legal and institutional structures in place where necessary. In any given case, it may be necessary to:

1. Address the *substance* of women's property rights through research and legal reform. This would lead to appropriate revisions of the national constitution as well as legislative and policy changes.
2. Make the necessary *structural* and institutional changes to ensure effective application of the law by the courts, administration, and enforcement agencies. The courts must build capacity to handle these cases, along with legal representation and counseling for women bringing cases and, perhaps most strategically, provide training for paralegals who can provide support services at the grassroots level.
3. Address the *cultural* aspects of shared attitudes and behaviors of the population, including the barriers placed by informal institutions, through education. This can be done through the media, public forums, and legal literacy programs as well as through awareness courses for lawyers.

At the international level, much can be done through public information and advocacy. There are plans to follow up the Kigali meeting of 1998 with a further international meeting, and it is hoped that tools will emerge that will give guidelines to countries on how to carry out effective measures. There is a need for further research and data on the situation of women's property rights on the ground and on the effects of actions that are being taken to address them. These experiences in turn can be shared among practitioners and widely disseminated to the public.

Starting from Good Practice

Although Uganda has not yet come close to achieving equal property rights for women (adequate and secure rights to property equal to those of men and not dependent upon a man in order to secure or enjoy them), its experience gives a clear positive example of how to change the situation on the ground. It is a start and it has begun to change people's attitudes, which is necessary so that laws that are already on the books can be enforced. The failures that result from lack of coverage and shortage of resources are clear. The courts in Uganda, as is typical of developing countries, are not yet properly implementing the relevant legislation due to bias toward customary law and practices that prevent women from inheriting property. But the paralegal networks are playing an increasingly important role. They help implement the new legislation while raising awareness of women's rights at the local level.

Uganda has also made progress in linking the efforts of central and local governments with networks of nongovernmental organizations to promote women's property rights, considerably enhancing the impact of its constitutional and legislative reforms. The infrastructure of training and support for paralegal officers to mediate cases of women's rights helps to make these reforms a reality at the grassroots level.

This and other good practices in all regions need to be systematically supported by international donors so that they can be replicated at the necessary scale. Above all, the richness of the experience of women and activists in communities in all regions of the world needs to be brought to light, documented, shared, publicly broadcast, and supported. There is the potential for a vast network of women's groups that can help inform policy and precipitate more effective global, regional, and national action.

NOTES

1. Among these Sylvie Lacroux, Marjolein Benschop, Wandia Seaforth, and Angela Hakizimana deserve specific mention.

2. The original paper prepared by the two authors was reviewed by members of the Huairou Commission and then presented in early 2000 as a *Position Paper on Land Management* during the parallel activities organized by the Commission on Sustainable Development Women's Caucus in preparation for its eighth session (CSD-8), and the Forty-Fourth Session of the Commission on the Status of Women. At that time it was summarized in the CSD NGO newsletter *Outreach 2000.* Subsequently, the ideas were used in a shorter article, on "Women's Land Ownership and Globalization," for the British Council magazine, authored by Diana Lee-Smith and Minu Hemmati, Chair of the CSD Women's Caucus. Three events on similar topics were organized by various people in parallel with the Special Session of the General Assembly, Beijing+5, in June 2000. Irene Tinker contributed to one of these debates, together with Gale Summerfield, based on their book on women's land and housing rights in Southeast Asia. The ideas have also fed into numerous other policy debates, discussions, and action initiatives, including those of the Huairou Commission and UN-HABITAT's Global Campaign for Secure Tenure. This version was specifically prepared, based on all this material, for this book.

3. This section is very similar to what was first presented in the *Position Paper on Land Management* addressed to the CSD in 2000, but it has been updated and additional references have been cited.

4. Nevertheless, the positions taken by the authors do not reflect the official views of UN-HABITAT or of the Huairou Commission, even though one of the authors still works for the former and both are members of the latter. The views expressed here, and any errors of fact or judgment, remain the responsibility of the authors alone.

5. In this paper we refer to both formal and informal institutions. Nobel laureate Douglas North's definition of institutions is appropriate: "Humanly devised constraints that shape human interaction."

6. Such buildings could include workplaces, including offices and workshops, barns, stores, and so on.

7. It is not the purpose of this paper to engage in debate on the extent of differences in poverty between men and women, only to explain differences in access to capital in the form of property that contribute to such differences.

8. Resolution UNCHS/13/13, endorsed by the General Assembly on 8 May 1991, "invites governments and the UNCHS (Habitat) to develop a closer cooperation with the Habitat International Coalition Women and Shelter Network and similar NGOs at national, regional and international levels."

On Loan from Home:
Women's Participation in Formulating Human Settlements Policies

Faranak Miraftab

To better understand the difficulties involved in gendering UN policies and programs in the area of human settlements, the Women and Habitat Programme of
the UN Centre for Human Settlements began gathering data in the early 1990s
on the situation of women compared to men in human settlements development
at the community, local, and national levels.[1] To do this, the program encouraged the participation of grassroots and professional women in several countries
of Africa, Latin America, and Asia. The study, referred to here as gender gaps
project, was completed in the late 1990s and was documented in individual country reports.

   This chapter offers a synthesis of these reports, highlighting the findings that
have been most useful to the research participants in different settings. It is intended to provide community-based organizations, researchers, professionals,
and activists concerned with gender equity issues in the development of human
settlements with information that may enhance their efforts to improve women's
living conditions and reduce gender gaps.

CONTEXT AND RATIONALE FOR THE STUDY

The need for the study was identified by grassroots and professional women in
the countries where the Women and Habitat Programme had been working with
community-based and nongovernmental organizations and women in local and

national governments. The lack of information on the factors affecting women in human settlements was seen as a serious obstacle to their identifying priorities and mobilizing around women's needs. The women repeatedly requested that the program provide data that concretely reflected the conditions in which they were working. In response, Habitat developed the agenda of Global Shelter Strategies for 2000, which stated that although women play a central role in the improvement of human settlements, they have little access to shelter and community resources and little influence over the decisions that affect them. In its new Strategic Vision and Security of Tenure Campaign, Habitat went on to identify women's empowerment as the main indicator of success for Global Shelter Strategies.

Phase one of the study, at the level of communities, was carried out in sixteen low-income communities across eight countries in Africa, Asia, and Latin America: Ghana, Senegal, Tanzania, Uganda, Zambia, Colombia, Costa Rica, and Sri Lanka. Phase two was carried out in Cuba, Colombia, Ecuador, Senegal, Tanzania, Uganda, Ghana, India, and the Philippines. The first phase identified ways to measure male and female differences in specific human settlements, comparing (for example) access to land, housing, income, and education. Its intent was to identify those problems women share with men as a result of their common social and economic deprivation and to distinguish where men's and women's situations diverge as measured by their access to resources. These comparisons are used as indicators of gender gaps at the community level and suggest which actions are needed to target the most important imbalances and specific problems. The data from phase one of the study will not be discussed here as it has been published elsewhere in detail (see Miraftab 2001).

The second phase is the focus of this chapter, which examines the gender gaps at various levels of authority in institutions responsible for decisions that affect women's lives at the community level in respect to the development of human settlements. The underlying assumption was that the existing gender gaps in resources within human settlements might be linked to gender gaps within the human settlement-related institutions. The second phase basically tried to understand how women professionals in decision-making positions are, or are not, able to address gender gaps that the first phase of the study had identified in human settlements. These data were seen as important by the women themselves in focusing efforts to improve their living conditions. A vast body of research highlights the point that although women play a significant role in shelter improvement, they are seldom included in the decisions that affect the conditions under which they live (Tinker and Summerfield 1999b; Moser 1987; Chant 1996; Miraftab 1997). The UN study under discussion in this chapter tried to precisely shed light on this problem by documenting gender gaps in key institutions responsible for training and making decisions for development of human settlements. This includes training in higher education fields such as architecture, engineering, and urban planning and professional and senior decision-making positions in public agencies and institutions such as the ministries or offices of public works, land, housing, and urban development, whatever they might be called in each specific country context.

METHODOLOGY

A central commitment of those who designed the process[2] was that the study should be carried out by women in their own communities. One shared assumption was that knowledge is power. The process of developing indicators was designed to demystify the process of social research. Information was gathered and analyzed with the participation of community women themselves, not just researchers who often treat the communities as sources of raw material and take from them the valuable knowledge they collect. The intent was not to produce statistically representative data for valid comparison across countries but to ensure that both the process of doing the research and knowledge of the outcomes, in terms of the overall gender gaps in human settlements development, would increase the awareness of community members and allow women to identify and organize around their own needs, contributing to their empowerment.

The present chapter reflects the results of such a participatory process. The study was carried out by a mixed team of women from communities and local NGOs, with at least one grassroots woman and one professional woman working together, ensuring that there would be an equal number of women from local communities and professionals gathering and evaluating the information. Key factors were identified in a process that relied on close interaction and dialogue between grassroots and NGO women. At different points throughout the process, workshops and meetings were organized for community women and professionals to identify indicators of gender gaps, evaluate their effectiveness, and adapt indicators and the methodology to their specific context.

Quantitative and qualitative information was collected from institutions dealing with the development of human settlements, such as universities, government departments, and ministries formulating policies and programs in the areas of housing, urban development, and public works in each country context. This included the analysis of personnel records of different government organizations at central and local levels, interviews with female and male employees at different levels of authority in these institutions, and an examination of the enrollment lists at major universities in each country.

Quantitative measures included the number of women and men at different levels of authority in decision-making agencies, and male and female enrollment in higher education in areas related to human settlements work. Qualitative measures included the perceptions of employees regarding gender equity at work; the presence or absence of gender-sensitive recruitment, evaluation, and promotion procedures; the existence of a support system for mothers; and links between each ministry's gender policies and the country's overall development policy.

Putting grassroots and professional women together to do research benefited the community women, helping them to understand their everyday lives in more analytical terms and to gain self-confidence and a stronger belief in their abilities. Similarly, professional women benefited by reflecting on their situations and recognizing the extent of their contributions and the gender disadvantages they experienced in their own workplaces. These interactions did not produce clear and measurable outcomes but did encourage processes invaluable to women's empowerment. Grassroots women who participated in the study acquired skills in data collection and analysis, and professional women learned about the real issues on the ground by working with community women and analyzing their problems.

BASIC FINDINGS: GENDER GAPS AT INSTITUTIONAL LEVELS

Several studies underline the importance of women's participation in policy decision making, through legislative or executive channels and in political or professional positions that influence formulation and implementation of policy and programs that directly affect women's lives (Beall 1997b; Hamadeh-Banerjee and Oquist 2000; Goetz 1995). Some stress that a greater number of women in these positions creates a critical mass that makes a difference in advocating women's interests and formulating women-friendly policies and programs (UNDP 1995; O'Regan 2000; Hamadeh-Banerjee 2000). Others stress the limitation of women's public presence in these institutions and the numeric goals involved in affirmative action and quota systems and underline the institutionalization of gender hierarchies and gendered structures of power (Lister 1997). They call for transformation in a range of individual and structural conditions

that may influence bringing about women-friendly politics and eventually policies (Bayes 1991; Kenworthy and Malami 1999).

In this light, there is a need to understand both the quantitative and qualitative
dimensions of gender disparities in determining shelter policies and programs.
In respect to the former, the absence of gender-aggregated information presents
an obstacle to forming policies that would help women gain ground. There is a
shortage of information on kinds of women's participation in public administration and policy making as well as the levels of their decision-making influence
(e.g., clerical versus senior professional positions). To address this shortcoming
in the present study, research teams in Cuba, Colombia, Ecuador, Senegal, Tanzania, Uganda, and Ghana reviewed the personnel files of government organizations and enrollment lists of universities and collected data in respect to quantitative gaps between men and women in terms of their access to relevant institutions
and the degree to which they hold authority positions within them. A summary
of the data sources used for each country case and the data collected by study
teams is presented in table 1.

Furthermore, to understand the qualitative dimension of gender disparities in
determining shelter policies and programs and to understand ideas and conditions that create direct and indirect obstacles to women's participation and thus
contribute to these gaps, study teams interviewed individual male and female employees at various levels of authority. They asked the employees about their perceptions of gender inequities in the workplace and their insights into how gender
interests are supported or silenced in processes of decision making. The quantitative and qualitative information gained by study teams in different countries
are the basis of the present chapter.

Quantitative Indicators of Gender Gaps

Table 1 summarizes the gender gaps that exist for the case study countries in professional decision making, levels of authority, and higher education. This reveals
the proportion of women to men in professional capacities and their levels of authority in shelter-related agencies and ministries, and in institutions of higher
education that train professionals in fields related to the development of human
settlements. In all cases, women constitute between 30 and 40 percent of government employees in human settlement-related government departments and
organizations at the municipal, provincial, and central levels. But the sample data
seem to suggest that the higher the level of authority, the lower the percentage of

women in those capacities. For example, in the case of Uganda, 35 percent of all rank employees in the sample are female, but of these female employees only 22 percent hold decision-making positions (10.5 percent in professional positions of authority, and 9.9 percent in the top senior positions). Sixty percent of them are in middle-ranked levels and 20 percent are in clerical/entry-level positions. Interestingly, this trend seems to persist across administrative levels of governance (e.g., central, regional, and district/local). In Ghana, for example, where the district level is the most powerful of the three, within the sample group women occupy only 8 percent of positions of authority at the district level, compared to 10 percent and 13 percent at the central and regional levels respectively.

In respect to the education of women and men in fields that prepare them for professional employment in areas related to the development of human settlements, the sample data suggest a very low participation by women. In developing countries, this has traditionally included the fields of architecture, engineering and, more recently, planning. The average percentages of women enrolled in these fields at the university level range from 7.5 percent in Tanzania to 26 percent in Cuba.

Some study teams argued that the low participation of women compared to men at the university level is closely linked to the lower levels of employment for women in these fields and to the barriers to the promotion and advancement of women in professional positions. The patriarchal assumptions that ascribe technical fields such as engineering, architecture, and planning to the "male" domain also play a role in lowering the number of female students enrolled in those fields. These factors produce a limited pool of qualified women who could enter professional positions in ministries and government agencies dealing with housing and human settlements.

Results from other study teams, such as the one in Ecuador, challenge this explanation, suggesting that institutional hurdles other than education are more important in explaining why fewer women are in these positions. The Colombian team, for example, reports that within its sample in areas typically seen as "technical" and therefore "male," a surprising 54 percent of the employees with postgraduate degrees are women. Yet their higher qualification is not directly reflected in their success in gaining positions of authority, since women constitute 43 percent of the directors and 32 percent of those in executive positions.

As several other studies also indicate, these findings challenge the assumption that the onus of change can be placed on individual women and their abilities.

Rather, it is the very structure of power and the nature of institutions dominated by patriarchal values and relations that need to change in order to make women's participation count (Baden 2000; Lister 1997).

Qualitative Insights into Gender Gaps

To understand the underlying factors that result in the gender gaps reflected in the quantitative data outlined above, it is necessary to understand the complex and subtle processes by which women's professional roles are often limited to areas with the least influence on policy and located at the lower levels of the power hierarchy. These exclusionary practices are not necessarily legal or formal. They can be enforced through social norms and value systems based on unspoken and unwritten rules. For example, none of the country case studies reports the existence of policies that directly call for gender discrimination or the exclusion of women. But most female employees interviewed underline their experience of gender discriminatory practices in their workplace.

The interviews indicate an important distinction between discriminatory gender *policies* and discriminatory gender *practices*. The latter are often carried out in subtle ways, so that institutions that have formal policies that support women may harbor gendered practices that limit women's credibility and advancement. These operate through mechanisms of self-exclusion by women themselves or imposed exclusion through widely shared assumptions that women cannot perform as well as men in these areas. Such patriarchal notions that ascribe social expertise to women and technical ability to men are often internalized by both women and men and play important roles in shaping a gendered pattern of professional activities. Hence, women are less likely to be recruited, supported, or given higher responsibilities in technical fields.

The synthesis of qualitative information obtained through the country case studies identified the following important issues: (1) the difference between gender differentiation and gender discrimination; (2) political gender considerations; (3) access to versus control of institutional resources; (4) stereotypes and gender discrimination in the workplace; and (5) neoliberal public-sector downsizing and the erosion of women's support.

GENDER DIFFERENTIATION VERSUS GENDER DISCRIMINATION

An important misconception obscuring gender inequities in the workplace is the tendency to misread the absence of gender differentiation as evidence of a lack of

TABLE 1 Percentage of Women in Official Human Settlements' Decision-Making Positions and Higher Education

Sample	Employees	Professionals	Authorities/Decision-making levels	Enrollment in higher education institutions
Cuba		47%	41%	26%
Personnel files for 3 institutions directly working with HS			Municipality 36%	Architecture 30%
5 W and 5 M in each institution (total 30) interviewed			Provincial 37%	Engineering 23%
Students' enrollment statistics from Ministry of Education			Central 11%	
Columbia		51%	41.5%	21% (1992–97)
Personnel files for 40 institutions at central and municipality levels			Central 37% (43% executive, 30% management)	Architecture 36%
27 W and 13 M interviewed			Municipality 46% (44% executive, 51% management)	Engineering 7%
List of universities missing				
Ecuador	39%		30%	21% (1992–97)
Personnel files for 21 government institutions (10 central, 11 regional and local)				Architecture 36%
60 W and M interviewed				Engineering 7%
Enrollment for 2 main universities				
Senegal		13% in government institutions	44%	17%
Personnel files for 13 ministries and local government and 11 other institutions		8% in other organizations		Administrative 8%
113 W interviewed				Engineering 18%
Universities' enrollment				Planning/Environmental management 25%

Tanzania	32%		Ministries 26% of top officials	7.5%
3 ministries related to HS		Ministries 34%	City commission (district, town, municipality) 10% of top officials	Architecture 10% (1993–98)
Local authorities (1 city, 2 municipality, 1 town, 6 district councils)		City/District, municipalities 66%		Engineering 5% (1992–97)
Enrollment lists for University of Dar el Salam				
Uganda	35%			19.5% (91–96)
7 ministries and 16 departments		60% middle level	22% of principals	Architecture 24%
Enrollment lists from education department of Makerere University		20% clerical		Engineering 15%
Ghana				14% (1997)
18 ministries, 18 government departments related to HS		22% of senior professionals	10.5% of authority level positions	Architecture, planning, building technology 18%
		Ministerial level 34%	Ministerial level 10% (of directors)	Engineering 10%
1 of 3 metropolitan assemblies		Central level government departments 19%	Regional level 13% in top decision-making level	
1 of 4 municipality assemblies		District level 14%	District level 8%	
8 district assemblies				

Key: M, men; HS, human settlements; W, women

Source: United Nations Center for Human Settlements, Women and Habitat Programme 1999

gender discrimination. An extensive body of feminist research has demonstrated that public policies' claims of "gender-blindness" in practice result in the marginalization of women's interests (Moser 1993; Sandercock 1998; Tinker 1990b). The field data obtained through these country case studies indeed show that male and female employees may misconceive the lack of flexibility and differentiation in their needs as proof of successful gender equity policies. This issue is clearly demonstrated in the Ecuadorian case in which 75 percent of respondents state that there is no discrimination in their workplace. But in further explaining their position, it becomes clear that they base this view on the absence of any formal distinction between male and female employees.

Other interviewees respond differently, revealing the critical flaw in this assumption and demonstrating that the equal treatment of unequal parties practically imposes a form of discrimination. Some point out that the absence of any consideration of women's child care roles results in inadequate support for maternity leave, on-site child care, and flexible schedules to allow for breast-feeding, which in turn squeezes women out of critical and demanding positions. Others, fearing backlash, declare they prefer "gender-blindness" or no gender differentiation in their workplace. They mention their opposition to "pro-woman" policies, concerned that where employers are required by law to support women's reproductive responsibilities, they are reluctant to hire women, hence further victimizing them. They declare that affirmative action policies, like support for maternity, can weaken women's opportunities for employment and promotion and make them unattractive to employers. This may continue to be a point of disagreement among the respondents, but it reveals that the relationship between gender differentiation and gender discrimination needs to be addressed.

Molyneux (1985) makes an important distinction between strategic and practical gender interests that is of much relevance to this discussion on the dilemma women face in pursuing their practical and strategic gender interests at work. In her view, practical gender interests are more immediate and reflect the daily responsibilities of women (and men); strategic gender interests are longer term and concern the transformation of relations between men and women. This distinction resonates with the conflict perceived by interviewees in terms of gender differentiation leading to, as opposed to ameliorating, gender gaps.

For example, considering the receipt of maternity leave as a practical gender need, many women believe the satisfaction of this need undermines their strategic gender interest in greater institutional influence and control of institutional resources, policies, and programs. Although maternity leave might be considered an entitlement for female employees, many respondents declared that it negatively affects how they are considered for promotion and advancement at work. They also believe their reproductive role in the family is equated with their lack of productivity at work.

This weary view of the conflict between practical and strategic gender interests in the enforcement of gender differentiated policies was held despite the fact that the adoption of affirmative action policies was quite limited in the countries examined in this study. Only Ecuador and Uganda had quotas for women in certain executive positions. Ecuador's law guarantees that 20 percent of positions of authority be filled by women, but at the time of the field research this law had only recently been passed, so its effects were not yet clear. The Ugandan constitution of 1994 promoted national processes of women's political participation, which led to a more recent local government act requiring women to hold at least one-third of council positions (UNCHS 2000). But this has had limited effect on the overall distribution of bureaucratic power among male and female government employees, as seen in table 1.

Women's fear of backlash as a result of gender equity policies underlines the need for institutional accountability (Kardam 1995). A system must be put in place that allows women to control the implementation of these policies and ameliorate their unintended negative effects. Women not only need policies that identify and respond to their gender interests, but also the specific mechanisms to control a transparent and accountable process that ensures their practical gender interests without undermining their strategic interests.

POLITICAL GENDER CONSIDERATIONS

Another important insight that emerged from the case studies is the significance of the wider context in which gender issues have been raised in each country. The Colombian and Ecuadorian case studies shed light on the political disadvantage women face in occupying top decision-making positions. What hinders or facilitates access to these positions in the public sector, they argue, is not gender per se, but the gendered implications of corruption and political favoritism. Where top executive positions are allocated by appointment rather than competition, male professionals without the proper political allegiances are similarly disadvantaged.

Politics and gender interact and deprive women of access to positions that have the "final say" or ultimate decision-making power. Women are usually less influential in the formal political arena and make up a smaller proportion of the pool of politically qualified candidates for the top professional positions. By default, therefore, fewer women exercise executive power. Worldwide, women occupy 12 percent of the seats in the national parliaments (UNDP 1999, cited in UNCHS 2000, 10); and their share of employees in professional, technical, and related occupations averages 42 percent (ranging from 12 to 70 percent) (1990 data in UNDP 1995, cited in Kenworthy and Malami 1999, 249). Many of the key professional administrative positions are politically generated and appointed. Hence, the limited influence of women in formal party politics directly affects their limited influence in key decision-making positions for development policies and strategies for shelter and human settlements.

As the Ecuadorian study team concludes, no gender equity can be expected without democracy, and no women's liberation can be expected within an authoritarian, hierarchical system. The structures and rules of institutions primarily protect and perpetuate the interests of those for whom the institutions were designed in the first place. Therefore, "getting the institutions right for women entails political activism across all social institutions and within individual organizations" (Goetz 1995, 10). Women's participation in policy decision making cannot be promoted if divorced from the larger sociopolitical processes shaping the distribution of these positions of power.

ACCESS TO VERSUS CONTROL OF INSTITUTIONAL RESOURCES

In Senegal, women in the sample group hold 44 percent of positions of authority, but respondents agree that women lack the final say in decisions. This underlines a significant distinction between access to and control over resources. Women can have access to institutions and resources as long as they do not challenge the status quo and control over those institutions and resources. In quantitative terms, this is reflected in the greater concentration of women in entry-level clerical positions and in qualitative terms in the different experiences of women who occupy senior positions versus those in clerical positions. In both Senegal and Columbia sample groups, among women in senior positions a greater percentage reported having experienced discrimination from their male colleagues at the workplace.

Greater discrimination at higher levels of authority may be explained by the fact that women in top positions are entering what many perceive as a male domain. Women's presence in decision-making roles is often perceived as a threat by male colleagues and is thus subject to greater resistance. In junior or clerical positions in male-dominated institutions, women are seen as operating in support roles, serving men, which is more consistent with patriarchal expectations. Women may thus have access to institutions but be denied effective power within them, as Goetz also notes (1995, 7).

ON "LOAN" FROM THE DOMESTIC REALM: STEREOTYPES AND GENDER DISCRIMINATION IN THE WORKPLACE

Overall, the findings of the country case studies emphasize the importance of gender stereotyping as the basis of the discriminatory treatment of women in the institutions and organizations studied. Stereotypes that identify women solely with their roles as mothers and homemakers invalidate women's specific needs and interests as workers and sources of material support for their family (del Rosario 1995, 107), and they extend to the workplace the stereotype that women are subservient to their husbands. This is reflected in the policies and regulations highlighted by different case studies.

The Senegal study offers a case in point. Female employees cannot claim their husbands and children as dependents, even when they are the financial heads of their families. In the case of Uganda, unmarried mothers may not benefit from entitlements related to children, as those are linked to the marital status of female employees. These regulations shed light not only on the power of stereotypes that ignore women's multiple roles including as family breadwinners but also show how the rights of women as individual employees are overwritten by their familial and marital status.

Another example, demonstrated by the Uganda study, is the specific support provided for female employees to retire upon marriage: a "privilege" not provided for men. A single female officer who holds a pensionable office has, upon marriage, the option of retiring with a marriage gratuity if she has completed the statutory period of years in the office. The assumption is that women would like to stay home and be cared for by their husbands and that home is the proper place for women to be if they have that option (that is, if they have a responsible husband). Facilitating the early retirement of female employees who marry is seen as a "women-friendly and supportive law." But the review of maternity support mechanisms in Uganda shows them to be quite inadequate. Such regulations have the effect of pushing married female employees out of the workforce rather than accommodating them so they can stay and advance in their careers.

In one of the case studies, there is a difference observed between the responses offered by single and married female employees. The single women are less likely than married women employees to report experiencing discriminatory policies and practices. The study concludes that there is more discrimination against married women based on the assumption that once women are married, they won't be able to perform as well as those who are single and who are still one step away from "domesticity." Other factors may be involved as well, including the differences in professional ranking of single and married women. Single women are likely to be younger and thus at the lower ranks; married women are more likely to be older and in higher positions and thus vulnerable to the earlier argument that the higher women move up in the organization, the more they are likely to be perceived as a threat.

The third example that clearly reveals the role of stereotypes is shown by the Tanzanian case study. It points out that when men are transferred in their jobs, no consideration is given to the possible transfer of their wives working in the same institution. The underlying assumption is that wives should follow their husbands, at whatever cost, including their professional career. This study found that the transfer of female employees' husbands often jeopardizes the professional advancement of women.

Clearly the social construction of gender roles contributes to women's institutional disadvantage in participation in the public domain and influencing decisions that affect their lives through human settlements. The stereotyping of men as "public" and women as "domestic" and the division of work at home (which sees women as mothers and subservient wives) are extended to their workplace rights and entitlements. Within the public domain, women are assumed to be "on loan" from the domestic realm. Their presence is seen as transitional, until they return to where they belong: the home.

NEOLIBERAL PUBLIC-SECTOR DOWNSIZING
AND THE EROSION OF WOMEN'S SUPPORT

Much recent literature has addressed the effects of neoliberal policies of government downsizing and privatization on women and disadvantaged populations (Benería and Feldman 1992; Aslanbeigui and Summerfield 2001; Miraftab 2005 forthcoming; Bakker 2003). These studies point out that the removal of the state from key social policies—justified as abandoning a "Nanny State"—has left the brunt of these policies to fall on women and on the poor (Kenway and Langmead 2000, 160); and that the logic of neoliberal capital accumulation relies on patriarchal gender roles in the realms of production and reproduction (Bakker 2003). Research has also demonstrated that flexibilization of production and the global trend of using women's casual labor are part and parcel of the privatization and decentralization strategies promoted within the neoliberal policy framework (Miraftab 2004).

In this project the observation made by the Ugandan team regarding the vulnerability of female employees in processes of government downsizing offers a clear example of the devastating impact of neoliberal policies on women. The Ugandan study found that the public-sector budget support for on-site day care centers (most critical to female employees) was among the first categories to be cut, followed by diminishing maternity supports. Furthermore, women, who are a larger percentage of the lower paid ranks of civil servants and whose entitlements are the easiest to eliminate from the public-sector budget, are the first to be laid off. It is these acts that the Ugandan team points to as having led to fewer female employees in the public sector, despite their newly institutionalized quota system that requires 30 percent of women at all levels of government.

The case studies do not provide longitudinal data, but the limited references made to adverse effects of recent trends suggest a critical need for close examination of the relationship between government downsizing and gender gaps in public institutions. This issue should be on a future research agenda.

FUTURE ACTIONS

The findings of this study show that different forms of women's disadvantage cannot be addressed in isolation from one another or divorced from the structures of inequality that exist in society at large. At the level of institutions, we observe that women's disadvantage and the discriminatory practices that limit their influence over decisions affecting the conditions of women in human settlements cannot be rectified without taking into account the patriarchal notions subscribed to by both male and female employees in the workplace. It is easier to address the gender gaps in policies and in legal documents on paper than to do so in practice, as these case studies show. Nevertheless, to improve the gender gaps identified by case studies at the professional level in government institutions that deal with the development of human settlements, certain possible "remedies" can be taken into consideration for future action. These include the following:

— Establish specific mechanisms to promote and protect gender equity in recruitment and promotion of women in all levels and fields of expertise at the workplace, disseminate those policies, and monitor their performance.

— Recognize differential needs of female employees compared to those of men and establish women's entitlement to adequate maternal support without a cost to their consideration for recruitment and promotion.

— Establish an effective monitoring system to secure the institution's accountability and commitment to its equity policies.

— Take measures to ensure gender units at all government agencies and each administrative level pursue women's interests and women's greater participation by frequent evaluation of institutions' gender equity policies. These units should be provided with political backing in order to operate as watchdogs and secure that gender equity policies are translated into actual practices at their agencies.

— Identify the levels at which (national, district, municipal) women are most disadvantaged and have low representation and make conscious organizational effort to entice women to work at those levels.

— Require governments to provide gender disaggregated data on their employees' profiles by levels of authority and professional fields and make those readily available to employees as an important measure in their gender equity performance.

— Ensure gender training up to the highest levels of authority and underline the importance of gender equity policies in the overall development policies of the country.

— Establish affirmative action to encourage and support education of female students at universities in technical fields in order to enhance women's participation at the higher levels of decision making in technical areas traditionally defined as men's domains of expertise. This requires addressing the factors that hamper the education of women at all levels, including the promotion of girls' education in science fields at primary and secondary levels.

— Examine the effects of decentralization and privatization on women as civil servants and identify whether these strategies and trends are further deteriorating women's conditions at the workplace; if so, recommend means of resistance before too much erosion of their rights has taken place.

— Last but not least, with the participatory method utilized by the UN's Women and Habitat Programme proving successful in its empowering process and outcome, promote this widely to various development agencies and research institutions involved in the development of human settlements.

The United Nation's Center for Human Settlements and its Women and Habitat Programme have correctly set empowerment of women in low-income human settlements as the ultimate goal of their research and project interventions. But this goal cannot be achieved without integrating the strategies that address the issue at the local community level and at the national and state professional levels. The problem of gender gaps in human settlement development cannot be addressed at the institutional level solely through training of professional women and their occupation of higher decision-making positions. This is for two reasons: First, women do not necessarily have a feminist consciousness when they formulate policy and project priorities; hence, their greater participation may not automatically result in women-friendly policies or projects (Lister 1997; O'Regan 2000; Rai 1995). Second, in the absence of women's access to resources at the community level, that is, access to land, income, time, and inheritance, security of shelter cannot be achieved by efforts to address the gaps at the institutional and professional levels.

To improve women's conditions of life in human settlements, closing the gender gaps at the professional and political levels, achieving formulation and implementation of policies that respond to the needs of women, and addressing their disadvantage are vitally important. But it is also crucial to understand and account for the interconnections between women's disadvantage at the professional and community levels. Women's limited ownership of land and housing must be understood in the broader sociopolitical context of institutionalized privilege within an interconnected web of social and political forces and processes that try to maintain patriarchy and capitalism. The lack of services in many human settlements means that girls will be absorbed for most of the workday in helping their mothers with domestic chores, limiting their access to education and thus to all other resources, including land and housing. But change and the surge for justice are inevitable. Women as agents of change challenge these policies and practices of oppression both at the level of communities and institutions through the informal and formal arenas of politics and policy making. Agendas for future action, hence, must be understood as closely interdependent, and intervention strategies must address the problem holistically, on all fronts and at all levels.

NOTES

1. I would like to thank the UN Gender and Habitat Programme and Mazingira Institute, in specific Annika Turkvis, Catalina Hinchey Trujillo, and Diana Lee-Smith, for inviting me to join the 1995 UN meeting on gender and urbanization which became the basis of my involvement with this project. My most sincere thanks to Catalina Hinchey Trujillo whose insights have been influential in more ways than she knows.

2. This includes Mazingira Institute and the UN Gender and Habitat Programme—for details of the process see Miraftab 1996.

In Theory and in Practice:
Women Creating Better Accounts of the World

Louise Fortmann

MAKING WOMEN VISIBLE

Throughout the nineteenth and much of the twentieth century, ideas of what was worthy of scholarship were highly gendered. Most social science research focused on men (usually white men) or male-dominated institutions. Finding "women" in an index or mentioned in the text was a considerable surprise, even an occasion for rejoicing. Then with Esther Boserup's 1970 book, *Woman's Role in Economic Development*, came a steady stream of scholarly works on women and rural development by such pioneers as Meena Acharya and Lynn Bennett (1981), Bina Agarwal (1986), Edna Bay (1982), Noel Chavangi (1984), Carol Colfer (1981), Elizabeth Croll (1985), Carmen Diana Deere (1982), Ruth Dixon (1978), Ann Fleuret (1977) Marilyn Hoskins (1980), Shimwayi Muntemba (1982), Dianne Rocheleau (1988), Gita Sen and Caren Grown (1987), Kathleen Staudt and Jane Jaquette (1982), and, of course, Irene Tinker (1976a, 1980b).[1]

Their work focused on invisible women—the invisible woman farmer, the invisible woman agroforester or forester, the invisible woman fisher—and made them visible to state agencies and donors as well as to other scholars. Much of the work focused on individual women or pried apart the notion of unitary households to identify women's roles, asking: What work do women do? What resources, in what quantities, do they have to work with? What are they responsible for? What costs do they bear? What benefits do they achieve? The picture that emerged was one of women whose work and knowledge were essential parts of rural livelihood systems and who were, in general, disadvantaged vis-à-vis men in most spheres of access to resources and power.

One could quite correctly conclude that this body of scholarship grew out of the women's movement. Under the banner of "the personal is political," analysis and critique were making gender discrimination visible in structures and processes ranging from the workplace, to the provision of health care, to access to education and credit, to prevailing discourses about intelligence and sexuality. However, this chapter looks at the body of scholarship in a different way, exploring the production of knowledge by and about women and rural development.[2] It takes as the starting point Donna Haraway's (1999, 75) assertion: "Feminists have to insist on a better account of the world." For her this is the goal of science (182), which I take to include the social sciences. How, this chapter asks, have and should we use women's theory and practice to develop better accounts of the world? It further assumes with Haraway (1999) that objectivity is not the "god-trick of seeing everything from nowhere" (176) but rather that objectivity is necessarily embodied and, therefore, all knowledges are situated and partial. Thus, the male scholars before Boserup were not able to pull off the "god-trick." Rather, their knowledge, situated in the partiality of the male gaze, led them to an account of the world that consisted of and privileged male agency, knowledge, and efficacy. Women's scholarship produced knowledge situated in the female gaze that gave a better account of the world by repicturing that world through women's agency, knowledge, and efficacy.

The chapter proceeds in three parts, each exploring how theory and practice rooted in situated knowledges can be used to develop better accounts of the world. Together they focus on what questions are asked, whose knowledge counts, and whose voices are permitted to be heard. Throughout, it is taken as given that women create knowledge through their practices including not only scholarly research and theory but also the everyday practices of producing livelihoods and raising families. The first section turns the idea of women as societal victims and perpetrators of environmental degradation inside out by asking about the adverse effects of discrimination against women on the environment. The second section explores the possibilities of analysis that combines the partial gazes of the global North and South. The third section argues for the practice of an interdependent science that eschews hierarchical notions of whose knowledge counts and what kinds of voices are permitted.

MAKING MULTI-SCALE EFFECTS OF GENDER DISCRIMINATION VISIBLE: AN ENVIRONMENTAL EXAMPLE

Making multi-scale environmental effects of gender discrimination visible requires us to consider two literatures, one at the intersection of women and the environment and the other on gendered property rights. Rural women in the global South often appear in the literature on the environment in one of three roles: victims, perpetrators, or manager/stewards. The literature, often written by women, on women as environmental victims has documented the adverse effects on women of environmental degradation and environmental projects that do not take them into account. Often women must walk farther for fuelwood (Karan and Iijima 1975) and water (UNEP 2004) as a result of environmental degradation. And some environmental projects have forced women to walk farther for fuelwood (the original Campfire program in Masoka, Zimbabwe, is a case in point) or destroyed their livelihood strategies (Schroeder 1997). The perpetrator literature portrays women's practices such as fuelwood collection as a cause (sometimes major) of environmental degradation (Van Horen and Eberhard 1995). Finally, the literature (also often written by women) documenting the knowledge and practices that enable women to be competent manager/stewards of natural resources on which they depend is extensive (Colfer 1981; M. Leach 1994; Rocheleau and Edmunds 1997).

Much of the literature on property and environment has focused on the debate about environmental outcomes of different property regimes: common, public, and private property (Ostrom 1991; McCay and Acheson 1987). Attention to gender in this literature is rare (Meinzen-Dick and Zwarteveen 2001). The literature on gendered property regimes demonstrates that generally women are less likely than men to have access to land in their own right or to own or control land or the crops they produce and are more likely than men to be landless or to lose access to land with a change in their marital status; when they are landowners, women have less land than men on average (Bruce 1990; Maboreke 1990; Ngqaleni and Makhura 1996; Verdery 1996; Agarwal 1994; Simbolon 1998; Dore 2000; Deere and Leon 2001; Whitehead and Tsikata 2003; Casolo 2004).[3]

These literatures pose situated knowledge at different scales. The literature on women as manager/stewards takes a micro-level view, focusing on the knowledge, practices, and livelihood strategies of individual women and their households.[4] The macro level appears in this literature in the form of institutions and structures that have adverse micro-level effects on women. The property regimes literature generally proceeds as if macro-level property institutions were gender neutral and focuses on their environmental effects. When the environmental degradation literature takes a gendered view, it focuses on macro-level environmental effects and looks to women's micro-level practices (real or imaginary) as a cause of environmental degradation. The following case study connects these partial and situated knowledges in asking the question: Do the adverse micro-level effects of macro-level institutions also have adverse effects at the macro level? Do the focus on and implicit willingness to accept gendered adverse outcomes at the micro level mask adverse societal level effects?[5]

An Example of Adverse Environmental Effects of a Gendered Property Regime

In a 1991–92 study of 27 percent of the households in two villages[6] in central Zimbabwe, 56 percent of the respondents had planted at least one tree in the homestead. But only 44 percent of the women planted trees in their homestead, in contrast to 83 percent of the men. To analyze homestead tree planting, logit models were used.[7]

The analysis showed that women, regardless of class, were significantly less likely to plant trees in the homestead than men. Taking the average value of each variable over the entire sample, the predicted probability of planting a tree is 58 percent. With all other variables held at their mean (average), men had an 83 percent probability of planting a tree in the homestead while the probability for women was only 43 percent. Wealth was not statistically significant at the .05 level. Poor and mid-level farmers were as likely as the wealthy to have planted at least one tree, although they were not necessarily planting for the same reasons. Poor men have a positive (and highly significant) probability of planting a tree. This analysis suggests that gender plays a more important role than wealth in the decision to plant trees on homestead property.

Why might gender adversely affect tree planting? It is not physical strength, as anyone knows who has done women's work: planting groundnuts, hauling water, collecting firewood, making groundnut butter (smooth, not chunky!) with a grinding stone. It is not women's lack of knowledge about or need for trees and tree products: in the study area for all but two categories of use, women knew far more tree species than men did. Neither age nor education had any statistical significance. Tree planting is neither culturally proscribed for women nor prescribed for men in the study area. Insecurity of land and tree tenure resulting from a gendered land tenure system is by far the most persuasive explanation.

This interpretation is strengthened by two additional pieces of data. First, women who are divorced in the village (all of whom who had lost all rights to the trees they had planted and tended during their marriage even when they stayed in the village) were emphatic that they would not plant trees in a new marital compound lest they once again be discarded and once again lose everything. Second, gender did not affect tree planting in the community woodlot where women retained their rights after a divorce as long as they continued to reside in the village. The latter finding must be approached with caution since women's tree planting in community woodlots may be done not on their own behalf but as an emissary of the household. Nonetheless, it is instructive that gender has adverse effects on tree planting when women's tenure is insecure and apparently has no such effects where their tenure is secure.

Although we must be cautious in drawing conclusions from a single study, these data are certainly suggestive. To the extent that the ecological stability and health of a society and its production systems depends on women's willingness to invest their labor in long-term investments (what Blaikie and Brookfield [1987] call landesque capital) such as tree planting, terracing, irrigation infrastructure, and fences, property and tenure systems that discriminate against women will have negative societal consequences. Since in many parts of Africa the productive rural population is still disproportionately made up of women, this finding should give pause to those concerned with maintaining or improving ecological conditions that can continue to sustain agricultural livelihoods. Clearly, property rights must enable and encourage women to be ecological stewards.[8]

The study also shows the importance of recognizing the partiality of one's knowledge. Better accounts of the world require not only making women visible but also making visible the multi-scale adverse effects that result from micro-scale adverse effects on women.

MAKING VISIBLE THE COMMONALITIES OF WOMEN
IN THE GLOBAL NORTH AND GLOBAL SOUTH

This section focuses on the need for and the possibilities of combining the partial knowledges of both theory and practice in the global North and global South. The following vignette exemplifies the problem at hand.

At a 2002 international meeting on community forestry networks,[9] the suggestion that participants break out by regional groups was met with a pained query from a prominent scholar and practitioner of development: "But what would the people from the North talk about?" The reply, "We would talk about community forestry networks in the North," left many dumbstruck. Practitioners and development scholars from the South as well as those from the North whose scholarship and practice were limited to the South could not imagine that rural people in the South had anything in common with rural people in the North.[10] The mirror image is the common belief of those in the North that the South has no relevance to them, despite the fact that the northern community forestry movement is firmly rooted in the community forestry experience of South and Southeast Asia.

These reactions are not surprising when one acknowledges that, with some exceptions,[11] scholarship on women (and other issues) in the global South and in the global North have been more or less distinct. Of course, some edited volumes (Rocheleau et al. 1996; Perry and Schenck 2001) as well as conferences include both. But more often than not, discussion of women in one geographical area takes place as if the other areas do not exist in any relevant way. This may reflect the time and money required to do comparative research effectively or the narrow focus of many scholarly studies. It may well mean that the everyday lives of women in one region are not imaginable to women in another. Or it may be because the altogether appropriate insistence that we pay attention to social embeddedness has led to a failure to ask if the macro-level structures and processes within which local communities operate are similar across regions. For example, all too often the working assumption seems to be that communities in countries where the Bretton Woods institutions influence (or dictate) policy or initiate projects are qualitatively different from communities in countries where they do not. Perhaps the position of a community is conflated with the power of the country where it is located. Whatever the reason, these partial gazes result in a failure to look at the similarity of the effects of institutions such as transnational corporations and NGOs on communities in the North *and* South.

Practice may provide the most effective pathway to better accounts of the world though combining the partial gazes and situated knowledges of the North and South. There are numerous examples of bridging practice involving institutional practitioners. An Indian forester with experience with Joint Forest Management in India directs a U.S. national community forestry organization. Community forestry practitioners from the North and South met at the Johannesburg summit and made common cause, forming the Global Caucus on Community Based Forest Management. The successful women's saving circles of the Grameen Bank came to the United States in the form of the ShoreBank in Chicago.

Commonalities are made visible at the personal level. When villagers from resource-dependent rural communities in the South visit rural resource-dependent communities in northern California, both groups almost inevitably make the same comment: "We never realized that they have the same problems we do. Now we know we are not alone." Thus members of the Hupa Nation in northern California and the villagers of Bawa, Mozambique, recognized that they both struggle to maintain culturally based natural resource use and management against government interference. On one occasion an African NGO staffer quipped that he never would have guessed that his country would have so much in common with a small California forest community; namely, that in both places major decisions are made in Washington, D.C., without consulting local people. The instant the words were out of his mouth, the political relationships that Cameroonians and the residents of Hayfork had in common became visible to everyone.

To return to scholarly practice, imagine what we might learn if we broke out of our geographic ghettos and did, for example, a study of the economic and social strategies of poor female household heads in the North and the South, or a study of the reasons for and effects of excluding wives from ownership of lineage land in parts of rural Africa and family farm corporation in the U.S. Midwest, or a study of the cultures and social consequences of physical and sexual abuse of women wherever they are.

Much mutual learning between North and South is clearly to be done. It is to further possibilities of mutual learning between civil and conventional scientists that the next section turns.

MAKING INTERDEPENDENT SCIENCE VISIBLE

The twenty-first century's most privileged form of knowledge production is conventional science. Conventional scientists are formally educated and use prescribed experimental and observational techniques. Their findings, often validated by statistical tests, networks of other scientists, and journals, are intended to be generalizable and may not translate easily into useful solutions to local problems.[12] Conventional science has been criticized for frequently being hostile to women and for privileging a narrow spectrum of possible ways of producing knowledge including both the questions that may be asked and the methods that may be used (Merchant 1980; Haraway 1999; Maddox 2002; Bug 2003; Conkey 2003; Gowaty 2003).

Civil science is a different way of producing knowledge. Civil scientists by and large work informally using experimental and observational techniques they and their predecessors have developed themselves. Their science depends on their knowledge of a particular set of social-ecological relationships. Their findings, validated by utility, are well suited to providing useful solutions to local problems but may not be generalizable. Civil science encompasses indigenous knowledge, traditional knowledge, local technical knowledge, and the ethnosciences.

Given the situated and partial nature of knowledge, one way to develop better accounts of the world would be through the collaboration of civil and conventional sciences. For the most part, there is relatively little interaction between the two modes of knowledge production but there are exceptions. For example, in the field of medicine, conventional scientists have used civil science as a source of information. A familiar example is the common or Madagascar periwinkle, *Catharanthus roseus*, which was traditionally used in different parts of the world to stop bleeding, as an astringent and a diuretic, and to treat diabetes, wasp stings, coughs, lung congestion and inflammation, sore throats, and eye irritation and infections. Two alkaloids, vincristine and vinblastine, found in the Madagascar periwinkle are used in drugs made by Eli Lilly to treat leukemia and a variety of cancers. While the Madagascar periwinkle story, without question, has had good outcomes for cancer patients, civil-conventional science interactions of this uni-directional sort are likely to have undesirable features. The relationship is generally hierarchical, privileging conventional science. It may also be extractive as demonstrated all too well by the problems of bioprospecting and biopiracy (Chapela 1994; Fairhead and Leach 2003; see also note 9 below).

A different mode of interaction is possible through interdependent science, a set of knowledge-producing practices intended to provide better accounts of the world through collaboration between conventional and civil scientists. Interdependent science does not privilege conventional science. Rather, it recognizes that good science integrates and acknowledges different actors and actions, including different ways of knowing, such as civil science. It recognizes practice as a mode of knowledge production (Chaiklin and Lave 1993; Holland and Lave 2000). It recognizes, as this essay has argued from the outset, that all science is embodied and that objectivity comes not from the "god-trick" but from the recognition of partiality. Its metric of objectivity is knowledge and explanatory power. It recognizes the multiple female and male voices in which better accounts of the world emerge, voices ranging from sparse passive-voice prose to chatty accounts and explanations, from the chants of a ritual healer to the thick description of an ethnographer and many more. Since its goal is the co-production of knowledge, it is likely to utilize participatory methods.[13]

Examples of interdependent science involving women and men demonstrate its potential. The combination of farmers' knowledge with the knowledge and technologies of conventional scientists in participatory plant breeding has shortened the time required to develop a new variety and increased the adoption of new varieties. For example, in Rwanda, "Farmer bush bean selections outperformed their own mixtures with average production increases of up to 38 percent; breeder selections in the same region on average showed negative or insignificant production increases" (Sperling 1996:45). Conventional scientists who have been involved in participatory plant breeding say they would never go back to doing plant breeding on their own because conventional plant breeding is more time consuming and less effective (Robin Buchara personal communication, 2000). Sally Humphries (personal communication, 2004) reports the commercial release of an improved bean variety by a research team of women and men Nicaraguan farmers working in collaboration with a conventional science agronomist. In the face of a dearth of knowledge about the ecology of commercially important floral greens, a team of women and men floral greens harvesters worked with a forest ecologist to develop experimental trials on the effects of harvesting on floral green production (Ballard et al. 2002; Ballard and Fortmann 2004). This research has provided information on which to base management policies. A team of women and men Zimbabwean villagers working with a rural sociologist and a botanist documented the use and management of 122 varieties of indigenous trees (Chidari et al. 1992). This was an important complement to the approach of the Forestry Commission, which concentrated on growing a few exotic species. In addition, the team also documented the extensive knowledge that women had of trees and their uses, knowledge that generally was greater than men's.

In addition to producing knowledge, the practice of interdependent science can empower the civil scientists including women. After the women and men of the Zimbabwe village research team presented their research findings at a well-attended village meeting, the Chairman of the Grazing Scheme (the *de facto* village head) rose to his feet and said, "I never thought we could learn anything from a woman, but we have." While this did not overturn patriarchal social relations in the village, it was an important step, a moment that no one could take away from the women research team members whose work and knowledge had been acknowledged.

CONCLUSIONS

This chapter has shown that women's research and practice has led to better accounts of the world through making neglected social actors and social relations visible, by bringing actors and social relations thought to be distinct into conversation with each other, and by embracing and utilizing difference and collaboration rather than hierarchy and extraction. To be sure, this is an ongoing project requiring the iteration of making things visible in each of the ways discussed here. For example, if women are to be participants in interdependent science, their knowledge of a particular subject in a particular place may first have to be made visible, the first step discussed above. Clearly, much remains to be done. Equally clearly, much has been accomplished. In theory and in practice, in the academy and in the household, farm field and forest, women have produced knowledge that we need for the lives of our children and grandchildren. One of our jobs as scholars is to collaborate in keeping that knowledge visible and validated.

NOTES

I would like to acknowledge the research assistance of Katariina Tuovinen and the critical comments of Emery Roe.

1. Despite its length, this list only scratches the surface of the numbers of brave and energetic women who did research on and published about women even when it put their own careers in jeopardy.

2. The focus of this chapter is limited to rural development both for reasons of manageability and because the literature on women and rural development has often been more applied than other feminist scholarship and research in women's studies. For genealogies of scholarly work on women in development see M. Leach (1994) and Rocheleau et al. (1996).

3. Mexico provides a case to the contrary. Hamilton (2002) argues that although land titling eliminated women's inheritance rights, because of ejidatarias' social status as mothers deserving their children's cooperation and the respect and aid of the community following their husband's death, they have generally been well provided for.

4. Meinzen-Dick and Zwarteveen (2001) note the general focus at the household or micro level and call for attention to the community or meso level. This chapter calls for further scaling up to the macro level.

5. Put in a more pithy fashion: is oppressing mother also bad for Mother Nature (and everybody else)?

6. The research project documented the management of trees and woodlands and their commercial and domestic uses as well as the factors affecting tree planting. There were 48 men and 106 women in the final sample. There are more women because men in many households worked in town most of the year and came home only occasionally.

7. Logit models are appropriate for situations in which individuals must make a choice between two options, in this case: to plant or not plant, and can be used to estimate probabilities—in this case, the probability that a person will plant a tree. This study is described in detail in Fortmann et al. 1997.

8. Although it is beyond the scope of this chapter, it is worth noting that land races developed, often by women, over a number of years using deliberate agronomic practices and seed selection are not recognized as deserving of legal protection (Kameri-Mbote and Cullet 1999). Thus, it can be argued that the right of women to intellectual products of their agricultural labor is as insecure as their rights to the physical means of production and their products. Kameri-Mbote and Cullet maintain that the current lack of protection of intellectual property rights at the level of the individual farmer "has contributed to the erosion of the genetic base necessary for the further development of agrobiodiversity" (24).

9. Community forestry is a set of institutional arrangements in which communities are involved wholly or in part in decision making about and benefits from forest management as well as contributing knowledge and labor to achieve healthy forests and social well-being (Cecilia Danks personal communication, 2003).

10. Similarly, many participants from the global South who attended a 2004 traveling workshop on community forestry in Alabama and California were quite surprised to discover that there were both forests and poor people in the United States.

11. Refugee studies are an exception in that they address questions of women from the South who find themselves in the North. These studies tend now, however, to address women from the North.

12. For an in-depth discussion of conventional, civil, and interdependent sciences see Ballard and Fortmann (2004).

13. There is informal evidence (but no systematically collected data) that suggests women are more likely to use participatory methods. Whether this is true is a question worth researching.

Women's Work: The Kitchen Kills More than the Sword

Kirk R. Smith

In spring 2003, the world stood in fear of SARS (severe acute respiratory syndrome), which killed 800 people in six months, mostly in East Asia. Travel in the area ground to a standstill, schools and businesses were closed, towns and villages barred entrance to strangers, and medical and public health agencies were put on high alert. All told, it caused a significant drop in GNP for the region, costing US$12–28 billion (Fan 2003). One of its scary features was its speed—its victims could proceed from first symptoms to death in five to six days (WHO 2004).

In developing countries, however, where children suffer from what might be called old SARS (that is, ALRI—acute lower respiratory infection, commonly leading to pneumonia), children die even faster. A child can be perfectly healthy when visited on Monday afternoon, but dead by Wednesday night. Although ALRI is theoretically treatable with antibiotics, there is little hope of finding and treating all such cases in time, given the lack of rural doctors and the conditions of rural roads. Once the infection takes hold in the deep lung, even antibiotics do not work. Prevention is the only answer.

New SARS is frightening, but its deaths amount to barely a drop in the torrent of death represented by old SARS. In the six months that new SARS killed 800, old SARS killed a million children less than 5 years old around the developing world. It kills more children than any other disease, making it the biggest source of lost life years in the world. In South Asia, for example, it is responsible for more than one-twelfth of the entire burden of disease. Indeed, ALRI in Indian children under five (one disease, in just one country and one age group) is responsible for 1.5 percent of the entire global burden of disease. More people die of old SARS in India every few hours than died in the entire global new SARS epidemic (WHO 2003a).

Unlike new SARS, ALRI normally does not threaten healthy adults. Businessmen who were afraid to fly to Hong Kong during the new SARS epidemic can walk with impunity through the slums of Kolkata, where children die hourly from ALRI, without fear of catching it. Unlike new SARS, ALRI does not make the news, directly affect the economy of a continent, or trigger emergency worldwide action. Nevertheless, it exacts a terrible toll.

My goal in this essay is to discuss what is currently known about the health impacts on women and their youngest children that stem from their exposure to indoor air pollution as a result of the use of poor fuels and unvented cookstoves.[1] I start, however, by asking a broader question: Within societies, which groups lose most from being underdeveloped, marginalized, and victimized by globalization or by being just plain poor? Although there are many ways to assess development and human welfare, I address this question here through health.

MEASUREMENTS OF HEALTH

Arguably, nearly every other welfare measure depends on health: economies cannot prosper, democracies cannot flourish, and schools cannot function without healthy people. It complicates things that causality also runs the other way. Health gains come through progress in income, political rights, and education. But the most important fact is that good health is as close as we have to a universal human desire. It is what makes all else possible, the necessary if not sufficient criterion for achieving all life's goals. But, like the monkey's paw in Jacobs's short story (Jacobs 1902), it does not guarantee wisdom or happiness.

But how do we measure health? At one end of the spectrum is the definition in the World Health Organization's 1946 constitution: "Health is a state of complete physical, mental, spiritual, and social well-being and not merely the absence of disease or infirmity."[2] At the other extreme are those who measure health by measuring death, for example, by age-adjusted mortality rates or life expectancy. Neither type of measure is satisfactory for my purpose here.

Given today's level of knowledge, the WHO definition seems impossible to operationalize. It cannot be used to make even simple comparisons across populations. Surveys of perceptions, which would seem the only way to derive mental and spiritual well-being, bring results that do not correlate well with physical measures. Australian Aborigines, for example, who by any physical measure suffer significant ill health by comparison to white Australians, typically rank themselves far healthier than their better-off neighbors, many of whom rank themselves in poor health although they are "objectively" in better physical health than 99.9 percent of all humans who ever lived (AIHW 1996). If we simply took people's own assessment of their health at face value and acted accordingly we would have a global public health system that focused resources on the anxious wealthy in the developed world. This hardly seems desirable. One day we may have a way to operationalize the WHO definition for policy purposes, but today we do not.

On the other end of the spectrum, death is clearly related to health, but it is obviously an inadequate measure. First, everyone dies and if they don't die of one thing then they die of another. Thus, health defined as the absence of death is never achieved. A second consideration is that the age of death is very important. The death of an 88 year old is sad but rarely tragic. Indeed, we often call deaths of the old "natural." There is no "natural" death for a 28 year old, however. Something went wrong. The economic, social, and emotional impact is much greater when the young die, even though the death certificate is the same length. Finally, death fails as a measure of ill health because it does not include nonfatal illness and injury, conditions that affect health but may not change death rates. This discussion suggests several criteria that would have to be met by a useful measure of ill health to be used for international comparisons (Murray and Lopez 1996):

It should be objectively derived and not subject to personal, local, temporary, and unrepeatable valuation.
It should combine death and disease.
It should include consideration of age and sex.
It should be blind to income, race, nation, class, religion, etc.; the illness and premature death of a 50-year-old female stockbroker in Sydney should be counted the same as that of the 50-year-old farmer's wife in Guatemala.

The only measure that has ever been seriously proposed that meets all these criteria is lost time. Premature death is measured by the years of lost life given the life expectancy of a person of that particular age and sex. Illness can be measured as a duration (years) times a severity factor, which varies from low values (e.g., 0.05) for minor illnesses or injuries to large values (e.g., 0.9) for major ones. The total lost life years from premature death and illness is a measure of a disease or risk factor within a population.

The idea behind this approach is that very few things other than potential life length are given as equally to everyone on Earth—certainly not income or wealth, the loss of which is sometimes used as a measure of ill health in some legal cases. Assuming we are each granted "three score and ten," the fact that some of us (the women farmers of Guatemala for instance) are not able to live out those years is an indication of their ill health. We believe that if women farmers had the nutrition, education, environment, medical care, and so on of the women stockbrokers in Sydney, they would live just as long and just as disease-free. The degree to which they do not, the lost life years, is a measure of their ill health that meets all the criteria above.

There are several different ways of calculating lost life years, each with certain methodological and presentational advantages and disadvantages (Murray et al. 2000). Here I use the disability-adjusted life year (DALY). By doing so I can tap the only complete coherent worldwide health database, the Global Burden of Disease database, which is published annually by the World Health Organization (WHO 2003a). With this measure of ill health, we can turn to the question at hand.

THE GENDERED HEALTH EFFECTS OF POVERTY

The groups that have the most ill health (those who lose the most DALYs) from underdevelopment are in general women and children, because they bear a disproportionate burden of disease in poor countries. Put another way, women and their youngest children are usually the biggest winners in development. Although there are risks in extrapolating cross-sectional data to longitudinal trends, table 1 shows that women and children typically bear more than their share of ill health in poor countries but less than their share in rich countries. Women's absolute burden (converted to annual lost healthy days per capita [DALDs] to avoid small fractions) is some 25 percent more than men in South Asia and 35 percent more in poor Sub-Saharan Africa.

By comparison, men's health in rich countries, although better than that of men in poor countries, does not improve as much as that of women and children. Data from western Europe and Sub-Saharan Africa show that women and children's health is better by a factor of six in western Europe, but men's health improves by only a factor of three. In contrast to poor countries, men in rich North America and western Europe are actually worse off than women and children in terms of burden per capita.

Why? Most bluntly, this may be because women are educable and men are

TABLE 1   Comparison of Ill-Health Borne by Women and Children at Different Levels of Development, 2002

| Region | Women and Children | | | Men |
	% of Population	% of Burden	DALD/capita	DALD/capita
South Asia	66	71	115	92.1
Poor Africa	70	76	233	173
North America	62	51	43.0	65.2
Western Europe	60	49	39.0	58.6

Key: DALD, daily annual lost days
Source: WHO 2003a

not. In general, men probably live less long than women in nearly all countries today because they seem not to be able to give up drinking, smoking, fighting, and other risky behaviors. Indeed, as shown in figure 1, ill health from this type of risk tends to increase during development. In poor countries, many men tend to work at physically demanding jobs that reduce risk of chronic diseases, but these jobs are commonly lost as countries develop. Looking at the noninfectious aspects of the disease burden for men (mainly heart disease, cancer, chronic lung disease, and intentional and unintentional injuries), in North America, for example, men lose 62 healthy days per year, which is only some 12 percent less than the 70 lost by men in South Asia.

DEADLY KITCHENS: COOKING, AIR POLLUTION, AND DISEASE

One risky behavior in which men have not indulged much in any culture, however, is routine household cooking. Evidence in recent years is creating a strong case that a significant portion of the disproportionate ill health borne by women and young children in poor countries is due to this ancient human occupation. In particular, the approximate half of family meals cooked daily in the world with solid fuels (biomass and coal) expose women and the children with them to large amounts of health-damaging air pollutants. Recent conservative estimates by the WHO (based on a large systematic search and assessment of the world literature and using common coherent methods of analysis across risk factors by 100 researchers in 30 institutions) put the burden at about 1.6 million deaths annually from use of poor quality fuels in simple household stoves. About 40 percent of these are of women and are from chronic obstructive pulmonary disease and lung cancer (Smith et al. 2004). The remainder are ALRI, mainly in the form of pneumonia in children under five. As discussed above, this category of disease causes

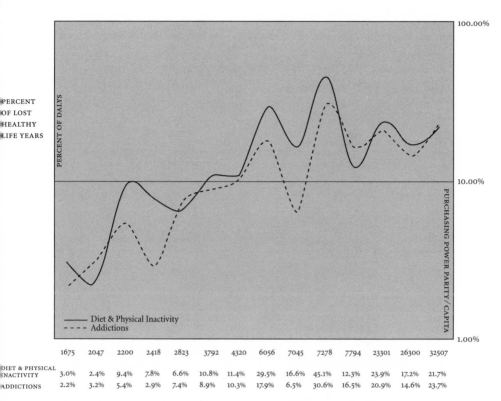

PERCENT
OF LOST
HEALTHY
LIFE YEARS

PERCENT OF DALYS

PURCHASING POWER PARITY / CAPITA

100.00%

10.00%

1.00%

—— Diet & Physical Inactivity
- - - - Addictions

	1675	2047	2200	2418	2823	3792	4320	6056	7045	7278	7794	23301	26300	32507
DIET & PHYSICAL INACTIVITY	3.0%	2.4%	9.4%	7.8%	6.6%	10.8%	11.4%	29.5%	16.6%	45.1%	12.3%	23.9%	17.2%	21.7%
ADDICTIONS	2.2%	3.2%	5.4%	2.9%	7.4%	8.9%	10.3%	17.9%	6.5%	30.6%	16.5%	20.9%	14.6%	23.7%

FIGURE 1   Addictions (Tobacco, Drugs, Alcohol), Diet, and Physical Inactivity. Note: Risks tending to increase during economic development. Risk is measured as percent of total lost healthy life years ranked by income per capita measured in purchasing power in fourteen world regions. Data source: WHO 2002.

the most ill health in the world, about 8 percent of the entire world burden in 2000 (Smith and Mehta 2003).

In South Asia, for example, the burden of disease from major risk factors is shown in figure 2 (Smith 2003). Note that the household-level environmental risks due to poor fuel and ventilation are almost as large as those from poor water and sanitation. In each country, both are exceeded only by malnutrition as causes of ill health. As the data show, nearly all the risks are born by women and children. Indeed, if the three risks—malnutrition, poor water and sanitation, and poor fuel and ventilation—in South Asia were lowered to their levels in developed countries, the difference between women's and children's ill health and that of men would reverse. Instead of women and children bearing 25 percent more lost DALD per capita, they would have some 5–10 percent fewer DALD than men.[3] At

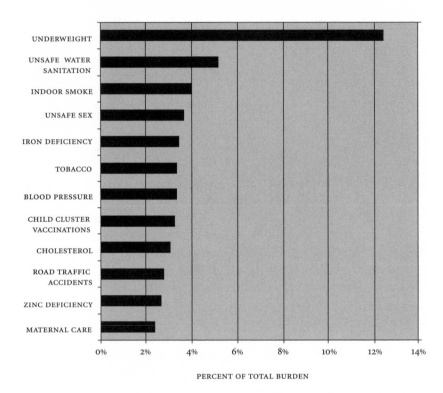

FIGURE 2 Top Risk Factors in South Asia in 2000. Note: Top twelve risk factors for ill-health in South Asia measured as percent of total lost healthy life years. Data source: WHO 2002.

about 85 DALD per capita, however, they would still be bearing twice the burden of women and children in rich countries.

There is growing evidence (not yet as strong as the evidence for ALRI, chronic obstructive pulmonary disease, and lung cancer) that exposures to household air pollutants are responsible for a range of other diseases that cause fewer deaths but have other characteristics that make them worrisome. Tuberculosis, in particular, seems to be related to these high exposures, a finding consistent with the extra tuberculosis risk experienced by smokers. Tuberculosis is particularly trouble-some in the world today not only because it is so highly infectious, but because, unlike most other infectious diseases, it is on the rise. This is largely attributable to the HIV epidemic but results in increasing the risk of non-HIV tuberculosis in-fection as well. Tuberculosis is hard to treat effectively and is becoming more so due to increasing resistance to drugs. Less well known is the fact that tuberculo-sis is also among the chief causes of ill health in women aged 15–44 in developing countries. In South Asia, for example, tuberculosis exceeds the impact of cardio-vascular disease and of sexually transmitted diseases, including HIV, and exerts more than two times the burden of cancer and three times that of nutritional dis-orders. This is the sex and age group that is the bulwark of society, those who provide the chief emotional and often material support for both the young and the old, and who frequently work longer hours than any other group.

Household pollution also has a direct impact, operating most likely through the special relationship between mother and child. Careful analysis of the Na-tional Family Health Survey in India, for example, shows not only an effect of indoor air pollution on respiratory disease in young children but also an effect on other types of childhood mortality, such as diarrhea (Hughes and Dunleavy 2000). There are probably two causal pathways by which this effect operates. The first, as with passive and active tobacco smoking, is that pregnant women's expo-sure to household pollution affects their unborn children. Several studies show, for example, that air pollution exposures in utero produce a greater risk of low birth weight, which in turn is associated with a range of diseases in children and, probably, adults. A second pathway is what might be called the "unhealthy mother effect." If the mother is ill because of poor indoor air, combined perhaps with other impacts of solid fuel use such as long hours in gathering fuel, then she will be less able to take good care of her children, increasing risk across disease types for them.

THE GUATEMALA STUDY

I am writing this at our research site in highland Guatemala where we are engaged in a randomized intervention trial to study the impact of indoor air pollution on childhood pneumonia and chronic lung and heart disease in women.[4] The project and the people here starkly illustrate the issues of women's and children's health in the poor communities of the Third World.

This week in the four hundred rural families with whom we are currently working, there were eight life-threatening pneumonias among children under one year old. We were able to catch and treat most of them successfully, but two children died before we could reach them. Along with her baby, a sixteen-year-old mother died during childbirth in spite of my driving her, with one of our doctors who was caring for her, to the nearest hospital seventy-five minutes away. Get-ting anywhere at this time of year is dirty and difficult. The rainy season is well under way and the dirt roads, some next to steep drop-offs, are muddy and slippery. Everything in and around the small adobe houses is damp and, at 3,000 m (9,843 ft.), cold.

Malnutrition is everywhere evident in these households with five to nine children, some 60 percent of whom are at least two standard deviations and 20 percent more than three standard deviations below the height-for-age norm. These data come only from the children who show up for the first day of school. What about the kids from the poorest and most remote villages?

Social health in our area is not well either. The institution of marriage has nearly disappeared in some communities. Alcoholism is widespread among men and boys, along with the domestic violence it encourages. Indeed, one of our mothers was recently kicked to death by her drunken husband. All measures of health were reduced by 40 years of vicious civil war in Guatemala, which resulted in widespread killings and disappearances in indigenous rural communities, and large refugee populations were created in Mexico and elsewhere. At least this terrible period is over; peace has been reestablished, people have returned to their land, and there is some democracy.

At the start of our work here, all the households used open indoor biomass fires for cooking and heating, a practice shared by about half the world's population. We gave at random improved woodstoves with chimneys to half the households and are monitoring to see if there are differences between the two groups in the health of the children and women. The other half will receive the same stove when the babies reach 18 months. Pollution levels in the kitchens before intervention commonly exceed prudent health standards by factors of 20 or 30.

Previous observational studies in Asia, Africa, and Latin America have indicated that children living with clean fuels or vented stoves have about half the rate of serious pneumonia compared to those in households with open or poorly vented biomass or coal stoves. The large global comparative risk study managed by WHO discussed earlier recently estimated that about one million children die prematurely because of this pollution (WHO 2002).

Although the consistency and number of observational studies showing a relationship between household indoor air pollution and child pneumonia provide a fairly persuasive argument for a connection between the two, the nature of such studies is such that it is impossible to firmly pin down the case for causality and identify the causal paths. To prove causality, it is necessary to conduct a randomized control trial, which we are doing for the first time.

To date, we have not broken the codes in our data collection to know whether the stoves are improving health, but we have learned much else. Our highly trained and dedicated local fieldworkers visit every household every week to evaluate each child's health and refer any child with any sign of illness to one of our three full-time doctors for further evaluation, treatment, and transport to the local hospital if required. By this method, all houses gain significant benefit, even if only half have the improved stove. Nevertheless, we are losing many children—twenty-five after a year, making the annual infant mortality rate nearly 100 per 1000, even with this intense delivery of medical care. In other words, more than one of ten infants die, mostly of diarrhea and pneumonia, for which highly effective treatments exist. In practice, however, it is virtually impossible to reach every child in time. Undoubtedly, we have cut the mortality rate much from its "natural" level, but clearly not enough. This shows the importance of prevention—treatment is not enough.

CONCLUSION

In many areas of development, there is today a sense of frustration, in part due to lack of resources that in turn is based on a sense that many development efforts have not worked well. But many health interventions, such as vaccinations, clean water, and sanitation, have made a dramatic difference in the health status of people living in developing countries. As with clean water and sanitation, improving health through prevention—that is, better fuels and ventilation—may not seem as economically cost effective as some well-known treatment options, such as oral hydration salts and antibiotics. The success of treatment options actually poses a challenge for public health and environmental scientists, for they seem to impose a handicap on preventative measures in the keen competition for the limited resources available to promote health in the Third World. A county like India, for example, is able to muster only about $23 per capita each year for all health expenditures, some 200 times less than what is spent in Europe or North America (WHO 2002). Given the intense competition for limited resources, those concerned with prevention must make the case that some of the health resources now spent on proven and cost-effective measures such as vaccines and antibiotics should be shifted, for example, to better sanitation and improved stoves. Better yet, of course, would be to expand the total available for these essential services across the board, taken if needed from military or other sectors. Nevertheless, one must be very sure that the preventative measures are really going to work before trying to make this case.

This creates a somewhat paradoxical fact: the evidence required to make a case for dissemination of a measure to improve health in the Third World has to be made much more rigorously than would be necessary in the First World. The air pollution levels in Third World housing, because they are one or more orders of magnitude above typical health-based standards, would require no special studies in the United States or Europe to justify action. The response would be, "You do not need to know exactly how much ill health is caused by these levels, you need just go out and fix it." In the Third World, however, the response is, "We have 30 randomized and other field trials on antibiotics and vaccines and know exactly how much ill health they stop and how much they cost. Where are your randomized trials, preferably done in different regions with standardized methods, so that we can calculate the cost-effectiveness exactly? Only then can we consider recommending that scarce health resources be targeted to lowering indoor air pollution."

Like clean water and sanitation (and unlike vaccines, oral rehydration salts, and antibiotics), preventative measures for indoor air pollution tend to have non-health benefits as well. Studies done in the 1980s showed that, in strict economic terms, the time-saving benefits from provision of clean water in households often exceed the health benefits, although there are obvious difficulties in and ongoing controversies about doing such calculations. This is also the case for improved stoves, which can reduce fuel consumption (saving time and money in fuel collection) and improve household hygiene (reducing cleaning time). In addition, there are difficult-to-quantify improvements in the quality of life due to lowering the risk of burns and scalds, improving the ergonomics of cooking, and providing clean stable working surfaces in the kitchen. We have often found in Guatemala, for example, that in anticipation of an improved stove being built, households will entirely revamp their kitchen or even build a new one ("We did not want to put the beautiful new stove in our old dirty kitchen"). This may be problematic for our nice neat experimental research design, but it is quite exciting from the standpoint of a potential donor wishing to introduce interventions that trigger other positive changes. In contrast, few people are energized to improve their households when their child receives a vaccination.

Even though there is demonstrable and substantial ill health (mainly) in women and young children from poor household hygiene today (see figure 3), making the case for improvements in household hygiene as a development measure requires showing their multiple benefits. Unfortunately, to date there have

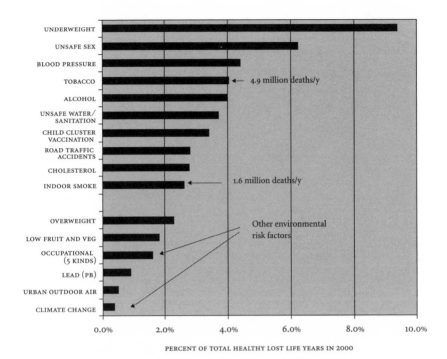

FIGURE 3   Global Burden of Disease from Top 10 Risk Factors Plus Selected Other Risk Factors. Measured as percent of total lost healthy life years. Note: From the WHO comparative risk assessment (WHO 2002), except those marked with *, which are derived from total outcomes. Data source: Smith and Ezzati 2005.

not been good coordination, common evaluation methods, and joint decision making among the different agencies, donors, and lenders, who each tend to have different emphases in their programs but as a group control the purse strings for such interventions. Along with strong advocacy, focused scholarly work is needed to develop and prove out the needed methods.

Like dirty water and lack of sanitation, dirty fuel and lack of ventilation are outcomes of poverty (see figure 4). Operating at the household level, these toxic pairs also produce major negative health impacts in the poorest groups, and mainly in women and young children. As shown in figure 3, they do decline sharply with development status along with the burden from lack of malaria control. It does not follow, however, that poverty alleviation is the right way to deal with them. Focusing only on ways to increase general income as a means to deal with these household risks is to relegate billions of people to much poorer health than they need to have, and to do so for many decades. Like clean water and

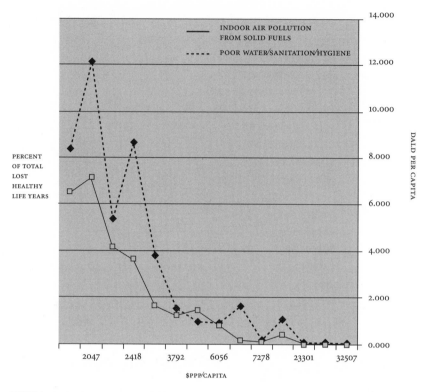

FIGURE 4 Risks Declining with Development. Three risk factors that tend to decrease during development. Note: Here risk is measured as percent of healthy lost life years ranked by income per capita as purchasing power in fourteen world regions. Data source: Smith and Ezzati 2005.

sanitation, however, targeted interventions in the household sector for cleaner fuels, chimney stoves, improved ventilation, and behavioral changes that affect air hygiene can achieve benefits in the near term, and at costs commensurate with other primary health interventions accepted by the world community. As with water and sanitation, however, there is no universal solution suitable for households worldwide but rather a need to distinguish the different needs in different areas and to seek innovative ways to encourage both top-down and bottom-up activities that can generate an even broader array of options in the future. As often noted by Irene Tinker (see the chapter by Tinker in this book, for example), the role of women, both as victims of the current situation and as actors in most feasible solutions, remains paramount.

NOTES

The subtitle of this chapter, "The Kitchen Kills More than the Sword," is a Latin proverb.

1. Because of the importance of indoor pollution for human security and human development, the editors solicited this chapter as a conceptual "think-piece" to bring this dimension into the discussion.

2. "Spiritual" was added in 1999.

3. The risk factors in figure 3 cannot be directly added in many cases. For example, some of the impacts in children of malnutrition are also captured in the diarrhea and ALRI attributed to poor water and sanitation and poor fuel and ventilation. If malnutrition were addressed first, therefore, there would be fewer impacts due to these environmental risk factors, and vice versa.

4. For more details, see http://ehs.sph.berkeley.edu/guat/.

III. Women's Mobilization and Power

Women's Movements in the Globalizing World: The Case of Thailand

Amara Pongsapich

Women's movements were significant political actors in Thailand in the 1970s and 80s. In this period, environment was a key issue. In the 1990s, however, the focus shifted toward "women and globalization." This essay focuses on the way the issue of women and environment is evolving from its role in the "growth-centered" development paradigm to its place in the emerging "human-centered" development paradigm. Human-centered development has been adopted by many development agencies, making poverty a key development issue. Women are among the stakeholders, and environmental issues compete with, but also overlap, these other priorities.

Women in Thailand have traditionally wielded more power in the household than is characteristic in many emerging economies, and women's groups have been active in movements advocating for environmental protection. In this essay I document several case studies where women are leading actors in movements committed to environmental protection and to a more human-centered approach to development. These are local movements, but they are also part of broader transnational networks that are redefining development priorities.

WOMEN AND THE ENVIRONMENT IN THE CONTEXT
OF GROWTH-CENTERED DEVELOPMENT

Growing awareness of environmental problems led to the organization of the United Nations Conference on the Human Environment in Stockholm (1972), which adopted the Action Plan for the Human Environment and initiated the United Nations Environment Program (UNEP). This conference was significant for introducing the concept of sustainable development and for the role of non-governmental organizations (NGOs) in presenting the views of the people. It set a new pattern for the relationship between the United Nations and NGOs in dealing with global issues.

In 1987 the World Commission on Environment and Development (WCED), under the chairmanship of Gro Harlem Brundtland, published its report, *Our Common Future*, which focused on sustainable development. As Annabelle Rodda observes, the report defined sustainable development as that which meets the needs of the present without compromising the ability of future generations to meet their own needs. The problem of world poverty was addressed without re-jecting economic growth: "We see instead the possibility for a new era of eco-nomic growth, one that must be based on policies that sustain and expand the en-vironmental resource base. And we believe such growth to be absolutely essential to relieve the great poverty that is deepening in much of the developing world" (Rodda 1991, 2).

Twenty years after the Stockholm Conference, in 1992, another UN Confer-ence on Environment and Development was held in Brazil. The overall agenda was basically the same as in 1972, but its main purpose was to create greater aware-ness and to set out principles and establish the agenda for the twenty-first cen-tury: Agenda 21.

The United Nations has also played a key role in recognizing the need to give women a greater role in economic development and a greater voice in political change. The recognition of International Women's Year in 1975 by a UN confer-ence in Mexico City and the subsequent adoption of the UN Decade for Women influenced the global development of women's movements. The Second World Conference on Women in 1980 in Copenhagen and the Third World Conference in 1985 in Nairobi involved grassroots women who were increasingly represented in parallel NGO conferences. By the Fourth World Conference on Women, held in Beijing in 1995, NGOs played a major role, working directly with the official dele-gations to shape the results. As momentum developed, a growing number of NGOs and grassroots women's groups participated, assisted by financial support from international NGOs, bilateral foreign assistance, and UN agencies.

The Nairobi Forward-Looking Strategies for the Advancement of Women (1985) provided guidelines for the monitoring and evaluation of activities taking place within many developing countries. Both government and nongovernmental organizations promoted women in development (WID) activities to improve the status of women. Research activities and indicators to monitor the status of women were developed, including the gender-related development index (GDI) and the gender empowerment measure (GEM) indexes.

As more women realized the need to involve men in the movement, the emphasis shifted to gender and development (GAD), and many men were recruited to help strengthen the efforts to improve the status of women. Meanwhile, the WID approach came under criticism from postmodern feminists who labeled it "patriarchal" on the grounds that women are urged to become involved in income-generating activities and participate in the market economy, which has always been male-centered. Recognizing that mainstream development strategies had not done much for women, and that WID was closely associated with efforts to improve women's position in the capitalistic development system rather than change that system, some scholars and activists in both the North and South began calling for a new approach to women's development. GAD focused on gender, that is, on the social construction of gender roles and relations (Marchand and Parpart 1995, 14). Although GAD was intended to draw in more men, not all men were convinced that these issues need to be raised or that the status of women should be made equal to that of men.

Building on many of the insights of both socialist and postmodernist feminism, the empowerment perspective argues for a development that is more squarely embedded in the particular experiences faced by women and men in the South. The empowerment approach deconstructs the discourse of development, seeing it as Western biased; it affirms the multiple realities of women, particularly their situated, localized character. In this process, Third World women become participants in, rather than recipients of, the development process (Chowdhry 1995, 36–39).

WOMEN'S ROLES IN THAI DEVELOPMENT

The early phase of the industrialization process in Thailand brought about many changes in families and communities. In this phase, only men migrated out to work for income; women were left in the domestic domain to take care of the children and the home. But with the full development of the cash economy, men were not able to earn sufficient cash to pay family expenses, and women had to leave home to work for cash as well. Someone else had to raise the children. It has been reported that during the economic boom, a visitor to a village found only children and grandparents. The men and women of working age had all left to work in the factories (Social Agenda Working Group 2001).

As organized in Thailand, factory work cannot accommodate married couples. Only men—married or unmarried—and unmarried women join the formal economic sector. Married women with children prefer to work in the informal sector, selling street foods, for example, which gives them the flexibility to look after small children. Industrialization has had a major impact on women and the family. The more industrialized the country became, the more women were alienated from their families. Migration split families, resulting in temporary single-parent households or broken homes. The loosening of kinship ties and the disappearance of residential extended families and mutual-aid units are consequences that are particularly hard on women. At the same time, many income-generating activities were initiated, promoted by both government and nongovernmental organizations, to help bring cash income to families. Home-based activities were introduced, including craft production as well as sub-contracted manufacturing to supply factories (Pongsapich et al. 2002).

The financial and economic crises in Asia in 1997 affected women in different ways. Women workers in the formal sector were affected in two stages. The first year after the crisis, workers in the financial sector were the first group to be hit, and men and women both were laid off. Women learned to shift from office work to self-employment in the informal sector. The second year after the crisis, women workers in factories were laid off. When the manufacturing sector collapsed, many women went home to their villages. Home-based work and local crafts became the alternative, and women learned to organize to survive.

Garment manufacturers cut costs by turning to subcontract work. Women who had experience with factory-style sewing machines organized to form networks. They invested in heavy-duty factory-style sewing machines and now work at home, awaiting orders from Bangkok that have to be turned around quickly. Precut slacks sent to the villages are returned within a few days. Women sew 14 to 15 hours a day to try to produce as many slacks as physically possible to make the most money in a short period. Then they wait for a new order. The men try to help by finishing small details or taking care of the necessary household chores during the rush period, although house cleaning and other household routine activities are often neglected during the few days when household manufacturing takes place. Each woman tries to sew about ten pairs of slacks, assembling all parts, attaching the pockets, sewing in the zipper, and then hemming. Pants with many pockets are paid a few baht more per pair. In all, each pair earned a seamstress only 17 baht in 2001, which is about US$0.40, and ten slacks were worth only approximately US$4.00–5.00 (Pongsapich and Bunjongjit 2003).

In 2003 the government began promoting its One Tambon (Subdistrict)/One Product (OTOP) program. Community members organize themselves to manufacture a product as a community enterprise, usually crafts or foods. Many women's groups produce attractive goods, and marketing is now the main problem. Since the government is promoting OTOP all over the country, women's groups are competing among themselves, and they are learning to cope for survival (Petprasert 1999).

NEW SOCIAL MOVEMENTS AND THE GROWTH OF CIVIL SOCIETY

The civil society movement is a form of new social movement, a concept Habermas (1981) reintroduced that has become a concrete reality during the past two decades. Andre Gunder Frank and Marta Fuentes (1989) argue that "new" social movements are really "old," but have some new features. Antiglobalization movements in particular demonstrate these new characteristics. In the new social movements paradigm, the definition of "politics" has moved beyond its traditional association with the nation-state, government, and political parties. The new social movements are "resistance movements" and "civil disobedience," not against any particular nation-state or government, but against a transnational identity that has been imposed by development theories and practices. The demand is for more space for ordinary people, for reducing the gap between the government and the people, and for asking for more humane government.

Social movements bring a shift from representative democracy to dialogic democracy, allowing for public discourse and negotiation and reinterpreting the meaning of democracy. In liberal theory, concepts of personal rights and social justice frequently come into conflict. Giddens (1994) suggests a concept of radical democratic theory that is more responsive to plural conditions. New social movements draw on theories of civil disobedience to argue that forms of political activity that are illegal may nonetheless be legitimate.

New social movements differ from civil society movements of the past. Voluntary organizations, nonprofit organizations, and nongovernmental organizations are usually viewed as community-based or civic groups that cooperate with the government. But this cooperation depoliticizes them. In contrast, the new social movements politicize civil society, raising concern over broad public issues rather than merely promoting the well-being of certain disadvantaged groups.

In theory and practice, the new social movements challenge conventional representative democracy and traditional concepts of government. They do not call for replacing "government" with "governance," but advocate for a more proactive strategy to bring social justice to global society. New social movements, which in many countries have taken the form of antiglobalization movements, are linked together transnationally and have a high degree of flexibility. They create a political space for negotiation with other supranational structures, which increases their ability to negotiate with the state as well.

The development of different forms of civil society organizations in Thailand can best be understood through a historical perspective. Traditional Buddhist temples performed the philanthropic function of providing for those in need and also served as community centers. Later on, different forms of organizations appeared with the arrival of missionaries and Chinese immigrants. The impact of Western influences, social heterogeneity, and the spread of communist ideology brought about changes in the activities of civil society organizations, which were viewed by the government at the time as possible threats to national security. In order to control activities of civil society groups, the government passed the National Cultural Act 1942 and established the National Cultural Commission. The act states that philanthropy and cultural promotion organizations need to be registered at the commission. Independent political and advocacy activities were not allowed.

During and after World War II, the government reasoned that the threat of communism from China justified exercising control over civil society organizations. The National Cultural Act promoted Thai culture and provided welfare and social services, but these were regulated by the government. Well-known groups that formed during this period include organizations belonging to the National Council of Women and the Social Welfare Council of Thailand, philanthropic organizations, school alumni groups, and Chinese dialect and clan associations. Some organizations operated under royal patronage; a few "royal projects" that operated as nonprofit organizations did not officially register.

The student uprising in 1973 led to the overthrow of the authoritarian military regime followed by the return of the right wing government in 1976. Many students and farmers joined the Communist Party of Thailand and some went into exile. In 1980, after the fall of the party and the government's amnesty announcement, many reoriented themselves to Thai society. Returnees formed many grassroots groups that focused mainly on rural and urban development; others organized advocacy activities. These groups are called nongovernmental organizations in contrast to the organizations established earlier by upper-class women, which are thought of as philanthropic. During the 1990s, politicized people's organizations such as the Forum of the Poor became very active.

As in the Philippines, in Thailand local activists played a key role in toppling the authoritarian military regime in 1986, and NGOs have played an active political role ever since. NGOs and civil society groups were recognized in the Sixth National Development Plan (1986–91), which stipulates that government and nongovernmental organizations should work together on development activities. During the Sixth Plan the NGO Coordinating Committee for Development (NGO-COD) was established. Approximately 220 organizations became members of NGO-COD (Pongsapich and Kataleeradabhan 1997). Other bodies include working groups for child welfare, primary health care, human rights, and slum development organizations, each with memberships of from twenty to thirty organizations.

The civil society movement became stronger during the 1990s when the need for political and social reforms was more widely recognized. The military coup d'état in February 1991 established an interim government led by Anand Panyarachun. After the April 1992 election, General Suchinda Kraprayoon, a leader of the 1991 coup, was nominated as prime minister. A coalition group led by the Student Federation of Thailand and the Confederation for Democracy opposed the Suchinda government. The protest ended in bloodshed in May 1992, indicating that political development lagged behind economic development. During the currency crisis of 1997–98 it became apparent that economic development was not that far advanced either.

In the 1990s, civil society organizations adopted the strategy of monitoring political as well as economic activities in the country. From 1992 to 1997, increasing demands were made for a new constitution and for the participation of the people in the drafting process. The 1997 constitution is the most advanced political reform in the region. Since the economic crisis of 1997, civil society groups have been monitoring the impact of economic and financial crises and putting the spotlight on corruption cases, through many groups including Poll Watch, Gender Watch, Corruption Watch, WTO Watch, and Social Watch. Civil society groups investigate the role of international financial institutions (the World

Bank, IMF, and the Asian Development Bank), and monitor poverty eradication programs.

Transnational civil society movements are also active in the Asian region, including transnational antiglobalization and antidam movements. Networking is now the dominant feature of civil society movements, and movements against dam construction are particularly strong. Antidam groups have linked together to exchange information on specific dam construction projects and have pooled financial and human resources to help organize demonstrations or mass rallies. For example, techniques used in the opposition to the Sardar Sarovar Dam on the Narmada River in India were transferred to Thailand to help the protest against the Pak Mun Dam. NGOs in Thailand have been able to stop or postpone construction of the Nam Choan Dam, the Kaeng Krung Dam, and others that were planned by the Royal Irrigation Department and the Electricity Generating Authority of Thailand (Pongsapich and Kataleeradabhan 1997).

HUMAN-CENTERED DEVELOPMENT: ENVIRONMENT AND POVERTY ISSUES

Women and development was a focus of the 1985 World Conference on Women, but the link between women and environment was only one of its many themes. By contrast, the role of women was highlighted in the UNEP State of the Environment Report 1988 and its subsequent publications on women and environment. According to Annabel Rodda:

> Women's contribution to making the environment a central issue has been significant. In 1962, the publication of Rachel Carson's *Silent Spring* focused attention on the dangers of pesticides. Since the 1970s, women's groups and organizations have been very active in promoting environmental awareness, education and protection. Women make up a large part of Western Europe's Green parties, both as members and party leaders. All over the developing world, women play a crucial role in environmental management; as farmers, stockbreeders, suppliers of fuel and water, they interact most closely with the environment. They are the managers, and often the preservers of natural resources. The crucial role of women in environmental issues has long been recognized in the developing countries. The empowerment of women is vital if they are to participate fully. (Rodda 1991, 5–6)

Women are often victims of ecological crises. In 1974, twenty-seven women of Reni in northern India took simple but effective action to stop tree felling. They threatened to hug the trees if the lumberjacks attempted to cut them down.

The women's protest known as the Chipko (Hindi for "to embrace or hug") movement also gave visibility to two basic complaints of local women: commercial felling by contractors damaged many standing trees, and teak and eucalyptus monoculture plantations were replacing valuable indigenous forests (K. Warren 1997, 5).

The Chipko movement attracted worldwide attention. The image of poor, rural women in the hills of northern India standing with their arms around trees was romantic and compelling. The Chipko movement can be considered an important success story in the fight to secure women's rights in the process of local community development through forestry and in environmental protection. There was a sustained dialogue between the Chipko workers (originally men) and the victims of the environmental disasters in the hill areas of Garhwal (chiefly women). Women, who were solely in charge of cultivation, livestock, and children, lost all they had because of recurring floods and landslides. Women were able to perceive the link between their victimization and the denuding of mountain slopes by commercial interests. Thus, sheer survival made women support the movement, with implications for possible changes in gender relationships in the Garhwali society (S. Jain 1991).

Changes in the agro-ecosystem may affect women and men differently. Declining swidden fallow time and lower yields mean more work for women, because in order to produce the same amount of food, women must cultivate more land or cultivate the same land more intensively. Sometimes available land is farther away. More intensive weeding is required, because the shorter fallow periods are less effective in suppressing weed growth. Loss of forest requires women to spend more time foraging at greater distances or to plant gardens to produce substitutes for forest products.

Peasant groups in Southeast Asia have responded in different ways. Civil society groups develop different coping strategies. In terms of natural resource management, they have recommended "alternative means." Alternative agriculture, alternative energy, alternative medicine groups are relative newcomers to Thai civil society and are linked to a network of branches dispersed in different parts of many countries. In cases of conflict over natural resource management, they have negotiated compromises with governments through long negotiation processes.

Data on gendered land use among the Tai in Northern Vietnam indicates that the collection of natural products varies by gender and age and is affected by the season, household needs, and the market. Women and men use different natural products to generate their shares of their families' livelihood. Women are more likely to collect plant products, while men are more likely to harvest timber and hunt and trap wild animals. Women gather a greater variety of natural products than do men and appear to spend much more time at gathering than do men. They have knowledge of medicinal plants. Both men and women have benefited from sales of forest products, so the depletion of wild plants and animals affects both women's and men's sources of income (Sowerwine 1999).

Women are more likely to use natural products directly, while men are more likely to sell natural products and use the income. As agricultural growth stagnates, forest resources dwindle, and population growth continues, more families may be forced to hire out their labor in order to purchase food. Only men are involved in this activity, which usually requires heavy physical labor for low pay. Poor women are especially likely to suffer as their labor (in swidden and forest) becomes the mainstay of their household economy (Ireson-Doolittle and Ireson 1999).

During 1980s, protests against reforestation plans to introduce monocropped tree plantations or other forms of commercial forestry occurred in most developing countries. NGOs encouraged local communities to make their voices heard. Local leaders were identified and activities organized to stop forest concessions. NGO-COD worked with grassroots groups. Debates on the question of whether people and the forest can coexist took place throughout the decade. The Royal Forestry Department took the position that hill people should be removed from conservation forest areas. However, ethnic hill people had been living in the forest areas prior to their demarcation, and many royal projects had supported hill people for decades. The issue of community forestry has not been resolved and resulted in three competing drafts of the Community Forestry Act by the government, political parties, and civil society (CUSRI 1988).

GRASSROOTS WOMEN AND THE PROTECTION OF THE ENVIRONMENT IN THAILAND: DEMAND FOR ACCESS TO NATURAL RESOURCES FOR THE POOR

The government recognition, in 1980, of the role of civil society in development activities spurred the formation of grassroots groups. They have worked together with middle-class student activists who settled in village and slum communities to work hand in hand with the poor. Together, grassroots groups and student activists questioned the goals of the standard development model, suggesting the need to shift from growth-centered to human-centered development. This change is especially relevant for organizations working with specific target groups. Organizations working with women and children, for example, realized that they needed to move away from welfare-oriented approaches to encourage more self-help and development that preserved the natural environment. They linked demands to meet the basic needs of the people to their basic rights. Women's development organizations were active and their work reached the grassroots level, with support of the government as well as NGOs.

Grassroots groups demanded that the people participate in the decision-making processes that determine development activities. Peasant movements became stronger, making demands at the village or provincial level and later moving their efforts to Bangkok to have their voices heard. Every year, during the dry season, peasant movements as well as urban poor movements gathered in front of the government house. The Forum of the Poor was unofficially recognized by the government in 1996; its encampment and rallies are a familiar sight to the Thai public. The Forum, or Assembly, of the Poor, is made of groups affected by government projects to build infrastructure and facilitate industrialization. Diverse groups (ranging from environmental NGOs, academics, civic groups, unidentified support groups and individuals, and the participants themselves) support its activities.

Villagers have joined together to make their needs known for many years. Available statistics indicate that during the boom period in 1988 there were 170 rallies, which some labeled "mobs." During the Chuan and Banharn governments in 1993 and 1994, there were 739 and 754 marches and rallies, respectively. Of these, 37 percent were environmentally related in 1993 and 44 percent in 1994 (Pintoptaeng 1998, 5).

In 1996, the Forum staged a monthlong encampment in Bangkok and obtained agreements in principle from the Banharn coalition government to compensate Forum members for land appropriations or losses of livelihood. The subsequent Chavalit government also agreed to allocate funds. During 1996–97, the Forum developed an agenda of seven issues. Five of these are rural, including the use of forests and land, the building of dams, land appropriation for government projects, the promotion of alternative agriculture, and the livelihood of small fishermen. The remaining issues are urban, related to slums and occupational health.

These seven concerns have remained the organization's priorities since 1998. But because of the impact of the 1997 economic crisis and the government's limited financial resources, the Forum is focusing its energies on monitoring and following up earlier agreements. To counter its relative powerlessness vis-à-vis the government, the Forum has publicized its campaign to seek justice with three mottoes: *sajja* (truthfulness), *ahinsa* (nonviolence), and *taba* (patience).

THE EMPOWERMENT OF GRASSROOTS WOMEN IN ENVIRONMENTAL ISSUES

The following cases show specific ways in which women have played key roles in grassroots organizations attempting to halt or shape government infrastructure projects.

Case 1: The Rasisalai Dam

The construction of this dam created an agrarian movement of peasants demanding their rights, mostly in the form of land that they were forced to evacuate for dam construction or forestry projects. Pha Kongtham or "Mae Pha" is the name people call a 60-year-old woman who has been working with men from these areas to demand a study on the social impacts of the dam.

In the case of the Rasisalai Dam, the government decided to give 363 million baht in compensation to 1,154 affected persons in October 1997. It created some confusion because many more people made demands based on claims to the same plots. In November 1999, another 57 million baht was made available for compensation of those who had been evacuated to make way for the reservoir and who had not received compensation earlier. The government disbursed additional funds in June 2000, only to face more demands. Mae Pha together with her villager colleagues demanded that investigation be made to clarify the contradicting claims. There were accusations of corruption. The minister then ordered the reservoir to be emptied to allow for a proper ownership survey to provide an accurate mapping of land ownership pattern prior to the construction of the dam so that compensation could be made accordingly. However, it turned out that even when the reservoir was drained, contradicting claims could not be resolved.

Mae Pha and her colleagues are members of the Forum of the Poor, which is continuously monitoring developments and taking steps to assure that future decisions are made with accountability, predictability, transparency, and participation—the four components of good governance. They have requested another study of the social impacts of the Rasisalai Dam, which is now being carried out.

Case 2: The Hin Grud Coal-Fired Plant

This case also illustrates how people are demanding the right to protect community resources and prevent new infrastructure projects. Jintana Kaewkhao is the woman leader who resisted the construction of the coal-fired plant. In 1998, it was difficult for residents of Prachuab Khirikhan province to understand why there should be three coal-fired power plants in one province. When the Electrical Generating Authority of Thailand (EGAT) together with the National Energy Policy Office (NEPO) agreed to adopt the Independent Power Producer Policy (IPP), the intention was to lessen the burden on the state energy authority by encouraging the private sector to generate power and supply it to EGAT at a profit. Each plant took the responsibility to identify power sources, decide the location of the plant, and choose the technology required to generate power. The three projects, one of which is EGAT's and the other two joint-ventures, each selected Prachuab Khirikhan due to its long coastline, which is suitable for transporting better quality imported coal from Indonesia and Australia. The use of local coal and inferior power plant design in Mae Moh, Lampang province in the north had caused severe air pollution, creating a notorious health hazard.

All three investors individually submitted their feasibility and environmental impact assessment studies to the Office of Environmental Policy and Planning (OEPP) of the Ministry of Science, Technology and Environment. OEPP approval of each of the studies passed separately from the National Environmental Board to the cabinet. Before construction, permission is required from the provincial office and the Department of Public Works in the Ministry of Interior. Consultation with local administration and public hearings are also required for all infrastructure construction. Public relations and information dissemination are considered vital initial steps for projects related to the environment.

Jintana Kaewkhao, a woman in her late forties, led the people of Hin Grud Village, the site where one of the plants is to be located, in protest against the construction of the coal-fired power plant in the village. The people demanded explanations of health hazards and the impact on air pollution and called for preventive measures.

In December 1998, people of Prachuab Khirikhan and their Subdistrict Administrative representatives marched to the South Highway that connects Bangkok with all southern provinces and blocked all traffic for many hours. The incident lasted overnight and perishable goods including seafood and vegetables were destroyed. Police troops were sent in and the rally was broken up after the Deputy Minister of Interior, who oversees the Department of Public Works, informed the protesters that the permission for construction had not been granted. The rally was broken up, but further negotiations and public hearings continued, citing the public's right to information as stated in the 1997 Constitution. As a result, EGAT put its project on hold indefinitely. The other two joint-venture plants continue to face resistance from the public. The Environmental Impact Assessment Studies were questioned and additional studies were required. Official public hearing sessions took place in 1999 and the new Environmental Impact Assessment reports are being scrutinized.

Case 3: The Khlong Dan Waste Water Treatment Plant

In 1993, the Pollution Control Department (PCD) counted 5,200 factories spilling out industrial waste in the city of Samut Prakan. The Ministry of Science and Environment decided to set up a wastewater treatment plant, and the cabinet approved a budget of 13.6 billion baht in October 1995. The Asian Development Bank (ADB) offered a loan for a turnkey project. The consortium of six construction firms who won the contract suggested some changes to the original design. Instead of two plants in the two areas where most of the factories are located, they advised constructing one big plant 20 km (12.4 miles) away at Khlong Dan. The budget was increased by 10 billion baht.

The relocation of the project onto the Klong Dan site threatened a highly productive fishery. The unusual currents around the river mouth create a unique marine environment in the mangroves of Khlong Dan that is especially good for shellfish farming. The villagers who depend on these fisheries were not consulted about the project, which they only found out about when the contractor erected a sign. Despite local protests, the project was not halted (*The Nation*, April 15, 2002).

Dawan Chantarahassadee, a grassroots woman in her forties, led a group of local people to protest. She represented a network that informed the public that some politicians and public servants had vested interests in the consortium of six construction firms undertaking the project. She urged the government to suspend the project, which she said lacked transparency. She and other opponents of the Khlong Dan project threatened to expose the alleged irregularities.

Meanwhile the Asian Development Bank established an inspection panel to investigate the case. According to the *Bangkok Post*, the ADB admitted it was wrong to lend money for the project because it breached the bank's principles of transparency and environmental conservation (*Bangkok Post*, April 10, 2002). On 26 March 2002, Dawan Chantarahassadee and another villager, Chalao Timthong, together with Narong Khomklom, the mayor of Khlong Dan, submitted a letter to Tadao Chino, president of the ADB. They expressed their concerns about the inspection process on the grounds that members of the Board Inspection Committee had not been able to visit the site. Despite that weakness, the inspection report made it clear that the ADB had made serious errors in the appraisal, approval, and implementation of the project, and they asked that the ADB stop its financial support. The investigation is still ongoing and the National Counter Corruption Committee is looking into the matter.

Case 4: The Thai/Malaysia Natural Gas Project

In May 2002, there was a protest against the government's decision to continue with a joint Thai-Malaysian natural gas project despite the opposition of grassroots groups. The government claimed that the joint venture project had been initiated in the early 1980s and should not be revoked. The project is designed to bring natural gas from a jointly owned seabed area bordering Thailand and Malaysia. A site in the Thai province of Songkhla, Lan Hoi Siaip, has been selected for the separation plant from which gas will be transported to the respective destinations. During the first five years, the gas is to be sent to Malaysia; after that, Thailand will use the gas.

Grassroots organizations in Songkhla province oppose the decision because they are concerned about the impact of downstream industrial development activities such as petroleum-related production plants or an industrial estate that appears in the master plan introduced by the National Economic and Social Development Board. Alisa Mudmoh, a woman Muslim leader, established a protest center at Lan Hoi Siap, a Muslim community that has been identified as the construction site. She worked closely with the protesters to negotiate with the government to stop the project. The government sent out a team to carry out a feasibility study to supplement the original one carried out earlier by a research team from Prince of Songkhla University. The government decided to relocate the project to a site 5 km (3.1 miles) away.

CHANGING THE DEVELOPMENT PARADIGM

These four cases demonstrate the different perceptions of two stakeholders, the people who are affected by these projects and development professionals. Women leaders have clearly demonstrated their ability to lead social movements for sustainability of the community and the environment. As political actors, the people claim a natural morality (J. Scott 1986, 1988) and call on the principle of environmental sustainability, while infrastructure developers adopt the modernization dynamic of industrial capitalist societies and label the natural morality environmentalists "antirationalist." Although many in environmental circles hold antidevelopment views, they have not been persuasive in the political arena where this discourse has been easily delegitimized by the dominant rationalist and modernization discourse.

The debate here is how to balance the instrumental rationality of industrialization with another instrumental rationality based on management of the environment and natural capital. The modernist paradigm emphasizes industrialization and economic development, but grassroots people want a human-centered development paradigm that is respectful of nature. Some have adopted James C. Scott's idea of "the moral economy" to counter conventional capitalist and bureaucratic arguments.

Another issue being debated is whether decisions should be centralized or localized. Should local people sacrifice their natural resources for the benefit of a broader, national public? Local people who have less political power and often less professional knowledge are disadvantaged compared to national policy advocates. Their only hope is to seek support from transnational networks. All four movements can also be viewed as resistance movements. They are not based on abstract arguments about globalization, but on the support of people who are directly impacted by these projects, especially women who must feed their families.

WOMEN AND POVERTY PROGRAMS

There has been a decline in the role of agriculture in the Thai economy since the 1960s. In many countries, urban infrastructure development has resulted in large-scale entry of women into urban labor markets. Yet, social policy and legislation have not kept up with the changes. The World Bank study *Voices of the Poor* (Narayan et al. 2000) states that poor people across a majority of communities report that women's roles are undergoing tremendous change. Male unemployment and deepening economic stress have placed greater responsibilities on women to seek paid work. Women are stepping outside of their household responsibilities to earn a living and help bring food to the table. Diversification of women's work is being observed everywhere. Both women's and men's traditional gender roles are changing, sometimes marginally, sometimes more dramatically. Increasingly, household budgets depend on women's earning capacities.

Although women may be working in larger numbers than ever outside the home, the demanding responsibilities of running a household seem to remain largely theirs. Meanwhile discrimination based on gender remains widespread and entrenched despite changing laws in some countries, limiting women's access to higher wages. At the household level, people perceive that major changes are underway in gender relations. With increased economic hardship and a decline in poor men's traditional livelihood strategies, more poor women have had to make their way into the informal economy, primarily in low-paying and often menial work. These changes are placing stress on households. Poor people mention domestic violence in many forms with greater frequency, which is due to the breakdown of traditional norms.

The UNDP Human Poverty Report (2000d) states that most development practitioners now agree that poverty is not about income alone but is multidimensional. The report also observes the gender insensitivity of most poverty programs which generally have weak theoretical and practical links between gender and poverty. Poverty programs have not incorporated gender as an important dimension, and gender programs have not done well in focusing on poverty. According to the report "Combating gender inequality is not the same thing as combating poverty." In attempting to "mainstream" their issues, "poverty programs and gender programs have often neglected the intersection between them—poor women" (UNDP 2000d).

The World Bank's *World Development Report 2000/2001* finds that in many countries women continue to be denied even basic legal rights. Poor women face a double disadvantage in access to resources and voice—they are poor, and they are women. Furthermore:

> Poor people have much less access to education and health care than the nonpoor, and the gender gap in these services is larger among poor people. The same is true for credit and agricultural extension services; unless strong countervailing measures are taken, the poor receive less than the nonpoor, and women receive the least. Studies from many countries show that agricultural extension agents focus on male farmers,

even though women are often the primary cultivators, because husbands work off the farm. So women are disadvantaged not only in land ownership, but in gaining access to the resources and information that would improve yields. (World Bank 2001b, 118)

Attempts to help women deal with poverty have been diverse. The one most closely related to the environment issue is land titling. The Rasisalai Dam protest led by Mae Pha is related to land and land titling for future use. When the dam was being constructed, people living in the area where the reservoir was to be constructed were relocated. Land in the reservoir area had no titles. People only knew where their plots were. These people to be relocated were to be given farmland as well as land for residence or be compensated in cash. Compensation has been given to some but not others, and an overall solution has not been found. In the process, however, land compensations were made to family units, not individuals. There is no plan to address women's needs for land.

In addition to land, any program to address women and poverty should incorporate issues of human security, which emphasizes two principles: freedom from want and freedom from fear (UNDP 1994). Personal insecurity in the form of family violence is increasingly reported, which is often linked to male control of housing and land, and other issues (such as food, health, environmental, political, and community security) have not been given sufficient importance. Security for women in all these areas has been neglected. Dawan, the woman leader protesting against the construction of the wastewater treatment plant, and her colleagues are insecure economically and environmentally. Their fishing occupation is being threatened, and the wastewater treatment plant may produce waste that is environmentally dangerous.

Jintana of Hin Grud, Prachuabkhirikhan province and Alisa Mudmoh in Songkhla will be less secure if the coal-fired plant and the natural gas separation plant are constructed. The people who support the protests do not want these development projects. They claim that their traditional way of life is preferable to the changes these projects will bring. Their personal and community security are threatened. They do not have freedom from fear.

In the late 1980s the World Commission on Environment and Development (the Brundtland Commission) drew attention to important links between increasing poverty and environmental degradation. It stated that many parts of the world were caught in a vicious downward spiral. Poor people were forced to overuse environmental resources to survive from day to day, and the impoverishment of their environment further impoverished them, making their survival even more difficult and uncertain (WCED 1987, 27). This linkage is called the poverty-environment hypothesis. However, this hypothesis was later criticized as too simplistic. "The two-way link between poverty and environmental degradation as the fundamental premise of mainstream sustainable development thinking tended to focus on only some of the relevant factors such as inadequate technical know-how and managerial capabilities, common property resource management, and pricing and subsidy policies. It ignored many other important factors, notably deeper socio-political changes and changes in cultural values" (Hayes 2001).

The UNDP Human Poverty Report (2000d) indicates that national poverty programs seldom have strong environmental and natural resources components. Although planners generally recognize that the environment and natural resources have implications for the poor, these have not been reflected in their anti-poverty programs or organizational structures. One attempt to link poverty and the environment is a collaborative project between the UNDP and the European Commission. The Poverty and Environment Initiative

> has tried to debunk several myths about the links between poverty and the environment. A central myth is that population growth and lack of resources compels the poor to damage the environment. This myth claims that the environmental damage then leads to a downward spiral of increased impoverishment and further environmental damage. But there is no such straightforward causal link between the two. Much depends on the specific situation and on public policies. Win-win solutions start with the assumption that the poor are part of the solution, not the source of the problem. In many areas it is private companies or state agencies that cause the most environmental damage — by felling forests, diverting water, polluting the air or saturating the land with chemicals. (UNDP 2000d, 98–99)

CONCLUSION: POVERTY PROGRAMS, WOMEN, AND THE ENVIRONMENT

Many now recognize that the growth-centered development paradigm is no longer appropriate, as it is producing weak growth and deepening inequities in the globalized economy. Gaps between developed and developing countries have been widening. The growth paradigm created competition among nations to the detriment of the disadvantaged nations who have fallen behind even further. Environmental degradation has been observed in most development activities, and this has exacerbated poverty.

Future economic development should not be at the cost of the environment and should not weaken human and social capital. Development plans need to adopt the social development paradigm proposed at the World Summit for Social Development in 1995 in Copenhagen and confirmed in Geneva in 2000, which states that special attention should be given to the poor, unemployed, and all vulnerable groups. Measures should be taken to ensure that the impact of global and national development does not result in increasing numbers of the poor. Cases in Thailand indicate clearly that the poor and women have been impacted negatively, both before and after the 1997 crisis.

Similarly, the unemployed—both men and women—who are affected by changing patterns of international trade need to be guaranteed a minimum standard of living. The economic and financial crisis that resulted from globalization showed that the new unemployed were unable to cope because governmental and private safety nets were inadequate or nonexistent. Traditional social capital was destroyed during the period of economic boom and further undermined during the crisis. In the next decade, appropriate mechanisms need to be developed at the global, regional, and national levels to respond to the negative impacts of development. Mechanisms need to be made available both for workers in export manufacturing units and for farmers in the agricultural sector.

Another shift has taken place since 2000, when civil society groups moved forward to protest the inadequacies of the idea of a New International Economic Order (NIEO), which was the development agenda of the United Nations in the 1970s, and has continued to be proposed. There is a need to propose a new international *social* order instead. The World Social Forum holds meetings in different locations parallel to the World Economic Forum that takes place in Davos every year to promote the view that future economic development should not be at the cost of social development.

At the transnational level, a group of women's movements have formed the International Gender and Trade Network (IGTN). IGTN supported the call that originated in Latin America for a global day of protest against the WTO on 13 September 2003; several women's networks held an International Women's Forum as part of the People's Forum in Cancun. Gigi Francisco, who was in Cancun for DAWN/IGTN, reported on 14 September (when the WTO meetings were cancelled):

> There is much jubilation among the NGOs and social movements in Cancun. Tonight is the night of celebrations. Once again the rapidity with which economies of the South are being pried open by the WTO, causing harm to their people's livelihoods,

has been halted. Critical to the outcome of the meeting were the impressive unity and solidarity among the developing countries in rejecting a trade agreement that is anti-development, and the close relationship between them and the NGOs and social movements throughout the Ministerial Meeting. Several mass actions inside and outside the WTO meeting perimeter were carried out to show dissatisfaction with the arrogance and high handedness of developed countries. (Francisco 2003)

If a human-centered development paradigm is to be adopted, vulnerable groups, including the poor and women, must be directly involved in the process, building on grassroots organizations and knowledge and with roles and space for other vulnerable groups, including the elderly, people with disabilities, and ethnic minorities. Subsidies and other measures may be necessary to enable vulnerable groups to become involved in producing for export and share the gains from international trade.

For women in social movements, the issues have shifted from placing the priority on gender equality and gender and development to gender and the environment and trade-related issues. The case studies presented here involved resistance to infrastructure projects that would have had negative effects on the environment and on the health or employment of people living nearby. The projects themselves are justified to support trade and growth-centered development activities, so it is logical that women's movements have gradually moved from environmental to trade issues. The government claims to be employing "dual track" development strategies that will promote a "sufficiency economy" as well as growth. This approach has lifted some women, who are involved in craft and food production, out of poverty. But this strategy is not enough, and the case studies presented here represent a more radical stance; they are antiglobalization movements, operating at the grassroots level.

T-Shirts to Web Links: Women Connect!
Communications Capacity-Building with Women's NGOs

Doe Mayer, Barbara Pillsbury, and Muadi Mukenge

There is a tradition in the Buganda ethnic group in Uganda that when the king marries he takes a young virgin into his household along with his wife. That girl is given a home and support, but she is taken out of school and deprived of a normal life. In 1998 when the current king married, women's groups in Uganda mobilized to rescue the 12-year-old girl who had been chosen for this "honor." Led by ISIS-WICCE *in Kampala, they e-mailed colleagues all over the world asking them to e-mail the king with their concerns about this traditional practice. After receiving a huge number of protest messages, the king decided the practice was not appropriate for a modern monarch and allowed the young girl to go back to her family and school.*

This true story illustrates how the Internet can strengthen the voices of women in parts of the world where they have traditionally been stifled. The Internet helps these groups connect to the world and to each other. But it also is a powerful tool for social change. The women's organizations in Uganda used their activism around this case to highlight the importance of education for girls and prevention of early marriage. They weren't just trying to rescue this one girl; there are thousands of girls in Uganda who do not finish school and who therefore lack the tools education gives them to improve their lives. By using the Internet to provoke international outcry, these groups both embarrassed the Buganda king into making a change and at the same time highlighted the broader public issues that are central to women's human rights.

Over the past two decades, women have come together worldwide to work for greater rights for women and girls. Thousands of women's nongovernmental organizations (NGOs) have organized to improve some particular aspect of women's lives (Naples and Desai 2002). To achieve their goals, these groups must engage in communication with others: community members and politicians, the media, and like-minded groups. Communication skills are central to an organization's success.

As the Buganda case illustrates, the ability to communicate effectively to diverse audiences is critical to making change happen. Bringing about change generally involves altering ways of thinking that are so deeply ingrained that few—whether villagers or political leaders—see that there is anything wrong. The communication strategies women's NGOs use to bring about change span a broad range, from slogan-bearing T-shirts to the Internet and Web sites. However, many if not most women's NGOs know they still have much to learn about communication and media campaigns.

THE PROJECT

Women Connect! was a five-year effort to support the desire of women's NGOs in developing countries to communicate more effectively. The Pacific Institute for Women's Health and the Annenberg Center for Communication at the University of Southern California, both based in Los Angeles, carried out the project collaboratively between 1997 and 2002. The goals of Women Connect! were to contribute to women's empowerment through collaboration, communications capacity-building, and information-sharing; and to help women strengthen their organizations and their ability to achieve their own objectives, especially in the areas of women's health and well-being, broadly defined. The project's operating hypothesis was that an organization maximizes its impact only by strengthening a broad range of communications capacities, including but not limited to information communication technologies.

Women's organizations are an important force for women's empowerment and for reducing inequity (Oxaal and Baden 1997). Women Connect! sought to help women's organizations use the power of information and communication tools to change women's lives.[1] The project focused on thirty NGOs in Zimbabwe, Zambia, and Uganda, but the lessons learned apply to communications work with women's groups throughout Africa, Asia, and Latin America.[2]

The project's emphasis on information technology was clearly ahead of the curve when it began in the mid-nineties, and the mainstream has now started to catch up. But the strategies it developed are still very current. Access to technology has greatly improved, but its use is still limited, especially in poor rural communities. This case study shows how communications can empower women's NGOs and speaks to three other important issues: how women's organizations empower women; how Northern organizations can best work with Southern (developing country) NGOs; and where women's health fits among priorities of women's NGOs.

ORIGINS OF THE PROJECT

Three distinct developments helped create the impetus for Women Connect!: the reconceptualization of women's empowerment that arose from the 1994 International Conference on Population and Development (ICPD), the expansion of health communication work, and the information technology boom.

The ICPD in Cairo: Women's Empowerment to
Improve Women's Reproductive Health

At the 1994 ICPD in Cairo, government delegates recognized that women's empowerment is an important goal in itself and essential for sustainable development; they also acknowledged that NGOs, especially women's NGOs, are playing key roles in population and family planning policies and programs. To be effective, responses to reproductive and sexual health challenges, such as HIV/AIDS, unintended pregnancy, and gender-based violence, require the involvement of women's NGOs and other civil society organizations with strong community ties (United Nations 1994, 22, 32). Women's organizations, which previously had been marginalized in development work, were increasingly being asked to join in as partners.

Health Communication: Training and
Programs with Government

Since the 1970s, international donor agencies have invested heavily in health communication efforts in developing countries, implemented largely through ministries of health. Millions of dollars have been dedicated to promoting family planning, nutrition, and child survival, and we have learned a great deal about how to communicate effectively with specific target audiences. Thousands of hours of training have helped personnel in ministries of health worldwide develop research, implementation, and evaluation skills in designing large-scale campaigns that use mass media, traditional media (such as posters, brochures, and folk drama), and person-to-person communication.[3] Evaluations showed positive results in changing attitudes and behavior, lowering birth rates, and saving lives (Piotrow et al. 1997, 11; Backer et al. 1992). An authoritative analysis of forty-eight health campaigns found that "7 to 10 percent more people in campaign communities changed their behavior than did in control communities" (Snyder 2001, 82). However, very little of this work was shared with women's or other NGOs, suggesting a serious gap that Women Connect! could address.

The Needs of Grassroots and Women's Organizations

Grassroots and community-based organizations develop in response to local or regional circumstances and typically act with tremendous enthusiasm and commitment to local and regional concerns. However, in spite of their understanding of problems in their communities and their desire to solve them, most NGOs have limited capacity to communicate effectively about these problems. Historically, these organizations have used various forms of traditional media—especially posters and brochures—to get their messages out to local rural and urban audiences, but they seldom thought strategically about how to use media to change attitudes. They were frequently unclear about whom they were trying to reach, and they rarely conducted research to gain a clear picture of what different people in their communities thought about the issues. They also rarely tested whether people understood the messages they were receiving or felt they were appropriate.

Many groups spent precious resources on outreach activities without knowing whether their efforts were having the desired effect. For example, if a donor gave money for work on HIV/AIDS, an organization might design a poster saying simply "AIDS is a killer" or produce a brochure telling people not to have unprotected sex. Often these were distributed without finding out what people really knew about AIDS or about pregnancy and sex and without studying what would convince people to accept new information, much less change their behavior. Organizations frequently produced messages that did not resonate with the local community, and the posters and brochures often ended up stacked on clinic shelves.

Often organizations talked down to their intended audiences or produced messages that were more effective in talking to themselves than in reaching their audiences. For example, a poster in Uganda told men to stop beating their wives because it is a "crime punishable by law"; this may have made the women who printed it feel better, but it is very unlikely that it changed men's behavior since the law was rarely enforced.

Groups need to understand clearly whom they are trying to reach and what messages might engage them. One common fallacy is thinking that all women or all members of the same ethnic group or tribe will think alike, when in fact there is significant diversity within any category. Messages must be geared to specific subgroups, especially when they challenge deeply held cultural beliefs. Class is the single most important determinant of health (Bunker, Gomby, and Kehrer 1989), but those who are educated and from upper middle classes may not understand the most appropriate messages for reaching less-advantaged people.

Effective campaigns involve appropriate audience research, pretesting of the messages and media, and evaluation of impact. Ideally, target communities will participate in the design and implementation of the campaign. The women's groups working with Women Connect! had a clear need to try these methodologies to increase the impact of their outreach efforts (Riaño 1994).

Information Communication Technology in Developing Countries

These three developments—the Cairo conference, the increased focus on health education, and the growth of grassroots movements and their greater role in international policy making—coincided with rapid advances in information communication technology (ICT) during the 1990s. Grassroots and community-based organizations often worked in relative isolation from like-minded groups within their own and other countries. As women's NGOs became increasingly aware of the power and the expanding use of ICT, they too aspired to get online.

The international donor community debated the appropriateness of introducing these new technologies in poorer countries. Many argued that it was premature where poverty was so great that basic needs for water, food, and shelter had not been met and where electricity and phone lines were lacking or unreliable. Still others asked why NGOs should worry about ICT when their access to conventional media (radio, television, newspapers) was still so limited (Lush et al. 2000, vi). These issues were especially debated in the African context (see Hafkin and Taggart 2001; Kole 2001).

But women's organizations in developing countries saw that ICT was being increasingly used by commercial enterprises and argued that they too could benefit. Many NGOs were already spending substantial sums on technologies—international phone calls, couriers, and faxes—that were costly ways to communicate.

As an NGO leader in Uganda put it, "The way the world is going, if you are not connected, you do not exist," adding that "Organizations, like individuals, also depend on information to plan, network and respond to societal needs."[4] The Economic Commission for Africa identified helping NGOs develop ICT capacity as a top priority (Economic Commission for Africa 1999).

THE PILOT PROJECT: WOMEN LINKING

Following the Cairo ICPD's recognition of the important role of women's NGOs,[5] it was a logical step to propose that the health communications work undertaken with government ministries be extended to women's NGOs. To achieve this, co-author Doe Mayer, director of the Program in Development Communication at the Annenberg Center for Communication at the University of Southern California, proposed a partnership and pilot project with the Pacific Institute for Women's Health, which had substantial experience working with developing country women's NGOs. The Pacific Institute was then engaged in worldwide evaluation research testing the conclusions drawn at Cairo through in-depth field studies with fifty-six women's NGOs in Africa, Asia, and Latin America that had received funding from the Global Fund for Women.[6] Mayer asked Dr. Barbara Pillsbury, a founder of the Pacific Institute and co-director of the Global Fund evaluation, to collaborate and identify a women's NGO appropriate for partnering in the pilot project. Carole Roberts, a specialist in educational technology, joined as technology coordinator.[7]

Mayer and the Pacific Institute chose to implement the pilot project in three African countries. A major factor was extremely active and enthusiastic women's rights movements in several countries, where women's NGOs played important roles in building civil society. Advocacy for reproductive and sexual health and rights figured prominently in these movements' agendas. Further, many of the African women's NGOs were enthusiastic about trying new approaches but were neophytes in thinking strategically about communications. As the continent of greatest need and with the least ability to acquire ICT without external collaboration and support, Africa provided a challenging test. Other efforts to provide ICT to Africa were in progress at the time, but these focused on governments and larger NGOs, not on the smaller more community-based women's organizations.[8] Finally, Africa faced the highest HIV/AIDS and maternal mortality rates in the world, a crisis that demanded new and imaginative approaches to communication (Parker et al. 2000).

The developing country partner for the pilot project was ACFODE (Action for

Development), a dynamic women's NGO in Kampala, Uganda, dedicated to improving the status and lives of Ugandan women by providing outreach and advocacy on such issues as inheritance rights, legal reform, and women's political participation in local and national government.

Women Linking, the pilot project, set out to test a two-pronged approach involving both communication campaigns and strategic use of media and ICT. Women Linking aimed to go beyond providing computers and "wiring" organizations to strengthening their ability to use all communication tools strategically. Although ICT is "sexier" than traditional media—posters, brochures, and such—we did not want participating groups to overlook the importance of using these other communications media well. In both components, women's health issues provided most of the content and were the central focus of case studies and materials shared with the participants.

Communication Campaigns and Strategic Use of Media

This project component introduced a scientific approach to communication campaigns, an emphasis new to most smaller NGOs. Many community-based groups have commonly used traditional media—such as posters, brochures, and folk drama—to reach their audiences. Although women's NGOs rely on these "small" media and face-to-face communication, the principles of mass media communication campaigns are relevant and appropriate to their work and can increase the success of their outreach efforts. A classic definition is that communication campaigns are "purposeful attempts to inform, persuade or motivate behavior changes in a relatively well-defined and large audience, generally for noncommercial benefits and/or society at large, typically within a given time period, by means of organized communication activities involving mass media and often complemented by inter-personal support" (Rice and Atkins 1989, 7). Women Linking thus included a component aimed at helping ACFODE develop a more strategic approach to communications, including planning and conducting media campaigns.

Information Communication Technology

The project's ICT component introduced new information technologies, especially e-mail and the Internet, to help link ACFODE with the world outside. Rejecting the view that Internet technology is too sophisticated and not appropriate for low-income women in developing countries, we argued that this is a crucial moment in history and that new technology is revolutionizing how we communicate and how we may mold the future. This innovation will either be profoundly empowering or leave the poor worse off, more isolated, and increasingly marginalized.

Because donors and Northern technical assistance organizations had already become involved in providing computers and software, many organizations already had computers but were not using them efficiently. Some groups kept their computer locked up in the boss's office under plastic or a heavy blanket; when organizations had several computers, they were often not networked and each had its own printer, a poor use of scarce resources. Our approach emphasized that technical connectivity alone is not enough, that the effective use of ICT requires much more than hardware, software, electricity, and a phone line. We believed it was critical to address how organizations incorporate ICT into their structures, including understanding the ways in which technology can change power relationships and affect organizational hierarchies. The project also took into account barriers to adoption or appropriate use. For example, some NGO directors were intimidated by ICT and resisted adopting these innovations, excluding younger staff members with interests and skills in these areas. The project emphasized ways that ICT used well could be empowering to both the organization and the women it serves.

Pilot Project Implementation and Results

In 1997, a two-person project team made two technical collaboration visits to Uganda to work with ACFODE.[9] The team provided training in communication campaign design and implementation to ACFODE members and other interested women's groups and conducted a workshop requested by ACFODE on advocacy techniques. The team connected ACFODE to e-mail and the Internet, conducted training in basic Web design and management, and set up a Web page online. Equally important, the project team provided training in the use of the new technology and led discussions about its potential and implications. The team set up a support committee within ACFODE to spearhead the innovation and identified local Ugandan consultants to work with the organization to provide additional technical and upgrade information as needed.

The results of this pilot project were instructive for designing an expanded follow-up project. A major lesson was that it took a compelling event, totally external to the project and ACFODE's work, for the ACFODE staff to get truly hooked on Internet use. In 1998, England's Princess Diana died in a car accident in Paris. Ugandans, who are part of the British Commonwealth, have great interest in the royal family. ACFODE staff, frustrated by the lack of information in Uganda's newspapers, turned to the Internet to get additional updates on the Diana story. This experience confirmed for them the importance of the Internet in connecting them to the broader world. Merely introducing technology does not automatically result in its use. It is only when people are personally motivated that they begin to incorporate it into their daily lives and begin to see the broader implications of what they can achieve.

A positive impact for ACFODE was its expanded capacity to attract and communicate with interested donors. Their Web site brought them an unsolicited major grant. A couple in the U.K. whose son had died in a plane crash after having lived in and loved Uganda wanted to commemorate him. The parents were impressed that ACFODE had a Web site, liked what ACFODE presented about itself, and contributed over US$80,000 to help ACFODE build a new training and resource center, named after their deceased son. Although Web sites should not be created simply in the hope of raising funds, many other Ugandan organizations became interested in developing Web sites as a result of ACFODE's success.

As anticipated, ACFODE saved money by using e-mail in place of long-distance faxing and phone calls. It also was able to use its network access to generate income. ACFODE members were invited to use the Internet for a small fee per connection or per e-mail message. Nonmembers were invited to use it too, but were required to pay more. For the many Ugandans with family members abroad, having such access nearby in their semi-urban community was a much-appreciated resource. Unfortunately, shortly after the project's final technical assistance visit, a number of the staff trained by Women Linking left AFCODE in a massive reorganization. A lesson for the follow-up project was not to put all eggs into one basket but to work with several organizations, given that staff turnover is frequent in many NGOs because they depend on grants and volunteer labor. Yet even when there is staff turnover in one organization, training and skills are not necessarily lost to the community. The primary technology person at ACFODE, who was terminated in the reorganization, subsequently moved to a women's umbrella organization, Uganda Women's Network (UWONET), where she shared her new skills with staff there.

WOMEN CONNECT!: THE PROJECT DESIGN

With the lessons learned from the pilot project, the Pacific Institute sought funding to expand to at least three African countries and approximately ten to fifteen organizations per country. In January 1999, the Gates Foundation awarded a grant of US$1 million dollars for the expanded project, called Women Connect! retaining the objectives, values, and assumptions that motivated the pilot project but defining them more clearly. The phrase "project design" is deceptively simple, but it involves critical decision making about how exactly to use available resources and confront the issues that are deeply imbedded in the competing ideologies that characterize all international development work.

Women's Health: Whose Agenda?

One of several crucial decisions the project team debated at length was the extent to which health, and specifically reproductive health, should be emphasized. This question cuts directly to the heart of several thorny issues in North-South cooperation. The dilemma was this. On one hand, it is well established that donor funding is much more available for work related to reproductive and sexual health (especially family planning, contraception, and HIV/AIDS) than for efforts to improve the status, or even health, of women more generally. On the other hand, NGOs in Southern developing countries resent being "donor-driven" and strongly prefer that Northern organizations do not impose agendas that divert them from their intended goals.

We wanted to show how a Northern organization could collaborate with Southern organizations while allowing them to pursue their own goals. We concluded that Women Connect! should not restrict its collaboration only to women's groups that were working on reproductive and sexual health. In fact, relatively few women's NGOs in Africa have reproductive health as their major focus, although many are tackling HIV/AIDS and violence against women. In Cairo in 1994 and at the Fourth World Conference on Women in Beijing in 1995, many women from Southern countries had made it clear that the health of women living in poverty depends directly on addressing other issues: food for their families, access to clean water, land, credit, inheritance, and other legal rights. In Zambia, for example, of the thirteen NGOs assessed for Women Connect!, ten included reproductive health as a priority area but gave greater importance to economic empowerment and land rights. As the NGO Coordinating Committee of Zambia put it, "Poverty needs to be tackled first so that women are empowered, and perhaps given the tools to seek positions of leadership. In that capacity, they are likely to make health a priority and that will translate into policies that will uplift the status of women in their constituent districts."

Women Connect! included an emphasis on women's health, with hopes of collaborating in the area of reproductive and sexual health but with a willingness to let women's health be interpreted very broadly, as "health and well-being." Project materials, including brochures and a Web site (www.women-connect .net), stated that Women Connect! would assist women's groups in appropriate use of media and technology "to communicate and advocate for the causes they feel are important in their communities — for example, women's reproductive and sexual health, inheritance rights for women, and the reduction of all forms of violence." This decision had both beneficial and problematic consequences.

Donor-Grantee Relationships: Hands-On or Hands-Off?

An additional issue in North-South cooperation is the extent to which a Northern donor or partner imposes reporting and other requirements on the Southern organization. Large donor agencies such as the U.S. Agency for International Development (USAID), United Nations Population Fund (UNFPA), or the World Bank use public monies and must report to the U.S. Congress or Northern governments on their impact. This translates into extensive reporting requirements to show precisely how the funds are used and with what results.

Although many NGOs welcome the financial support, these requirements are usually onerous for small organizations. In Uganda, for example, one women's NGO began as a local affiliate of an international feminist organization, the Holland-based Women's Global Network on Reproductive Rights. Initially calling itself the Network on Reproductive Rights, Uganda, it soon changed its name to Safe Motherhood Initiatives to facilitate and gain income by doing project work for USAID and UNFPA. Eventually, contemplating taking on a multimillion dollar health and nutrition contract with the World Bank, the founder recognized she and her staff were burned out from being donor-driven, working on agendas that were not their own. She decided to say no to the World Bank's millions and work instead, on a much smaller scale, on violence against women. Representatives of some thirty women's NGOs in Nicaragua expressed similar concerns in convening a workshop on how to have successful collaboration with Northern organizations.

The Global Fund for Women provided an alternative model. In contrast to the hands-on approach of the major donors, the Global Fund takes a hands-off approach to grant making. It defines its mission as "to assist women and women's organizations to transform their societies," and its basic premise is that women's groups know best what is needed to improve the lives of women in their communities and that there is a gap between large-scale funding agencies with set agendas and the capacities and flexibility needed by small-scale local women's groups. The Global Fund provides small grants (up to US$15,000 at that time) to women's groups without defining what specific issues grantees must address — except that their work fit within a broad women's rights context (Global Fund for Women 2002). It usually asks only for an end-of-project report, thus imposing only the barest minimum of paperwork.

The Pacific Institute for Women's Health had worked with the Global Fund and appreciated its hands-off approach. Women Connect! sought to incorporate these values, but to intervene more directly by emphasizing a specific skills area — media and communication strategies — and by providing training and technical assistance in these areas. The intent was to find an optimal middle ground between the open Global Fund model on one hand and narrow technical assistance on the other. Participating NGOs would have the freedom to select the content of activities they would carry out, but would do so within the general areas of media and technology as we presented them. This decision also had both beneficial and problematic consequences.

Although we were positioning Women Connect! in this middle ground, we were committed to working in accord with values articulated by Southern women's NGOs. These included transparency, building on and giving credit to work already done by others, collaboration (thus "technical collaboration" rather than "technical assistance"), information sharing, partnerships, capacity building, and follow-through to maximize sustainability. This institutional development approach focused on the group's organizational needs rather than solely on the delivery of a fixed technical content.

Project Objectives

Given the above considerations, we agreed on the following project objectives. In health, we wanted to strengthen the capacity of women's NGOs to improve the health of women in their communities, especially reproductive health. In the area of communication and the strategic use of media, we would provide technical assistance to women's NGOs in media and campaigns for effective publicity, outreach, and advocacy activities. We wished to increase technical ICT skills and contribute to the use of ICT for the advancement of women's health and well-being. The project also focused on networking to expand collaborative relationships among women's NGOs and strengthen peer-support for organizations in Africa and elsewhere. Finally, Women Connect! would assist women's groups to develop mutually beneficial long-term relationships with mass media professionals, an objective that was added in response to requests from women's groups who made it clear during the needs assessment that they lacked effective relationships with the local mass media.

IMPLEMENTING THE PROJECT

The Women Connect! project consisted of five complementary activities: needs assessments, training workshops, technical collaboration, distribution of health information and materials, and small grants.

The project team made assessment visits to nine countries in Africa and selected Zimbabwe, Zambia, and Uganda as the three project countries. In each country a local researcher familiar with the NGO community, communication strategies, and health issues visited NGOs that seemed appropriate to the project. From a wider sample of NGOs, the researcher identified ten to fifteen groups per country that best met the project criteria and conducted a needs assessment with each, focusing on their communication priorities related to women's health. The assessment confirmed that women saw reproductive health as embedded in a broad range of concerns that influence a woman's life and therefore her health, including safe motherhood, access to the political arena, protection from all forms of violence, access to property, and socioeconomic advancement. Among groups working on health issues, the most common priority was tackling HIV/AIDS (both prevention and care) and working to prevent other sexually transmitted infections. A total of 30 organizations, all having some explicit emphasis on health in their work, were selected and invited to participate in training workshops.

In each country the project identified a leading local NGO to link Women Connect! to a network of grassroots women's groups and co-host a Media Strategy and Information Technology Workshop. The project also identified several professionals in each country to participate in the workshop as trainers and co-facilitators. Immediately prior to the workshop, the project team made site visits to participating NGOs to meet their directors and communications, advocacy, and training staff to further explain the project and generate interest and commitment. The workshop lasted four days, two days on media strategies and campaigns and two on information communication technology. Training was highly interactive and based on the most current research on how adults learn. Women Connect! also provided ongoing technical collaboration to individual groups through local project facilitators in each country, on-site visits by the U.S.-based project team, and e-mail relationships and feedback from the project team to each participating organization.

The Pacific Institute for Women's Health reviewed, compiled, and provided to each NGO a large collection of the latest health-related materials most appropriate to the needs and the literacy levels of the communities it served. It also provided a list of health information Web sites appropriate for use with community groups.

Training alone is not enough to make something happen. Often in the development field, training workshops are conducted assuming that participants will go back to their organizations and implement the new ideas and skills from the workshop. Previous experience had taught us that this is not enough—and, in fact, it rarely happens. NGOs are often unable to carry out new activities, despite interest and good intent, without additional funding. We saw small grants (ranging from US$3,500 to $5,000 per organization) as a means of putting steam in the engine. Following the workshops we worked with each of the participating NGOs to help them prepare a small-grants proposal.

In total, the Pacific Institute awarded US$121,500 in small grants to 26 organizations in order that they conduct a one-year project on some aspect of communications presented in the training. In some cases the group used the small grant as a pilot project. For example, the Uganda Media Women's Association (UMWA) used its small grant for a teen pregnancy pilot project in a slum area of Kampala with the goal of raising more money and expanding elsewhere. Evaluations by the grantee organizations emphasized the significant role of the small grants in allowing them to use the tools introduced in the workshops.

Although the pilot project, Women Linking, had provided a computer, Women Connect! did not. It worked only with organizations that already had phone lines, electricity, and some computer knowledge, providing elements that were often lacking but essential for taking advantage of the computers: basic software, virus protection, surge protection against lightning (a major cause of modem failure in Africa), and subscriptions to e-mail and the Internet along with the training in e-mail and Internet use.

Project Management, Monitoring, and Evaluation

The project was managed by a team based at the Pacific Institute for Women's Health, itself a small women's NGO. It was assisted in Africa by local researchers, trainers, and technical support advisors.[10] In each country a local consultant was hired to monitor and facilitate the groups' progress on their small grants projects. Whenever possible we hired African women out of the conviction that providing appropriate role models is crucial for helping women stretch their ideas of what they can do. In particular, it was important to employ women with technology skills, as technology is a male-dominated area where women often feel incompetent.

The Women Connect! team also visited the participating NGOS periodically to identify problems, successes, opportunities for collaboration, and technical assistance needs. Because each NGO had different needs, structures, and target audiences, these visits were extremely important. As one participant expressed it, "Women Connect! has been a very user-friendly program. The fact that donors come to the ground is important. We have donors who live in Kampala who have not even come to see what we do. It is very important for donors to know . . . what the problems are and how they can be resolved" (Morna 2001).

A variety of methods were used to evaluate and document progress. These included baseline organizational needs assessments, workshop evaluations, site visits, technical staff feedback, and, from the NGOS that received the small grants, a six-month and year-end report, self-evaluation, and case studies. A final external evaluation was carried out in 2001 by a South African communication specialist also knowledgeable about NGOS (Morna 2001; Morna and Khan 2000).

Sustainability was a major concern. From the outset we had hoped that other sources of funding could be found that would support the African organizations with which Women Connect! had worked. This became increasingly important as the groups showed dedication and desire to capitalize on the momentum of activities initiated under the small grants program. The Global Fund for Women became the principal partner for this and has re-granted the majority of the Women Connect! groups in all three countries for further communications work. Some European donors (e.g., Denmark's Danida) have also begun to launch communication initiatives, and it is likely that many of our partner organizations will be able to leverage their experience to attract additional funding. German donors have helped one NGO partner, NAWOU in Uganda, to develop a Web site, and Jekesa Pfungua in Zimbabwe has now integrated communication strategies into all of its work, which is being funded by European donors as well as the Global Fund. The Zimbabwe Women's Resource Center and Network continues to operate an Internet café opened with Women Connect! funding. The Zambia Association for Research and Development, which is now primarily funded by European donors, has strengthened its use of ICT in all program activities, even offering technical assistance to other local NGOs. The five Web sites developed as part of Women Connect! activities in 2000 remain operational today.

CASE STUDIES FROM ZIMBABWE, ZAMBIA, AND UGANDA
Zimbabwe

Women Connect! began working in Zimbabwe in 1999, a time of significant social and political change. The women's movement in Zimbabwe was gaining momentum after a series of progressive rulings on women's rights, but there were legal setbacks on rights to land. The country itself was experiencing economic shocks and severe political tensions. Record numbers of women were assaulted and raped, without access to counseling or treatment for infections. Women's NGOs saw their work multiply in all sectors but faced budget shortages due to donor pullout on the grounds of government corruption and instability. Many NGOs were heavily scrutinized by the government and reduced their public outreach for fear of being mistaken for members of the political opposition.

Emboldened by the media strategies training with Women Connect!, five organizations took on media projects funded by its small grants program. These included a grassroots newsletter that addresses community needs in reproductive health and social services; a community publishing initiative that involves villages in producing media on AIDS, domestic violence, and rape; and a media campaign on women's rights launched during an annual advocacy event called 16 Days of Activism. Four other groups completed ICT projects, using e-mail and the Internet to network with affiliate organizations, to research information on health issues, and to repackage data for distribution to their target audiences. All groups effectively demonstrated that they could increase women's access to reproductive health information.

Case Study: The Zimbabwe Women's Bureau

The Zimbabwe Women's Bureau (ZWB) is a well-established NGO with activities in thirteen regions of the country and facilities that include a training center for community-based organizations. Priorities include poverty alleviation, home building and improvement, small business promotion, and business management training. Its training team develops projects based on perceived needs at the grassroots level. With Women Connect! training and support, ZWB undertook an ICT capacity-building initiative, yielding significant improvement in the management and productivity of the organization's activities.

ZWB went further with ICT than initially planned, taking the initiative to download health information from the Internet, translate it, and share it via ZWB's monthly local-language newsletter with target communities in both urban and rural districts. Using downloaded information, ZWB raised community awareness about reproductive health and rights, impacts of HIV/AIDS on women, home-based care for AIDS patients, rape, female genital cutting and other harmful traditional health practices, informed consent, prevention of infectious diseases, and male responsibility in reproductive and sexual health. ZWB continues to carry out health communications work with additional funding from the Global Fund for Women.

Zambia

In Zambia, a network of women's organizations (the NGO Coordinating Committee) was attempting to use media and information communication technology more effectively. Despite their resolve, their ability to use these tools remained extremely limited and sporadic. Among NGOs participating in the project, Zambian NGOs faced the most serious organizational challenges, from limited staff technical capacity to high turnover. Nevertheless, the women's movement in Zambia is quite active and has worked diligently in dealing with a government that has not always been responsive to women's needs. In fall 2000, after several years of lobbying, the national legislature adopted a National Gender Policy. Women's organizations have key roles to play in implementing this policy, and the potential benefits to women's health are significant. There are provisions to study the prevalence of particular medical conditions in women, to build additional and appropriate facilities, and to facilitate women's access to medical care. Such measures are needed in a country where five times more girls are HIV infected than boys in the same fifteen to nineteen age group (Nanda 2000, 14).

Both the NGO sector and government have worked to develop HIV/AIDS prevention messages and care programs. They have had some impact, as indicated by the decrease in the national prevalence of HIV-infected adults. Research by NGOs into the HIV education needs of their communities resulted in suggestions to disseminate prevention information through traditional leaders, at Bible study groups, and at community plays. Women Connect! trained staff from eight NGOs and funded six of them for small grants projects, three dealing with HIV/AIDS, one promoting women in nontraditional roles, and the others promoting women in decision making.

Case Study: Zambian National Association of Disabled Women

The mission of the Zambian National Association of Disabled Women (ZNADWO) is to promote the welfare of women with disabilities and to be a voice for their concerns, promoting education, training, and employment possibilities for disabled women. ZNADWO chose to use both traditional media and ICT to get its messages out. It established an Internet connection and provided training to staff and members on e-mail and Internet skills and in strategies for conducting health research. Its e-mail connection is particularly useful to disabled women, allowing them to connect and learn from women in disabled groups in other countries from Australia to Zimbabwe.

As part of its Women Connect! project, ZNADWO repackaged health information from existing print sources into a simple hard-copy format appropriate for the low literacy levels characteristic of its audience. In January 2001, ZNADWO convened a workshop on HIV/AIDS specifically for disabled women, including deaf and blind women. Disabled women need contraception and protection from sexually transmitted infection and unwanted pregnancy. "Disabled women end up depending on men in exchange for money, and men abandon them after sex," according to Francisca Muyenga, ZNADWO's director. The group is considering a variety of media channels to reach disabled women with prevention messages, such as providing radios in each branch office where weekly radio listening clubs can be scheduled. Muyenga has negotiated with health clinics for free services for disabled women who present a ZNADWO membership card, and she takes male and female condoms to disabled women when she makes visits throughout the country. ZNADWO has worked hard to meet its project objectives despite a volunteer staff and limited resources. The only NGO without a computer at the time of Women Connect! training, ZNADWO wrote a proposal and secured funding for a computer from a donor identified by the project.[11]

Uganda

In Uganda, NGOs have taken the initiative to integrate traditional media and information communication technology in innovative ways. Six of the eleven participating organizations downloaded information from the Internet and repackaged it into other forms of traditional media for their target audiences. Since each

NGO works with different target groups, in different regions and with different secondary media, projects vary. Ugandan NGOs have a long history and coexist with a government that is at the forefront of including women in parliamentary and other decision-making roles. However, there are still significant socioeconomic barriers to women's advancement. Ugandan NGOs did not succeed in getting a domestic relations bill to protect women in regard to marriage, property rights, and child custody rights passed. The 17-year civil war continues in northern Uganda, where many women continue to face sexual violations and lack of access to education, and there is widespread indifference to the plight of women who suffer domestic abuse.

Case Study: Uganda Media Women's Association

The Uganda Media Women's Association (UMWA) has launched a strategy to reach teenage girls with reproductive and sexual health information. Sex work, teen pregnancy, and HIV infection among poor young girls have reached alarming rates; an estimated 40 percent of all Ugandan teenage girls become pregnant. With its grant, UMWA carried out a media campaign involving teens of ages fourteen to nineteen. The target community was in a slum area in the capital of Kampala, next to the world-renowned Makerere University. The project needs assessment was followed by a workshop attended by over one hundred young people who spoke candidly about their lives. Their stories were documented in the UMWA newsletter, where some girls wrote that they resort to prostitution as a way of earning a living and in the process end up with unwanted pregnancies and sexually transmitted diseases, including HIV/AIDS. Others said that since they can't afford to pay school fees, they don't have enough to keep them busy and consequently become sexually active.

The teens themselves helped design messages on sexual responsibility and safety for T-shirts, caps, and posters that were produced and disseminated in the community. UMWA learned which messages would resonate with youth and which were ineffective. The teens stressed that UMWA's outreach has to sensitize health service providers to not reprimand youth when they seek reproductive or sexual health services. Otherwise, youth won't seek the help they need. The young people called for more health centers in the community and explained that they often don't have money to buy condoms and birth control pills. Purchase of contraceptives also competes with alcohol and drugs, they said, which some use to forget their problems. One result of UMWA's media campaign is that news about its activities has spread by word of mouth, and young people in other neighborhoods now want to participate.

OVERALL RESULTS

The Women Connect! project established an important foundation for future efforts. In these three African countries, leading women's organizations and individuals have engaged in strategic thinking about effective communication, often for the first time, and many have incorporated these new skills and strategies into their work. Eager to build on the momentum established with their small grants, they now have a year's experience in doing more effective planning, research, implementation, and monitoring. Their efforts have shown results under very challenging circumstances. As a woman from the Musasa Project in Zimbabwe expressed it, "What Women Connect! did was to plant a seed that can be watered and cultivated. There is no going back."

Communication Campaigns and Strategic Use of Media

Organizations that undertook media projects succeeded in achieving significant results with limited funds, according to the external evaluation (Morna 2001, 38). The media projects funded by Women Connect! small grants yielded immediate tangible benefits. Eight organizations conducted media campaigns on topics including reproductive health, domestic violence, HIV/AIDS, women in decision making, gender stereotypes, and women and the law. Others produced T-shirts, stickers, posters, flyers, and information sheets on specific women's health and empowerment themes. One organization conducted research on why its advocacy work was failing to yield the desired results and produced recommendations for a more effective media strategy. Two organizations worked with communities in producing their own publications, a newsletter and a training manual with a strong emphasis on gender and health.

Two organizations produced calendars, one of which was an innovative motivational calendar emphasizing new gender roles for women and men (produced by the Zambia Association for Research and Development, ZARD) (Morna 2001, 71-73). That such projects can have a significant impact on individuals' lives is illustrated by what happened with one of ZARD's gender-role calendars. A couple in Nakonde, Zambia, had withdrawn their fourteen-year-old daughter from school to enter her into an arranged marriage. A social worker visited the family to try to persuade them to allow the girl to continue her education.

The parents refused. However, the social worker had heard of the role-model calendar produced in Lusaka by ZARD. He traveled all the way from Nakonde to Lusaka, more than 1,000 km (621 miles), to collect one calendar that he took to the family. Upon seeing the photographs, especially those of the female pilot, female mechanic, and female photographer, the couple decided their daughter could go back to school and continue with her education, so that one day she could be like one of the women in those pictures. "This was a happy ending to a situation that could have destroyed the young girl's life," in the words of one of ZARD's members.[12]

Perhaps the most important impact on the participating organizations was their recognition of the need for public opinion research and needs assessments. By actually doing needs assessment, the NGOs acquired important information about the levels of knowledge, attitudes, and practices of their target audiences that often differed from their initial assumptions (Mukenge 2002). Sheila Kawamara, then director of the Uganda Women's Network, assessed its previous efforts to lobby for changes in the domestic relations bill: "The campaign had largely been one where we talked to ourselves as women or to the already converted. We realize now that we have pointed fingers and not understood people's problems and realities . . . There is a strong and urgent need to look at these issues from the eyes of the people we are trying to reach" (D. Mayer and Mukenge 2001, 16).

Information Communication Technology

The participants also gained skills in ICT. Lead women's organizations learned to use the Internet to link with each other and with the outside world. They learned about the range of possible applications of ICT and the need to be careful in making choices. Many are saving through the use of e-mail in place of long-distance telephone and faxes. The evaluator noted immediate tangible benefits in the area of ICT (Morna 2001, 71–73). In terms of connectivity, nine organizations that did not have e-mail or Internet access became connected. Two (in Zimbabwe and Uganda) set up Internet cafés that also function as Internet learning centers. Both Internet cafés are training sister groups, women parliamentarians, and others in how to use the Internet and are providing access for those without connectivity in their own organizations.

Five organizations established Web sites and nine repackaged information from the Internet for dissemination to key constituencies via radio or print. On the basis of its repackaging of Internet information on reproductive health, the Association of Uganda Women Medical Doctors (AUMWD) was a finalist in the Stockholm ICT Challenge Awards in 2001.

As the needs assessment showed, women's NGOs often have poor communications with the local mass media. The project hired local public relations and mass media professionals to work with the women's groups on how to think more strategically about relationships with the mass media and how to cultivate mutually beneficial long-term relationships. More needs to be done, but the participating groups are now much more effective in getting their issues into the local newspapers, radio, and television.

Because Women Connect! made reproductive and sexual health issues the main content of its substantive training, even participating NGOs that did not have health as a focus of their work were able to strengthen their competencies in the health area. Participating NGOs also generated important data on women's health. They, and the women in their communities, now have more up-to-date information, ongoing access to current information through the Internet, and greater motivation and ability to share this information. Using downloaded health information, the Uganda Private Midwives Association broadcast radio programs presenting health tips on prenatal care, safe motherhood, and infant nutrition. The online newsletter of the AUMWD presented data and case studies on breast and cervical cancers, HIV prevention and treatment, and reproductive health.

Feminists and women's organizations generally place high value on networking and collaboration but often find it difficult and too time consuming to carry out, especially given limited budgets and the fact that many members are volunteers doing NGO work on top of full-time jobs.[13] The project encouraged collaboration and, in some cases, it took. In Zimbabwe two organizations worked together effectively to launch a media campaign on reducing violence against women. The groups divided the labor: the YWCA produced drama, print media, and organized an essay contest and community march. Musasa, a domestic violence group, produced radio programs, a Web site, co-hosted a community forum, participated in the march, and networked to involve other organizations.

In Uganda, women's organizations identified ways to collaborate on the health components of their small-grants projects. Innovative approaches included sharing strategies on effective counseling skills; identifying professionals that do counseling and referring clients (instead of failing to provide follow-up assistance); training parents on parent-child communication about sexuality and reproductive and sexual health; setting up mechanisms to inform women about sources of health information (e.g., midwife clinics and women's rural information clubs); providing taped discussions of radio health programs to women's clubs in rural areas; addressing adolescent needs (e.g., building self-esteem, use of reproductive health services, encouraging groups to join the "Straight Talk" exchange in which teens anonymously submit questions on relationships and sexual health); and using the e-mail listserv of the Women of Uganda Network to share experiences and seek information.

The small grants program was perhaps the most important capacity-building aspect of the project. It gave participants the opportunity to learn by doing. In addition to using e-mail and Web sites more effectively, the evaluation concluded that "those who undertook media campaigns have recognized the need to build a communications dimension into all their work and to have a clear communications strategy" (Morna 2001, 72).

All the participating women's groups had suggestions for ways to improve the project, but most were very positive about what they accomplished with their small grants, particularly its effectiveness in training staff. As Debbie Serwadda, then program coordinator for Hope After Rape in Uganda, observed, "There was a culture of investing in us from the start. . . . This small grant project has completely revolutionized our lives! Oh, the excitement to just sit at a desk and be able to access information from as far as Australia! . . . We surely will not let down the women and children of Uganda" (Pacific Institute for Women's Health 2000).

LESSONS FOR FUTURE WORK IN MEDIA AND ICT

Communication Campaigns and Strategic Use of Media

An important finding from the project is that it is very important for women's organizations to conduct community-based research, including needs assessments and pretests, to be certain their messages are communicating clearly to their intended audiences. The process may be time consuming and expensive, but groups quickly learn that different target audiences receive messages in different ways and have to be reached in different ways. A second conclusion is that women's NGOs engaged in advocacy and outreach should consider mounting campaigns using multiple forms of media, such as booklets, radio, posters, and drama, as has been shown in other studies. The most effective campaigns have clear objectives and can measure their results.

A third lesson is that women's organizations can be more successful if they learn how to relate effectively to mass media professionals. They must become known to reporters as local "experts," and it is essential to respect journalists' deadlines. It is also useful to design exciting and visual media events. Organizations that have good relationships with mass media professionals are generally much more satisfied with how they are portrayed.

The Use of ICT

In terms of the impact of ICT, Women Connect! showed that women's NGOs can help bridge the digital divide through repackaging information from the Internet to share with their constituencies (Mukenge 2002). Ten of the NGOs participating in the project (nine of these getting connected for the first time) succeeded in using this approach.

Introducing new technology into an organization puts pressure on systems, relationships, communication, and management styles. Will the system of one person opening up regular mail be transferred intact to opening up e-mail? Who will have access to the Internet and e-mail? In many developing countries, computers are typically tools for secretaries, not managers. Using the Internet makes it necessary for management and other people in the organization to develop technology skills, which may change the hierarchical relations in the organization. For ICT to be managed, NGOs must designate a staff member to provide oversight and leadership on ICT issues.

There are no "one size fits all" solutions. Each organization has unique needs and must find its own way to integrate ICT into its work. ICT cannot be used occasionally or superficially and still be effective. Organizations must internalize ICT in their activities, strategically and gradually. Organizations just beginning to develop ICT capacity should resist the urge to design sophisticated approaches and applications (e.g., Web sites) that are beyond their capacity to maintain.

The experiences of Women Connect! also suggest lessons about how one set of goals important to the funding organization—women's health—can be integrated into the goals women's NGOs set for themselves. Although many groups had identified other priorities, reproductive and sexual health and rights figure prominently among the issues of highest concern in communities where NGOs work. Domestic violence, HIV/AIDS, sexually transmitted infections, cervical cancer, and safe motherhood emerged as priorities in all three countries. Violence against women is so common and its ramifications so great (including unwanted pregnancy, sexually transmitted infection, abortion, and depression) that it should always be considered a women's health issue.[14] Unsafe abortions continue to take place where stigma against teenage pregnancy or pregnancy among unmarried women remains extremely high. Women want information on family planning options and available services. So do adolescents, but they still face a stigma when seeking reproductive health services and, as a result, most shy away. In all cases, poverty is a major factor in determining knowledge of and access to proper health services.

The project showed that women are eager to learn techniques of negotiating safe sex to protect themselves from sexually transmitted infections, especially HIV. In many places awareness is high, but many women lack the power to negotiate safe sex. For this reason, there is great interest in new innovations such as emergency contraception and other woman-controlled methods of contraception and disease prevention, including microbicides.

Finally, ICT can help meet the great demand for up-to-date health information. Downloading and "repackaging" information from Internet sources on women's health emerged as an objective of several organizations after the project supplied them with lists of Web sites providing information on women' health topics. These groups saw an opportunity to cheaply and quickly access new information instead of relying on outdated resources in their libraries. Groups, especially in Uganda, took the initiative to find Internet information, download it, adapt it to the local context, simplify it for readability, in some cases translate it into the local language, and print and distribute it in brochures, booklets, and newsletters to those who have no access to the Internet. This remains an important area for technical collaboration.

According to the final evaluation, "Women Connect! walked a perpetual tightrope between having groups identify their own goals and at the same time ensuring a realistic set of options." As the evaluation noted, "In an effort to achieve the former, the program ran the risk of losing focus and effectiveness. . . . The broad range of themes, and loose coordination between the various components, despite strenuous efforts by the project implementers to achieve greater synergy, limited their impact. While the desire to define women's health and well-being broadly is commendable, this may have contributed to a lack of sufficient focus" (Morna 2001, 73).

In retrospect, the design was indeed overly ambitious for its time frame. Women Connect! offered an unusual opportunity to the project designers (who had worked for many years for large agencies on projects that were already quite well formulated at the time they became involved) to design a major intervention based on their own values. The project offered a rare opportunity to plan and carry out an innovative project from the ground up.

When the project was over, we asked ourselves what we might have done differently without compromising our values and convictions. We were committed to combining strategic use of media with technology, and we were committed to a broad definition of "women's health and well-being." How could we have had greater focus, efficiency, and impact?

We could have chosen fewer countries to work in and fewer organizations to work with. We could have clustered groups more for structured collaboration around their topics of interest. And, if we had had more time and more money, we could have paid the local project facilitators to work more closely with the participating groups. This would have been more efficient without compromising our values or those of the groups with whom we worked.

Yet it seems to us that the project was definitely worth doing. In countries that are politically unstable, with problems ranging from no electricity to galloping inflation, extremely high maternal mortality and HIV rates and ethnic tensions, it is necessary to take a long view. Women Connect! made it possible for an important set of women leaders and organizations to think differently about how to be more effective in their communications, how to employ ICT within a broader strategy, and how to use information "to change the lives of women," in the words of Lilian Mashiri of the Zimbabwe Women's Resource Centre and Network (D. Mayer 2002).

Women's NGOs are an important force for women's empowerment and development, improving living conditions and possibilities for women, especially those living in poverty in a world of harsh inequalities. They bring ethical issues to the fore and are committed to improving lives of citizens in their societies. The women's rights issues with which so many are involved translate directly into citizens' rights more broadly. Their level of commitment constitutes a major engine for strengthening civil society. In today's environment, empowerment is often envisaged as an individual rather than a collective force, emphasizing entrepreneurship and individual self-reliance. Yet it is not just individuals but organizations that drive development and improve the political environment in which economic and social institutions operate. Women's organizations cooperate to challenge power structures that inhibit development and subordinate women and other marginalized groups. They employ a variety of approaches, but their impact depends on increasing their skills and capacities, including in the strategic use of all forms of communication, for outreach and advocacy and to stay connected locally and internationally.

Women Connect! set many things in motion.[15] Most of the women's organizations in Africa that were our partners are continuing to use their new learning and are sharing it with other women's groups. Some groups were able to translate their new skills into advocacy work, using e-mail to raise awareness on issues relating to women's health and empowerment, for networking, and to apply for funding with new donors. By strengthening communication capacity, these organizations became more effective in getting their messages out, in using and sharing information with others, improving health and well-being, and having greater influence in their communities and countries.

NOTES

1. The authors express their deep appreciation for contributions to this work by Carole Roberts, technology coordinator for Women Linking and Women Connect! and by Colleen Lowe Morna, evaluation consultant.

2. Primary funding was provided by the Annenberg Center for Communication at the University of Southern California and the Bill and Melinda Gates Foundation (called the William F. Gates Foundation at the time). Additional funding was provided by the Wallace Global Fund, with institutional support from the John D. and Catherine T. MacArthur Foundation.

3. The Academy for Educational Development (AED) and the Johns Hopkins University Center for Communications Programs (JHU/CCP) were among the leaders in this work.

4. Deborah Kaddu-Serwadda, Hope After Rape, Kampala, Uganda (in Morna 2001, 17).

5. The Pacific Institute for Women's Health, a Los Angeles–based nonprofit organization founded in 1993, is dedicated to improving the health and well-being of women and girls locally and globally. The institute takes a comprehensive approach to the complex realities of women's lives and works through applied research and evaluation, advocacy, community involvement, and training.

6. The Global Fund for Women, based in San Francisco, makes grants to seed, support, and strengthen women's rights groups in developing countries.

7. As technology coordinator, Roberts developed the plan for the project's technology component and provided ICT training, technical collaboration, and guidance for both the pilot project and the expanded Women Connect!.

8. ICT efforts focused on governments, and larger NGOs included the Leland Project of USAID and the DevCom initiative of the World Bank.

9. The team consisted of Doe Mayer, project director and media campaign trainer, and Carole Roberts, technology coordinator.

10. The U.S.-based team at the Pacific Institute consisted of project director Doe Mayer; program officer Muadi Mukenge; technology coordinator Carole Roberts; part-time co-director Barbara Pillsbury; and a part-time administrative assistant and occasional advisors.

11. Go to http://www.annenberg.edu for four lively Women Connect! videos presenting ZNADWO and three other participating organizations.

12. Patrick Sapallo, Zambian Association for Research and Development.

13. Some women's NGOs do collaborate effectively in mobilizing around specific issues that need pressure from women's advocates (e.g., legislation before parliament on women's issues). This sort of mobilization is especially strong in Uganda, where it is coordinated by the Uganda Women's Network (UWONET).

14. For a communications toolkit for ending violence against women, see Drezin and Lloyd-Laney 2003.

15. Women Connect! has also had a significant impact on the overall program of the Pacific Institute for Women's Health. The institute has integrated elements of Women Connect! into all its work with women's organizations in Africa, Asia, Latin America, and the United States. It has included communications components in other reproductive health training and has established a small-grants initiative, the Action Grants Program, to improve the impact of Pacific Institute training and technical assistance to women's NGOs and youth-serving organizations worldwide. For further information, see http://www.women-connect.net and http://www.piwh.org.

Empowerment Just Happened:
The Unexpected Expansion of Women's Organizations

Irene Tinker

Empowerment just happened. No man, planning economic development for the developing countries, intended to empower women. Indeed, leading theorists such as Walt Rostow and Edward Banfield had a negative view of women, assuming their support for traditional values and religion would impede progress. These attitudes were so embedded in U.S. society that on many university campuses women professors, from chemists to psychologists, were forced into home economics departments (Nerad 1998). In the 1960s, women in the United States began to rebel against their socially constructed roles and demanded passage of the Equal Rights Amendment. "Uppity Women Unite" was our motto. Together we altered policies in the Congress and help shift the development paradigm to include women. This shift meant that resources began to flow to women in villages and slums and supported the elite women who organized them. Women broke out of their patriarchal shackles and began to accumulate power.

Women have traditionally formed groups for savings, harvesting, or community support. During the suffragist era, educated women's organizations became global. The crucial difference in the last half of the twentieth century was that male goals for economic transition undermined the sexual division of labor. This in turn required a change in women's roles. Importantly, because of the focus on agriculture and food security, development planners provided resources for women in rural areas that encouraged this change. To reach them, planners hired educated women to form village women into groups in order to improve health, limit population, alter fuel consumption, or reduce the drudgery of food production. New technologies, new ideas, new credit, all flowed downward. In turn, the organizers and the women involved observed and critiqued the plans and began to demand new programs, new policies, new laws. Without resources, social movements are difficult to sustain. This time, the launching of socioeconomic transformations led to a shift in gender relations at home and in the world. From the standpoint of the planners, empowerment was an unintended result.

Taking this opportunity, women around the globe have made unprecedented gains toward equality and justice within the family and the state. Societies everywhere have been challenged by this most significant social movement of the late twentieth century. The movement began in trickles in the rural towns and villages, in suburban homes, in national and international meetings, in legislation, and in flows of economic assistance. In the past, isolated groups of women would have been inhibited by geography. But in the last quarter of the twentieth century, women could connect making use of rapid improvements in communications and travel. These many groups converge, as streams do, into mighty rivers, but they are also influenced by the rain blowing in from distant places bringing new ideas and information. The streams may be sluggish or swift, the rivers may have dams or rapids, the rain may fall on deserts or in swamps. But as the waters—the many local feminisms—converged, they formed an irresistible force: the global women's movement.

History records how women's status has varied by culture, government, religion, and agricultural systems. Throughout history, women expanded their societal roles during crises, when wars have left them in charge at home or recruited them to combat roles. But when the crises subsided, patriarchy was reasserted, perhaps under a different guise. This pattern persists today but, because the current epoch has bound the world together as never before, women can no longer be so easily isolated and controlled. The spread of women's organizations and networks, nationally and internationally, have made women everywhere more aware of their human rights, more willing to demand change, and more capable of sustained organization.

My perspective of these profound transformations has been formed by over fifty years of research and study of the social, economic, and political changes in the global South coupled with organizing and participating in nongovernmental organizations in the United States—from think tanks, to civil rights and women's rights groups, to political parties, salons, and university classes. Drawing on these diverse experiences, I want to analyze two of the many paths to women's personal empowerment and how they have led to changes in gender relations within family, community, and country.

The story is not straightforward. Causality is ambiguous and inconsistent; no one path serves all women. But two distinct factors are constant. First, women organized are more powerful than disparate voices. Second, international economic development has undermined subsistence and traditional farming communities, altering the sexual division of labor and opening cracks in the foundations of patriarchal control. Development programs not only encouraged women to organize but also provided them with funding, training, and a broader worldview.

Leaders in developing countries wanted modernization and economic development but no diminution of their political power. Such selective change might have been possible in the past, but not today. As China struggles to expand markets but maintain communism or Iran seeks nuclear power while increasing the autocratic control of its mullahs over democratically elected leaders, young people hook up on the Internet, families watch foreign television, and newscasts show women in high-level decision-making positions in governments, business, and international institutions.

Fifty years ago the communications age had barely begun as rapid economic development began to challenge the social order that kept women in their place. Planners did not intend to alter traditional power relationships. But as women organized to support economic development, empowerment happened anyway. Advocates, who promoted the inclusion of women in economic development or the recognition of women's human rights at the United Nations and other international agencies, were themselves empowered. At the national level, as employment opportunities in the government and in development organizations expanded, the number and variety of women's organizations soared, giving visibility to their leaders and their causes. At the village level, women recipients of economic projects that had been designed to reduce their time burden or increase their income were empowered. From Mexico City (1975) to Beijing (1995), UN Conferences for Women brought together representatives of all these organizations in an explosive mix of jubilation, intellectual ferment, and growing demands for equal human rights.

In this chapter, I trace the growing power of women in these interrelated spheres—international, national, and local—showing how they reinforced each other through organizing and networking. Because rapid socioeconomic change can be profoundly distressing, I also take note of the ways women as well as men have challenged the basic premise of gender equality or deliberated its implications. The first section shows how disparate concerns about the changing roles and status of women in developing countries culminated in the effort to recognize the differential impact of development programming on women in the Plan of Action of the UN First Conference on Women in Mexico in 1975. The second section discusses three initiatives from this Mexico meeting as they influenced opportunities for women in government, in research, and in development agencies. The final section reviews the much more abundant literature on the consequences of international development programs designed to address the economic activities and responsibilities of poor women with a focus on the intended and unintended results of such initiatives.

The chapter asserts that whatever the activities or interventions, organizing women provided the foundation for increases in economic, human, social, and material capital for both the organized and the organizers. How this new capital was utilized varied from country to country, and culture to culture, and in some cases provoked backlash as patriarchal laws were challenged. Women understood that they needed to safeguard their new status and possibilities and that these had to be secured by law. Today, women are flexing the still growing power of the women's movement and demanding access to political structures at all levels of government. Marilena Da Souza, a coordinator of a broom factory in the Amazon, captured the importance of groups. "Alone you are nothing. If you think you are nobody, you are nobody. Together, we have courage, we have new ideas. Together we float" (as quoted in Rogow 2000, 27).

SEIZING THE HISTORIC MOMENT

The confluence of three historic seismic shifts allowed women to seize the initiative for advancing social justice around the world, causing upheavals in traditional sex-age-race-class hierarchies, to utilize Ester Boserup's formulation (1990): the crumbling of the colonial order; the establishment of the United Nations; and the reinvigoration of both the international and U.S. women's movements.

Developing Countries

The world after World War II witnessed the success of nationalist movements in Asia and Africa. In their fight against the imperial powers, nationalist leaders frequently recruited the help of women in their struggles for freedom and equality. With independence, the male leadership could hardly deny women at least formal rights. Thus, the constitutions of the newly independent countries granted equal rights to women and men in civil matters. Customary or family law remained a source of contention and discrimination. Nonetheless, the right to vote and hold office represented a significant advance. Indeed, France scrambled to allow women to vote only when their former colonies were doing so.

Many women leaders of nationalist movements were appointed to high governmental positions; others began to organize locally to ensure their new freedoms were not compromised.[1] The idea of using development aid money for women was first proposed by Inga Thorsson to the Swedish Parliament in 1963; in her report of visits in Africa she described women as "an especially ill-fated group" (Himmelstrand 1977). In 1969, the Swedish International Development Agency (SIDA) funded two positions in the recently established United Nations Economic Commission for Africa to ensure a voice for women at the policy level (M. Snyder 1995). Margaret Snyder, later the founding director of UNIFEM, the UN Fund for Women, was one of the women appointed (M. Snyder 2004). As more development agencies adopted such programs, women around the world began to organize in order to demand some access to the program funds.

Danish economist Ester Boserup was among those who studied the agricultural systems in former colonies to recommend ways to increase production.[2] Her research in India in the 1950s convinced her that the prevailing theories about agricultural development were inaccurate and failed to measure women's economic activity on or off the farm. Her ideas were reinforced and expanded by subsequent research in Africa, resulting in her ground-breaking book *Woman's Role in Economic Development*, which appeared in 1970. She discussed the changing sexual division of labor caused by economic development in a radio broadcast meant to popularize her research; the lecture was widely distributed by the International Labor Organization (ILO). Further exposure came in 1971 when the *Development Digest*, a publication of the U.S. Agency for International Development (USAID), published an abstract of her book for dissemination around the world. Her identification with women's roles in economic development was solidified when she acted as rapporteur of the UN Interregional Expert's Meeting on the topic (Boserup 1970, 1999; Tinker 2003b, 2004a, 2004b). By the mid-1970s, Ester Boserup had become an icon for the emerging women in the development movement.

United Nations

The establishment of the United Nations provided a forum for the newly independent countries that were deeply concerned with development issues. Their power grew as the stalemate in the Security Council moved the focus from security issues to the General Assembly, where they proclaimed a UN Development Decade that was patterned on the Marshall Plan that had spurred the recovery in Europe. Applied in developing countries, this approach magnified income disparities and increased the gross domestic product at the same time. The World Bank shifted its focus from infrastructure to poverty and population growth; the ILO worried about inadequate industrialization in the developing world and began to study the informal sector; the Food and Agricultural Organization strove to increase food production in face of frequent shortages and predicted famine. This shift in development thinking from infrastructure toward people allowed such questions as who grows food, who is poor, and who makes fertility decisions to enter the development debate.

The UN Commission on the Status of Women (CSW) was concerned from its inception with the advancement of women, passing resolutions that eventually became the influential Convention on the Elimination of All Forms of Discrimination Against Women (CEDAW). At the beginning, women from developed countries dominated the CSW, reflecting the distribution of power in the UN itself. In this period, the CSW's primary issues were education and citizenship rights. Not until 1962 was an Arab delegate, Aziza Hussein, appointed to replace an Israeli as the representative for the Middle East. She introduced two new and controversial issues to CSW, including family planning and the status of women in Islam (Hussein 2004).

Interest in economic development was lodged in the Department of Economic and Social Affairs of the UN Economic and Social Council; a section on social planning was set up in 1966. The head of this section, economist Gloria Scott, organized a seminar in Sweden in 1972 to explore new ideas to ameliorate the socioeconomic disparities associated with development. Although not on the agenda, women clearly emerged as an issue during the discussion. To capture this insight, Scott inserted the phrase "integration of women in development" in her report and then collaborated with the CSW to convene another experts' meeting that put women into the development debate. Ester Boserup was invited to serve as rapporteur.[3]

U.S. Women's Movement

Political turmoil grew intense in the United States by the late 1960s. The civil rights movement and anti-Vietnam protests activated women as well as men. Rebelling against the dismissive attitude of the male leadership of both groups, women came together on university campuses, at the workplace, in the suburbs, and in the cities to demand equality. This reinvigorated women's movement created an excitement throughout the country; formal and informal groups of women began to challenge male-dominated institutions and organizations. Women demanded equal rights to jobs and education; the campaign for an Equal Rights Amendment (ERA) to the U.S. Constitution, though unsuccessful in the end, became a rallying point.

Opposition to the ERA was grounded in the conservative South and among the religious right. But the ERA's declaration of full equality also worried some women labor leaders, such as Esther Peterson who was vice chairman to chair Eleanor Roosevelt of the Kennedy Commission, set up in 1960. Peterson believed that the ERA would undermine the long-fought-for special protection for working women. Only subsequent changes in federal laws that expanded health and safety provisions to include men as well made it possible for her to support the ERA (Peterson 1983).

ERA supporters generally viewed protective legislation, such as restrictions on night shifts or hours worked, as obstacles to increased work opportunities for women. The conviction that women are the same as men was a basic tenet of this new women's activism. In a society where income is often seen as the marker for success, women demanded equal access to work because an outside job was valued over homemaking. Any concessions might undermine the march to equality.

Yet, if both parents work, who cares for the children? Or does equality at work translate into double days for women? These points continue to be contentious, affecting both planning and policy in the United States and around the world — to say nothing of women's lives. Many feminists looked at the social support for motherhood in Europe and elsewhere and saw weakness. On campuses, some scholars contested this *essentialism* as a danger to women's equality, but others began to emphasize the value of women's difference (Gilligan 1982), and more recent research has shown that there are some innate differences (e.g., Baron-Cohen 2003). By contrast, most women in Europe and Latin America did not perceive a fundamental conflict between calling for equality and recognizing that women are different from men. Indeed, some women in former communist countries have argued that they had experienced the effects of "women's equality" in the workplace, and they had not been good for women (Jaquette and Wolchik 1998).

As the women's movement gathered strength in the 1970s, Congress and the administration, pushed by activist groups in Washington, passed laws to guarantee equal treatment in education, sports, credit, employment, pensions, and social security. These are rights of citizenship and are easily put into law. Policies to address women's health or the needs of displaced homemakers required increased government expenditures, but these too were passed.[4] However, once women began to lobby for legislation that encroached on sexual mores (by asking funds for centers to treat victims of rape or domestic violence or legalization of abortion), congressional support began to wane (Tinker 1983b). As in developing countries, men were reluctant to give up patriarchal control.

Organizing took place on university campuses as well. Graduate women and sympathetic women faculty formed caucuses to initiate courses on women and demand recognition of women's studies in the curriculum and within their academic disciplines (Howe 2000). Under pressure, professional associations set up committees to explore women's issues at conferences and on campuses. In Washington, D.C., I helped form such a group within the Society for International Development; it became known as Women in Development or SID/WID. Talks at our brown-bag meetings by members studying development or doing research in the field confirmed what was then a startling indictment: economic development was having an adverse impact on women.

Presentation of this viewpoint at a 1973 Department of State briefing on the upcoming UN World Conference for Women convinced Mildred Marcy, of the U.S. Information Agency, that the issue of women must be included in the pending legislation revising the U.S. Foreign Assistance Act. Through her connections in the Senate, Marcy secured support for an amendment, which she wrote based on UN terminology, to "integrate women into development." Senator Charles Percy—a Republican in a Republican administration—was asked to introduce the amendment, although he had little understanding of its import. Once the phone calls and faxes (it was before the age of e-mail) started pouring in, however, he became a knowledgeable champion of WID, introducing a resolution at the UN General Assembly and co-chairing the U.S. delegation to Mexico City.[5]

These three initiatives—the Swedish development assistance in Africa, the UN Experts Seminar in NYC, and the WID amendment to the U.S. Foreign Assistance Act—had an impact on the direction and scope of international economic assistance programs in the 1970s. The original development paradigm was under attack. Funding for infrastructure and industry had increased the disparity of incomes in developing countries, prompting the World Bank to make poverty a high priority issue. At the time, little data was sex disaggregated and development programs assumed families were the basic economic unit for planning, ignoring women's roles and needs. Through the American Association for the Advancement of Science, where I was the head of international science and whose chair at that time was Margaret Mead, I convened a seminar in Mexico City prior to the UN Conference for Women which brought together over one hundred women and men who had studied the problem. In preparation, my staff abstracted all available literature on the topic in French, Spanish, and English (Tinker and Bo Bramsen 1976; Buvinic 1976).

The new direction was championed at the UN World Conference for Women in Mexico City in June 1975 where two new UN agencies were created specifically for women: the UN Voluntary Fund for Women—now UNIFEM—and the International Research and Training Institute for the Advancement of Women, INSTRAW. Major bilateral donors searched for programs that could reach poor women in rural and urban settings. Scholars documented the negative impact of many development programs on women, noted women's lower entitlements within families, and showed the perilous existence of many women-headed households (Buvinic et al. 1983; Chant 1997a; Elson 1992; Folbre 1988; Papanek 1990; A. Sen 1990). The impact of subsequent structural adjustment programs, initiated by the World Bank in the 1980s to force borrowing governments to contain spending, fell heavily on women as social programs were decimated (Acosta-Belén and Bose 1995; Benería and Feldman 1992; Moghadam 1995; Monteon 1995; Owoh 1995).

WOMEN'S INTERNATIONAL POLICY LEADERSHIP

The women mentioned above—advocates, scholars, and practitioners—not only influenced development policy within the UN and its agencies, bilateral assistance programs, and the burgeoning nongovernmental organizations (NGOs), they were themselves empowered.[6] Including women in development programs meant that agencies created new offices and hired more women professionals;

land grant universities with large agricultural projects funded by USAID set up new programs both on campus and in the field. The UN system, bombarded by demands for greater equity in its own workforce, increased the number of women in decision-making positions and promoted Finnish Helvi Sipila as the first assistant secretary general when she headed the Mexico City conference. UNIFEM and INSTRAW both provided opportunities for women to rise within the international system.

The World Bank also set up an office for women, but it was minimally funded and soon outpaced by the newer office on environment (G. Scott 2004). Over twenty years later, and despite a recent publication on *Engendering Development Through Gender Equality in Rights, Resources and Voice* (World Bank 2001a), the perception persists that the Bank does not support its own poverty reduction or social goals sufficiently. On the contrary, many researchers have argued, many Bank projects add to the immiseration of women (O'Brien at al 2000; World Bank 2001a; Valdisavljevic and Zuckerman 2003). Nonetheless, there are more women in professional positions within the Bank as countries who fund the Bank have pressured it to hire more women. Although not all women professionals support women's programs, the presence of more women who do (and some men who do) makes advocacy within the institution more acceptable and less likely to hurt one's career.

The resistance to WID in the World Bank and other multilateral economic institutions is examined in a path-breaking study of how global social movements are contesting global governance. The authors compare the women's movement to the environmental and labor movements in terms of their impact on the International Monetary Fund, the World Trade Organization, and the World Bank. They write that while these multilateral economic institutions are "moving beyond their interstate mandates to actively engage civil society actors in numerous countries," the women's movement has not been as successful as environmental and labor movements in reforming institutions or changing policies (O'Brien et al. 2000, 2).

An in-depth study of women in the World Bank documents the difficulties women have had in trying to influence the Bank. The authors suggest two reasons that women have been less effective. First, they argue that there is no single international women's movement and no agreed upon women's agenda, although there are women's movements in the plural. Further, they note that deep resistance to gender equality exists among women as well as men because the vision championed by feminists would fundamentally change current approaches to social organization (O'Brien et al. 2000, 32).

These two propositions are related. The variety of local feminisms reflects the tremendous differences among cultures and societies making a single agenda illusive despite the fact that women everywhere are struggling for equality in all the many facets of their lives (Basu 1995; Tinker 2004d). Underlying much of the debate over immediate goals is whether equality means "the same" or "different"; whether social or individual goals should prevail; whether the dominant market system can be adjusted for greater equity. Opportunities and obstacles which women encounter as the socioeconomic transformation engulfs their lives demand distinct responses from women's organizations.

In Bank negotiations, the distance between local women's groups and the international institutions is huge. Women in the South and North frequently disagree about the causes of economic injustice. Women in the periphery also have trouble being heard by international development NGOs working in their countries. Because these women often lack the training and sophistication of lobbyists in Washington and New York, the male-dominated international NGOs often make policy for them and ignore their input. Even when executive directors of the Bank have pressured for women's programs (O'Brien et al. 2000, 33, 59, 65), women in the South, who would potentially benefit from these policies, feel marginalized. The U.S. women's movement, which is an effective lobby, does not pressure the Bank on behalf of women's groups in the South. In contrast to the cooperation that exists among international environmental groups, the "U.S. women's movement has not thrown its weight behind the gender and development issues. . . . Gender equity issues are still seen as more controversial, and more 'culturally specific' than are concerns with the environment or even human rights" (O'Brien et al. 2000, 65).

Contesting Global Governance underscores how radical women's challenges to the existing order really are, much more so than is true of the environmentalists or trade unionists. Their conclusions illustrate both the remarkable expansion of women's power and its limitations. A single programmatic solution may be impossible; advocates for women's empowerment must understand the tremendous variation of cultures in which women live before trying to recommend appropriate programs or evaluate progress, but the vision of a just and equitable world — whatever its definition — anchors the global women's movement.

Women's Studies Versus Women in Development

In the United States, little interaction takes place between women's studies and women in development organizations. As the U.S. women's movement grew during the seventies, its activities diverged. Consciousness-raising groups exploded in the suburbs; committees on the status of women were formed in cities and states. Courses on women were introduced on most college and university campuses, but largely in the humanities. Women doing comparative research in developing countries added to the knowledge of women's subordination and patriarchy but were challenged at home and abroad. In the United States, minority women, often calling themselves "Third World" women, demanded inclusion of race in the curriculum. As academic women strove for power and acceptance on liberal arts campuses, they focused increasingly on theoretical analysis—first Marxist, then postmodern (Howe 2000). These critiques took place in a climate of fierce antigovernment attitudes, spawned by the civil rights movement and the Vietnam War, which was suspicious of government actions and programs on campuses, from military recruitment to government-sponsored research.

By contrast, the growing WID community was lodged primarily in agricultural universities where government funding was the rule. Research on economic development was applied, not theoretical. USAID funded programs provided scholarships for women from developing countries—real Third World women. These conflicting perspectives produced a confrontation at the first Women's Studies Association meeting in Kansas in 1979, when U.S. minority women accosted women panelists from developing countries. This confrontation opened a gap between WID and women's studies that has continued to shape women's studies curricula for two decades. In an effort to heal this breach and encourage a more global viewpoint, in the late 1990s the Ford Foundation offered grants to thirteen women's studies programs to add comparative and international studies to their offerings.

Area studies women, writing about the impact of colonialism and development on women, were also caught in the controversies between scholars from the North and the South. African and Muslim women in particular questioned the right as well as the ability of white Christian scholars to understand their countries. Such a debate had already split the African Studies Association into two distinct professional groups. At a 1976 conference, convened at the Wellesley Center for Research on Women and organized by the women's committees of the area studies associations, the explosiveness of the debate hampered further cooperative research for several years. As funding sources pushed for collaborative research, area studies associations emphasized the participation of scholars from the region, including women (Flora 2004).

North-South Perspectives

The lack of international perspective and the ethnocentrism of many U.S. women leaders led to clashes at the Mexico City conference as well. Many women from the developing world rejected the feminists' emphasis on individualism at the expense of family and community; they argued that women's problems were due as much to international economic exploitation as to patriarchy. The North-South division was exacerbated by U.S. foreign policy that rejected demands for a new international economic order at Mexico City and efforts to include the pro-Palestinian stance held by a majority of UN members; these issues were included in the separate Declaration of Mexico City that the United States voted against. These global political issues persisted at the women's conferences in Copenhagen and Nairobi (Winslow 1995).

The nadir of U.S. foreign policy regarding women came at the Second World Conference for Women held in Copenhagen in 1980. Preparations for the Copenhagen conference included funds for research. Lucille Mair, secretary general of the conference, broadened the viewpoints of women and international development by channeling these funds to women from the developing world. As a result, the documentation for the conference inserted women into the three most contentious issues of the period: apartheid, Israel and Zionism, and underdevelopment. Language that linked Zionism with racism, which the United States had consistently opposed in all UN documents, was incorporated into the conference document. Despite the feminist bent of the U.S. delegation, the State Department insisted that the delegation vote against the conference document (Tinker and Jaquette 1987).

The Third UN Conference on Women in Nairobi in 1985 was held during less contentious times. A Peace Tent fostered dialogue between Israelis and Arabs; South Africa was in transition to majority rule. A group of women scholars from the South offered a distinctive analysis on the relationship between macroeconomic policies and gender issues. The group, called Development Alternatives with Women for a New Era (DAWN), was convened by Devaki Jain in Bangalore, India, in 1984. Through regional meetings and debates, DAWN presented their compelling manifesto, *Development, Crises, and Alternative Visions: Third World Women's Perspectives*, at the NGO Forum (Sen and Grown 1985), challenging the failure of WID to examine structural issues of international inequality. The DAWN network continues to publish on development policy issues (Antrobus 2004; Jain 2003, 2004).

Clearly, policy leaders in both South and North benefited from the increased funding from national or international sources to study, organize, and support women. Project priorities during the 1980s focused on providing opportunities for women to earn an income. The egalitarian bias of Western feminists affected their assessments of project success. If a woman used her microcredit loan to buy a pedicab for her husband, Northern feminists criticized this, while many Southern writers emphasized the positive effect on family welfare and lauded such action. Lucille Mair reiterated the unease of women in the South who argued that poor women already worked; they did not need to be "integrated" into development. For them the problem was not *exclusion* but *inclusion* in a system that uses the sexual division of labor and class differences to exploit women (1986).

By the end of the UN Decade for Women in 1985, a global women's movement existed that encompassed many viewpoints and distinct feminisms (Basu 1995). The energy of the U.S. women's movement, which had helped propel the inclusion of women in development programming in the 1970s, was splintered; a majority of both scholars and activists focused on national issues and identity politics. In the early 1980s, those concerned with international development formed their own professional association, the Association for Women in Development (AWID), to unite the women on campuses with those carrying out programs for donor agencies and those conducting action research. Generally, these women were trying to convince development agencies that their programs would be more effective if they paid attention to women's concerns and de-institutionalized male bias (Miller and Razavi 1998b). Confrontation was not considered a useful tactic; rather the most effective approach was to redesign and broaden existing programs.

As the World Bank moved to support neoliberal economic policies in the 1980s, the WID office did not challenge the overall model but defended the Bank to outside critics (O'Brien et al. 2000, 24–66) while seeking compensatory programs to counter the negative effects of structural adjustment programs on women, which were being demonstrated by research often funded by the Bank itself (Elson 1992). Few women in the Bank, whatever their nationality, viewed themselves as part of the women's movement; most considered that too radical. Lacking strong critics pursuing a transformative agenda, the gender unit in the Bank has been unable appreciably to affect Bank's policies.[7]

IMPACT OF UN DIRECTIVES ON GOVERNMENTS AND WOMEN'S ORGANIZATIONS AT THE NATIONAL LEVEL

The 1975 Mexico City conference gave international visibility to women's concerns; the recognition of the adverse impact of economic development on women resulted in increased funding for studies and projects by bilateral and international donor agencies, by foundations, and by nongovernmental organizations. The Plan of Action, which passed by acclamation, included three directives for national governments that have continued to influence both development and empowerment strategies. The Plan instructed governments to prepare a report on the status of women in their country; to set up a focal point for women, that is, a bureau or office dedicated to women's issues and called "national machineries" in UN parlance; and to ensure that women are included in their economic planning. The outcome of these initiatives is described below.

Reports on the Status of Women and Their Impact

In order to prepare a status of women report, governments had to collect sex-disaggregated data for critical indicators such as education, employment, and health. Such data provided, for the first time, a clearer view of women's inferior status that could then be used as an argument for development planning. Government ministries had to alter their census or questionnaire forms to provide the necessary data. Collecting and analyzing these data provided employment for women in the government and universities, and dissemination of the data often sparked local debate.

The starkness of gender inequality revealed in these data was given prominence as the UN and the World Bank included these statistics in their annual reports. Disparities in work, education, health, and income were laid bare. Development programs that had championed growth over the quality of life were rejected in favor of development as a tool for social justice; UNDP's *Human Development Reports* use the status of women as a critical measure of human capacity.

Women lawyers in many countries researched the gap between laws and practice and formed groups to teach women about their legal rights (Schuler 1986). As the conflicts between civil laws and customary and family law became evident, some women's organizations began to challenge patriarchal dominance and demand changes in the privileged traditional practices from inheritance rights to land and home ownership to the application of sharia law within civil society.[8]

Established women's organizations based on charitable contributions and committed to good works were joined by more activist groups.[9] Many more women were energized by the new opening for action and worked tirelessly as volunteers. These leaders grew in skill and self-confidence as leaders of women-only organizations. Women in trade unions and in political parties formed caucuses within these male-dominated institutions to press for greater attention to women's issues and sometimes, in frustration, formed their own organizations. Questions arose about what should be women's highest priority in a given country: survival needs or challenging patriarchy? Work issues of union women, women farmers, and domestic help were often seen as distinct from those of educated feminists in many countries (Basu 1995), although in revolutionary Nicaragua, women for a time bridged this gap (Chinchilla 1995).

The attempt to form a cohesive national women's movement has been well documented in India. The Committee on the Status of Women in India, operating under the aegis of the Indian Council for Social Science Research (ICSSR), was headed by Vina Mazumdar. Demand for research was so great that grants were often given to independent scholars (Gulhati 2003) and newly formed groups. For example, Devaki Jain formed the Institute for Social Studies Trust in 1975 in order to receive funding from ICSSR to conduct time allocation studies. For the next decade she produced a series of influential reports while providing technical services for grassroots organizations and engaging in advocacy. Jain convened the meeting where DAWN was established in 1984; DAWN took her views on development alternatives to the international level. Tensions between advocacy and research "meant that reports did not get published or put into high quality formats" (Jain 2003, 276), a familiar problem of action-research centers. Once the report on the Status of Women in India was completed, the government appointed advisory committee recommended that an autonomous institution be set up with a mandate to continue research on women's issues. In 1980, the Centre for Women's Development Studies was set up with Mazumdar as director (Sharma 2003).

Such research centers in India and elsewhere[10] relied heavily on the Ford Foundation and European agencies for much of their support. Despite this, at many international conferences these policy leaders from the South experienced increased discomfort with the "almost tedious reference to 'third world women.' Agendas as well as knowledge bases came from Northern women" (Jain 2003,

269–70; see also Mohanty 2003). DAWN provided an alternative vision for development and established a strong network of women scholars from the global South.

In many countries, feminist groups joined opposition movements against governments that were corrupt or authoritarian. With the advent of new democratic administrations, tension arose between women choosing to join the government and those who preferred to retain the high ground outside government (Jaquette 1994; Waylen 1997). Constitutional reforms have provided opportunities for cooperation, especially those in South Africa, Uganda, and most recently in Kenya (Gituto et al. 1998; Goetz and Hassim 2003). Current demands for quotas of women in decision-making positions are bringing women into the legislative and executive branches of governments in ways that will change the predominant male culture of the institutions.

National Machineries

Most governments did in fact set up a focal point within the bureaucracy: in the prime minister's office, in a ministry charged with welfare, or in some cases in a new women's ministry. Foreign donors often provided start-up funds, but governments were slow to provide additional resources, a fact that underscores the "shallowness of national commitment" (Goetz 1998, 62). The effectiveness of women's advocacy depended more on the attitudes of the men in positions of power than on where the office was placed in the formal government structure. To succeed, these offices needed presidents and prime ministers who were receptive to new policies and supportive of the staff. When this strategy worked, strong women in the ruling political party often provided the political muscle. Peggy Antrobus writes of her experience in Jamaica in 1979:

> Yes, Manley was very supportive. I was Director of the Women's Bureau, and it was situated in the Office of the Prime Minister. But this was in large measure thanks to the effectiveness of the leadership of women in the ruling party. Without these women Jamaica's national machinery would have been as ineffective as those machineries are everywhere, unless women are organized politically. (Personal communication, 22 September 2003)

Many one-party states in Africa established women's ministries, but the goal of these units was more often to enhance the party's policies than improve women's status. In communist and many one-party states, women were organized from the top down through a mass organization that served both as a communication system for party declarations and as a control mechanism, but rarely advanced women's views of their own needs.

Dorienne Rowan-Campbell (then Wilson-Smillie) writes of her attempts as the first director for the Women and Development Programme at the Commonwealth Secretariat to support the various women's offices in the organization's fifty-four member countries. Noting that this traditional civil service was quite flexible because rules were few and decisions were made by gentlemen's agreement, she writes: "Not being a gentleman, I felt I was free to challenge the rules. . . . We achieved what we did in part because the organization did not perceive the types of changes being instituted as important or even possible." Her staff analyzed the women's bureaus, held workshops on why these offices were not performing, and published resulting case studies in *Ladies in Limbo: The Fate of Women's Bureaux*. She observed that, although these new offices in developing countries provided opportunity for women, those hired often lacked requisite skills. To address this problem, the Programme initiated training sessions for these women and supported research centers to produce reports they could understand and use (Rowan-Campbell 2004).

Realizing that without political will and adequate resources women's machineries were isolated and ineffective, feminists turned to alternative strategies. Embracing the academic concept of gender, critics of WID believed that using a different term that focused attention on gender relations would be more effective and gain cooperation from male decision makers turned off by "feminist" advocacy. They argued that "women-only" programs marginalized women. The result of this paradigm shift within the donor community was to rename policy offices gender and development (GAD) and institute the mainstreaming of women's programs (see "Mainstreaming Gender in International Organizations," p. 53 in this book). In the field, gender programs were designed to examine gender relationship and to allow men as well as women to benefit from resources.

In my view, this shift has not necessarily meant a gain for women. The substitution of GAD for WID had the potential to undercut the political clout of the women's movement; indeed some critics think that was its original purpose. Instead, the promise of robust insights, gender has become a euphemism for women in programming or an alternative to sex in census forms, a politically correct usage that has dulled the analytical power of the term. Goetz found that the use of gender in the field was problematic: not only is it hard to translate but it expresses a "particularly Anglo-America feminist understanding of the social construction of gender" (Goetz 1998, 53; see also "What Is Justice?" in this book, p. 107). The confusion is illustrated by the widespread strategy of producing "*gender* budgets" of national and agency expenditures to document the paltry amounts of government budgets spent on *women* (see Budlender et al. 2002).

Mainstreaming was an attempt to promote women's issues throughout national ministries by insisting that gender be considered in all foreign assistance programming. Like so many good ideas, however, its implementation has often weakened women's programming. The WID/GAD focal points did provide more positions for women and helped staff develop a capacity for strategic planning, but lack of adequate sex-disaggregated data as well as limited resources undermined attempts to influence program budgets. Budget constraints had impeded WID efforts, but because GAD programs (and hence their resources) were spread through many ministries, their effect was often diluted. Women professionals often tried to avoid assignment to such marginalized units—GAD and WID alike—for fear these jobs would negatively affect their careers (Goetz 1998; Jahan 1995). The need for a central focus for information and research prompted most universities to strengthen their women's studies teaching units, pressured by faculty and students alike. But lack of similar internal and external pressure meant that bureaucracies tended to fall back into their usual habits, even when there were explicit directives from political leaders.

The most obvious way to increase the pressure is to ensure that women occupy executive and legislative positions. In many countries, the campaign for quotas for women in all executive and legislative decision-making positions has asked that 30 percent of seats in parliament be designated for women. Thirty percent representation is deemed necessary to provide a critical mass needed to bring about significant changes in policies and procedures. The political visibility of this demand has escalated in the past decade as both the UN Division on the Advancement of Women and the European Union have supported the concept (Gierycz 2001; Jaquette 1997). The 30 percent target quickly became a goal at the 1995 Fourth World Conference for Women held in Beijing (UNIFEM 2000, 9). The widespread interest in the issue of representation in legislative bodies has now been added to the earlier focus on economic and social issues as a means for women to protect and expanded their rights. The possibility of electing women increased in the 1990s as countries instituted democratic governments to replace former dictatorships.

To date over twenty-five countries have adopted legal or constitutional quotas for women in legislatures, primarily at the national level but also at the local level.[11] The Inter-Parliamentary Union regularly updates it data on the numbers of women in national legislatures, and posts results on its Web site (http://www .ipu.org). The Institute for Democracy and Electoral Assistance in Stockholm also tracks elections globally (http://www.idea.int). The latest published data indicates that women hold at least 30 percent of the seats in parliaments in eleven countries; another twenty-three countries have at least 20 percent of seats occupied by women.[12] Although many of these are developed countries, six are in Africa, six are in South America and the Caribbean, three are in former communist countries, and four are in currently communist countries (UNDP 2002b, 226–29).

The impact of the quotas on numbers of women elected varies by electoral systems, so that the understanding of the actual impact of more women in the legislatures on policy and laws will be a long-term project. Extensive studies of state legislatures and the Congress in the United States suggest that once a critical mass of women is present, it does influence types and direction of legislation (Swers 2001). Institutional cultures as well as societal norms loom as major obstacles in most countries (Tinker 2004d), but the view that women's different perspectives should be represented has found broad support along with the call for greater equality. Despite the many hurdles, women are moving into the formerly male bastion of politics; not all of them support feminist agendas, but many do focus on what is happening to women and families.

National Programming for Economic Development

The third directive of the Mexico City Plan of Action was to include women in economic planning. Literature assessing the impact of economic development on women focused initially on grassroots or community-level beneficiaries. But the employment opportunities available in development programs themselves are frequently overlooked. As a result of WID and antipoverty programs, governments and NGOs began to hire educated women as staff both in agency headquarters and in the field. Women riding scooters in Bangladesh or Cameroon in order to reach rural women certainly encouraged young girls to dream of alternatives to a life in the fields. While international development NGOs frequently hired women, the men who headed local NGOs or government agencies retained many gender stereotypes and resisted women's new mobility and visibility on the grounds that women were violating traditional norms. Even when efforts were made to protect women from these criticisms, such as the Grameen Bank's special residential centers in rural towns, cultural pressures on the women themselves were often severe.

Special provisions for women were debated in a recent action-learning project with the BRAC (Bangladesh Rural Advancement Committee), "the world's largest indigenous private sector development organization" with 15,000 staff and 1.6-million village-based members (Rao and Kelleher 1997, 123). As donors pressured BRAC to live up to its stated goals of gender equity and women's empowerment, women staff increased to 20 percent. Promotion is difficult when constraints on women's mobility contrast with men's freedom to travel night or day by any available means. "While the organization is attempting to accommodate women's needs, it is doing so in an incremental fashion, essentially leaving intact the dominant organizational culture, space, and ways of working which are themselves gendered. Thus, women in effect have to fit into a system that was made to fit men" (Rao and Kelleher 1997, 131).

Although women staff within male-dominated agencies and NGOs were able to affect programming, many joined ranks to set up their own development organizations such as the Self-Employed Women's Association (SEWA) and Working Women's Forum in India, Proshika in Bangladesh, the Green Belt Movement in Kenya, or the Glass of Milk Program in Peru. The charismatic leaders of such organizations expounded their innovative programs at international meetings and UN conferences; their ideas led to new policies and programs.

Ela Bhatt's experience with unions led her to start SEWA, a union of workers who had no employers. Her exposure to the feminist movement as well as her observation of methods used by community development programs led her to promote a form of organizing poor women that conflated these perspectives: women working at home could be organized and provided with services and protections. When the ILO decided to promote the Convention on Home Work in the 1990s, SEWA representatives found themselves in opposition to many trade union organizers from the global North who condemned home-based work as exploitative. In contrast, many women in the global South perceived home-based work as an important source of income that was consistent with their household responsibilities.

Yet all of these women workers need protection, and as more women in the North were beginning to work at home with computers, home-based work took on a different connotation. SEWA helped organize HomeNet International, a net-work of groups supporting home-based work. Together, these women convinced the trade unionists that organizing women in their communities, as SEWA and other development organizations do, provides an alternative to the way tradi-tional unions organize women workers. The 1996 Convention recognizes that homeworkers can be independent or produce for an employer. Governments who ratify it are expected to pass laws that treat homeworkers the same as other wage earners (Prügl 1999; Prügl and Tinker 1997).

Expanding her work with the informal sector, Ela Bhatt helped form WIEGO: Women in the Informal Economy, Globalizing and Organizing, in 1997. This umbrella group brought together researchers, practitioners, and activists from North and South who were concerned with home-based women workers. Their goal is to put this topic on the international agenda through broad participation in international meetings and by sponsoring action-research projects around the world to expand data on the informal economy and especially women's partici-pation in it.[13] An innovative study is tracing "value chains"—finding where value is added—for two distinct activities associated with women: garments and pro-cessed food and forest products. The hope is that a better understanding of where value is added will allow women lower on the chain to claim a greater share of the market price of the products. At a WIEGO conference in Ahmedabad in 2002, the importance of working with governments to address issues faced by infor-mal economy workers was emphasized. The mayor of Ahmedabad listened as a multiracial delegation from Durban discussed how they are engaging with men and women who work in the informal economy to coordinate services already available to these street vendors and to create new markets for them.

Roiling the Waters

In this way, the streams of educated activist women at the national level often merged with those in government, in research centers, and in development groups, working nationally and internationally for empowerment of women at all socioeconomic levels. While tensions between women in and outside the government were evident in some countries, in most places symbiotic relation-ships evolved. Insiders provided contracts and grants to local women's organiza-tions and research centers.[14] Outsiders produced marches, articles, and reports that strengthened the arguments of women in government for new programs. All benefited from funding flowing through development agencies and foundations. These women expanded on the issues raised by women in the field and local women's organizations and led the fight to alter policies and laws inhibiting women's equality at national and international levels. When structural adjustment policies were invoked in the mid-1980s, women documented their effects and influenced their implementation over time (Datta and Kornberg 2002).

The series of UN World Conferences on Women with their NGO forums grew impressively in size and complexity from Mexico City to Beijing. They provided space on official delegations and on panels at the forums for bureaucrats, advocates, and practitioners to meet fellow nationals as well as women from around the world. Sectoral issues expanded at each conference to include health, housing, and technology. These issues often reflected North/South disparities, but the view that "women's rights are human rights," declared at the 1993 UN World Conference on Human Rights and enshrined in the Beijing Platform for Action (United Nations 1995), unite women everywhere.

Equally important, the parallel NGO forums allowed women from around the world to meet and exchange ideas. Newly formed women's organizations often challenged older organizations for women. In India the split was between charitable elite women's groups and activist change agents (Tinker 2003b), while in much of Latin American there was a gap between feminist groups of educated women and working women from trade union backgrounds (Basu 1995) and domestic workers (Chaney and Castro 1989). All the ferment at local, national, and international levels created layers of women organized, interacting, disagreeing, and uniting to confront customary constraints, educate themselves and others, or campaign for change laws and practices that limited women's rights (Bystydzienski and Sekhon 1999).

ALTERING CULTURE THROUGH ECONOMIC DEVELOPMENT — BUT NOT ON PURPOSE

When international development policies began to consider how to empower people, not merely build infrastructure, programs addressing basic human needs were initiated to provide a safety net as rapid economic transformation resulted in increasing income disparities. Most early programs ignored the gender aspects of these programs. But, women as well as men had to benefit from new programs, or old patterns would reassert themselves once funding disappeared. Indoor toilets required buckets of water that women had to carry; improved cook stoves were sometimes less efficient in terms of women's time; literacy programs or health clinics held in midday meant lost time for farming. The fundamental flaw of these programs was ignorance of women's economic importance to family livelihood. Statistical methods introduced by the ILO in the 1930s defined work as labor for remuneration, effectively making women's unpaid family labor invisible (Benería 2001). Early foreign assistance programs, designed by economists, assumed that women did not work.

Women's Economic Subsistence Work

Time constraints helped explain women's sporadic attendance at classes or clinics held during working hours—which for women was twelve to fourteen hours per day: fetching water and fuelwood; planting, weeding, harvesting, processing and cooking food; taking care of family members; and maintaining the home. These necessary subsistence activities were invisible to economists and census takers, but these income-substituting chores become income producing in more advanced societies and therefore should be counted as economic contributions to the nation. Rapid deforestation added to women's work as they trekked farther and farther for fuelwood supplies. Wangari Maathai, Nobel Peace Prize recipient for 2004, formed the Greenbelt Movement in Kenya in 1977 to counter desertification while providing women with income and a source of fuel. The Nobel citation notes: "She has taken a holistic approach to sustainable development that embraces democracy, human rights and women's rights in particular. She thinks globally and acts locally."

The appropriate technology community responded to the drudgery by introducing faster ways to grind grain and designing more efficient cook stoves (Tinker 1987c, 1980b). Such technology was introduced to villagers through community organizations set up by national and international NGOs. These improved technologies not only reduced time spent but had nutritional and health consequences such as reducing indoor pollution when cooking (Smith et al. 1981), or making up nutritional needs of underfed women (Batliwala 1985). Though these solutions were sometimes inappropriate, the attention and organizing women received were important steps for increasing their capacity.

Income needs grew as subsistence economies were monetized. Women needed to buy pots and cloth and pay school fees (Huston 1979). Early efforts to form groups for knitting and sewing (skills presumed to be female, even in countries where men are tailors and weavers) seldom produced income. Most craft-based activities such as basketry or pottery did not survive the departure of rural development workers who market the products for free. These efforts to help the poor earn income were based on Western stereotypes and lacked adequate market studies.

Existing Employment

More successful were projects assisting women who were already working. SEWA organized women working in the informal sector and doing the most menial jobs—those collecting trash for reselling, carrying loads of wood on their heads, or stuffing cloth with scraps from textile factories to make mattresses. From vegetable sellers to *bidi* rollers; each occupation has its own section. Bhatt notes that the informal economy in India today employs well over 90 percent of the Indian workforce, provides some 63 percent of the GDP, 55 percent of the savings, and 47 percent of the exports. In its 30 years of existence, SEWA has organized 418,000 women, 92 percent from minorities and 7 percent Muslims, seeking the women out in the street or in their homes (Bhatt 2000). Without any employers to negotiate with, SEWA lobbies the government for favorable laws and regulations to benefit its members. Because they lacked a regular wage, many women frequently had to take out loans at usurious interest so, in 1974, SEWA established a bank. Additional financial services are now offered including enterprise and health insurance as well as home loans. Literacy classes are offered, and members are recruited to be local and regional leaders, for which they are offered a small fee (Rose 1992).

In 2002, I visited Khulsum, a Muslim tea seller in Ahmedabad, India, who had also been a SEWA organizer for fifteen years. In return for walking around the nearby slum to check on SEWA members and try to recruit more, she received 35 rupees a day. Shortly after this visit, Hindu mobs burned most of these slums, targeting Muslims. Khulsum's shanty and teacart were both burned, but the insurance offered by SEWA for 85 rupees per year covered her assets in her home and outside up to 5,000 rupees.

Because of caste constraints, few women sell prepared food in India. But in Southeast Asia and in Africa, street food vendors are predominantly female. In 1980, I began a fifteen-year study of women and men who make and sell food on the streets in seven countries (Tinker 1997b).

At the enterprise level, three findings stand out: except in Africa, the family cooperates in the enterprise; profits are invested in children not in the business; and income from street food vending is often greater than that earned by local white collar workers. The greatest obstacles to vendors were onerous government regulations that often resulted in "street cleaning" which left their carts and utensils broken. Municipal authorities in the study towns changed these policies once they understood the economic importance of street foods. These authorities also provided access to clean water because they understood that the major health risk in street foods came from washing hands and dishes in dirty water. The Food and Agricultural Organization, which issues directives on health safety to governments, continues to work with cities and vendors to improve health standards.

Microcredit in Perspective

The street foods study underscores the experience of SEWA: negotiations with governments to change regulations may be the best approach to improve the income of poor entrepreneurs. Available credit is most useful when it is not tied to specific productive uses. These observations provide a critical counterpoint to much of the research and policy on microcredit.

When small funds became available through microcredit schemes in the early 1980s, they allowed women to expand entrepreneurial activities doing what they knew how to do: raise goats and chickens, make or sell food, pound rice, even buy a pedicab for male relatives to use. The rapid adoption of microcredit programs in the developing world showed that there is tremendous demand for credit— at reasonable rates—among the poor. Promotion of microcredit as the answer to poverty among women has become so insistent that many observers fear that spending on this single solution will undercut other needed programs. Clearly, the focus on one particular path to empowering poor women should be suspect and needs careful evaluation of its advantages and pitfalls.

The Grameen Bank exemplifies the predominant microcredit approach. Participants form small solidarity groups which act as collateral for individual loans. Because of their superior repayment rates, women now make up over 90 percent of the bank's membership. Promoted as a minimalist approach that avoids costly social services that were common in earlier poverty programs, the concept of group responsibility for loans to the poor has been introduced in countries as diverse as Nepal, Rwanda, and the United States (Acharya 2000; Clark and Kays 1999; Edgcomb et al. 1996; Servon 1999; Tinker 2000).

The strong social movement foundation of Grameen Bank is frequently overlooked; the bank requires its members to follow Sixteen Decisions designed not only to encourage banking discipline but also to encourage women to practice social goals such as not paying dowry when their daughters marry, not overspending on weddings and funerals, and limiting family size. In other words, the Grameen Bank trains the poor to reduce traditional social spending as well as to save and utilize credit. Further, members are provided information about health and family planning along with financial and marketing issues at the required weekly meetings. In recent years, in order to increase international support, the Grameen Bank has downplayed this social aspect and claims it is simply a bank.

Although alternative microfinance institutions are now extensively used around the world (Otero and Rhyne 1994; Mehta et al. 1995; Sebstad and Cohen 2001), the Grameen model still appears to many agencies and NGOs as the panacea for poverty alleviation. International donors sponsored a Microcredit Summit in 1997 in Washington to announce a goal of reaching 100 million poor with credit facilities, primarily along the Grameen model, by 2005.[15] This initiative rekindled critics who are worried about concentrating on a single method of assisting poor women; the rosy view of microcredit masks serious issues about targeting and commercialization and causes confusion about microfinance as a substitute for social welfare (Burjorjee et al. 2002). Cynics comment that the Grameen Bank has been "lavishly supported by donors" because it is "an ideal channel for donor assistance, since it is relatively standardized" (Harper 2002, 9).

Economic complaints center on the profitability of the microenterprises; existing women entrepreneurs are more likely to show a profit than those starting a business the first time (Kabeer 1998b). Others claim that women are mere conduits for loans controlled by male family members (Goetz and Sen Gupta 1996). Such critics ignore the cultural context of rural Bangladesh where studies show that women's access to funds itself seems to raise their status within the family and reduce domestic violence (Schuler et al. 1999). Further, research indicates most women use credit both for their own projects and also for family enterprises such as farming and selling the harvest, which are typically male activities. Todd (1996), who observed Grameen members in their villages for a year, found that women often serve as family managers and that their ability to improve the family income increases their status and self-confidence. Their acumen was evident in the ways they circumvented strict rules for use of loans and bought land *in their own names* for their husbands to farm—bank members are supposed to own no more than .25 ha (.62 acre) of land although they may take out loans to build a house on land they hold in their own name. The Grameen model also rigidly controls the use of loans for productive activities, ignoring the fungibility of cash expenditures between social needs. Yet data indicate that family finances improved, whatever the success of the women's enterprise, simply because loans from the bank, though not negligible, were available at a much lower rate than through local moneylenders.

The highly disciplined Grameen model seems uniquely adapted to Bangladesh. Explaining why India has preferred self-help groups, Harper suggests that "Bangladesh has less experience of any form of democracy than India" which has a more diverse and individualist society (2002, 9). Because self-help groups set up and run their own banks, members themselves become skilled in finance. This contrasts with a large staff needed to visit and monitor rural Grameen centers. Given the geographic isolation and the traditional culture that persists in rural areas of Bangladesh, most of this staff are men. Training members to run their own banks, a common practice in Latin America as well as in India, creates an intermediate level of empowered women. Such upward mobility for members, which provides income and leadership opportunities to less educated women, is a feature of organizations led by women. In Bangladesh, empowerment for women awaits the generation of daughters of Grameen Bank and BRAC members who are now in school.

Use and Misuse of Microfinance Programs

Development organizations worry that the Grameen Bank model is too narrow: although it claims to be a bank, members have difficulty withdrawing the money they save as part of each loan. Accumulated assets of members have funded much of its growth. Alternative models put more street on banking functions, which allow easy deposits and withdrawals. SEWA's bank is now located in one of the most modern buildings in Ahmedabad; their members enter confidently, often with their husbands trailing them as they conduct their business. Even street kids in Delhi have launched their own bank under the auspices of the local voluntary agency, Butterflies. Located at the Old Delhi Railway Station, where kids shelter at night, the bank keeps their meager income safe; older children have even started taking loans to start their own enterprises.

As the popularity of microcredit explodes, the danger of offering too much credit to the poor is worrying many observers. One of the most vociferous is Farhad Mazhar, an editor of the Bangla journal *Chinta* (*Reflection*). In an e-mail to me on 25 July 1999 she wrote: "Politically we always resisted the bizarre idea that indebting poor contributes to 'development.' The idea that poor women of Bangladesh are empowered by being indebted to credit institutions run by middle class male patriarchal structures built upon the existing web of patriarchal relations, obligations and oppressions—is the biggest joke of our time."

Concerns over indebtedness increase when groups offering credit compete for customers, something that might happen as the targets of the Microcredit Summit are reached. Will the poor run up debts just as so many Americans do with multiple credit cards, paying off one card with credit from another? Something similar happened in Nepal when the rural credit bank allowed a single borrower to have several loans of differing length; the program collapsed with no apparent injury to the borrowers. In Bangladesh, with its tighter group membership structure, neither borrowing too much nor failing to pay back seems likely.

Some academics argue that offering credit to women for work-intensive low-profit activities condemns women to continued drudgery. Many microfinance programs have responded by assisting in the development of new opportunities from catering or craft businesses to the Grameen Bank cell phone project. But offering credit to the poor is about more than setting up a microenterprise. Required group meetings are a font of information and support as regular meetings of otherwise isolated and hardworking women open the world to them. Women exchange ideas about dealing with male violence as well as male interference with loans. Most groups promote literacy and often provide such training. Women members enhance their personal and social skills while learning how to set up and run their enterprises. Increased self-confidence as well as income encourages women to send their daughters to school.

Observers agree that at least among users of Grameen loans, violence against women falls as women's economic importance increases (Hashimi et al. 1996), perhaps because access to the loans, which are used by the family as well as by the women, are through the women themselves. A particularly poignant case was recently recorded by Edward Miguel in his paper "Poverty and Witch Killing." In Tanzania, "households near subsistence kill (or expel) relatively unproductive members to safeguard the nutritional status of other members," justifying their actions by accusing the old women of being witches. Miguel notes that witch killings in South Africa dropped after old age pensions were introduced in the 1990s (2003, 1).

Both SEWA and the Grameen Bank offer home loans to women. The power and sense of control that comes from owning one's own house is incalculable in these patriarchal societies. Houses can be used as a place of work, a source of food, provide income through renting, and protection from being evicted should a husband desert or divorce (Tinker 1995a). A woman's right to own a house is traditional within Islam, and laws have been changed in India to allow it. But in many parts of Africa, the material power that comes from accumulation of assets is still not guaranteed to women. Women throughout the continent are taking on this issue (see "Unequal Rights" in this book, p. 159; Tinker 1999d).

Credit is a universal need; the poor are not different in this. Moneylenders have prospered giving usurious loans, and traditional loan circles, often based on family, did not reach the poor. When poor women can borrow at a reasonable rate of 16 percent per year, rather than 40 percent per month, the standard of living of the household improves even if the enterprise loses money.

Local Leading to National Political Action

Spontaneous protests have erupted in India over government actions that directly affect women's livelihood, such as the use of nontimber resources or legalizing of toddy, a cheap local liquor, to increase state taxes. Established women's organizations quickly absorbed and supported these new issues. The emergence of the Chipko movement, women in the Himalayan foothills who hugged trees to prevent their harvesting, documented the negative consequences of rapid economic growth not only on the poor but also on the environment. Recognizing the indigenous knowledge of such women about the sustainable uses of field and forest, women have organized to support traditional agricultural practices in Ladakh and elsewhere (Angeles and Tarbotton 2001), against high dams that would deprive many peasants of their land, and against "biopiracy" of golden rice or the neem tree (Shiva 2001). In Bihar, local women organized to obtain land in their own names (Agarwal 1994).

Increased radio and television coverage of such events spread the word, and soon spontaneous groups of village women arose protesting local inequities. Women in hill tribes in Maharashtra shamed husbands who beat their wives by banging kitchen pots outside the offending man's house. Dalit (formerly called untouchable) women joined with devadasis (temple dancers) to protest the dedication of girls to serve in temples as "brides" of the gods—a sort of sanctioned prostitution. In central India local women challenged government sanctioned toddy shops because cheap liquor was increasing domestic violence while encouraging their husbands to spend their paychecks on the liquor; the shops were closed (Verghese 1997).

This ferment was widely reported and helped spur the creation of reserved seats in local councils. Under laws passed in 1993, one-third of all seats in local councils in India must be filled by women, a goal that is achieved by rotating the reserved constituencies so that no seat is permanently a woman's seat. While such provisions might be seen as preventing continuity, many women become so respected that they are elected to general seats. To date over one million women have been elected to local bodies.

In Argentina and Chile, women led nonviolent protests against the "disappeared." Such action under authoritarian governments was dangerous; the women counted on their identity as mothers. In Peru, women organized communal kitchens and organized boycotts against rising prices and supplied milk to children and communal kitchens in poor neighborhoods during the economic crisis of the 1980s (Jaquette and Wolchik 1998, 5). A similar protest by Indonesian women in 1998 helped precipitate a regime change. "Acting under the cover of the traditional concept of the role of women, young women intellectuals started the sales of affordable milk for infants." Encouraged by widespread support, the women led a demonstration in front of Hotel Indonesia; three women observers were mistakenly arrested (Bianpoen 2000, 286). The organizer of the group writes that "They were very much aware that the shift—*from milk to politics*—was a protest against the government's masculine paradigm of power and violence which had brought the country to economic ruin" (Roosseno 2000, xi).

The groups that organize such demonstrations are often evanescent; established organizations are usually too embedded in the system to contest it. But South Africa offers an example of women countering the party of which they were an integral part. The Rural Women's Movement which had agitated against forced removals and Bantustans, worried that a return of power to tribal chiefs, as proposed in the draft constitution which made the bill of rights subordinate to customary law, would legitimize women's subordination (Kemp et al. 1995; Hassim 2003). In 1992, the Women's National Coalition was formed from eighty-one groups and thirteen regional alliances of women's groups plus the women's caucuses or "gender desks" of all major parties. This coalition declared a Women's Charter for Effective Equality and lobbied successfully for reversing the order and making customary law answer to civil law. The amended constitution was passed in 1997.

Such protests, initiated by small groups, merge local concerns into national and eventually into international policies. The examples presented here merely suggest the activities of hundreds of others.[16] The political climate in a given country is key to the success of such demonstrations: challenging authoritarian regimes must be done with care; few protests take place in communist countries. In Eastern Europe as in the Philippines, where gender equality was widely assumed, women tended not to organize separately but rather joined men in contesting government actions (Jaquette and Wolchik 1998; Roces 2000).

ACCUMULATING PERSONAL, ECONOMIC, SOCIAL, MATERIAL, AND POLITICAL POWER

In less than four decades, organized women everywhere have coalesced into what has been described as the dominant social movement that emerged in the late twentieth century, a global women's movement, with varied priorities and practices but united in its goal of empowering women. For millennia, women came together to harvest, worship, and support others in their tribes or villages. In the past 150 years, suffragists formed national and international associations for business, charitable, and educational goals. Many international women's organizations achieved representation in the United Nations, which allowed them to provide guidance and support to the new wave of the women's movement.

What made the quantum leap from disparate organizations to a diverse global women's movement—with local, national and international affects—possible? My argument is that the recognition by the international development community of women's economic roles made a critical difference, and it is an understanding that has been championed by women around the globe. But recognition without funding would not have had the results inscribed in this chapter. Funds flowed to researchers and activists; women did not have to be wealthy to travel to international conferences or to focus on studies of women, or to write books such as this for an audience created by the rise of the women's movement. Opportunities for women to be paid to study or work with women grew. Funding reached poor rural and urban women through NGOs and community development projects. Current efforts to ensure that women share in and benefit from the information society are also funded by international agencies, and the spread of rapid global communications has increased the speed by which ideas flow.

When economic aid began to flow, few planners considered the possible dislocation of the relations between men and women, which were viewed as established behaviors, firmly embedded in local traditions. Today, theses changes are identified with the West, and nationalists and religious fundamentalists in many countries fulminate against "cultural imperialism." But these leaders do not desire less developed economies, only a return to unchallenged patriarchal control. Thus in many ways, women's status has become hostage to cultural change. Only women in their own countries and societies can counter this trend. But the intellectual support from other countries and examples of women's growing empowerment are essential for their success. The combination of resources available through development and the power of local organizing contributed to women's empowerment at various socioeconomic levels through myriad channels and organizations. No one planned it, but women seized the opportunities and empowerment happened.

NOTES

1. For historic roots of women's organizing see Basu 1995 for a global view; Jayawardena 1986 or Tinker 2003b for Asia; Kumar 1993 for India; Oey-Gardiner and Bianpoen 2000 for Indonesia; Weiss and Gilani 2001 for Pakistan; F. Miller 1981 for Latin America; M. Snyder 2004 for Africa.

2. Observing women's agricultural activities in India and Africa, Boserup found little recognition of this in economic literature and determined to document her insights. Her works on agriculture and population were equally provocative in their fields. For a summary of her influence see Tinker 2003b and 2004b. Boserup completed a significant review of her evolving ideas in *My Professional Life and Publications 1929–1998*, which should be more widely known. For a succinct statement of her views on women and development see Boserup 1990.

3. Gloria Scott, author of the phrase "integration of women in development," explains how she convinced the UN Commission on the Status of Women that economics was critical in her chapter "Breaking New Ground" in Fraser and Tinker 2004.

4. Displaced homemakers were women in the fifties and sixties who rushed into marriage with the expectation that they would be financially secure for life. As the divorce rate climbed in the seventies, perhaps due to consciousness-raising among the wives, such women were without protection before changes were made to guarantee them a portion of their husband's pension or social security. The women who lobbied for these changes wrote about their struggles and successes in *Women in Washington: Advocates for Public Policy* (Tinker 1983b).

5. For the story of the Percy Amendment to the U.S. Foreign Assistance Act of 1973, see Tinker 1983a. The WID focus on poor women was frequently ignored by critics who argued that women were not a homogeneous category and that class was a predominant classification. See Jaquette and Staudt, this volume.

6. Twenty-seven women pioneers of the women in development movement from around the world tell their own stories in Fraser and Tinker 2004.

7. Many activists scorned women in governmental agencies, a topic that was hotly debated in Latin America (Jaquette 1994). In *Missionaries and Mandarins*, Miller and Razavi examine the distinct strategies of women working to transform state institutions, the critics/activists/missionaries outside versus the femocrats/mandarins working inside (1998b). In the United States, this approach was utilized during the period of major change in laws affecting women in the 1960s and 70s (Tinker 1983b).

8. Women Living Under Muslim Law is one of the most courageous groups; they provide women with the divergent interpretations of sharia law so that they can question local prac-

tice. Women in India confronted the courts over a widow's rights to support in the Shah Bano case (Kumar 1993). Ethnic practices were at the center of the Otieno case in Kenya.

9. India provides an example of these competing groups (Kumar 1993). See also Tinker 2004d.

10. Peggy Antrobus, head of the Women's Bureau in Jamaica, was involved in several such organizations before heading the DAWN secretariat for several years.

11. India requires that 33 percent of all panchayat or local council seats as well as one-third of elected heads of these councils must be occupied by women and secures this figure with reserved seats. See Tinker 2004a,d.

12. As of March 2002, those legislatures with the highest percentage of women are Sweden 42.7; Denmark 38.0; Finland 36.5; Norway 36.4; Iceland 34.9; Netherlands 32.9; Germany 31.8; Argentina 31.3; New Zealand 30.8; Mozambique 30; South Africa 29.8. The 23 countries with at least 20 percent of the seats occupied by women: Belgium, Switzerland, Austria, Spain, Poland, and Bulgaria in Europe; Canada and Australia; Barbados, Trinidad and Tobago, and Sao Tome and Principe in the Caribbean; Guyana and Nicaragua in Central America; Namibia, Tanzania, Uganda, and Rwanda in Africa; communist countries of Cuba, China, Laos, Vietnam; plus Seychelles, Turkmenistan.

13. Martha A. Chen at Harvard's Kennedy School is the coordinator of regionally based directors of programs investigating major issues of the sector. More information on http://www.wiego.org.

14. Projects to support heads of these various offices and to strengthen their impact on programming were a major activity of the WID office of the Commonwealth Secretariat. See Rowan-Campbell 2004.

15. This highly publicized meeting included 2,900 delegates from 137 countries and included Hillary Rodham Clinton, Grameen Bank founder Mohammad Yunus, and SEWA founder Ela Bhatt. More information is on http://www.microcreditsummit.org.

16. Two edited books appeared in 1995 in time for the Beijing conference; authors in Amrita Basu's *The Challenge of Local Feminisms* recount stories of a multitude of organizations; Alida Brill's *A Rising Public Voice: Women in Politics Worldwide* contains personal stories of outstanding leaders.

Acronyms

ACFVA	Advisory Committee on Voluntary Foreign Aid
ADB	Asian Development Bank
ACFODE	Action for Development (Uganda)
AID/WID	Women in Development Office, USAID
AIDS	acquired immunodeficiency syndrome
ALRI	acute lower respiratory infection
APEC	Asia Pacific Economic Cooperation
AUMWD	Association of Uganda Women Medical Doctors
BRAC	Bangladesh Rural Advancement Committee
CPM	capability poverty measure
CEDAW	Convention on the Elimination of All Forms of Discrimination Against Women (UN), 1979
CGA	Country Gender Assessment
CIDA	Canadian International Development Agency
CLACSO	Latin American Council of Social Sciences
COPD	chronic obstructive pulmonary disease
CSD	Commission on Sustainable Development (UN)
CSW	Commission on the Status of Women (UN)
DAWN	Development Alternatives with Women for a New Era
DALD	Daily Annual Lost Days (per capita)
DALY	Disability Adjusted Life Year
ECOSOC	Economic and Social Council UN
EGAT	Electrical Generating Authority of Thailand

ERA	Equal Rights Amendment (U.S.)
EU	European Union
FTZ	free trade zone
GAD	gender and development
GDI	gender-related development index (UN)
GEM	gender empowerment measure (UN)
GNP	gross national product
GIDP	Gender in Development Program (UNDP)
GPA	Gender Plan of Action (USAID)
HDI	human development index (UN)
HIV	human immunodeficiency virus
HPI	human poverty index (UN)
HRS	Household Responsibility System (China)
ICPD	International Conference on Women's Population and Development (UN; Cairo, 1994)
ICSSR	Indian Council for Social Science Research
ICT	information communication technology
IGTN	International Gender and Trade Network
ILO	International Labor Organization
IMF	International Monetary Fund
INSTRAW	International Research and Training Institute for the Advancement of Women (UN)
ISIS-WICCE	Ugandan women's NGO
IWY	International Women's Year (1975)
NAFTA	North American Free Trade Area
NATO	North Atlantic Treaty Organization
NAWOU	National Women's Organization of Uganda
NEPO	National Energy Policy Office (Thailand)
NGO	nongovernmental organization
NGO-COD	NGO Coordinating Committee for Development (Thailand)
NIEO	New International Economic Order
NOW	National Organization of Women
OAS	Organization of American States
OECD	Organization for Economic Cooperation and Development
OEPP	Office of Environmental Policy and Planning (Thailand)
OTOP	One Tambon/One Product program (Thailand)
PCD	Pollution Control Department (Thailand)

PPA	participatory poverty assessment
PRAS	participatory rural appraisal methodologies
PREM	Poverty Reduction and Economic Management (World Bank)
SAP	structural adjustment program
SARS	severe acute respiratory syndrome
SEWA	Self-Employed Women's Association (India)
SIDA	Swedish International Development Agency
TVES	township and village enterprises (China)
UMWA	Uganda Media Women's Association
UN	United Nations
UNDAW	UN Division for the Advancement of Women (Secretariat of the CSW)
UNDP	UN Development Program
UNEP	UN Environment Program
UNESCO	United Nations Educational, Scientific and Cultural Organization
UNFPA	UN Fund for Population Activities (now UN Population Fund)
UN-HABITAT	UN Human Settlements Programme
UNHCR	UN High Commission for Refugees
UNICEF	UN International Children's Emergency Fund
UNIFEM	UN Fund for Women
UNRISD	UN Research Institute on Social Development
USAID	US Agency for International Development
UWONET	Uganda Women's Network
WCED	World Commission for Environment and Development
WEDO	Women's Environment and Development Organization
WHO	World Health Organization
WID	women and development
WIEGO	Women in the Informal Economy, Globalizing and Organizing
WTO	World Trade Organization
YWCA	Young Women's Christian Association (Zimbabwe)
ZARD	Zambia Association for Research and Development
ZNADWO	Zambian National Association of Disabled Women
ZWB	Zimbabwe Women's Bureau

Bibliography

Abric, Jean Claude. 1994. *Pratiques Sociales et Représentations*. Paris: Presses Universitaires de France.

Acharya, Meena. 2000. "Economic Dimensions of Governance in Nepal." Kathmandu: Tanka Prasad Acharya Memorial Foundation.

Acharya, M., and L. Bennett. 1981. *The Status of Women in Nepal, Volume II, Part 9, The Rural Women of Nepal: An Aggregate Analysis and Summary of 8 Village Studies*. Kathmandu, Nepal: Centre for Economic Development and Administration, Tribhuvan University.

Ackerly, Brooke A., and Susan Moller Okin. 1999. "Feminist Social Criticism and the International Movement for Women's Rights as Human Rights." In *Democracy's Edges*, edited by I. Shapiro and C. Cordon, 134–62. Cambridge: Cambridge University Press.

Ackerman, John. 2004. "Co-Governance for Accountability: Beyond 'Exit' and 'Voice.'" *World Development* 32 (3): 447–63.

Acosta-Belén, Edna, and Christine Bose. 1995. "Colonialism, Structural Subordination and Empowerment: Women in the Development Process in Latin America and the Caribbean." In *Women in the Latin American Development Process*, edited by Christine Bose and Edna Acosta-Belén, 15–36. Philadelphia: Temple University Press.

ACVFA (Advisory Committee on Voluntary Foreign Aid). 2000. *New Agenda for Gender Equality*. Washington, D.C.: USAID.

ACWF (All China Women's Federation). 2003. "Women's Rights in Land Contract Are Outlined in the Law." http://www.women.org.cn/womenorg/English/english/whatisnws/2002-4.htm.

Agarwal, Bina. 1996. "From Mexico 1975 to Beijing 1995." *Indian Journal of Gender Studies* 3 (1): 21–25.

———. 1994. *A Field of One's Own: Gender and Land Rights in South Asia*. Cambridge: Cambridge University Press.

———. 1986. *Cold Hearths and Barren Slopes: The Woodfuel Crisis in the Third World*. London: Zed Books.

AIHW. 1996. *Australia's Health 1996*. Canberra: Australian Institute of Health and Welfare.

Albelda, Randy. 1997. *Economics and Feminism: Disturbances in the Field*. New York: Twayne Publishers.

Alvarez, Sonia. 1999. "Advocating Feminism: The Latin American Feminist NGO 'Boom.'" *International Feminist Journal of Politics* 1 (2): 181–209.

Anastasakos, Kiki. 2002. "Structural Adjustment Policies in Mexico and Costa Rica." In *Women in Developing Countries: Assessing Strategies for Empowerment*, edited by R. Datta and J. Kornberg, 113–27. Boulder: Lynne Rienner.

Anderson, Jeanine. 1990. "Sistemas de género e identidad de mujeres en culturas marcadas del Perú." *Revista Peruana de Ciencias Sociales* 2 (1): 77–117.

Anderson, Mary B. 1991. "An Analysis of Operational Experiences in Integrating Women into Development." SWID/1991/WP2. New York: UNIFEM.

Andina, Michèle, and Barbara Pillsbury. 1998. *Trust: An Approach to Women's Empowerment—Lessons Learned from an Evaluation on Empowerment and Family Planning with Women's NGOs.* Los Angeles: Pacific Institute for Women's Health.

Andreas, Carol. 1985. *When Women Rebel: The Rise of Popular Feminism in Peru.* Westport, Conn.: Lawrence Hill.

Angeles, Leonora C., and Rebecca Tarbotton. 2001. "Local Transformation Through Global Connection: Women's Assets and Environmental Activism for Sustainable Agriculture in Lahakh, India." Special issue, *Women's Studies Quarterly* 29 (1 and 2): 99–115.

Annenberg Center for Communication. 1996. *Summary Report on Communication and Empowerment: Use of Media and Information Technologies in Developing Countries, a Symposium Presented by the Development Communication Program.* University of Southern California, April.

Antrobus, Peggy. 2004. "A Caribbean Journey." In *Developing Power: How Women Transformed International Development*, edited by Arvonne Fraser and Irene Tinker, 138–48. New York: Feminist Press.

Apodaca, Clair. 2000. "The Effects of Foreign Aid on Women's Attainment of Their Economic and Social Human Rights." *Journal of Third World Studies* 17 (2): 205–19.

Appadurai, Arjun. 1990. "Disjunction and Difference in the Global Cultural Economy." In *Global Culture: Nationalism, Globalization and Modernity*, edited by Mike Featherstone, 295–310. London: Sage.

Appleton, Simon. 1991. "Gender Dimensions of Structural Adjustment: The Role of Economic Theory and Quantitative Analysis." *IDS Bulletin* 22 (1): 17–22.

Arnold, Denise. 1997. *Más allá del silencio. Las fronteras de género en los Andes.* La Paz: ILCA-CIASE.

Arriagada, Irma. 1998. "Latin American Families: Convergences and Divergences in Models and Policies." *CEPAL Review* 65: 85–102.

Aslanbeigui, Nahid, Steven Pressman, and Gale Summerfield, eds. 1994. *Women in the Age of Economic Transformation: Gender Impact of Reforms in Post-Socialist and Developing Countries.* London: Routledge.

Aslanbeigui, Nahid, and Gale Summerfield. 2001. "Risk, Gender, and Development in the 21st Century." *International Journal of Politics, Culture, and Society* 15 (1): 7–26.

———. 1989. "The Impact of the Responsibility System on Women in Rural China: A Theoretical Application of Sen's Theory of Entitlement." *World Development* 17 (3): 343–50.

Babb, Florence. 1999. *Mujeres y Hombres en Vicos, Perú: Un caso de Desarrollo Desigual.* En Genero y Desarrollo II, Materiales de Enseñanza del Diploma de Estudios de Género, 95–116. Lima: Facultad de Ciencias Sociales, Universidad Católica del Perú.

Backer, Thomas E., Everett M. Rogers, and Pradip Sopory. 1992. *Designing Health Communication Campaigns: What Works?* Newbury Park, Calif.: Sage.

Baden, Sally. 2000. "Gender, Governance and Feminization of Poverty." In *Women's Politi-*

cal Participation and Good Governance: 21st Century Challenges, edited by Lina Hamadeh-Banerjee, 27–40. New York: UNDP.

———. 1999. "Gender, Governance and the 'Feminization of Poverty.'" Background Paper Prepared for Management Development and Governance Division, UNDP.

Baden, Sally, and Anne Marie Goetz. 1998. "Who Needs [Sex] When You Can Have [Gender]?" In *Feminist Visions of Development: Gender, Analysis and Policy*, edited by Cecile Jackson and Ruth Pearson, 19–38. London: Routledge.

Baden, Sally, and Kirsty Milward. 1997. *Gender Inequality and Poverty: Trends, Linkages, Analysis and Poverty Implications*. Brighton: Institute of Development Studies, Bridge Report no. 30.

Bakker, Isabella. 2003. "Neoliberal Governance and the Reprivatization of Social Reproduction: Social Provisioning and Shifting Gender Orders." In *Power, Production and Social Reproduction*, edited by Isabella Bakker and Stephen Gill, 66–82. New York: Palgrave McMillan.

———, ed. 1994. *The Strategic Silence: Gender and Economic Policy*. London: Zed Books.

Baldez, Lisa. 2002. *Why Women Protest: Women's Movements in Chile*. Cambridge: Cambridge University Press.

Ballard, H., D. Collins, A. Lopez, and J. Freed. 2002. *Harvesting Floral Greens in Western Washington as Value-Addition: Labor Issues and Globalization*. Meeting of the International Association for the Study of Common Property, Victoria Falls, Zimbabwe.

Ballard, Heidi, and Louise Fortmann. 2004. "Collaborating Experts: Integrating Civil and Conventional Science to Inform Management of Salal (*Gaultheria shallon*)." In *Fostering Integration: Concepts and Practice in Resource and Environmental Management*, edited by Kevin Hanna and D. Scott Slocombe. Oxford: Oxford University Press.

Bardhan, Kalpana, and Stephan Klasen. 1999. "UNDP's Gender Related Indices: A Critical Review." *World Development* 27: 6, 985–1010.

Baron-Cohen, Simon. 2003. *The Essential Difference: The Truth About the Male and Female Brain*. New York: Basic Books/Perseus Publishing.

Barrig Maruja. 2001. *El Mundo al Revés. Imágenes de la Mujer Indígena*. Buenos Aires: CLACSO/ASDI.

Bartle, John R., and Marilyn Marks Ruben. 2002. *The Potential of Gender Budgeting: Has Its Day Come?* Paper delivered to a Panel on Democratizing the Budgetary Process. Association for Budgeting and Financial Management Annual Conference 12 October 2002, Kansas City, Mo.

Basch, Linda, special ed. 2004. "Women, Human Security and Globalization." *Peace Review: A Journal of Social Justice* 16 (1).

Basu, Amrita, ed., and Elizabeth McGrory. 1995. *The Challenge of Local Feminisms*. Boulder: Westview Press.

Batiwala, Srilatha. 1982. "Rural Energy Scarcity and Nutrition: A New Perspective." *Economic and Political Weekly* 27 (9): 329–33.

Baulch, Bob. 1996. Editorial. "The New Poverty Agenda: A Disputed Consensus." *IDS Bulletin* 27 (1): 1–10.

Baumann, Theo. 1999. "Sobre Autonomía." The Hague, unpublished manuscript.

Baxi, Upendra. 2004. Presentation at the Conference on Gender, Governance and Globalisation, University of Warwick, 17–18 September.

Bay, E. 1982. *Women and Work in Africa*. Boulder: Westview Press.

Bayes, Jane. 1991. *Women and Public Administration: International Perspectives*. Binghamton: Haworth.

Baylies, Carolyn. 1996. "Diversity in Patterns of Parenting and Household Formation." In *Good Enough Mothering? Feminist Perspectives on Lone Motherhood*, edited by E. Bortolaia Silva, 76–96. London: Routledge.

Beall, Jo. 1997a. "Households, Livelihood and the Urban Environment: Social Development Perspectives on Solid Waste Disposal in Faisalabad City, Pakistan." Ph.D. thesis. Department of Geography, London School of Economics.

———. 1997b. "Participation in the City: A Gender Perspective" In *A City for All: Valuing Difference and Working with Diversity*, edited by Jo Beall, 38–48. London: Zed Books.

———. 1996. "Social Security and Social Networks among the Urban Poor in Pakistan." *Habitat International* 19 (4): 427–45.

Bebbington, Denise Humphreys, and Arelis Gomez. 2000. "Rebuilding Social Capital in Post Conflict Regions: Women's Village Banking in Ayacucho, Peru and in Highland Guatemala." Paper given at the Latin American Studies Association meeting, Miami, 16–18 March.

Benería, Lourdes. 2003. *Gender, Development and Globalization: Economics as if People Mattered*. New York: Routledge.

———. 2001. "The Enduring Debate over Unpaid Labour." In *Women, Gender and Work: What Is Equality and How Do We Get There?* edited by Martha Fetherolf Loutfi, 85–109. Geneva: ILO.

———. 1999. "The Enduring Debate over Unpaid Labour," *International Labour Review*, 138 (3): 287–309.

Benería, Lourdes, and Shelley Feldman, eds. 1992. *Unequal Burden: Economic Crises, Persistent Poverty and Women's Works*. Boulder: Westview Press.

Benería, Lourdes, and Martha Roldán. 1987. *The Crossroads of Class and Gender: Industrial Homework, Subcontracting and Household Dynamics in Mexico City*. Chicago: University of Chicago Press.

Benería, Lourdes, and Gita Sen. 1981. "Accumulation, Reproduction, and Women's Roles in Economic Development: Boserup Revisited." *Signs* 7 (2): 279–98.

Benschop, Marjolein. 2002. *Rights and Reality: Are Women's Equal Rights to Land, Housing and Property Implemented in East Africa?* Nairobi: United Nations Human Settlements Programme (HABITAT).

Bergeron, Suzanne. 2003. "The Post-Washington Consensus and Economic Representations of Women in Development at the World Bank." *International Feminist Journal of Politics* 5 (3): 397–419.

———. 2001. "Political Economy Discourses of Globalization and Feminist Politics." *Signs* 26 (4): 983–1006.

Berkovitch, Nitza. 1999. *From Motherhood to Citizenship: Women's Rights and International Organizations*. Baltimore: Johns Hopkins University Press.

Bhatt, Ela R. 2000. "Self Employment as Sustainable Employment." Keynote speech at the Public Event on the Social Summit+5 organized by the Swiss Development Cooperation, Berne, Switzerland.

Bianpoen, Carla. 2000. "Women's Political Call." In *Indonesian Women: The Journey Continues*, edited by Mayling Oey-Gardiner and Carla Bianpoen, 283–302. Canberra: Australian National University.

Bibars, Iman. 2001. *Victims and Heroines: Women, Welfare and the Egyptian State*. London: Zed Books.

———. 1996. "Social Security and Social Networks among the Urban Poor in Pakistan." *Habitat International* 19 (4): 427–45.

Blaikie, Piers, and Harold Brookfield. 1987. *Land Degradation and Society*. London: Routledge.

Blanc-Szanton, Cristina. 1990. "Gender and Inter-Generational Resource Allocation among Thai and Sino-Thai Households." In *Structures and Strategies: Women, Work and Family*, edited by Leela Dube and Rajni Palriwala, 79–102. New Delhi: Sage.

Blumberg, Rae Lesser. 1995. Introduction to *Engendering Wealth and Well-Being*, edited by Rae Lesser Blumberg, Cathy A. Rakowski, Irene Tinker, and Michael Monteon, 1–14. Boulder: Westview Press.

Blumberg, Rae Lesser, Cathy A. Rakowski, Irene Tinker, and Michael Monteon, eds. 1995. *Engendering Wealth and Well-Being: Empowerment for Global Change*. Boulder: Westview Press.

Bortolaia Silva, Elizabeth. 1996. Introduction to *Good Enough Mothering? Feminist Perspectives on Lone Motherhood*, edited by E. Bortolaia Silva, 1–9. London: Routledge.

Boserup, Ester. 1999. *My Professional Life and Publications 1929–1998*. Copenhagen: Museum Tusculanum Press, University of Copenhagen.

———. 1990. "Economic Change and the Roles of Women." In *Persistent Inequalities: Women and World Development*, edited by Irene Tinker, 14–24. New York: Oxford University Press.

———. 1970. *Woman's Role in Economic Development*. London: Allen and Unwin.

Bossen, Laurel. 2000. "Women Farmers, Small Plots, and Changing Markets in China." In *Women Farmers and Commercial Ventures: Increasing Food Security in Developing Countries*, edited by Anita Spring, 171–89. Boulder: Lynne Rienner Publishers.

Bourque, Susan, and Kay Warren. 1981. *Women of the Andes: Patriarchy and Social Change in Two Peruvians Towns*. Ann Arbor: University of Michigan Press.

Bradshaw, Sarah. 1996a. "Female-Headed Households in Honduras: A Study of their Formation and Survival Survival in Low-income Communities." Unpublished Ph.D. thesis. Department of Geography, London School of Economics.

———. 1996b. "Inequality within Households: The Case of Honduras." Paper presented at symposium "Vulnerable Groups in Latin American Cities." Annual Conference of the Society of Latin American Studies, University of Leeds, 29–31 March.

———. 1995a. "Female-Headed Households in Honduras: Perspectives on Rural-Urban Differences." Special issue, *Third World Planning Review* 17 (2): 117–31.

———. 1995b. "Women's Access to Employment and the Formation of Women-Headed Households in Rural and Urban Honduras." *Bulletin of Latin American Research* 14 (2): 143–58.

Braidotti, Rosi. 1997. "Uneasy Transitions: Women's Studies in the European Union." In *Transitions/Environments/Translations: Feminisms in International Politics*, edited by Joan W. Scott, Cora Kapland, and Debra Keates, 355–72. New York: Routledge.

Brandt, Loren, Jikun Huang, Guo Li, and Scott Rozelle. 2002. "Land Rights in China: Facts, Fictions, and Issues." *China Journal* 47: 67–97.

Brautigam, Deborah. 2000. *Aid Dependence and Governance*. Prepared for the Division of Development Cooperation, Swedish Ministry of Foreign Affairs, Expert Group on Development Issues.

Bridge Report. 2001. "The Feminization of Poverty." Brighton: Institute of Development Studies, University of Sussex, *Bridge Report* no. 59.

Brill, Alida, ed. 1995. *A Rising Public Voice: Women in Politics Worldwide*. New York: Feminist Press.

Brohman, John. 1996. *Popular Development: Rethinking the Theory and Practice of Development*. Oxford: Blackwell Publishers.

Brown, Katrina, and Andrine Lapuyade. 2001. "A Livelihood from the Forest: Gendered

Visions of Social, Economic and Environmental Change in Southern Cameroon." *Journal of International Development* 13: 1131–49.

Bruce, John. 1990. "Legal Issues in Land Use and Resettlement." World Bank Background Paper for Zimbabwe Agricultural Sector Memorandum. Harare: Zimbabwe.

Bruce, Judith, and Cynthia Lloyd. 1992. *Finding the Ties That Bind: Beyond Headship and the Household*. New York/Washington, D.C.: Population Council/International Center for Research on Women.

Brydon, Lynne, and Karen Legge. 1996. *Adjusting Society: The IMF, the World Bank and Ghana*. London: I. B. Tauris.

Brysk, Alison. 2000. *From Tribal Village to Global Village: Indian Rights and International Relations in Latin America*. Palo Alto: Stanford University Press.

Budlender, Debbie. 2002. *A Global Assessment of Gender Responsive Budgeting*. www.hdrc.undp.org.in/Gndrinitv/wrkppr/genderbudgets.pdf.

Budlender, Debbie, Diane Elson, Guy Hewitt, and Tanni Mukhopadhyay. 2002. *Gender Budgets Make Cents*. London: Commonwealth Secretariat.

Budowksi, Monica, and Laura Guzmán. 1998. "Strategic Gender Interests in Social Policy: Empowerment Training for Female Heads of Household in Costa Rica." Paper prepared for the International Sociological Association XIV World Congress of Sociology, Montreal, 26 July–1 August.

Bug, Amy. 2003. "Has Feminism Changed Physics?" *Signs* 28 (3): 881–99.

Bullock, Susan. 1994. *Women and Work*. London: Zed Books.

Bunker, John P., Deanna S. Gomby, and Barbara H. Kehrer, eds. 1989. *Pathways to Health*. Menlo Park, Calif.: Henry J. Kaiser Family Foundation.

Burga, Manuel. 1988. *Nacimiento de una Utopía. Muerte y Resurrección de los Incas*. Lima: Instituto de Apoyo Agrario.

Burgess, Robin. 2000. "Land Distribution and Welfare in Rural China." Available at www.Worldbank.org/research/abcde/washington_12/papers_12.html.

Burjorjee, Denna M., Rani Deshpande, and C. Jean Weidemann. 2002. "Supporting Women's Livelihoods: Microfinance that Works for the Majority. A Guide to Best Practices." New York: UN Capital Development Fund, Special Unit for Microfinance.

Buvinic, Mayra. 1995. *Investing in Women*. Washington, D.C.: International Center for Research on Women, Policy Series.

———. 1990. "The Vulnerability of Women-Headed Households: Policy Questions and Options for Latin America and the Caribbean." Paper presented at the Economic Commission for Latin America and the Caribbean Meeting on Vulnerable Women, Vienna, 26–30 November.

———. 1976. *Women and World Development: An Annotated Bibliography*. Overseas Development Council under the auspices of the American Association for the Advancement of Science.

Buvinic, Mayra, and Geeta Rao Gupta. 1993. "Responding to Insecurity in the 1990s: Targeting Woman-Headed Households and Woman-Maintained Families in Developing Countries." Paper presented at the International Workshop "Insecurity in the 1990s: Gender and Social Policy in an International Perspective." London School of Economics and European Association of Development Institutes, London, 5–6 April.

Buvinic, Mayra, Margaret Lycette, and William P. McGreevey, eds. 1983. *Women and Poverty in the Third World*. Baltimore: Johns Hopkins University Press.

Buvinic, Mayra, and Nadia Youssef. 1978. *Women-Headed Households: The Ignored Factor in De-*

velopment Planning. Monograph submitted to the Office of Women in Development, U.S. Agency for International Development, March.

Bystydzienski, Jill M., and Joti Sekhon, eds. 1999. *Democratization and Women's Grassroots Movements*. Bloomington: Indiana University Press.

Cabral, Elena. 1999. *China's Hidden Epidemic*. New York: Ford Foundation Report, Winter.

Cadena, Marisol de la. 1997a. *La decencia y el respeto: raza y etnicidad entre los intelectuales y las mestizas cusqueñas*. Working paper no. 86. Lima: Instituto de Estudios Peruanos.

———. 1997b. "Matrimonio y Etnicidad en Comunidades Andinas. Chitapampa. Cuzco." In *Más allá del silencio. Las fronteras de género en los Andes*. Arnold, Denise compiladora. La Paz: ILCA-CIASE.

———. 1992. *Las mujeres son más indias: etnicidad y género en una comunidad del Cusco*. In Ediciones de las Mujeres no. 16, 25-45. Santiago: Isis Internacional.

Cagatay, Nilüfer. 1998. *Gender and Poverty*. New York: UNDP, Social Development and Poverty Elimination Division, Working Paper 5.

Cagatay, Nilufer, Diane Elson, and Caren Grown. 1995. Introduction to *World Development* 23 (11): 1827-36.

Calderon, Edna Elizabeth. 1998. "Land Issues in Guatemala." Presentation given at the Kigali meeting: "Peace for Homes, Homes for Peace, Inter-Regional Consultation on Women's Land and Property Rights in Situations of Conflict and Reconstruction," Kigali, Rwanda, 16-19 February. http://www.undp.org/unifem/resources/.

Canessa Andrew. 1997. "Género, Lenguaje y Variación en Pocovaya, Bolivia." In *Más allá del silencio. Las fronteras de género en los Andes*, edited by Denise Arnold. La Paz: ILCA-CIASE.

Carothers, Thomas. 1999. *Aiding Democracy Abroad: The Learning Curve*. Washington, D.C.: Carnegie Endowment for International Peace.

Casolo, Jennifer. 2004. *"Voz y Voto* In Deed? Reworking of Land Rights, Gender and Power in Post-Hurricane Mitch Honduras." Unpublished master's thesis. Department of Geography, University of California at Berkeley.

CEDPA. 1995. *Training Trainers for Development*. The CEDPA Training Manual Series. Washington, D.C.: Center for Development and Population Activities.

CEPAL (Comisión Económica para América Latina). 2001. *Panorama Social de América Latina 2000-2001*. Santiago: CEPAL.

Chaiklin, Seth, and Jean Lave, eds. 1993. *Understanding Practice: Perspectives on Activity and Context*. Cambridge: Cambridge University Press.

Chambers, Robert. 1995. "Poverty and Livelihoods: Whose Reality Counts?" *Environment and Urbanisation* 7 (1): 173-204.

———. 1989. "Vulnerability: How the Poor Cope."*IDS Bulletin* 20 (2): 1-9.

———. 1983. *Rural Development: Putting the Last First*. Harlow: Longman.

Chandler, Ralph C., and Jack C. Plano. 1982. *The Public Administration Dictionary*. New York: Wiley.

Chaney, Elsa, and Maria Garcia Castro, eds. 1989. *Muchachas No More: Household Workers in Latin American and the Caribbean*. Philadelphia: Temple University Press.

Chant, Sylvia. 2003. "Female Household Headship and the Feminisation of Poverty: Facts, Fictions and Forward Strategies." London: London School of Economics, Gender Institute New Working Paper Series, Issue 9.

———. 2002. "Whose Crisis? Public and Popular Reactions to Family Change in Costa Rica." In *Exclusion and Engagement: Social Policy in Latin America*, edited by Christopher Abel and Colin Lewis, 349-77. London: Institute of Latin American Studies, University of London.

———. 1999. "Women-Headed Households: Global Orthodoxies and Grassroots Realities." In *Women, Globalisation and Fragmentation in the Developing World*, edited by Haleh Afshar and Stephanie Barrientos, 91–130. Houndmills, Basingstoke: Macmillan.

———. 1997a. *Women-Headed Households: Diversity and Dynamics in the Developing World*. Houndmills, Basingstoke: Macmillan.

———. 1997b. "Women-Headed Households: Poorest of the Poor? Perspectives from Mexico, Costa Rica and the Philippines." *IDS Bulletin* 28 (3): 26–48.

———. 1996. *Gender, Urban Development and Housing*. New York: UNDP.

———. 1994. "Women, Work and Household Survival Strategies in Mexico, 1982–1992." *Bulletin of Latin American Research* 13 (2): 203–33.

———. 1991. *Women and Survival in Mexican Cities: Perspectives on Gender, Labour Markets and Low-Income Households*. Manchester: Manchester University Press.

———. 1985. "Single-Parent Families: Choice or Constraint? The Formation of Female-Headed Households in Mexican Shanty Towns." *Development and Change* 16 (4): 635–56.

Chant, Sylvia, and Nikki Craske. 2003. *Gender in Latin America*. London: Latin America Bureau.

Chant, Sylvia, and Matthew Gutmann. 2000. *Mainstreaming Men into Gender and Development*. Oxford: Oxfam.

Chant, Sylvia, and Cathy McIlwaine. 1995. *Women of a Lesser Cost: Female Labour, Foreign Exchange and Philippine Development*. London: Pluto.

Chapela, I. H. 1994. "Bioprospecting in the Information Age: A Critical Analysis of Pharmaceutical Searches through Biodiversity." In *Emerging Connections: Biodiversity, Biotechnology and Sustainable Development*, edited by J. Feinsilver, 27–46. Washington, D.C.: Panamerican Health Organization/Interamerican Institute for Cooperation in Agriculture.

Charlton, Sue Ellen M., Jana Everett, and Kathleen Staudt, eds. 1989. *Women, the State, and Development*. Albany: State University of New York Press.

Chavangi, N. A. 1984. *Cultural Aspects of Fuelwood Procurement in Kakamega District*. Working Paper no. 4. Nairobi: Kenya Woodfuel Development Programme.

Chen, Fu, Liming Wang, and John Davis. 1998. "Land Reform in Rural China Since the Mid-1980s." Food and Agricultural Organization (FAO), http://www.fao.org/sd/Ltdirect/Ltan0031.htm.

Chen, Kai, and Colin Brown. 2001. "Addressing Shortcomings in the Household Responsibility System: Empirical Analysis of the Two-Farmland System in Shandong Province." *China Economic Review* 12: 280–92.

Chidari, Gift, Francisca Chirambaguwa, Patricia Matsvimbo, Anna Mhiripiri, Hilda Chanakira, James Chanakira, Xavier Mutsvangzwa, Angeline Mvumbe, Louise Fortmann, Robert Drummond, and Nontokozo Nabane. 1992. "The Use of Indigenous Trees in Mhondoro District." Centre for Applied Social Sciences, University of Zimbabwe NRM Occasional Paper 5.

China Daily. 2003. "Reforms Make Life and Travel Much Easier." 8 August. http://www2 .chinadaily.com.cn/en/doc/2003-08/08/content_252954.htm. Accessed 5 July 2005.

Chinchilla, Norma Stoltz. 1995. "Revolutionary Popular Feminism in Nicaragua: Ideologies, Political Transitions and the Struggle for Autonomy." In *Women in the Latin American Development Process*, edited by Christine Bose and Edna Acosta-Belén, 242–70. Philadelphia: Temple University Press.

Chowdhry, Geeta. 1995. "Women and Development: A Critique." In *Feminism/Postmodernism/Development*, edited by Marianne Marchand and Jane Parpart. London: Routledge.

Chua, Amy. 2003. *World on Fire: How Exporting Free Market Democracy Breeds Ethnic Hatred and Global Instability.* New York: Doubleday.

Clark, Peggy, and Amy Kays. 1999. *Microenterprise and the Poor: Findings from the Self-Employment Learning Project Five Year Survey of Microentrepreneurs.* Washington: The Aspen Institute.

Cloud, Kathleen. 1994. "Women, Households and Development: A Policy Perspective." In *Capturing Complexity: An Interdisciplinary Look at Women, Households and Development,* edited by Romy Borooah, Kathleen Cloud, Subadra Seshadri, T. S. Saraswithi, Jean T. Peterson, and Amita Verma, 60–83. New Delhi: Sage.

Cockburn, Cynthia. 1991. *In the Way of Women: Men's Resistance to Sex Equality in Organizations.* London: Macmillan.

Cohn, Carol, Helen Kinsella, and Sheri Gibbings. 2004. "Women, Peace and Security: Resolution 1325." *International Feminist Journal of Politics* 6 (1): 130–40.

Colfer, C. 1981. "Women and Men and Time in the Forests of East Kalimantan." *Borneo Research Bulletin,* 75–85.

Collins, Susan M. 1990. "Lessons from Korean Economic Growth." *American Economic Review, Papers and Proceedings* 80 (2, May): 104–7.

Commission on Human Security. 2003. *Human Security Now: Protecting and Empowering People.* New York. http://www.humansecurity-chs.org.

Conkey, Margaret W. 2003. "Has Feminism Changed Archeology?" *Signs* 28 (3): 867–80.

Connelly, M. Patricia, Tania Murray Li, Martha MacDonald, and Jane L. Parpart. 2000. "Feminism and Development: Theoretical Perspectives." In *Theoretical Perspectives on Gender and Development,* edited by Jane L. Parpart, M. Patricia Connelly, and V. Eudine Barriteau, 51–160. Ottawa, Canada: International Development Research Center.

Cooper, William. 1991. "Overview." In Joint Economic Committee, *China's Economic Dilemmas in the 1990s: The Problems of Reforms, Modernization, and Interdependence.* Washington, D.C.: USGPO: 335–39.

Cornwall, Andrea. 2002. "Making a Difference? Gender and Participatory Development." In *Shifting Burdens: Gender and Agrarian Change under Neoliberalism,* edited by Shahra Razavi, 197–232. Bloomfield, Conn.: Kumarian Press.

Council of Europe. 1998. *Gender Mainstreaming: Conceptual Framework, Methodology and Presentation of Good Practice.* Strasbourg: Council of Europe Publishing.

Croll, Elisabeth. 2000. *Endangered Daughters: Discrimination and Development in Asia.* London: Routledge.

———. 1999. "Report from the Field: Involuntary Resettlement in Rural China: The Local View." *China Quarterly* 158: 468–83.

———. 1994. *From Heaven to Earth: Images and Experiences of Development in China.* London: Routledge.

———. 1985. *Women and Rural Development in China: Production and Reproduction.* Geneva: International Labor Office.

Crowther, Sarah. 2000. "NGOs and Local Organizations: A Mismatch of Goals and Practices?" In *New Roles and Relevance: Development NGOs and the Challenge of Change,* edited by David Lewis and Tina Wallace, 165–75. Bloomfield, Conn.: Kumarian Press.

CUSRI. 1988. *People and Forestry in Thailand: Status, Problems, and Prospects.* Proceedings of the Seminar organized by Chulalongkorn University Social Research Institute. 8–9 September.

Dagron, Alfonso Gumucio. 2001. *Making Waves: Stories of Participatory Communication for Social Change.* New York: Rockefeller Foundation.

Dalder, Ivo H., and James M. Lindsay. 2003. *America Unbound: The Bush Revolution in Foreign Policy*. Washington, D.C.: Brookings Institution Press.

Darlington, Patricia S. E., and Becky Michele Mulvany. 2002. "Gender, Rhetoric and Power: Toward a Model of Reciprocal Empowerment." *Women's Studies in Communication* 25 (2): 139–72.

Datta, Rekha. 2002. "The State, Development, and Empowerment in India." In *Women in Developing Countries*, edited by R. Datta and J. Kornberg, 79–92. Boulder: Lynne Rienner.

Datta, Rekha, and Judith Kornberg, eds. 2002. *Women in Developing Countries: Assessing Strategies for Empowerment*. Boulder: Lynne Rienner.

Davin, Delia. 1998. "Gender and Migration in China." In *Village Inc.: Chinese Rural Society in the 1990s*, edited by Flemming Christiansen and Junzuo Zhang, 230–40. Honolulu: University of Hawaii Press.

Deere, Carmen Diana. 1982. "The Division of Labor by Sex in Agriculture: A Peruvian Case Study." *Economic and Development and Cultural Change* 30 (4): 795–811.

Deere, Carmen Diana, and Magdalena Leon. 2001. *Empowering Women: Land and Property Rights in Latin America*. Pittsburgh: University of Pittsburgh Press.

Delphy, Christine, and Diana Leonard. 1992. *Familiar Exploitation: A New Analysis of Marriage in Contemporary Western Societies*. Cambridge: Polity Press.

Del Rosario, Virginia O. 1995. "Mainstreaming Gender Concerns: Aspects of Compliance, Resistance, and Negotiation." *IDS Bulletin* (special issue on Getting Institutions Right for Women in Development) 26 (3): 102–18.

Denegri, Francesca. 2000. *Soy Señora. Testimonio de Irene Jara*. Lima: Instituto de Estudios Peruanos, Centro Flora Tristán, El Santo Oficio.

Desai, Vandana, and Robert Potter, eds. 2001. *The Companion to Development Studies*. London: Edward Arnold.

DFID (Department for International Development). 2000. *Poverty Elimination and the Empowerment of Women*. London: DFID.

Dijkstra, A. Geske, and Lucia Hanmer. 2000. "Measuring Socio-Economic Gender Inequality: Toward an Alternative to the UNDP Gender-related Development Index." *Feminist Economics* 6 (2): 41–75.

Direct Line 11: Gender Equality and the Advancement of Women. 1996. Memorandum from James Gustave Speth, Administrator, UNDP to all Resident Representatives, UNDP; Resident Coordinators. 22 November. http://www.undp.org/gender/policies/dline11.html. Accessed 25 June 2001.

Dixon, R. 1978. *Rural Women at Work: Strategies for Development in South Asia*. Baltimore: Johns Hopkins University Press.

Dong, Xiao-yuan. 1996. "Two-Tier Land Tenure System and Sustained Economic Growth in Post-1978 Rural China." *World Development* 24 (5): 915–28.

Dong, Xiao-yuan, Paul Bowles, and Samuel Ho. 2002. "The Determination of Employee Share Ownership in China's Privatized Rural Industries: Evidence from Jiangsu and Shandong." *Journal of Comparative Economics* 30 (2): 415–37.

Dore, E. 2000. "Property, Households and Public Regulation of Domestic Life: Dinomo, Nicarauigua, 1840–1900." In *Hidden Histories of Gender and the State in Latin America*, edited by E. Dore and M. Molyneux, 147–71. Durham: Duke University Press.

Douglas, Mary. 1991. *Pureza y Peligro. Un análisis de los Conceptos de Contaminación y Tabú*. Madrid: Siglo XXI Editores.

Drèze, Jean. 1990. *Widows in Rural India*. London: London School of Economics, Suntory-

Toyota International Centre for Economics and Related Disciplines, Development Economics Research Programme no. 26.

Drezin, Jenny, and Megan Lloyd-Laney, eds. 2003. "Making a Difference: Strategic Communications to End Violence Against Women." A tool kit from the UNIFEM Strategic Communications Workshop Series. New York: United Nations Development Fund for Women.

Duncan, Jennifer, and Li Ping. 2001. "Women and Land Tenure in China: A Study of Women's Land Rights in DongFang County, Hainan Province." RDI Reports on Foreign Aid and Development no. 110, Rural Development Institute, Seattle.

Dwyer, Daisy, and Judith Bruce, eds. 1988. *A Home Divided: Women and Income in the Third World*. Stanford: Stanford University Press.

Eccher, Celita. 1999. "At Copenhagen+5 Prepcom, a Sense of Déjà vu." *DAWN Informs* 2 (August) (1).

Economic Commission for Africa. 1999. *Report of Expert Consultation on the Capacity: Building Needs of African NGOs and Civil Society Organisations*. Addis Ababa.

Edgcomb, E. J. Klein, and P. Clark. 1996. *The Practice of Microenterprise in the US: Strategies, Costs, and Effectiveness*. Washington, D.C.: Aspen Institute.

Egziabher, Axumite G., Diana Lee-Smith, Daniel G. Maxwell, Pyar Ali Memon, Luc J. A. Mougeot, and Camillus J. Sawio. 1994. *Cities Feeding People: An Examination of Urban Agriculture in East Africa*. Ottawa: International Development Research Council.

Ehrenreich, Barbara, and Arlie Russell Hochschild, eds. 2003. *Global Woman: Nannies, Maids and Sex Workers in the New Economy*. New York: Metropolitan Books.

Elliott, Carolyn. 2003. "Civil Society and Democracy; A Comparative Review Essay." In *Civil Society and Democracy*, edited by Carolyn Elliott, 1–39. New Delhi: Oxford University Press.

Elson, Diane. 2004. "Human Rights and Corporate Profits: The UN Global Compact—Part of the Solution or Part of the Problem?" In *Global Tensions: Challenges and Opportunities in the World Economy*, edited by Lourdes Benería and Savitri Bisnath, 45–64. New York: Routledge.

———. 2003. "Gender Justice, Human Rights, and Neo-Liberal Economic Policies." In *Gender Justice, Development, and Rights*, edited by Maxine Molyneux and Shahra Razavi, 78–104. Oxford: Oxford University Press.

———. 1998. " 'Talking to the Boys': Gender in Economic Growth Models." In *Getting Institutions Right for Women in Development*, edited by Anne Marie Goetz, 155–70. London: Zed Books.

———. 1995a. "Gender Awareness in Modeling Structural Adjustment." *World Development* 23 (11): 1851–68.

———. 1995b. "Male Bias in Macro-economics: The Case of Structural Adjustment." In *Male Bias in the Development Process*, 2nd ed., edited by Diane Elson, 164–90. Manchester: Manchester University Press.

———. 1992. "From Survival Strategies to Transformation Strategies: Women's Needs and Structural Adjustment." In *Unequal Burden: Economic Crises, Persistent Poverty and Women's Works*, edited by Lourdes Benería and Shelley Feldman, 36–48. Boulder: Westview Press.

———. 1991. "Structural Adjustment: Its Effects on Women." In *Changing Perceptions: Writings on Gender and Development*, edited by Tina Wallace with Candida March, 39–53. Oxford: Oxfam.

———. 1989. "The Impact of Structural Adjustment on Women: Concepts and Issues." In *The IMF, the World Bank and the African Debt, Vol 2: The Social and Political Impact*, edited by Bade Onimode, 55–74. London: Zed Books.

Engle, Patrice. 1995. "Father's Money, Mother's Money and Parental Commitment: Guatemala and Nicaragua." In *Engendering Wealth and Well-Being*, edited by Rae Lesser Blumberg, Cathy A. Rakowski, Irene Tinker, and Michael Monteon, 155–79. Boulder: Westview Press.

Enloe, Cynthia. 2000. *Maneuvers: The International Politics of Militarizing Women's Lives*. Berkeley: University of California Press.

Entwisle, Barbara, Gail E. Henderson, Susan E. Short, Jill Bouma, and Fengying Zhai. 1995. "Gender and Family Businesses in Rural China." *American Sociological Review* 60 (February): 36–57.

Eschle, Catherine. 2003. " 'Skeleton Women': Feminism and Social Movement Resistances to Corporate Power and Neoliberalism." Paper presented at annual conference of the International Studies Association, Portland, Ore., 25–28 February.

———. 2002. "Engendering Global Democracy." *International Feminist Journal of Politics* 4 (3, December): 315–41.

Escobar, Arturo. 1995. *Encountering Development: The Making and Unmaking of the Third World*. Princeton: Princeton University Press.

Fairhead, James, and Melissa Leach. 2003. "Practicing 'Biodiversity' in Guinea: Nature, Nation and International Convention." *Oxford Development Studies* 31 (4): 427–40.

Faludi, Susan. 1991. *Backlash: The Undeclared War on American Women*. New York: Crown.

Fan, X. F. 2003. *SARS: Economic Impacts and Implications*. Manila: Asian Development Bank.

Feijoó, María del Carmen. 1999. "De Pobres Mujeres a Mujeres Pobres." In *Divergencias del Modelo Tradicional: Hogares de Jefatura Femenina en América Latina*, edited by Mercedes González de la Rocha, 155–62. Mexico City: Centro de Investigaciones y Estudios Superiores en Antropología Social/Plaza y Valdés Editores.

Ferber, Marianne, and Julie Nelson. 2003. *Feminist Economics Today: Beyond Economic Man*. Chicago: University of Chicago Press.

Ferguson, Kathy E. 1984. *The Feminist Case Against Bureaucracy*. Philadephia: Temple University Press.

Fernández, Blanca, and María Amelia Trigoso. 2001. *Las Mujeres Rurales en el Perú. Propuestas para la Equidad*. Lima: Centro de la Mujer Peruana Flora Tristán.

Fernandez-Armesto, Felipe. 2003. *Ideas that Changed the World*. New York: DK Publishing.

Fisher, William F., and Thomas Ponniah, eds. 2003. *Another World Is Possible: Popular Alternatives to Globalization at the World Social Forum*. London: Zed Books.

Fleuret, A. 1977. "The Role of Women in Rural Markets: Lushoto, Tanzania." Paper presented at the First Women and Anthropology Symposium, Sacramento, California.

Flora, Cornelia Butler. 2004. "The Ford Foundation and the Power of International Sisterhood." In *Developing Power: How Women Transformed International Development*, edited by Arvonne Fraser and Irene Tinker, 277–87. New York: Feminist Press.

———. 1982. "Incorporating Women into International Development Programs: The Political Phenomenology of a Private Foundation." In *Women in Developing Countries: A Policy Focus*, edited by Kathleen Staudt and Jane S. Jaquette, 89–106. Binghamton: Haworth.

Flores Galindo, Alberto. 1992. *Dos Ensayos sobre José María Arguedas*. Lima: Cuadernos de SUR, Casa de Estudios del Socialismo.

———. 1987 *Buscando un Inca: Identidad y Utopía en los Andes*. Lima: Instituto de Apoyo Agrario.

Flynn, Steven. 2004. *America the Vulnerable*. New York: HarperCollins.

Folbre, Nancy. 2001a. "Debating Business: Women and Liberalization at the Council on Foreign Relations." *Signs* 26 (4): 1259–64.

———. 2001b. *The Invisible Heart: Economics and Family Values*. New York: New Press.

Folbre, Nancy. 1994. *Who Pays for the Kids? Gender and the Structures of Constraint*. London: Routledge.

———. 1991. "Women on Their Own: Global Patterns of Female Headship." In *The Women and International Development Annual*, vol. 2, edited by Rita S. Gallin and Ann Ferguson, 69–126. Boulder: Westview Press.

———. 1988. "The Black Four of Hearts: Toward a New Paradigm of Household Economics." In *A Home Divided: Women and Income in the Third World*, edited by Daisy Dwyer and Judith Bruce, 248–62. Stanford: Stanford University Press.

Fonseca, Claudia. 1991. "Spouses, Siblings and Sex-Linked Bonding: A Look at Kinship Organisation in a Brazilian Slum." In *Family, Household and Gender Relations in Latin America* edited by Elizabeth Jelin, 133–60. London: Kegan Paul International/Paris: UNESCO.

Ford Foundation. 2001. *Summary of Gender and Property Rights Workshop*. In Chinese.

Fortmann, L., C. Antinori, and N. Nabane. 1997. "Fruits of Their Labors: Property Rights and Tree Planting in Two Zimbabwe Villages." *Rural Sociology* 62 (3): 295–314.

Francisco, Gigo. 2003. "Cancun." *DAWN Informs*. September.

Frank, Andre Gunder, and Marta Fuentes. 1989. "Ten Theses on Social Movements." *World Development* 17 (2) (February): 179–91.

Fraser, Arvonne. 1995. "The Convention on the Elimination of All Forms of Discrimination Against Women." In *Women, Politics and the United Nations*, edited by Anne Winslow, 77–94. Westport, Conn.: Greenwood Press.

Fraser, Arvonne, and Irene Tinker, eds. 2004. *Developing Power: How Women Transformed International Development*. New York: Feminist Press.

Fraser, Nancy. 1998. "From Redistribution to Recognition? Dilemmas of Injustice in a 'Post-Socialist' Age." In *Feminism and Politics*, edited by Anne Phillips, 430–60. Oxford: Oxford University Press.

Frum, David, and Richard Perle. 2004. *How to Win the War on Terror*. New York: Random House.

Fukuda-Parr, Sakiko. 1999. "What Does Feminisation of Poverty Mean? It Isn't Just Lack of Income." *Feminist Economics* 5 (2): 99–103.

Fuwa, Nobuhiko. 2000. "The Poverty and Heterogeneity Among Female-Headed Households Revisited: The Case of Panama." *World Development* 28 (8): 1515–42.

Gao, Xiaoxian. 1994. "China's Modernization and Changes in the Social Status of Rural Women." In *Engendering China: Women, Culture, and the State*, edited by Christina Gilmartin, Gail Hershatter, Lisa Rofel, and Tyrene White, 80–97. Cambridge, Mass.: Harvard University Press.

Garcilaso, de la Vega, Inca. 1991. *Comentarios Reales de los Incas*, two volumes. Lima: Edición, Indice Analítico y Glosario de Carlos Araníbar. Fondo de Cultura Económica.

Geldstein, Rosa. 1997. *Mujeres Jefas de Hogar: Familia, Pobreza y Género*. Buenos Aires: UNICEF-Argentina.

Giddens, Anthony. 1994. *Beyond Left and Right: The Future of Radical Politics*. Stanford: Stanford University Press.

Gierycz, Dorota. 2001. "Women, Peace, and the United Nations: Beyond Beijing." In *Gender, Peace and Conflict*, edited by Inger Skjelsbaek and Dan Smith, 14–31. Oslo: International Peace Research Institute.

Gilligan, Carol. 1982. *In a Different Voice: Psychological Theory and Women's Development*. Cambridge, Mass.: Harvard University Press.

Gituto, Billington Mwangi, and Wanjuki Mukabi Kabira. 1998. *Affirmative Action: The Promise of a New Dawn*. Nairobi: The Collaborative Centre for Gender and Development.

Global Fund for Women. 2002. *The Global Fund for Women: Annual Report 2001–2002*. Palo Alto, Calif.: Global Fund for Women.

———. 1996. *The Global Fund for Women: The Ninth Year, 1995–1996 Annual Report*. Palo Alto, Calif.: Global Fund for Women.

———. 1989. *Pathways to Health: The Role of Social Factors*. Menlo Park, Calif.: Global Fund for Women.

Goetz, Anne Marie. 2001. *Women Development Workers. Implementing Rural Credit Programs in Bangladesh*. New Delhi: Sage.

———. 1998. "Mainstreaming Gender Equality to National Development Planning." In *Missionaries and Mandarins*, edited by Carol Miller and Shahra Razavi, 42–86. London: Intermediate Technology Publications.

———, ed. 1997a. *Getting Institutions Right for Women in Development*. London: Zed Books.

———. 1997b. "Introduction." In *Getting Institutions Right for Women in Development*, edited by Anne Marie Goetz, 1–30. London: Zed Books.

———. 1997c. "Local Heroes: Patterns of Fieldworker Discretion in Implementing GAD Policy in Bangladesh." In *Getting Institutions Right for Women in Development*, edited by Anne Marie Goetz, 176–99. London: Zed Books.

———. 1995. "Institutionalizing Women's Interests and Gender-Sensitive Accountability in Development." *IDS Bulletin* 26 (3): 1–10.

Goetz, Anne Marie, and Rina Sen Gupta. 1996. "Who Takes the Credit? Gender, Power, and Control Over Loan Use in Rural Credit Programs in Bangladesh." *World Development* 24 (1): 45–63.

Goetz, Anne Marie, and Shireen Hassim. 2003. *No Shortcuts to Power: African Women in Politics and Policy-Making*. London: Zed Books. Originally published in *Journal of Modern African Studies* 2002 (40): 549–75.

Gold, Elizabeth. 1991. "Lessons Learned in Private Enterprise." Washington, D.C.: GENESYS for the Office of Women in Development, USAID.

González de la Rocha, Mercedes. 1999a. "A Manera de Introducción: Cambio Social, Transformación de la Familia y Divergencias del Modelo Tradicional." In *Divergencias del Modelo Tradicional: Hogares de Jefatura Femenina en América Latina*, edited by Mercedes González de la Rocha, 19–36. Mexico City: Centro de Investigaciones y Estudios Superiores en Antropología Social/Plaza y Valdés Editores.

———, ed. 1999b. *Divergencias del Modelo Tradicional: Hogares de Jefatura Femenina en América Latina*. Mexico City: Centro de Investigaciones y Estudios Superiores en Antropología Social/Plaza y Valdés Editores.

———. 1994a. "Household Headship and Occupational Position in Mexico." In *Poverty and Well-Being in the Household: Case Studies of the Developing World*, edited by Eileen Kennedy and Mercedes González de la Rocha, 1–24. San Diego: Center for Iberian and Latin American Studies, University of California, San Diego.

———. 1994b. *The Resources of Poverty: Women and Survival in a Mexican City*. Oxford: Blackwell.

———. 1988a. "Economic Crisis, Domestic Reorganisation and Women's Work in Guadalajara, Mexico." *Bulletin of Latin American Research* 7 (2): 207–23.

———. 1988b. "De Por Qué las Mujeres Aguantan Golpes y Cuernos: Un Análisis de Hogares sin Varón en Guadalajara." In *Mujeres y Sociedad: Salario, Hogar y Acción Social en el Occidente de México*, Luisa Gabayet, Patricia García, Mercedes González de la Rocha, Silvia Lailson, and Augustín Esobar, 205–27. Guadalajara: El Colegio de Jalisco/CIESAS del Occidente.

González de la Rocha, Mercedes, and Alejandro Grinspun. 2001. "Private Adjustments:

Households, Crisis and Work." In *Choices for the Poor: Lessons from National Poverty Strategies*, edited by Alejandro Grinspun, 55–87. New York: UNDP.

Gowaty, Patricia Adair. 2003. "How Feminism Changed Evolutionary Biology." *Signs* 28 (3): 901–21.

Graeff, Judith A., John P. Elder, and Elizabeth Mills Booth. 1993. *Communication for Health and Behavior Change: A Developing Country Perspective*. San Francisco: Jossey-Bass Publishers.

Graham, Carol. 2003. "Can Happiness Research Contribute to Development Economics?" Washington, D.C.: Brookings Institution.

Graham, Hilary. 1987. "Being Poor: Perceptions and Coping Strategies of Lone Mothers." In *Give and Take in Families: Studies in Resource Distribution*, edited by Julia Brannen and Gail Wilson, 56–74. London: Allen and Unwin.

Green, Maia. 2002. "Social Development: Issues and Approaches." In *Development Theory and Practice: Critical Perspectives*, edited by Uma Kothari and Martin Minogue, 52–70. Houndmills, Basingstoke, Hampshire: Palgrave.

Grosh, Margaret. 1994. *Administering Targeted Social Programs in Latin America: From Platitudes to Practice*. Washington, D.C.: World Bank.

Guamán Poma de Ayala, Felipe. 1980. *El Primer Nueva Crónica y Buen Gobierno*, edited by John Murra and Rolena Adorno. Mexico City: Siglo XXI Editores-Instituto de Estudios Peruanos.

Habermas, Jurgen. 1981. "New Social Movements." *Telos* 49 (fall): 33–37.

Hackenberg, Robert, Arthur Murphy, and Henry Selby. 1981. "The Household in the Secondary Cities of the Third World." Paper prepared in advance for the Wenner-Gren Foundation Symposium, "Households: Changing Form and Function," New York, 8–15 October.

Haddad, Lawrence. 1991. "Gender and Poverty in Ghana: A Descriptive Analysis of Selected Outcomes and Processes." *IDS Bulletin* 22 (1): 5–16.

Haddad, Lawrence, L. R. Brown, A. Richter, and L. Smith. 1995. "The Gender Dimensions of Economic Adjustment Politics: Potential Interactions and Evidence to Date." *World Development* 23 (6): 881–97.

Hafkin, Nancy, and Nancy Taggart. 2001. *Gender, Information Technology, and Developing Countries: An Analytic Study*. Washington, D.C.: Academy for Educational Development.

Halberstam, David. 2001. *War in a Time of Peace: Bush, Clinton and the Generals*. New York: Scribner.

Hall, Rodney Bruce, and Thomas J. Biersteker. 2002. "Conclusion and Directions." In *The Emergence of Private Authority in Global Governance*, edited by R. Hall and T. Biersteker, 3–22. Cambridge: Cambridge University Press.

Hamadeh-Banerjee, Lina. 2000. "Women's Agency in Governance." In *Women's Political Participation and Good Governance: 21st Century Challenges*, edited by Lina Hamadeh-Banerjee, 7–13. New York: UNDP.

Hamadeh-Banerjee, Lina, and P. Oquist. 2000. "Overview: Women's Political Participation and Good Governance: 21st Century Challenges." In *Women's Political Participation and Good Governance: 21st Century Challenges*, edited by Lina Hamadeh-Banerjee, 1–5. New York: UNDP.

Hamilton, S. 2002. "Neoliberalism, Gender and Property Rights in Rural Mexico." *Latin American Research Review* 37 (1): 119–43.

Haraway, Donna. 1999. "Situated Knowledges: The Science Question in Feminism and the Privilege of Partial Perspective." In *The Science Studies Reader*, edited by Mario Biagioli, 172–88. New York: Routledge.

————. 1997. *Modest_Witness@Second_Millennium.FemaleMan_Meets_OncoMouseTM Feminism and Technoscience*. New York: Routledge.

Harcourt, W., ed. 1999. *Women @ Internet: Creating New Cultures in Cyberspace*. London: Zed Books.

Harper, Malcom. 2002. "Indian Self-Help Groups and Bangladesh Grameen Bank Groups: A Comparative Analysis." Ahmedabad, India: Friends of Women's World Banking, India.

Harris, Olivia. 1985. *Complementariedad y Conflicto. Una visión andina del hombre y la mujer*. Cuzco: Revista Allpanchis 15 (21): 17–42.

Hartsock, Nancy. 1981. *Money, Sex and Power: An Essay on Domination and Community*. New York: Longman.

Harvey, Penélope. 1989. "Género, autoridad y competencia lingüística. Participación política de la mujer en los pueblos andinos." Documento de Trabajo no. 33. Lima: Instituto de Estudios Peruanos.

Hashimi, S. M., S. R. Schuler, and A. P. Riley. 1996. "Rural Credit Programs and Women's Empowerment in Bangladesh." *World Development* 24 (4): 635–53.

Hassim, Shireen. 2003. "Representation, Participation and Democratic Effectiveness: Feminist Challenges to Representative Democracy in South Africa." In *No Shortcuts to Power: African Women in Politics and Policy-Making*, edited by Anne Marie Goetz and Shireen Hassim, 81–109. London: Zed Books.

Hawkesworth, Mary E. 2001. "Democratization: Reflections on Gendered Dislocations in the Public Sphere." In *Gender, Globalization and Democratization*, edited by Rita Mae Kelly, Jane H. Bayes, Mary Hawkesworth, and Brigitte Young, 223–36. Lanham, Md.: Rowman and Littlefield.

Hayes, Adrian. 2001. "Poverty Reduction and Environmental Management." In *Poverty, Environment and Development*, edited by Adrian Hayes and M. V. Nadkarni, 253–68. Bangkok: UNESCO.

Held, David, and Mathias Koenig-Archigugi, eds. 2003. *Taming Globalization: Frontiers of Governance*. London: Polity.

Hellman, Judith Adler. 1992. "The Study of New Social Movement in Latin America and the Question of Autonomy." In *The Making of Social Movements in Latin America: Identity, Strategy and Democracy*, edited by Arturo Escobar and Sonia E. Alvarez, 52–61. Boulder: Westview Press.

Helzner, Judith, and Bonnie Shepard. 1997. "The Feminist Agenda in Population and Voluntary Organizations." In *Women, International Development, and Politics: The Bureaucratic Mire*, edited by Kathleen Staudt, 167–82. Philadelphia: Temple University Press.

Herz, Barbara, and Gende B. Sperling. 2004. *What Works in Girls' Education: Evidence and Policies from the Developing World*. New York: Council on Foreign Relations.

Heyzer, Noeleen, ed. 1995. *A Commitment to the World's Women: Perspectives on Development for Beijing and Beyond*. New York: UNIFEM.

Higer, Amy J. 1999. "International Women's Activism and the 1994 Cairo Women's Conference." In *Gender Politics in Global Governance*, edited by Mary K. Meyer and Elisabeth Prügl, 122–41. Lanham, Md.: Rowman and Littlefield.

Himmelstrand, Karin, 1977. "Women in Development: A Swedish View." Presented at a colloquium organized by Canadian International Development Agency in Ottawa, 6–8 June.

Hirschmann, David. 2002. "Aid Dependence, Sustainability and Technical Assistance: Designing a Monitoring and Evaluation System in Tanzania." *Public Management Review* 5 (2): 225–44.

Hirschmann, David. 1998. "Civil Society in South Africa: Learning from Gender Themes." *World Development* 26 (2): 227–38.

———. 1995a. "Democracy, Gender and US Foreign Assistance: Guidelines and Lessons." *World Development* 23 (8): 1291–1302.

———. 1995b. "Managing Equity and Gender in an Agricultural Program in Malawi." *Public Administration and Development* 15 (1): 21–40.

———. 1990. "The Malawi Case: Enclave Politics, Core Resistance and 'Nkhoswe No. 1.' " In *Women, International Development, and Politics: The Bureaucratic Mire*, edited by Kathleen Staudt, 163–79. Philadelphia: Temple University Press.

HIVOS. 1996. Policy Document: *Gender, Women and Development*. The Hague.

———. 1995. "Cultura y Desarrollo. La política de cultura de Hivos." The Hague.

———. 1993a. *Política de HIVOS 1993–1998 para América Latina*. The Hague.

———. 1993b. "Report. Women in Development: Central America." The Hague.

Ho, Peter. 2001. "Who Owns China's Land? Policies, Property Rights and Deliberate Institutional Ambiguity." *China Quarterly* 166: 394–421.

Hoddinott, John, and Lawrence Haddad. 1991. *Household Expenditures, Child Anthropomorphic Status and the Intra-Household Division of Income: Evidence from the Côte d'Ivoire*. Oxford: University of Oxford, Unit for the Study of African Economics.

Holland, Dorothy, and Jean Lave, eds. 2000. *History in Person: Enduring Struggles, Contentious Practice, Intimate Identities*. Santa Fe: School of America Research Press.

Hoskins, M. 1980. "Community Forestry Depends on Women." *Unasylva* 32 (130): 27–32.

Howe, Florence, ed. 2000. *The Politics of Women's Studies: Testimony from 30 Founding Mothers*. New York: Feminist Press.

Howell, Jude, and Jenny Pearce. 2001. *Civil Society and Development: A Critical Exploration*. Boulder: Lynne Rienner.

Hughes, G., and M. Dunleavy. 2000. *Why Do Babies and Young Children Die in India? The Role of the Household Environment*. Washington, D.C.: South Asia Office, World Bank.

Huntington, Samuel P. 1991. *The Third Wave: Democratization in the Late Twentieth Century*. Norman: University of Oklahoma Press.

Huntington, Suellen. 1975. "Issues in Woman's Role in Economic Development: Critique and Alternatives." *Journal of Marriage and the Family* 37 (4, November): 1001–12.

Hussein, Aziza. 2004. "Crossroads: The UN, Status of Women Commission and NGOs." In *Developing Power: How Women Transformed International Development*, edited by Arvonne Fraser and Irene Tinker, 3–13. New York: Feminist Press.

Huston, Perdita. 1979. *Third World Women Speak Out*. New York: Praeger.

ICSC (International Civil Service Commission). 1998. *Gender Balance in the United Nations Common System: Progress, Prognosis, Prescription*. New York. ICSC.

ILO Gender Audit 2001–02. 2002. Report to the Director-General. Geneva: ILO-GENDER.

———. 2001. *Gender! A Partnership of Equals*. International Labor Organization, Bureau for Gender Equity, http://www.ilo.org/public/english/bureau/ . . . r/beijing5/contribu/ briefing/approach.htm. Accessed 14 June 2001.

———. 1999. *Gender Equality and Mainstreaming in the International Labor Office*. Circular no. 564, 17 December, Geneva: International Labour Office.

———. 1994. *Women and Work: Selected ILO Policy Documents*. Geneva: International Labour Office.

ILO Governing Body. 2004. *Sixteenth Item on the Agenda: Composition and Structure of the Staff*. 289th Session, Geneva, March 2004; GB.289/PFA/16: International Labor Office.

————. 2001. *Tenth Item on the Agenda: Composition and Structure of the Staff.* 280th Session, Geneva, March 2001; GB.280/PFA/10: International Labour Office.

————. 2000. *Fifth Item on the Agenda: Governing Body Symposium on Decent Work for Women— The ILO's Contribution to Women 2000: Gender Equality, Development and Peace for the Twenty- First Century (New York, 5–9 June 2000). ILO Action Plan on Gender Equality and Mainstreaming in the ILO.* 277th Session (March), GB.277/5/2, Geneva: International Labour Office.

International Labor Organization (ILO) and United Nations Research and Training Institute for the Advancement of Women (INSTRAW). 1985. *Women in Economic Activity: A Global Statistical Survey (1950–2000).* Geneva: ILO.

IPAZ (Instituto para la Paz). 2000. *Núcleos Rurales de Administración de Justicia. Sistematización de Experiencias.* Ayacucho: IPAZ.

"Iraqi Council to Debate Plan for Transition." 2004. *Los Angeles Times,* 31 January: 1.

Ireson-Doolittle, Carol, and W. Randall Ireson. 1999. "Cultivating the Forest: Gendered Land Use among The Tay in Northern Vietnam." In *Women's Rights to House and Land,* edited by Irene Tinker and Gale Summerfield, 115–130. Boulder: Lynne Rienner.

Isbell, Billie Jean 1997. "De immaduro a duro: lo simbólilco feminino y los esquemas andinos de género." In *Mas Allá del silencio: Las fonteras de género en los Andes,* edited by Denise Arnold. La Paz: ILCA-CIASE.

————. 1976. "La otra mitad esencial: un estudio de complementariedad sexual andina." *Estudios Andinos* 5 (1): 37–55.

Jackson, Cecile. 2002. "Disciplining Gender?" *World Development* 30 (3): 497–509.

————. 1998. "Rescuing Gender from the Poverty Trap." In *Feminist Visions of Development: Gender, Analysis and Policy,* edited by Cecile Jackson and Ruth Pearson, 39–64. London: Routledge.

————. 1997a. "Actor Orientation and Gender Relations at a Participatory Project Interface." In *Getting Institutions Right for Women in Development,* edited by Anne Marie Goetz, 162–75. London: Zed Books.

————. 1997b. "Post Poverty, Gender and Development." *IDS Bulletin* 28 (3): 145–55.

————. 1996. "Rescuing Gender from the Poverty Trap." *World Development* 24 (3): 489–504.

Jackson, Cecile, and Ruth Pearson, eds. 1998. *Feminist Visions of Development: Gender, Analysis and Policy.* London: Routledge.

Jacobs, W. W. 1902. "The Monkey's Paw." In *Lady of the Barge.* London: Harper and Brothers.

Jahan, Rounaq. 1995. *The Elusive Agenda: Mainstreaming Women in Development.* London: Zed Books.

Jain, Devaki. 2004. "A View from the South." In *Developing Power: How Women Transformed International Development,* edited by Arvonne Fraser and Irene Tinker, 128–37. New York: Feminist Press.

————. 2003. "Building a Service Station Brick by Brick: The Institute of Social Studies Trust." In *Narratives from the Women's Studies Family: Recreating Knowledge,* edited by Devaki Jain and Pam Rajput, 259–86. New Delhi: Sage.

Jain, Shobita. 1991. "Standing Up for Trees: Women's Role in the Chipko Movement." In *Women and the Environment: A Reader: Crisis and Development in the Third World,* edited by Sally Sontheimer, 163–78. New York: Monthly Review Press.

Jaquette, Jane S. 2003. "Feminism and the Challenges of the 'Post-Cold War' World." *International Feminist Journal of Politics* 5 (3): 331–54.

————. 2001. "Women and Democracy: Regional Differences and Contrasting Views." *Journal of Democracy* 12 (3): 111–25.

Jaquette, Jane S. 1997. "Women in Power: From Tokenism to Critical Mass." *Foreign Policy* 108: 23-37.

———. 1995. "Losing the Battle/Winning the War: International Politics, Women's Issues, and the 1980 Mid-Decade Conference." In *Women, Politics and the United Nations*, edited by Anne Winslow, 45-59. Westport, Conn.: Greenwood Press.

———, ed. 1994. *The Women's Movement in Latin America: Participation and Democracy*. Boulder: Westview Press.

———. 1990. "Gender and Justice in Economic Development." In *Persistent Inequalities: Women and World Development*, edited by Irene Tinker, 54-69. New York: Oxford University Press.

———, ed. 1989. *The Women's Movement in Latin America: Feminism and the Transition to Democracy*. London: Allen and Unwin.

———. 1983. "Women and Modernization Theory: A Decade of Feminist Criticism." *World Politics* 34 (2): 267-84.

Jaquette, Jane S., and Kathleen Staudt. 1985. "Women as 'At-Risk Reproducers': Women and US Population Policy." In *Women, Biology and Public Policy*, edited by Virginia Sapiro, 235-68. Beverly Hills: Sage.

Jaquette, Jane S., and Sharon L Wolchik. 1998. Introduction to *Women and Democracy: Latin America and Eastern and Central Europe*, edited by Jane Jaquette and Sharon Wolchik, 1-28. Baltimore: Johns Hopkins University Press.

Jayawardena, Kumari. 1986. *Feminism and Nationalism in the Third World*. London: Zed Books.

Jelin, Elizabeth, and Eric Hershberg, eds. 1996. *Construir la Democracia. Derechos Humanos, Ciudadanía y Sociedad en América Latina*. Caracas: Nueva Sociedad.

Joachim, Jutta. 1999. "Shaping the Human Rights Agenda: The Case of Violence Against Women." In *Gender Politics in Global Governance*, edited by Mary K. Meyer and Elisabeth Prügl, 142-60. Lanham, Md.: Rowman and Littlefield.

Jodelet, Denise. 1988. *La Representación Social: fenómenos, concepto y teoría, en Psicología Social*. II Tomo, edited by Serge Moscovici, 470-94. Barcelona: Ediciones Paidós.

Joekas, Susan P. 1991. "Lessons Learned from the Advanced Developing Countries." Washington, D.C.: GENESYS for USAID.

Jonasdottir, Anna G. 1988. "On the Concept of Interests, Women's Interests, and the Limitations of Interest Theory." In *The Political Interests of Gender*, edited by Anna Jonasdottir and Kathleen Jones, 33-65. London: Sage.

Judd, Ellen R. 1994. *Gender and Power in Rural North China*. Stanford: Stanford University Press.

Kabeer, Naila. 1999. "Resources, Agency, Achievements: Reflections on the Measurement of Women's Empowerment." *Development and Change* 30: 435-64.

———. 1998a. "Jumping to Conclusions? Struggles over Meaning and Method the Study of Household Economics." In *Getting Institutions Right for Women in Development*, edited by Anne Marie Goetz, 91-107. London: Zed Books.

———. 1998b. " 'Money Can't Buy Me Love'? Reevaluating Gender, Credit and Empowerment in Rural Bangladesh." Brighton: Institute of Development Studies discussion paper no. 363.

———. 1997. "Tactics and Trade-Offs: Revisiting the Links Between Gender and Poverty." *IDS Bulletin* 28 (3): 1-25.

———. 1996. "Agency, Well-Being and Inequality: Reflections on the Gender Dimensions of Poverty." *IDS Bulletin* 27 (1): 11-21.

———. 1994. *Reversed Realities; Gender Hierarchies in Development Thought*. London: Verso.

———. 1989. *Monitoring Poverty as if Gender Mattered: A Methodology for Rural Bangladesh.* Brighton: Institute of Development Studies, discussion paper no. 255.

Kameri-Mbote, P., and P. Cullet. 1999. *Agrobiodiversity and International Law.* Biopolicy International Series no. 22. Nairobi: African Centre for Technology Studies.

Kandiyoti, Deniz. 1998. "Gender, Power and Contestation: Rethinking Bargaining With Patriarchy." In *Feminist Visions of Development: Gender, Analysis and Policy,* edited by Cecile Jackson and Ruth Pearson, 135–51. London: Routledge.

Kanji, Nazneen. 1991. "Structural Adjustment Policies: Shifting the Social Costs of Reproduction to Women." *Critical Health* 34: 61–67.

Karan, P. P., and Shigeru Iijima. 1975. "Environmental Stress in the Himalaya." *Geographical Review* 75 (1): 71–92.

Kardam, Nuket. 2004. "The Emerging Gender Equality Regime from Neoliberal and Constructivist Perspectives in International Relations." *International Feminist Journal of Politics* 4 (1): 85–109.

———. 1997a. "The Adaptability of International Development Agencies: The Response of the World Bank to Women in Development." In *Women, International Development, and Politics: The Bureaucratic Mire,* edited by Kathleen Staudt, 136–50. Philadelphia: Temple University Press. Originally published in 1990.

———. 1997b. "Making Development Organizations Accountable: The Organizational, Political and Cognitive Contexts." In *Getting Institutions Right for Women in Development,* edited by Anne Marie Goetz, 44–60. London: Zed Books.

———. 1995. "Conditions of Accountability for Gender Policy: the Organizational, Political and Cognitive Contexts." *IDS Bulletin* 26 (3): 11–22.

———. 1991. *Bringing Women In: Women's Issues in International Development Programs.* Boulder: Lynne Rienner.

Keck, Margaret E., and Kathryn Sikkink. 1998. *Activists beyond Borders: Advocacy Networks in International Politics.* Ithaca: Cornell University Press.

Kelly, Rita Mae, Jane H. Bayes, Mary Hawkesworth, and Brigitte Young, eds. 2001. *Gender, Globalization and Democratization.* Lanham, Md.: Rowman and Littlefield.

Kemp, Amanda, Nozizwe Madlala, Asha Mooodley, and Elaine Salo. 1995. "The Dawn of a New Day: Redefining South African Feminism." In *The Challenge of Local Feminisms,* edited by Amrita Basu with Elizabeth McGrory, 131–62. Boulder: Westview Press.

Kennedy, Eileen. 1994. "Development Policy, Gender of Head of Household, and Nutrition." In *Poverty and Well-Being in the Household: Case Studies of the Developing World,* edited by Eileen Kennedy and Mercedes González de la Rocha, 25–42. San Diego: Center for Iberian and Latin American Studies, University of California, San Diego.

Kenway, Jane, and Diane Langmead. 2000. "Fast Capitalism, Fast Feminism, and Some Fast Food for Thought." In *Global Feminist Politics, Identities in a Changing World,* edited by Ali Suki, Kelly Coate, and Wangui wa Goro, 154–75. London: Routledge.

Kenworthy, Lane, and Melissa Malami. 1999. "Gender Inequality in Political Representation: A Worldwide Comparative Analysis." *Social Forces* 78 (1): 235–69.

Kittay, Eva Feder. 1999. *Love's Labor: Essays on Women, Equality and Dependency.* New York: Routledge.

Kole, Ellen S. 2001. "Appropriate Theorizing about African Women and the Internet." *International Feminist Journal of Politics* 3 (2): 155–79.

Krook, Mona Lena. 2003. "Get the Balance Right!: Global and Transnational Campaigns to Promote Gender-Balanced Decision-Making." Paper presented at the International Studies Association Annual Meeting, Portland, Ore.

Kucynski, Pedro Pablo, and John Williamson. 2003. *After the Washington Consensus*. Washington, D.C.: Institute of International Economics.

Kumar, Radha. 1993. *A History of Doing*. New Delhi: Kali for Women; London: Verso.

Kumari, Ranjana. 1989. *Women-Headed Households in Rural India*. New Delhi: Radiant Publishers.

Landuyt, Katerine. 1999. *Gender Mainstreaming: A How-To Manual*. International Labor Organization, Bureau for Asia and Pacific, http://www.ilo.org/public/english/region/asro/mdtmanila/gender. Accessed 30 January 2001.

Langer, Ana, Rafael Lozano, and José Luís Bobadilla. 1991. "Effects of Mexico's Economic Crisis on the Health of Women and Children." In *Social Responses to Mexico's Crisis of the 1980s*, edited by Mercedes González de la Rocha and Agustín Escobar, 195–219. San Diego: Center for US-Mexican Studies.

Lapiedra, Aurora. 1985. "Roles y Valores de la Mujer Andina." *Cuzco: Revista Allpanchis* 21 (25): 43–63.

Lappe, Frances Moore, and Anna Lappe. 2002. *Hope's Edge: The Next Diet for a Small Planet*. New York: Tarcher/Penguin.

Lavallé, Bernard. 1999. *Amor y Opresión en los Andes Coloniales*. Lima: Instituto de Estudios Peruanos, Instituto Francés de Estudios Andinos, Universidad Particular Ricardo Palma.

Leach, Fiona. 1999. "Women in the Informal Sector: The Contribution of Education and Training." In *Development with Women*, 46–62. Oxford: Oxfam.

Leach, M. 1994. *Rainforest Relations: Gender and Resource Use among the Mende of Gola, Sierra Leone*. Washington, D.C.: Smithsonian Institution Press.

Lee-Smith, Diana. 2001. "Gender Equality: Addressing Women's Concerns." *UN Chronicle* 38 (1): 50–51.

———. 1997. *"My House Is My Husband: A Kenyan Study of Women's Access to Land and Housing."* Lund, Sweden: Thesis 8, Lund University Department of Architecture and Development Studies.

Lee-Smith, Diana, and Catalina Hinchey Trujillo. 1992. "The Struggle to Legitimize Subsistence: Women and Sustainable Development." *Environment and Urbanization* 4 (1) April: 77–86.

Lensink, R., and H. White. 1997. *Aid Dependence: Issues and Indicators*. Groningen: Report prepared for the Swedish Ministry of Foreign Affairs Expert Group on Development Issues.

Levey, Lisbeth A. 2000. *Wired for Information: Putting the Internet to Good Use in Africa*. Nairobi: Project for Information Access and Connectivity (PIAC). http://www.piac.org.

Lewis, David. 1993. "Going It Alone: Female-Headed Households, Rights and Resources in Rural Bangladesh." *European Journal of Development Research* 5 (2): 23–42.

Lewis, David, and Tina Wallace, eds. 2000. *New Roles and Relevance: Development NGOs and the Challenge of Change*. Bloomfield, Conn.: Kumarian Press.

Li, Zongmin. 2003. "Women's Land Rights in Rural China: A Synthesis." Beijing: Ford Foundation Office.

———. 1999. "Changing Land and Housing Use by Rural Women in Northern China." In *Women's Rights to Land and House*, edited by Irene Tinker and Gale Summerfield, 241–64. Boulder: Lynne Rienner.

Liebowitz, Debra J. 2002. "Gendering (Trans)National Advocacy: Tracking the Lollapalooza at 'Home.'" *International Feminist Journal of Politics* 4 (2): 173–96.

Lind, Amy. 1997. "Gender, Development and Urban Social Change: Women's Community Action in Global Cities." *World Development* 25 (8): 1205–23.

Lister, Ruth. 1997. *Citizenship: Feminist Perspectives.* New York: New York University Press.

Lloyd, Cynthia, and Anastasia Gage-Brandon. 1993. "Women's Role in Maintaining Households: Family Welfare and Sexual Inequality in Ghana." *Population Studies* 47: 115–31.

Longwe, Sara Hlupekile. 1995a. "A Development Agency as a Patriarchal Cooking Pot: The Evaporation of Policies for Women's Advancement." In *Women's Rights and Development,* compiled by Mandy MacDonald, 18–29. Oxfam: Oxford.

———. 1995b. *A Commitment to the World's Women: Perspectives on Development for Beijing and Beyond,* edited by N. Heyzer, 126–40. New York: UNIFEM.

López, Sinesio. 1997. *Ciudadanos Reales e Imaginarios. Concepciones, Desarrollo y Mapa de la Ciudadanía en el Perú.* Lima: Instituto de Diálogo y Propuestas.

Lotherington, Ann Therese, and Anne Britt Flemmen. 1991. "Negotiating Gender: The Case of the International Labour Organization." In *Gender and Change in Developing Countries,* edited by Kristi Anne Stolen and Mariken Vaa, 273–307. London: Norwegian University Press.

Lubin, Carol Riegelman, and Anne Winslow. 1990. *Social Justice for Women: The International Labor Organization and Women.* Durham: Duke University Press.

Lush, D., H. Rushwayo, and F. Banda, eds. 2000. *Into or Out of the Digital Divide? Perspectives on ICTs and Development in Southern Africa.* Lusaka: Panos Southern Africa.

Lutz, C., and J. L. Collins. 1993. *Reading the National Geographic.* Chicago: University of Chicago Press.

Lycklama, Geertje, Virginia Vargas, and Sakia Wieringa, eds. 1998. *Women's Movements and Public Policy in Europe, Latin America, and the Caribbean.* New York: Garland.

Maboreke, M. 1990. "The Gender Dimensions of the Land Question in Zimbabwe." Paper presented at the Conference on Land Policy in Zimbabwe after Lancaster, Harare, Zimbabwe.

Maddox, Brenda. 2002. *Rosalind Franklin: The Dark Lady of DNA.* New York: Harper Collins.

Mailer, Norman. 2003. "The White Man Unburdened." *The New York Review of Books* 17 July: 4–6.

Mair, Lucille. 1986. "Women: A Decade Is Time Enough." *Third World Quarterly* 8 (2): 583–93.

Mallee, Hein. 1998. "Rural Labor Mobility in China." In *Village Inc.: Chinese Rural Society in the 1990s,* edited by Flemming Christiansen and Junzuo Zhang, 212–29. Honolulu: University of Hawaii Press.

Marchand, Marianne H., and Jane L. Parpart, eds. 1995. *Feminism/Postmodernism/Development.* London: Routledge.

Marchand, Marianne H., and Anne Sisson Runyan, eds. 2000. *Gender and Global Restructuring: Sightings, Sites and Resistances.* London: Routledge.

Marcoux, Alain. 1997. "The Feminization of Poverty: Facts, Hypotheses and the Art of Advocacy." Rome: Report of Women and Population Division, FAO.

Marks, Eleanor. 2001. "The Women in Development Movement's Effect on Economic Development Policies of the United Nations, 1975–85. Unpublished dissertation, Boston University.

May, Julian. 2001. "An Elusive Consensus: Definitions, Measurement and the Analysis of Poverty." In *Choices for the Poor: Lessons from National Poverty Strategies,* edited by Alejandro Grinspun, 23–54. New York: UNDP.

Mayer, Doe. 2002. "Melding Digital and Traditional Media for Social Change in Africa." Four videos from *Women Connect!* http://www.annenberg.edu.

Mayer, Doe, and Muadi Mukenge. 2001. *Women Connect!: Improving Women's Reproductive Health and Empowerment Through Women's NGOs. A Final Report to the Bill and Melinda Gates Foundation*. Los Angeles: Pacific Institute for Women's Health.

Mayer, Enrique. 1996. "Reflexiones sobre los Derechos Individuales y Colectivos: Los Derechos Etnicos." In *Construir la Democracia. Derechos Humanos, Ciudadanía y Sociedad en América Latina*, edited by Elizabeth Jelin and Eric Hershberg, 171–78. Caracas: Nueva Sociedad.

Mayoux, Linda. 2002. "Women's Empowerment or the Feminisation of Debt? Towards a New Agenda in African Microfinance." Paper given at One World Action Conference, London, 21–22 March. http://www.oneworldaction.org/Background.htm.

Mazingira Institute. 1992–2003. *Settlements Information Network Africa (SINA) Newsletter*. Nairobi: Mazingira Institute.

McCay, B., and J. Acheson. 1987. *The Question of the Commons*. Tucson: University of Arizona Press.

McClenaghan, Sharon. 1997. "Women, Work and Empowerment: Romanticising the Reality." In *Gender Politics in Latin America: Debates in Theory and Practice*, edited by Elizabeth Dore, 19–35. New York: Monthly Review Press.

McIlwaine, Cathy. 2002. "Perspectives on Poverty, Vulnerability and Exclusion." In *Challenges and Change in Middle America: Perspectives on Mexico, Central America and the Caribbean*, edited by Cathy McIlwaine and Katie Willis, 82–109. Harlow: Pearson Education.

———. 1997. "Vulnerable or Poor? A Study of Ethnic and Gender Disadvantage among Afro-Caribbeans in Limón, Costa Rica." *European Journal of Development Research* 9 (2): 35–61.

Mehta, Rekha, Simel Esim, and Margaret Simms. 2000. *Fulfilling the Beijing Commitment: Reducing Poverty, Enhancing Women's Economic Options*. Washington, D.C.: International Center for Research on Women.

Mehta, R., A. Drost-Maasry, and R. Rahman. 1995. *Credit for Women: Why Is It So Important?* Washington, D.C.: International Center for Research on Women.

Meier, Lucille Mathurin. 1986. "Women: A Decade Is Time Enough." *Third World Quarterly* 8 (2): 583–93.

Meinzen-Dick, Ruth S., Lynne R. Brown, Hilary Sims Feldstein, and Agnes R. Quisumbing. 1997. "Gender, Property Rights and Natural Resources." *World Development* 25 (8): 1303–15.

Meinzen-Dick, Ruth, and Margreet Zwarteveen. 2001. "Gender Dimensions of Community Resource Management: The Case of Water Users' Associations in South Asia." In *Communities and the Environment: Ethnicity, Gender, and the State in Community-Based Conservation*, edited by Arun Agrawal and Clark C. Gibson, 63–88. New Brunswick: Rutgers University Press.

Menjívar, Rafael, and Juan Diego Trejos. 1992. *La Pobreza en América Central*, 2nd ed. San José, Costa Rica: FLACSO.

Merchant, Carolyn. 1980. *The Death of Nature: Women, Ecology and the Scientific Revolution*. San Francisco: Harper and Rowe.

Meyer, Mary K., and Elisabeth Prügl, eds. 1999. *Gender Politics in Global Governance*. Lanham, Md.: Rowman and Littlefield.

Mies, Maria, and Vandana Shiva. 1993. *Ecofeminism*. London: Zed Books.

Miguel, Edward. 2003. "Poverty and Witch Killing." Department of Economics, University of California, Berkeley. Forthcoming, *Review of Economic Studies*.

Miller, Carol. 1998. "Gender Advocates and Multilateral Development Organizations: Promoting Change from Within." In *Missionaries and Mandarins*, edited by Carol Miller and Shahra Razavi, 138–71. London: Intermediate Technology Publications.

Miller, Carol, and Shahra Razavi. 1998a. Introduction to *Missionaries and Mandarins*, edited by Carol Miller and Shahra Razavi, 1–19. London: Intermediate Technology Publications.

———, eds. 1998b. *Missionaries and Mandarins, Feminist Engagement with Development Institutions*. London: Intermediate Technology Publications.

Miller, Francesca. 1981. *Latin American Women: The Search for Social Justice*. Hanover, N. H.: University Press of New England.

Mindry, Deborah. 2001. "Nongovernmental Organizations, 'Grassroots,' and the Politics of Virtue." *Signs* 26 (4, summer): 1187–1211.

Ministerio de Asuntos Exteriores de Holanda, Departamento de Cooperación y Desarrollo. 1992. *Un Mundo de Diferencia. Un nuevo marco para la cooperación y el desarrollo en la década del 90*. Traducción no oficial al español. San José de Costa Rica: Interpress Service.

Miraftab, Faranak. Forthcoming 2005. "Privatization of Public Service and Municipal Housekeeping: The South African Case." *International Journal of Urban and Regional Research*.

———. 2005. "Making Neoliberal Governance: The Disempowering Work of Empowerment." *International Planning Studies* 9 (4): 239–59.

———. 2004. "Neoliberalism and Casualization of Public Sector Services: The Case of Waste Collection Services in Cape Town, South Africa." *International Journal of Urban and Regional Research* 28 (4): 874–92.

———. 2001. "Risks and Opportunities in Gender Gaps to Access Shelter: A Platform for Intervention." *International Journal of Politics, Culture, and Society* 15 (1): 143–60.

———. 1997. "Revisiting Informal Sector Homeownership: The Relevance of Household Compositions for Housing Options of the Poor." *International Journal of Urban and Regional Research* 21 (2): 303–22.

———. 1996. *Women's Empowerment: Participation in Shelter Strategies at the Community Level in Urban Informal Settlements*. Nairobi, Kenya: UNCHS.

Moghadam, Valentine. 1998. "Gender and the Global Economy." In *Revisioning Gender*, edited by Myra Feree, Judith Lorber, and Beth Hess, 128–60. London: Sage.

———. 1997. *The Feminisation of Poverty: Notes on a Concept and Trend*. Normal: Illinois State University, Women's Studies Occasional Paper no. 2.

———. 1995. "Gender Dynamics of Restructuring in the Semiperiphery." In *Engendering Wealth and Well-Being*, edited by Rae Lesser Blumberg, Cathy A. Rakowski, I. Tinker, and Michael Monteon, 17–37. Boulder: Westview Press.

Mohanty, Chandra Talpade. 2003. *Feminism without Borders: Decolonizing Theory, Practicing Solidarity*. Durham: Duke University Press.

Molyneux, Maxine. 2001. *Women's Movements in International Perspective: Latin America and Beyond*. Houndmills, Basingstoke: Palgrave.

———. 1998. "Analyzing Women's Movements." In *Feminist Visions of Development: Gender, Analysis and Policy*, edited by Cecile Jackson and Ruth Pearson, 65–88. London: Routledge.

———. 1996. "State, Gender and Institutional Change in Cuba's 'Special Period': The Federación de Mujeres Cubanas." London: University of London, Institute of Latin American Studies, Research Papers no. 43.

———. 1985. "Mobilization Without Emancipation? Women's Interests, the State, and Revolution in Nicaragua." *Feminist Studies* 11 (2, summer): 227–54.

Molyneux, Maxine, and Shahra Razavi, eds. 2003. *Gender Justice, Development and Rights*. Oxford: Oxford University Press.

———. 2003. Introduction to *Gender Justice, Development and Rights*, edited by Maxine Molyneux and Shahra Razavi, 1–44. Oxford: Oxford University Press.

Momsen, Janet Henshall. 2004. *Gender and Development*. London: Routledge.

Monteon, Michael. 1995. "Gender and Economic Crises in Latin America: Reflections on the Great Depression and the Debt Crisis." In *Engendering Wealth and Well-Being*, edited by Rae Lesser Blumberg, Cathy A. Rakowski, I. Tinker, and Michael Monteon, 39–62. Boulder: Westview Press.

Moore, Henrietta. 1988. *Feminism and Anthropology*. Cambridge: Polity.

Moore, Henrietta, and Megan Vaughn. 1994. *Cutting Down Trees: Gender, Nutrition and Agricultural Change in the Northern Province of Zambia, 1890–1990*. Portsmouth, N.H.: Heinemann.

Morna, Colleen Lowe. 2001. "Learning to Link: An Evaluation of the Women Connect! Project of the Pacific Institute for Women's Health." Johannesburg: Gender Links.

Morna, Colleen Lowe, and Zohra Khan. 2000. *Net Gains: African Women Take Stock of Information and Communication Technologies*. Johannesburg: Gender Links.

Morvaridi, Behrooz. 1995. "Macroeconomic Policies and Gender Relations: The Study of Farming Households in Two Turkish Villages." In *Engendering Wealth and Well-Being*, edited by Rae Lesser Blumberg, Cathy A. Rakowski, I. Tinker, and Michael Monteon, 135–52. Boulder: Westview Press.

Moser, Caroline. 1998. "The Asset Vulnerability Framework: Reassessing Urban Poverty Reduction Strategies." *World Development* 26 (1): 1–19.

———. 1997. *Household Responses to Poverty and Vulnerability*, Volume 1: *Confronting Crisis in Cisne Dos, Guayaquil, Ecuador*. Washington, D.C.: World Bank, Urban Management and Poverty Reduction Series no. 21.

———. 1996. *Confronting Crisis: A Comparative Study of Household Responses to Poverty in Four Poor Urban Communities*. Washington, D.C.: Environmentally Sustainable Development Studies and Monographs Series no. 8.

———. 1993. *Gender Planning and Development: Theory, Practice and Training*. New York: Routledge.

———. 1989a. "Gender Planning in the Third World: Meeting Practical and Strategic Gender Needs." *World Development* 17 (11): 1799–1825. Note: pages cited in text are from a manuscript version of this article (cited below).

———. 1989b. "The Impact of Structural Adjustment at the Micro-Level: Low-Income Women, Time and the Triple Role in Guayaquil, Ecuador." In *Invisible Adjustment*, vol. 2, edited by UNICEF, 137–61. New York: UNICEF, Americas and Caribbean Office.

———. 1988? "Gender Planning in the Third World." Unpublished manuscript.

———. 1987. "Women, Human Settlements, and Housing: A Conceptual Framework for Analysis and Policy Making." In *Women, Human Settlements, and Housing*, edited by Caroline Moser and Linda Peake, 12–32. New York: Tavistock Publications.

Moser, Caroline, Michael Gatehouse, and Helen Garcia. 1996a. *Urban Poverty Research Sourcebook. Module I: Sub-City Level Household Survey*. Washington, D.C.: UNDP/UNCHS/World Bank—Urban Management Programme, Working Paper Series 5.

———. 1996b. *Urban Poverty Research Sourcebook. Module II: Indicators of Urban Poverty*. Washington, D.C.: UNDP/UNCHS/World Bank—Urban Management Programme, Working Paper Series 5.

Moser, Caroline, and Cathy McIlwaine. 1997. *Household Responses to Poverty and Vulnerability, Volume 3: Confronting Crisis in Commonwealth, Metro Manila, Philippines*. Washington, D.C.: World Bank, Urban Management Programme.

Moser, Caroline, Annika Tornqvist, and Bernice van Bronkhorst. 1999. *Mainstreaming Gender and Development in the World Bank: Progress and Recommendations*. Washington, D.C.: World Bank.

———. 1998. "Mainstreaming Gender into Social Assessments." In *Social Development Notes.* http://www.worldbank.org/gender/assessment/maingen.htm. Accessed 30 January 2001.

Mosesdottir, Lilja. 1995. "The State and the Egalitarian, Ecclesiastical and Liberal Regimes of Gender Relations." *British Journal of Sociology* 46 (4): 624–42.

Moynihan, Daniel Patrick. 1975a. *A Dangerous Place.* New York: Little, Brown.

———. 1975b. "The United States in Opposition." *Commentary* 59 (3): 31–44.

Mueller, Adele. 1986. "The Bureaucratization of Feminist Knowledge: The Case of Women in Development." *Resources for Feminist Research* 15 (1): 36–38.

Mukenge, Muadi. 2004. "Women's NGOs and Social Change in Uganda, Zambia and Zimbabwe: How Information Technology Can Enhance Women's Health in Africa." In *Science and Technology in Africa,* edited by Paul Zeleza and Ibulaimu Kakoma. Trenton, N.J.: Africa World Press.

Muntemba, S. 1982. "Women as Food Producers and Suppliers in the Twentieth Century: The Case of Zambia." *Development Dialogue* (1–2): 29–50.

Murphy, Josette. 1997. *Mainstreaming Gender in World Bank Lending: An Update.* Washington, D.C.: World Bank.

Murray, C. J., J. A. Salomon, and C. Mathers. 2000. "A Critical Examination of Summary Measures of Population Health." *Bulletin of the World Health Organization* 78 (8): 981–94.

Murray, C. J. L., and A. D. Lopez, eds. 1996. *The Global Burden of Disease: A Comprehensive Assessment of Mortality and Disability from Diseases, Injuries, and Risk Factors in 1990 and Projected to 2020.* Global Burden of Disease and Injury Series. Cambridge, Mass.: Harvard School of Public Health on behalf of the World Health Organization and the World Bank.

Murray, Úna. 2001. *Gender Capacity Building Report.* Prepared for the Bureau for Gender Equality, http://www.ilo.org/public/english/bureau/gender/new/capacity.htm. Accessed 14 June 2001.

Muthwa, Sibongile. 1993. "Household Survival, Urban Poverty and Female Household Headship in Soweto: Some Key Issues for Further Policy Research." Paper given in seminar series "The Societies of Southern Africa in the 19th and 20th Centuries: Women, Colonialism and Commonwealth," Institute of Commonwealth Studies, University of London, 19 November.

Nanda, Priya. 2000. *Health Sector Reforms in Zambia: Implications for Reproductive Health and Rights.* Takoma Park, Md.: Center for Health and Gender Equity.

Naples, Nancy, and Manisha Desai, eds. 2002. *Women's Activism and Globalization: Linking Local Struggles and Transnational Politics.* New York: Routledge.

Narayan, Deepa, Robert Chambers, Meera K. Shah, and Patti Petesch. 2000. *Voices of the Poor: Crying Out for Change.* Washington, D.C.: World Bank.

National Bureau of Statistics. 2000. *China Statistical Yearbook.* Beijing: China Statistics Press.

———. 2002. *China Statistical Yearbook.* Beijing: China Statistics Press.

———. 2003. *China Statistical Yearbook.* Beijing: China Statistics Press.

National Cancer Institute. 1997. *Making Health Communication Programs Work: A Planner's Guide.* Washington, D.C.: National Institutes of Health.

Nerad, Maresi. 1998. *The Academic Kitchen: A Social History of Gender Stratification at the University of California, Berkeley.* Albany: SUNY Press.

Netherlands Ministry of Foreign Affairs. 1992. *Un mundo de diferencia: Un nuevo marco para la cooperación y el desarrollo en la década de los 90.* Costa Rica: Interpress Service (unofficial translation).

Ngqaleni, M., and M. T. Makhura. 1996. "An Analysis of Women's Status in Agricultural Development in Northern Province." In *Land, Labour, and Livelihoods in Rural South Africa*

Volume Two: KwaZulu-Natal and Northern Province, edited by Micheal Lipton, Mike de Klerk, and Merle Liptons, 335–56. South Africa: Indicator Press.

NOVIB. 1997. *Más poder, menos pobreza. Política de NOVIB con respecto a género y desarrollo hasta el año 2000*. The Hague: Netherlands Organization of International Cooperation.

Nussbaum, Martha. 2003. "Capabilities as Fundamental Entitlements: Sen and Social Justice." *Feminist Economics* 9 (2–3): 33–59.

———. 2000. *Women and Human Development: The Capabilities Approach*. Cambridge: Cambridge University Press.

———. 1999. *Sex and Social Justice*. Oxford: Oxford University Press.

Nussbaum, Martha, and Jonathan Glover, eds. 1995. *Women, Culture and Development: A Study of Human Capabilities*. Oxford: Oxford University Press.

Oboler, Susana. 1996. *El Mundo es Racista y Ajeno. Orgullo y Prejuicio en la sociedad limeña contemporánea*. Working Paper no. 74. Lima: Instituto de Estudios Peruanos.

O'Brien, Robert, Anne Marie Goetz, Jan Aart Scholte, and Marc Williams. 2000. *Contesting Global Governance: Multilateral Economic Institutions and Global Social Movements*. Cambridge: Cambridge University Press.

Oey-Gardiner, Mayling, and Carla Bianpoen, eds. 2000. *Indonesian Women: The Journey Continues*. Canberra: Australian National University.

Oppong, Christine. 1997. "African Family Systems and Socio-Economic Crisis." In *Family, Population and Development in Africa*, edited by Aderanti Adepoju, 158–82. London: Zed Books.

O'Regan, Valerie. 2000. *Gender Matters: Female Policymakers' Influence in Industrialized Nations*. Westport, Conn.: Praeger.

Ortiz Rescaniere, Alejandro. 2001. *La Pareja y el Mito. Estudios sobre las concepciones de la persona y de la pareja en los Andes*, 3rd ed. Lima: Fondo Editorial de la Pontifica Universidad Católica del Perú.

Ossio, Juan. 1973. "Guamán Poma: Nueva Corónica o Carta al rey. Un intento de aproximación a las categorías de pensamiento del Mundo Andino." In *Ideología Mesiánica del Mundo Andino*, 153–213. Lima: Ignacio Prado Pastor Ediciones.

Ostrom, E. 1991. *Governing the Commons: The Evolution of Institutions for Collective Action*. Cambridge: Cambridge University Press.

Otero, Maria, and Elizabeth Rhyne, eds. 1994. *The New World of Microenterprise Finance: Building Healthy Financial Institutions for the Poor*. West Hartford, Conn.: Kumarian Press.

Owoh, Kenna. 1995. "Gender and Health in Nigerian Structural Adjustment: Locating Room to Maneuver." In *Engendering Wealth and Well-Being*, edited by Rae Lesser Blumberg, Cathy A. Rakowski, I. Tinker, and Michael Monteon, 181–94. Boulder: Westview Press.

Oxaal, Zöe, and Sally Baden. 1997. *Gender and Empowerment: Definitions, Approaches and Implications for Policy*. Brighton: Institute of Development Studies, University of Sussex, *Bridge Report* no. 40.

Pacific Institute for Women's Health. 2000. *Women Connect!* Workshop Evaluation, Harare, Zimbabwe, October.

Panos. 2000. *Signposts on the Superhighway: African Gender*. Lusaka, Zambia: Panos Southern Africa.

Paolisso, Michael, and Sarah Gammage. 1996. *Women's Responses to Environmental Degradation: Case Studies From Latin America*. Washington, D.C.: International Center for Research on Women.

Papanek, Hanna. 1990. "To Each Less Than She Needs, From Each More Than She Can Do:

Allocations, Entitlements, and Value." In *Persistent Inequalities: Women and World Development*, edited by Irene Tinker, 162–81. New York: Oxford University Press.

Parker, Warren, Lynn Dalrymple, and Emma Durden. 2000. *Communicating Beyond AIDS Awareness: A Manual for South Africa*. Auckland Park, South Africa: Department of Health.

Parpart, Jane L. 2001. "Gender and Empowerment: New Thoughts, New Approaches." In *The Companion to Development Studies*, edited by Vandana Desai and Robert Potter, 338–42. London: Edward Arnold.

———. 1995. "Deconstructing the Development 'Expert': Gender, Development, and the 'Vulnerable Groups.'" In *Feminism/ Postmodernism/ Development*, edited by Marianne H. Marchand and Jane L. Parpart, 221–43. London: Routledge.

Parpart, Jane L., M. Patricia Connelly, and V. Eudine Barriteau, eds. 2000. *Theoretical Perspectives on Gender and Development*. Ottawa, Canada: International Development Research Center.

Peace for Homes. 1998. "Peace for Homes, Homes for Peace, Inter-Regional Consultation on Women's Land and Property Rights in Situations of Conflict and Reconstruction, Kigali, Rwanda, 16–19 February 1998." Report of a meeting organized by UNIFEM, UNCHS, UNHCR, UNDP. Nairobi: UN-HABITAT.

Pearson, Ruth, and Cecile Jackson. 1998. "Interrogating Development: Feminism, Gender and Policy." In *Feminist Visions of Development: Gender, Analysis and Policy*, edited by Cecile Jackson and Ruth Pearson, 1–17. London: Routledge.

People's Daily. 2003. "Law Protects Long-Term Land Use of China's Farmers." March 2. http://english.people.com.cn/200303/02/print20030302_112533.html.

Perry, Susan, and Celeste Schenck. 2001. *Eye to Eye: Women Practising Development Across Cultures*. London: Zed Books.

Peterson, Esther. 1983. "The Kennedy Commission." In *Women in Washington: Advocates for Public Policy*, edited by Irene Tinker. Beverly Hills: Sage.

Peterson, V. Spike. 2002. "Rewriting (Global) Political Economy as Reproductive, Productive and Virtual (Foucauldian) Economies." *International Feminist Journal of Politics* 4 (1): 1–30.

Peterson, V. Spike, and Anne Sisson Runyon. 1999. *Global Gender Issues*. Boulder: Westview Press.

Petprasert, Narong. 1999. *Community Enterprise: A Possible Route*. Bangkok: Thailand Research Fund.

Pharmacology of Vinblastine, Vincristine, Vindesine and Vinorelbine http://biotech.icmb.utexas .edu/botany/vvv.html. Accessed 8 December 2004.

Phillips, Anne. 2002. "Multiculturalism, Universalism, and the Claims of Democracy." In *Gender Justice, Development and Rights*, edited by Maxine Molyneux and Shahra Razavi, 115–38. Oxford: Oxford University Press.

———, ed. 1998. *Feminism and Politics*. Oxford: Oxford University Press.

Pietila, Hilkka. 2002. *Engendering the Global Agenda: The Story of Women and the United Nations*. Geneva: UN Non-Governmental Liaison Service.

Pintoptaeng, Praphat. 1998. *Street Politics: 99 Days of Forum of the Poor and History of the Protest Rallies in Thai Society*. Bangkok: Krirk University. In Thai.

Pinzás, Alicia 2001. *Jerarquías de género en el Mundo Rural*. Lima: Centro de la Mujer Peruana Flora Tristán.

Piotrow, Phyllis Tilson, D. Lawrence Kincaid, Jose G. Ramon, and Ward Rinehart. 1997. *Health Communication: Lessons from Family Planning and Reproductive Health*. Westport, Conn.: Praeger.

Pongsapich, Amara, and Naruemol Bunjongjit. 2003. *Expansion of Employment Opportunities for Women in Thailand: Promotion of Working Women's Economic and Social Empowerment in Thailand*. A report submitted to the International Labour Office, Bangkok.

Pongsapich, Amara, and Nitaya Kataleeradabhan. 1997. *Thailand Nonprofit Sector and Social Development*. Bangkok: Chulalongkorn University Social Research Institute.

Pongsapich, Amara, Rakawin Leechanawanichphan, and Naruemol Bunjoingjit. 2002. "Social Protection in Thailand." In *Social Protection in Southeast and East Asia*, edited by Erfried Adam, Michael von Hauff, and Marei John, 313–62. Singapore: Friedrich Ebert Stiftung.

Portocarrero, Gonzalo, and Patricia Oliart. 1989. *El Perú desde la Escuela*. Lima: Instituto de Apoyo Agrario.

Power, Margaret. 2002. *Right Wing Women in Chile: Feminine Power and the Struggle Against Allende, 1964–1973*. University Park: Pennsylvania State University Press.

PRATEC (Proyecto Andino de Tecnologías Campesinas). 2001. *Comunidad y Biodiversidad. El Ayllu y su organicidad en la crianza de la diversidad de la chacra*. Lima: PRATEC.

Presser, Harriet B. 1997. "Demography, Feminism and the Science-Policy Nexus." *Population and Development Review* 23 (2) (June): 295–331.

Prosterman, Roy, Brian Schwarzwalder, and Ye Jianping. 2000. "Implementation of 30-Year Land Use Rights for Farmers Under China's 1998 Land Management Law: An Analysis and Recommendations Based on a 17 Province Survey." Seattle: RDI Reports on Foreign Aid and Development no. 105, Rural Development Institute.

Prügl, Elizabeth. 1999. *The Global Construction of Gender: Home-Based Work in the Political Economy of the 20th Century*. New York: Columbia University Press.

Prügl, Elisabeth, and Mary K. Meyer. 1999. "Gender Politics in Global Governance." In *Gender Politics in Global Governance*, edited by Mary K. Meyer and Elisabeth Prügl, 3–18. Lanham, Md.: Rowman and Littlefield.

Prügl, Elizabeth, and Irene Tinker. 1997. "Microentrepreneurs and Homeworkers: Convergent Categories." *World Development* 25 (9): 1471–82.

Przeworski, Adam. 1998. "Culture and Democracy." In *World Culture Report*, 127–46. Paris: UNESCO.

Quisumbing, Agnes, Lawrence Haddad, and Christine Peña. 1995. *Gender and Poverty: New Evidence from Ten Developing Countries*. Washington, D.C.: International Food Policy Research Institute, Food Consumption and Nutrition Division, Discussion Paper no. 9.

Radcliffe, Sarah. 1998. "Indigenous Women and the Nation-State in the Andes." Paper presented in a seminar on "Gender, Rights and Justice in Latin America." Institute of Latin American Studies, University of London.

Rai, Shirin M, ed. 2003. *Mainstreaming Gender, Democratizing the State? Institutional Mechanisms for the Advancement of Women*. Manchester: Manchester University Press.

———. 1997. "Gender and Representation: Women MPs in the Indian Parliament, 1991–96." In *Getting Institutions Right for Women in Development*, edited by Anne Marie Goetz, 104–20. London: Zed Books.

———. 1995. "The Experience of Women in Institutions: Leadership, Power and Representation." Special issue, *IDS Bulletin* 26 (3): 110–16.

Rakodi, Carole. 1999. "A Capital Assets Framework for Analysing Household Livelihood Strategies: Implications for Policy." *Development Policy Review* 17: 315–42.

Randall, Vicky. 1998. "Gender and Power: Women Engage the State." In *Gender, Politics and the State*, edited by Vicky Randall and Georgina Waylen, 185–205. London: Routledge.

Rao, Aruna, and David Kelleher. 1997. "Engendering Organizational Change: The BRAC

Case." In *Getting Institutions Right for Women in Development*, edited by Anne Marie Goetz, 123–39. London: Zed Books.

Rao, Aruna, Rieky Stuart, and David Kelleher, eds. 1999. *Gender at Work: Organizational Change for Equality*. Hartford, Conn.: Kumarian Press.

Razavi, Shahra, ed. 2003. *Agrarian Change, Gender, and Land Rights*. Oxford: Blackwell.

———. 2002. Introduction to *Shifting Burdens: Gender and Agrarian Change under Neoliberalism*, edited by Shahra Razavi, 1–34. Bloomfield, Conn.: Kumarian Press.

———. 1999. "Gendered Poverty and Well-Being: Introduction." *Development and Change* 30 (3): 409–33.

———. 1998. "Becoming Multilingual: The Challenge of Feminist Policy Advocacy." In *Missionaries and Mandarins: Feminist Engagement with Development Institutions*, edited by Carol Miller and Shahra Razavi, 20–41. London: Intermediate Technology Publications.

———. 1997. "Fitting Gender into Development Institutions." *World Development* 25 (7): 1111–25.

Rees, Teresa. 1998. *Mainstreaming Equality in the European Union: Education, Training and Labour Market Policies*. New York: Routledge.

Riaño, P., ed. 1994. *Women in Grassroots Communication: Furthering Social Change*. Thousand Oaks, Calif.: Sage.

Rice, Ronald E., and Charles K. Atkin. 1989. *Public Communication Campaigns*. Newbury Park, Calif.: Sage.

Richardson, D., and L. Paisley, eds. 1998. *The First Mile of Connectivity: Advancing Telecommunications for Rural Development Through a Participatory Communication Approach*. Rome: UN FAO.

Richardson, James L. 2001. *Contending Liberalisms in World Politics: Ideology and Power*. Boulder: Lynne Rienner.

Richardson, Pat, and Karen Langdon. 2000. "Microenterprise and Microfinance: New Kids on the Block." In *New Roles and Relevance: Development NGOs and the Challenge of Change*, edited by David Lewis and Tina Wallace, 177–86. Bloomfield, Conn.: Kumarian Press.

Roberts, Carole, and Mona Masri. 1999. *Women Connect! Technology Workshop Resource Guide*. Los Angeles: Pacific Institute for Women's Health.

Roberts, Penelope. 1989. "The Sexual Politics of Labour in Western Nigeria and Hausa Niger." In *Serving Two Masters: Third World Women in Development*, edited by Kate Young, 27–47. New Delhi: Allied Publishers.

Roces, Mina. 2000. "Negotiating Modernities: Filipino Women 1900–2000." In *Women in Asia: Tradition, Modernity and Globalisation*, edited by Louise Edwards and Mina Roces, 112–38. Ann Arbor: University of Michigan Press.

Rocheleau, Dianne. 1988. "Women, Trees and Tenure: Implications for Agroforestry." In *Whose Trees: Proprietary Dimensions of Forestry*, edited by L. Fortmann and J. W. Bruce, 254–72. Boulder: Westview Press.

Rocheleau, Dianne, and David Edmunds. 1997. "Women, Men and Trees: Gender, Power and Property in Forest and Agrarian Landscapes." *World Development* 25 (8): 1351–71.

Rocheleau, Dianne, Barbara Thomas-Slayter, and Ester Wangari. 1996. "Gender and Development: A Feminist Political Ecology Perspective." In *Feminist Political Ecology: Global Issues and Local Experiences*, edited by Dianne Rocheleau, Barbara Thomas-Slayter, and Ester Wangari, 3–23. London: Routledge.

Rogers, E. M., and D. Storey. 1987. "Communication Campaigns." In *Handbook of Communication Science*, edited by C. Berger and S. Chaffee, 817–46. Newbury Park, Calif.: Sage.

Rogow, Debbie. 2000. "Alone You Are Nobody, Together We Float: The Manuela Ramos Movement." Introduction and afterword by Judith Bruce. *Quality/Calidad/Qualite*, no. 10. New York: Population Council.

Robinson, Fiona. 1999. *Globalizing Care: Ethics, Feminist Theory, and International Relations.* Boulder: Westview Press.

Rodda, Annabel. 1991. *Women and the Environment.* Women and World Development Series. London: Zed Books.

Roosseno, Toeti Heratt. 2000. "Foreword." In *Indonesian Women: The Journey Continues*, edited by Oey-Gardiner, Mayling, and Carla Bianpoen, vii–xi. Canberra: Australian National University.

Rose, Kalima. 1992. *Where Women Are Leaders: The SEWA Movement in India.* London: Zed.

Rostworowski, María. 1988. *Estructuras Andinas de Poder. Ideología Religiosa y Política.* Lima: Instituto de Estudios Peruanos.

Rowan-Campbell, Dorienne. 2004. "Coordinating Commonwealth Countries for WID." In *Developing Power: How Women Transformed International Development*, edited by Arvonne Fraser and Irene Tinker, 237–48. New York: Feminist Press.

Rowbotham, Sheila, and Swasti Mittner. 1994. *Dignity and Daily Bread: New Forms of Organizing among Poor Women in the Third World and the First.* London: Routledge.

Rowe, John. 1976. "El Movimiento Nacional Inca del siglo XVIII." In *Tupac Amaru II-1780. Sociedad Colonial y Sublevaciones Populares*, edited by Alberto Flores Galindo, 11–66. Lima: Retablo de Papel Ediciones.

Rowlands, Jo. 1996. "Empowerment Examined." In *Development and Social Diversity*, 86–92. Oxford: Oxfam.

Rozelle, Scott, Xiao-yuan Dong, Linxiu Zhang, and Andrew Mason. 2002. "Gender Wage Gaps in Post-Reform Rural China." *Pacific Economic Review* 7 (1): 157–79.

Rozelle, Scott, and Guo Li. 1998. "Village Leaders and Land Rights Formation in China." *American Economic Review*, May, 433–38.

Rozelle, Scott, Guo Li, and Loren Brandt. 1998. "Land Rights, Farmer Investment Incentives, and Agricultural Production in China." Conference draft, Ford Foundation and World Bank Conference on Land Tenure, Land Markets, and Productivity in Rural China, Beijing.

Rozelle, Scott, and Albert Park. 1998. "Reforming State-Market Relations in Rural China." *Economics of Transition* 6 (2): 461–80.

Ruggie, John Gerard. 1993. "Multilateralism: The Anatomy of an Institution." In *Multilateralism Matters: The Theory and Praxis of an Institutional Form*, edited by J. G. Ruggie, 3–47. New York: Columbia University Press.

Ruiz Bravo, Patricia, Eloy Neyra, Nora Cárdenas, and Tesania Velásquez. 1998. *Prácticas y Representaciones de Género.* Informe Final de Investigación. Manuscrito. Lima: Proyecto REPROSALUD-Movimiento Manuela Ramos.

Safa, Helen. 1995. *The Myth of the Male Breadwinner: Women and Industrialisation in the Caribbean.* Boulder: Westview Press.

Safa, Helen, and Peggy Antrobus. 1992. "Women and the Economic Crisis in the Caribbean." In *Unequal Burden: Economic Crises, Persistent Poverty and Women's Works*, edited by Lourdes Benería and Shelley Feldman, 49–82. Boulder: Westview Press.

Safilios-Rothschild, Constantina. 1990. "Socio-Economic Determinants of the Outcomes of Women's Income-Generation in Developing Countries." In *Women, Employment and the Family in the International Division of Labour*, edited by Sharon Stichter and Jane Parpart, 221–28. Basingtoke: Macmillan.

Sandercock, Leonie. 1998. *Towards Cosmopolis*. New York: Wiley.

Sapiro, Virginia. 1981. "When Are Interests Interesting? The Problem of Political Representation of Women." *American Political Science Review* 75 (3): 701-16.

Sarin, Madhu. 1991. "Improved Stoves, Women and Domestic Energy." *Environment and Urbanization* 3 (2, October): 51-56.

Sassen, Saskia. 2001. Background paper to chapter 5 of *Cities in a Globalizing World: Global Report on Human Settlements, 2001*. Nairobi: UN-HABITAT.

Schalkwyk, Johanna. 1998. *Building Capacity for Gender Mainstreaming: UNDP's Experience*. http://www.undp.org/gender/capacity/mid-term_review.html.

Schirmer, Jennifer. 1993. "The Seeking of Truth and the Gendering of Consciousness: The CoMadres of El Salvador and the CONAVIGUA Widows of Guatemala." In *Viva: Women and Popular Protest in Latin America*, edited by Sarah Radcliffe and Sallie Westwood, 30-64. London: Routledge.

Schroeder, R. A. 1997. " 'Re-claiming' Land in the Gambia: Gendered Property Rights and Environmental Intervention." *Annals of the Association of American Geographers* 87 (3): 487-508.

Schuler, Margaret. 1986. *Empowerment and the Law: Strategies of Third World Women*. Washington, D.C.: OEF International.

Schuler, S. R., S. M. Hashimi, and S. H. Badal. 1999. "Men's Violence Against Women in Rural Bangladesh: Undermined or Exacerbated by Microcredit Programmes?" *Development in Practice* 8 (2): 112-26.

Schwarzwalder, Brian. 2001. "China's Farmers Need Long-Term Land Tenure Security, Not Land Readjustment." *Transitions Newsletter*, World Bank. http://www.worldbank.org/html/prddr/trans/augsepoctoo/pages21-23.htm.

Scott, Alison MacEwen. 1994. *Divisions and Solidarities: Gender, Class and Employment in Latin America*. London: Routledge.

Scott, Catherine V. 1995. *Gender and Development: Rethinking Modernization and Dependency Theory*. Boulder: Lynne Rienner.

Scott, Gloria. 2004. "Breaking New Ground at the UN and in the World Bank." In *Developing Power: How Women Transformed International Development*, edited by Arvonne Fraser and Irene Tinker, 14-25. New York: Feminist Press.

Scott, James C. 1990. *Domination and the Arts of Resistance: Hidden Transcripts*. New Haven: Yale University Press.

———. 1988. *Weapons of the Weak: Everyday Forms of Peasant Resistance*. New Haven: Yale University Press.

———. 1986. *The Moral Economy of the Peasants*. New Haven: Yale University Press.

Seager, Joni. 2000. *The State of Women in the World Atlas*, new ed. London: Penguin Reference.

Sebstad, Jennifer, and Monique Cohen. 2001. *Microfinance Risk Management and Poverty*. Washington, D.C.: World Bank.

Secretaría de Gobernación. 1996. *Alianza par la Igualdad: Programa Nacional de la Mujer, 1995-2000*. Mexico City: Secretaría de Gobernación.

Selby, Henry, Arthur Murphy, and Stephen Lorenzen. 1990. *The Mexican Urban Household: Organising for Self-Defense*. Austin: University of Texas Press.

Sen, Amartya K. 1999. *Development as Freedom*. New York: Knopf.

———. 1992. *Inequality Reexamined*. Cambridge, Mass.: Harvard University Press.

———. 1990. "Gender and Cooperative Conflicts." In *Persistent Inequalities: Women and World Development*, edited by Irene Tinker, 123-49. New York: Oxford University Press.

Sen, Amartya K. 1987a. *Gender and Cooperative Conflicts*. Helsinki: World Institute for Development Economics Research, Working Paper no. 18.

———. 1987b. *Hunger and Entitlements*. Amsterdam: North Holland Press.

———. 1985. *Commodities and Capabilities*. Helsinki: United Nations University, World Institute for Development Economics Research.

———. 1981. *Poverty and Famines*. Oxford: Clarendon Press.

Sen, Gita, and Caren Grown. 1987. *Development Crises and Alternative Visions: Third World Women's Perspectives*. New Delhi: DAWN (Development Alternatives for Women for a New Era).

Servon, L. J. 1999. *Bootstrap Capital: Microenterprises and the American Poor*. Washington, D.C.: Brookings Institution Press.

Shanthi, K. 1994. "Growing Incidence of Female Household Headship: Causes and Cure." *Social Action* (New Delhi) 44: 17-33.

Shapiro, Ian, and Caisano Hacker Cordon. 1999. "Outer Edges and Inner Edges." In *Democracy's Edges*, edited by I. Shapiro and C. Cordon, 1-16. Cambridge: Cambridge University Press.

Sharma, Kumud. 2003. "The Discourse Between Studies, Institutions, and Critical Pedagogy: Centre for Women's Development Studies." In *Narratives from the Women's Studies Family: Recreating Knowledge*, edited by Devaki Jain and Pam Rajput, 300-13. New Delhi: Sage.

Shiva, Vandana. 2001. "Golden Rise and Neem: Biopatents and the Appropriation of Women's Environmental Knowledge." Special issue, *Women's Studies Quarterly* 29 (172): 12-23.

Sicular, Terry. 1991. "China's Agricultural Policy During the Reform Period." In *China's Economic Dilemmas in the 1990s: The Problems of Reforms, Modernization, and Interdependence*, ed. Joint Economic Committee, 340-64. Washington, D.C.: U.S. Government Printing Office.

Silverblatt, Irene. 1990. *Luna, Sol y Brujas. Género y Clases en los Andes Coloniales*. Cuzco: Centro de Estudios Regionales Andinos Bartolomé de las Casas.

Simba, Margaret, and Graham Thom. 2000. " 'Implementation by Proxy': The Next Step in Power Relationships Between Northern and Southern NGOs." In *New Roles and Relevance: Development NGOs and the Challenge of Change*, edited by David Lewis and Tina Wallace, 213-22. Bloomfield, Conn.: Kumarian Press.

Simbolon, I. J. 1998. "Peasant Women and Access to Land: Customary Law, State Law, and Gender-Based Ideology, The Case of Toba-Batak (North Sumatra)." Unpublished Ph.D. dissertation: Landbau Universiteit Wageningen.

Skjelsbaek, Inger, and Dan Smith, eds. 2001. *Gender, Peace and Conflict*. Oslo: International Peace Research Institute.

Smith, K. R. 2003. "Indoor Air Pollution and Acute Respiratory Infections." *Indian Pediatrics* 40 (9): 815-19.

Smith, K. R., and Ezzati Majid. 2005. "How Environmental Health Risks Change with Development: The Environmental Risk and Epidemiologic Transitions Revisited." *Annual Review of Energy and Resources* 30 (in press).

Smith, K. R., J. Ramakrishnan, and P. Menon. 1981. "Air Pollution from the Combustion of Traditional Fuels: A Brief Summary." Honolulu: East-West Center Working Paper WP-81-5.

Smith, K. R., and S. Mehta. 2003. "The Burden of Disease from Indoor Air Pollution in Developing Countries: Comparison of Estimates." *International Journal of Hygiene and Environmental Health* 206 (4-5): 279-89.

Smith, K. R., S. Mehta, and M. Maeusezahl-Feuz. 2004. "Indoor Smoke from Household

Solid Fuels." In *Comparative Quantification of Health Risks: Global and Regional Burden of Disease due to Selected Major Risk Factors*, edited by M. Ezzati, A. D. Rodgers, A. D. Lopez, and C. J. L. Murray, 1437–95. Geneva: World Health Organization.

Smith, Peter H., Jennifer L. Troutner, and Christine Hünefeldt, eds. 2004. *Promises of Empowerment: Women in Asia and Latin America*. Lanham, Md.: Rowman and Littlefield.

SNV (Servicio Holandés de Cooperación al Desarrollo). 1993. *Rumbo a espacio para Mujeres. Mujeres y la Política de Desarrollo del SNV (1993–1998)*. The Hague: SNV.

———. 1998. *Nota Estratégica sobre Igualdad de Género*. The Hague: Gender and Development Training Centre.

Snyder, Leslie B. 2001. "How Effective Are Mediated Health Campaigns?" In *Public Communication Campaigns*, 3rd ed., edited by Ronald E. Rice and Charles K. Atkin, 181–90. Thousand Oaks, Calif.: Sage.

Snyder, Margaret. 2004. "Walking My Own Road: Economic Commission of Africa and UNIFEM." In *Developing Power: How Women Transformed International Development*, edited by Arvonne Fraser and Irene Tinker, 37–49. New York: Feminist Press.

———. 1995. *Transforming Development: Women, Poverty, and Politics*. London: Intermediate Technology Publications.

Snyder, Margaret C., and Mary Tadesse. 1995. *African Women and Development*. London: Zed Books.

Social Agenda Working Group. 2001. *Restructuring for Poverty Eradication Program*. Data File, Social Agenda Forum 1, April 27.

Sorensen, Georg. 1998. *Democracy and Democratization: Processes and Prospects in a Changing World*. Boulder: Westview Press.

Sowerwine, Jennifer. 1999. "New Land Rights and Women's Access to Medicinal Plants in Northern Vietnam." In *Women's Rights to House and Land*, edited by Irene Tinker and Gale Summerfield, 131–42. Boulder: Lynne Rienner.

Spalding, Karen. 1974. *De Indio a Cmpesino*. Lima: Instituto de Estudios Peruanos.

Sperling, Louise. 1996. "Results, Methods and Institutional Issues in Participatory Selection: The Case of Beans in Rwanda." In *Participatory Plant Breeding*. Proceedings of a Workshop on Participatory Plant Breeding 26–29 July 1995. Wageningen, The Netherlands, 44–56. Rome: IPGRI.

State Statistical Bureau. 1986. *Statistical Yearbook*. Beijing: Statistical Publishing House.

Staudt, Kathleen. 1998. *Politics, Policy and Gender: Women Gaining Ground*. West Hartford, Conn.: Kumarian Press.

———. 1997. "Gender Politics in Bureaucracy: Theoretical Issues in Comparative Perspective." In *Women, International Development, and Politics: The Bureaucratic Mire*, edited by Kathleen Staudt, 3–36. Philadelphia: Temple University Press.

———. 1985. *Women, Foreign Assistance and Advocacy Administration*. New York: Praeger.

Staudt, Kathleen, and Jane S. Jaquette, eds. 1982. *Women in Developing Countries: A Policy Focus*. Binghamton: Haworth.

Staudt, Kathleen, Shirin M. Rai, and Jane Parpart. 2001. "Protesting World Trade Rules: Can We Talk About Empowerment?" *Signs* 26 (4, summer): 1251–57.

Stavenhagen, Rodolfo. 1996. "Los Derechos Indígenas: algunos problemas conceptuales." In *Construir la Democracia. Derechos Humanos, Ciudadanía y Sociedad en América Latina*, edited by Elizabeth Jelin and Eric Hershberg, 151–69. Caracas: Nueva Sociedad.

Stavig, Ward. 1996. "Amor y Violencia Sexual. Valores Indígenas en la sociedad colonial." Lima: University of South Florida-IEP. Colección Mínima 34.

Stienstra, Deborah. 2000. "Dancing Resistance from Rio to Beijing: Transnational Women's

Organizing and United Nations Conferences." In *Gender and Global Restructuring: Sitings, Sites and Resistances*, edited by Marianne H. Marchand and Anne Sisson Runyan, 209–24. London: Routledge.

———. 1994. *Women's Movements and International Organizations*. New York: St. Martin's Press.

Stiglitz, Joseph. 2002. *Globalization and Its Discontents*. New York: Norton.

Stone, Linda. 1997. *Kinship and Gender: An Introduction*. Boulder: Westview Press.

Summerfield, Gale, ed. 2001. "Risks and Rights in the 21st Century." Special issue, *International Journal of Politics, Culture and Society* 15 (1).

Summerfield, Gale, and Nahid Aslanbeigui. 1992. "Feminization of Poverty in China?" *Development* 4: 57–61.

Swers, Michele. 2001. "Research on Women in Legislatures: What Have We Learned, Where Are We Going?" *Women in Politics* 23 (1 and 2): 167–85.

Sylvester, Christine. 2001. *Gendering World Politics; Issues and Approaches in the Post-Cold War Era*. New York: Columbia University Press.

———. 1998. "Homeless in International Relations? Women's Place in Canonical Texts and Feminists Reimaginings." In *Feminism and Politics*, edited by Anne Phillips, 44–66. Oxford: Oxford University Press.

Tasies Castro, Esperanza. 1996. "Mujer, Pobreza y Conflicto Social." *Ciencias Sociales* 71 (San Jose, Costa Rica): 32–39.

Taylor, Charles. 2001. *El Multiculturalismo y la "política del reconocimiento,"* 2nd ed. Mexico City: Fondo de Cultura Económica.

Thomas-Slayter, Barbara P. 2003. *Southern Exposure: International Development and the Global South in the Twenty-First Century*. Westport, Conn.: Kumarian Press.

Tiano, Susan. 2001. "From Victims to Agents: A New Generation of Literature on Women in Latin America." *Latin American Research Review* 36 (3): 183–203.

Tibaijuka, Anna Kajumulo. 2001. Keynote address to the workshop "Building Capacities for Mainstreaming Gender in Development Strategies." Organized by UNCTAD in preparation for the UN Conference on the Least Developed Countries (LDC III). Cape Town, South Africa, 21–23 March.

Tickner, J. Ann. 1992. *Gender in International Relations*. New York: Columbia University Press.

Tilly, Charles. 1998. *Durable Inequality*. Berkeley: University of California Press.

Tinker, Irene. *Tinker's works are listed in a separate section at the end of the bibliography.*

Tinsman, Heidi. 2002. *Partners in Conflict: The Politics of Gender, Sexuality and Labor in the Chilean Agrarian Reform, 1950–1973*. Durham: Duke University Press.

Tisdell, Clem, Kartik Roy, and Ananda Ghose. 2001. "A Critical Note on UNDPs Gender Inequality Indexes." *Journal of Contemporary Asia* 31 (3): 385–99.

Todd, Helen. 1996. *Women at the Center: Grameen Bank Borrowers After One Decade*. Boulder: Westview.

Townsend, Janet Gabriel. 1999. "Empowerment Matters: Understanding Power." In *Women and Power: Fighting Patriarchies and Poverty*, edited by Janet Gabriel Townsend, Emma Zapata, Jo Rowlands, Pilar Alberti, and Marta Mercado, 19–46. London: Zed Books.

Tripp, Aili. 2000a. "Rethinking 'Difference': Comparative Perspectives from Africa." *Signs* 25 (3): 649–75.

———. 2000b. *Women and Politics in Uganda*. Madison: University of Wisconsin Press.

———. 1994. "Gender, Political Participation and the Transformation of Associational Life in Uganda and Tanzania." *African Studies Review* 37 (1): 107–32.

True, Jacqui. 2003a. *Gender, Globalization, and Postsocialism: The Czech Republic after Communism*. New York: Columbia University Press.

———. 2003b. "Mainstreaming Gender in Global Public Policy." *International Feminist Journal of Politics* 5 (November): 368–96.

True, Jacqui, and Michael Mintrom. 2001. "Transnational Networks and Policy Diffusion: The Case of Gender Mainstreaming." *International Studies Quarterly* 45 (March): 27–57.

Tsikata, Y. M. 2001. *Owning Economic Policy Reforms: A Comparative Study of Ghana and Tanzania*. Helsinki: United Nations University/WIDER.

Uçarer, Emek M. 1999. "Trafficking in Women: Alternate Migration or Modern Slave Trade?" In *Gender Politics in Global Governance*, edited by M. K. Meyer and E. Prügl, 230–44. Lanham, Md.: Rowman and Littlefield.

United Nations. 2002. *Gender Mainstreaming: An Overview*. New York: United Nations Office of the Special Adviser on Gender Issues and Advancement of Women.

———. 2001. Transcript of press conference by Secretary-General Kofi Annan at U.N. Headquarters, 27 June 2001. Press release SG/SM/7865.

———. 2000. *The World's Women 2000: Trends and Statistics*. New York: United Nations.

———. 1995. Platform of Action [Report of the Fourth UN Conference on Women, Beijing, 1995.] A full copy of the Platform can be accessed at http://www.un.org.womenwatch/daw/beijing/platform. Accessed 12 July 2005.

———. 1994. *Report of the International Conference on Population and Development. Cairo, 5–13 September 1994*. New York, A/CONF.171/13/Rev.1. http://www.un.org/News/Press/docs/2001/sqsm7865.dco.htm.

UNCHS. 2000. *Policy Paper on Women and Urban Governance*. Nairobi, Kenya: UNCHS.

UNDAW. 2000. *Beijing +5, Women 2000: Gender Equality, Development and Peace for the 21st Century*. New York: UN Division for the Advancement of Women.

———. 1991. "Women and Households in a Changing World." In *Women, Households and Change*, edited by Eleanora Barbieri Masini and Susan Stratigos, 30–52. Tokyo: United Nations University Press.

UN Department of Public Information. 1996. *Platform for Action and the Beijing Declaration*. New York: United Nations.

UNDP (United Nations Development Program). 2003. *Transforming the Mainstream: Gender in UNDP*. New York: UNDP.

———. 2000. *Assessment of Gender Mainstreaming in Sub-Saharan Africa: A Review of UNDP Supported Activities*. New York: UNDP.

———. 2002a. *Gender Equality: Practice Note*. New York: UNDP.

———. 2002b. *Human Development Report 2002: Deepening Democracy*. New York: Oxford University Press.

———. 2001. *Human Development Report 2001*. New York: Oxford University Press.

———. 2000a. *Human Development Report 2000*. New York: Oxford University Press.

———. 2000b. *Gender in Development: Policies*. http://www.undp.org/gender/policies/. Accessed 30 January 2001.

———. 2000c. *Guidance Note on Gender Mainstreaming*. http://www.undp.org/gender/policies/guidance.html. Accessed 12 June 2001.

———. 2000d. *Overcoming Human Poverty*. UNDP Poverty Report 2000. New York: UNDP.

———. 1998. *Background Paper of the Policy for Gender Balance in Management Phase II (1998–2001)*. www.undp.org/gender/gb_bkground.html. Accessed 12 June 2001.

———. 1997. *Human Development Report 1997*. New York: Oxford University Press.

UNDP. 1996. *Human Development Report 1996*. New York: Oxford University Press.

———. 1995. *Human Development Report 1995*. New York: Oxford University Press.

———. 1994. *Human Development Report 1994*. Delhi: Oxford University Press.

———. 1990. *Human Development Report 1990*. New York: Oxford University Press.

———. n.d. *Human Development Report: Analytical Tools for Human Development*. www.undp.org/hdro/anatools.htm. Accessed 18 June 2001.

United Nations Development Program (UNDP) and the United Nations Population Fund (UNPF) Executive Board. 2004. *Item 20 of the Provisional Agenda: Gender in UNDP: Management Response to "Transforming the Mainstream: Gender in UNDP."* DP/2004/31. New York: United Nations.

———. 2001. *Item 9 of the Provisional Agenda: Annual Report of the Administrator for 2000: Results-Oriented Annual Report (ROAR) for 2000*. DP/2001/14/Add.1. New York: United Nations.

UNEP (United Nations Environment Program). 2004. "Women and The Environment." Nairobi: UNEP.

UNESCO. 1997. *Male Roles and Masculinities in the Perspective of a Culture of Peace*. Report, Export Group Meeting, Oslo, 24–28 September. Paris: UNESCO.

UN-HABITAT. 2001a. *Gendered Implementation of the Habitat Agenda*. Nairobi: United Nations Human Settlements Programme (HABITAT).

———. 2001b. *The State of the World Cities 2001*. Nairobi: United Nations Human Settlements Programme (HABITAT).

———. 2001c. *Draft Policy Position Paper on Women and Secure Tenure*. Nairobi: United Nations Human Settlements Programme (HABITAT).

———. 2001d. *Declaration on Cities and Other Human Settlements in the New Millennium*. Nairobi: United Nations Human Settlements Programme (HABITAT).

———. 2000. *Women and Gender in Habitat since 1995: Implementing the Beijing Platform for Action at Local Level*. Nairobi: United Nations Human Settlements Programme (HABITAT).

———. 1999. *Women's Rights to Land, Housing and Property in Post-Conflict Situations and During Reconstruction: A Global Overview*. Land Management Series no. 9, Nairobi: United Nations Human Settlements Programme (HABITAT).

———. 1998. *The Istanbul Declaration and the Habitat Agenda*. Nairobi: United Nations Human Settlements Programme (HABITAT).

UNHCHR (United Nations High Commission on Human Rights). 2003. *Women's Equal Ownership, Access to and Control over Land and the Equal Rights to Own Property and to Adequate Housing*. Resolution 2003/22. United Nations High Commission on Human Rights, E/CN.4/RES/2003/422.

———. 2002. *Women's Equal Ownership, Access to and Control over Land and the Equal Rights to Own Property and to Adequate Housing*. Resolution 2002/49. United Nations High Commission on Human Rights, E/CN.4/RES/2002/49.

———. 2001. *Women's Equal Ownership of, Access to and Control over Land and the Equal Rights to Own Property and to Adequate Housing*. Resolution 2001/34. United Nations High Commission on Human Rights, E/CN.4/RES/2001/34.

———. 2000. *Women's Equal Ownership of, Access to and Control over Land and the Equal Rights to own Property and to Adequate Housing*. Resolution 2000/13. United Nations High Commission on Human Rights, E/CN.4/RES/2000/13.

———. 1999. *Women and the Right to Development*. Resolution 1999/15. United Nations High Commission on Human Rights, Sub-Commission on the Promotion and Protection of Human Rights, E/CN.4/Sub.2/RES/1999/15.

———. 1998. *Women and the Right to Land, Housing and Property and Adequate Housing*. Resolution 1998/15, United Nations High Commission on Human Rights, Sub-Commission on Prevention of Discrimination and Protection of Human Rights, E/CN.4/Sub.2/RES/1998/15.

———. 1997. *Women and the Right to Adequate Housing and to Land, Housing and Property*. Resolution 1997/19. United Nations High Commission on Human Rights, Sub-Commission on Prevention of Discrimination and Protection of Minorities, E/CN.4/Sub.2/RES/1997/19 (now the Sub-Commission on the Promotion and Protection of Human Rights).

UNICEF. 1997. *Role of Men in the Lives of Children: A Study of How Improving Knowledge About Men in Families Helps Strengthen Programming for Children and Women*. New York: UNICEF.

UNIFEM. 2000. *Progress of the World's Women 2000*. New York: UNIFEM.

———. 1996. *UNIFEM in Beijing and Beyond*. New York: UNIFEM.

United States Agency for International Development (USAID). 2000. *Women in Development: The USAID Commitment*. Washington, D.C.: Women in Development Office.

USAID. 1998. *Leland Initiative, Making the Internet Count: Effective Use of the Internet in Seven Steps*. http:// www.usaid.gov/regions/afr/leland.

U.S. General Accounting Office. 1993. *Foreign Assistance: U.S Has Made Slow Progress in Involving Women in Development*. Report to Congressional Requesters, GAO/NSIAD-94-16. Washington, D.C.: USGAO.

Valcárcel, Luis Enrique. C1927. *Tempestad en los Andes*. Lima: Populibros Peruanos.

Valderrama, Mariano. 2001. *Mito y Realidad de la Ayuda Externa. América Latina al 2002*. Lima: Ayuda en Acción, ActionAid, ALOP (Asociación Latinoamericana de Organizaciones de Promoción).

Valderrama, Mariano, and Federico Negrón. 2001. *El Financiamiento Externo de las ONG en el Perú*. Avances. Documento de Trabajo no. 1. Lima: CEPES.

Valderrama, Ricardo, and Carmen Escalante. 1997. "Ser Mujer: Warmi kay. La mujer en la Cultura Andina." In *Más allá del silencio. Las fronteras de género en los Andes*, edited by Denise Arnold, 153–69. La Paz: ILCA-CIASE.

Valdisavljevic, Aleksandra, and Elaine Zuckerman. 2003. *Structural Adjustment's Gendered Impacts: The Case of Serbia and Montenegro*. Washington, D.C.: Gender Action.

Van Horen, C., and A. Eberhard. 1995. "Energy, Environment and the Rural Poor in South Africa." *Development Southern Africa* 12 (2): 197–211.

Vargas Llosa, Mario. 1996. *La Utopía Arcaica. José María Arguedas y las Ficciones del Indigenismo*. Mexico City: Fondo de Cultura Económica.

Varley, Ann. 2001. "Gender, Families and Households." In *The Companion to Development Studies*, edited by Vandana Desai and Robert Potter, 329–34. London: Edward Arnold.

———. 1996. "Women-Headed Households: Some More Equal Than Others?" *World Development* 24 (3): 505–20.

VeneKlasen, Lisa. 2002. *The Politics of Gender Budget Work: Linking Research and Advocacy. Some Research Gaps in Gender Budget Work from an Advocacy Perspective*. International Center for Research on Women, Conference on "Engendering Macroeconomics, International Trade and Public Finance," 13 May.

Verdery, K. 1996. *What Was Socialism and What Comes Next?* Princeton: Princeton University Press.

Verghese, Jamila. 1997. *Her Gold and Her Body*, rev. ed. New Delhi: Vikas.

Viravong, Manivone. 1999. "Reforming Property Rights in Laos." In *Women's Rights to Land and House*, edited by Irene Tinker and Gale Summerfield, 153–62. Boulder: Lynne Rienner.

Vosko, Leah F. 2001. "Labour and Hegemony in a Different Register? *Decent Work* and the

Shifting Role of the ILO." Presented at the 42nd Annual Convention of the International Studies Association, Chicago, 22–24 February.

Walker, Cherryl. 2002. "Land Reform in Southern and Eastern Africa: Key Issues for Strengthening Women's Access to and Rights in Land." Report on a desktop study commissioned by the Food and Agricultural Organization (FAO) subregional office for Southern and Eastern Africa, Harare, Zimbabwe.

Wank, Christine U. 2003. "Constructing Gender: The Concept(s) of Gender Mainstreaming and the Case of the European Union." Presented at International Studies Association Annual Convention, 15 February–1 March, Portland, Ore.

Warren, Adria. 1999. "Chinese Women's Housing Rights: An International Legal Perspective." In *Women's Rights to Land and House*, edited by Irene Tinker and Gale Summerfield, 165–77. Boulder: Lynne Rienner.

Warren, Karen J., ed. 1997. *Ecofeminism: Women, Culture, Nature*. Bloomington: Indiana University Press.

Warren, Kay B., and Jean E. Jackson. 2002. Introduction to *Indigenous Movements, Self-Representation and the State in Latin America*, edited by Kay B. Warren and Jean E. Jackson, 1–46. Austin: University of Texas Press.

Wartenburg, Lucy. 1999. "Vulnerabilidad y Jefatura en los Hogares Urbanos Colombianos." In *Divergencias del Modelo Tradicional: Hogares de Jefatura Femenina en América Latina*, edited by Mercedes González de la Rocha, 77–96. Mexico City: Centro de Investigaciones y Estudios Superiores en Antropología Social/Plaza y Valdés Editores.

Waylen, Georgina. 1997. "Women's Movements, the State and Democratization in Chile: The Establishment of SERNAM." In *Getting Institutions Right for Women in Development*, edited by Anne Marie Goetz, 90–103. London: Zed Books.

———. 1996. *Gender in Third World Politics*. Buckingham, England: Open University Press.

Weekes-Vagliani, Winifred. 1992. "Structural Adjustment and Gender in the Côte d'Ivoire." In *Women and Adjustment Policies in the Third World*, edited by Haleh Afshar and Carolyne Dennis, 117–49. Houndmills, Basingstoke: Macmillan.

Weiss, Anita M., and S. Zulfiqar Gilani, eds. 2001. *Power and Civil Society in Pakistan*. New York: Oxford University Press.

West, Lois A. 1999. "The United Nations Women's Conferences and Feminist Politics." In *Gender Politics in Global Governance*, edited by Mary K. Meyer and Elisabeth Prügl, 177–93. Lanham, Md.: Rowman and Littlefield.

White, Sarah. 1996. "Depoliticizing Development: The Uses and Abuses of Participation." *Development Practice* 6 (1): 6–15.

Whitehead, Ann, and Matthew Lockwood. 1999. "Gendering Poverty: A Review of Six World Bank African Poverty Assessments." *Development and Change* 30 (3): 525–55.

Whitehead, Ann, and Dzodzi Tsikata. 2003. "Policy Discourses on Women's Land Rights in Sub-Saharan Africa: The Implications of the Re-turn to the Customary." *Journal of Agrarian Change* 3 (1 and 2): 67–112.

Whitworth, Sandra. 1994. *Feminism and International Relations: Towards a Political Economy of Gender in Interstate and Non-Governmental Institutions*. New York: St. Martin's Press.

Wichterich, Christa. 2001. "From Passion to Profession? Mehr Fragen als Antworten zu Akteurinnen, Interessen und Veränderungen politischer Handlungsbedingungen der neuen internationalen Frauenbewegung." *Zeitschrift für Frauenforschung und Geschlechterstudien* 19 (1 and 2): 128–37.

Wiegman, Robyn, ed. 2002. *Women's Studies on Its Own*. Durham: Duke University Press.

Williams, Chris, and Diana Lee-Smith. 2000. "Feminization of Poverty: Re-Thinking Poverty Reduction from a Gender Perspective." *Habitat Debate* 6: 4.

Willis, Katie. 1994. "Women's Work and Social Network Use in Oaxaca City, Mexico." Unpublished D. Phil. dissertation, Nuffield College, Oxford.

———. 1993. "Women's Work and Social Network Use in Oaxaca City, Mexico." *Bulletin of Latin American Research* 12 (1): 65–82.

Winslow, Anne, ed. 1995. *Women, Politics and the United Nations*. Westport, Conn.: Greenwood Press.

Witthaus, Gabi. 1999. *Edutainment Facilitator's Guide*. Houghton, South Africa: Soul City.

Wolf, Eric. 1966. "Pathways Toward a Global Anthropology." In *The Underdevelopment of Development: Essays in honor of André Gunder Frank*, edited by Sing Chew and Robert Denemark. London: Sage.

Women Watch. 2000. Fact Sheet no. 1, Prepared for Beijing +5. New York: Women Watch.

Women's Edge. 2000. "Notes from the Edge: China, the WTO, and Women." http://www.womensedge.org/notesfromtheedge/apri12000.htm.

Worby, Paula. 1998. "Organising for a Change: Guatemalan Refugee Women Re-Affirm their Right to Land." Presentation at "Peace for Homes, Homes for Peace, Inter-Regional Consultation on Women's Land and Property Rights in Situations of Conflict and Reconstruction," Kigali, Rwanda, 16–19 February. http://www.undp.org/unifem/resources/.

World Bank. 2004. *Implementing the Bank's Gender Mainstreaming Strategy: Second Annual Monitoring Report*, FY 03. http://www.worldbank.org/gender/overview/ssp/FY03Annual_Gender_Monitoring_Report_Jan04.pdf. Accessed 15 October 2004.

———. 2003a. *Gender and Development in the World Bank*. http://www.worldbank.org/gender/overview/aboutgnet.htm. Accessed 23 June 2003.

———. 2003b. Mainstreaming Gender. http://www.worldbank.org/gender/overview/mainstreaming.htm. Accessed 23 June 2003.

———. 2002a. *China Country Gender Report*. East Asia Environment and Social Development Unit.

———. 2002b. *Integrating Gender into the World Bank's Work: A Strategy for Action*. Washington, D.C.: World Bank. http://www.worldbank.org/gender/overview/ssp/home.htm.

———. 2002c. *Report of the Sixth Meeting of the World Bank External Gender Consultative Group*. 6–10 May. http://www.worldbank.org/gender/partnerships/EGCG%20Report_May6-9%202002.doc. Accessed 15 October 2004.

———. 2001a. *About Gender and Development in the World Bank*. http://www.worldbank.org/gender/info/aboutgnet.htm. Accessed 26 June 2001.

———. 2001b. *Engendering Development Through Gender Equality in Rights, Resources and Voice*. New York: Oxford University Press.

———. 2001c. *World Development Report 2000/2001: Attacking Poverty*. New York: Oxford University Press.

———. 2000. *Advancing Gender Equality: World Bank Action since Beijing*. Washington, D.C.: World Bank.

———. 1999a. *The Gender Dimension of Development: Operational Policy 4.20*. Based on *Enhancing Women's Participation in Economic Development: A World Bank Policy Paper* (1994). Washington, D.C.: World Bank. http://www.worldbank.org/gender/how/termr2.htm. Accessed 25 January 2001.

———. 1999b. *Report on the Fourth Annual Meeting of the External Gender Consultative Group*. 16 November. http://www.worldbank.org/gender/how/egcg4th.pdf. Accessed 26 June 2001.

World Bank. 1994. *Enhancing Women's Participation in Economic Development.* Washington, D.C.: World Bank.

———. 1992. *China: Strategies for Reducing Poverty in the 1990s.* Washington, D.C.: World Bank.

World Commission on Dams. 2000. *Dams and Development: A New Framework for Decision-Making.* London: Earthscan Publications.

World Commission on Environment and Development. 1987. *Our Common Future.* Oxford: Oxford University Press.

World Health Organization (WHO). 2004. *Scientific Research Advisory Committee on Severe Acute Respiratory Syndrome (SARS). Report of the first meeting, Geneva Switzerland, 20–21 October 2003.* Geneva: World Health Organization.

———. 2003a. Global Burden of Disease Estimates for 2002, http://www3.who.int/whosis/menu.cfm?path=whosis,burden,burden_estimates&language=english. Accessed April 22, 2004.

———. 2003b. "Suicide Rates." http://www.who.int/mental_health/prevention/suicide/suiciderates/en/ (accessed Oct. 25, 2004).

———. 2002. *World Health Report: Reducing Risks, Promoting Healthy Life.* Geneva: World Health Organization.

Wratten, Ellen. 1995. "Conceptualising Urban Poverty." *Environment and Urbanisation* 7 (1): 11–36.

Xinhua. 1999. "Chinese Rural Women Involved in Socioeconomic Development." 28 October.

Yang, Li, Denise Hare, and Xi Yen-sheng. 2004. "Women's Rights to Land Under China's Land Contract System." Paper presented at the International Workshop on "Women and Development in Post-Reform China." The Center for China's Economic Research, Beijing University, 21–22 June.

Yates, Rachel. 1997. "Literacy, Gender and Vulnerability: Donor Discourses and Local Realities." *IDS Bulletin* 28 (3): 112–21.

Young, Kate. 1992. "Household Resource Management." In *Gender and Development: A Practical Guide,* edited by Lise Østergaard, 135–64. London: Routledge.

Youssef, Nadia, and Mayra Buvinic. 1978. "Women-Headed Households." Washington, D.C.: AID/WID.

Zalewski, Marysia. 1993. "Feminist Standpoint Theory Meets International Relations Theory." *Fletcher Forum* 17: 2.

Zein-Elabdin, Eiman, and S. Charusheela, eds. 2004. *Post-Colonialism Meets Economics.* London: Routledge.

ZGTJNJ (Zhongguo Tongji Nianjian, China Statistical Yearbook). 1988, 1989, 1996, 2000. Beijing: China Statistical Publishing House.

Zhang, Heather Xiaoquan. 1999. "Understanding Changes in Women's Status in the Context of the Recent Rural Reform." In *Women of China: Economic and Social Transformation,* edited by Jackie West, Zhao Mingua, Chang Xiangqun, and Cheng Yuan, 45–66. United Kingdom: Anthony Rowe.

Zhang, Jane Youyun. 2000. Presentation at OECD/NCM ministerial-level conference: Gender Mainstreaming, Competitiveness and Growth. 23–24 November, Paris. http://www.norden.org/gender/taler/. Accessed 27 June 2001.

Zhang, Weiguo. 1998. "Rural Women and Reform in a North Chinese Village." In *Village, Inc.: Chinese Rural Society in the 1990s,* edited by Flemming Christiansen and Zhang Junzuo, 193–211. Honolulu: University of Hawaii Press.

Zhou, Jian-Ming. 2000. "Principal Forms of Land Consolidation and Expansion in China." Department of Economics, European University Institute, Tuscany, Italy/ FAO. http://www.fao.org/DOCREP/x7069t/x7069to8.htm.

Zuckerman, Elaine, and Ashley Garrett. 2003. "'Do Poverty Reduction Strategy Papers (PSRPS) Address Gender?' A Gender Audit of 2002 PSRPS." http://www.genderaction.org.

Zuckerman, Elaine, and Wu Qing. 2003. Reforming the World Bank: Will the New Gender Strategy Make a Difference? A Study with China Case Examples. Washington, D.C.: Heinrich Boll Foundation.

WORKS BY IRENE TINKER

Sole Author

Tinker, Irene. 2004a. "Contesting Wisdom, Changing Policies: The Women in Development Movement." In Developing Power: How Women Transformed International Development, edited by Irene Tinker and Arvonne Fraser, 65–77. New York: Feminist Press.

———. 2004b. "Ester Boserup." In David A. Clark, ed., Elgar Companion to Development Studies. Cheltenham, UK: Edward Elgar Publishing.

———. 2004c. "Introduction: Women Transforming International Development." In Developing Power: How Women Transformed International Development, edited by Irene Tinker and Arvonne Fraser, xiii–xxx. New York: Feminist Press.

———. 2004d. "The Many Paths to Power: Women in Contemporary Asia." In Promises of Empowerment: Women in Asia and Latin America, edited by Peter H. Smith, Jennifer L. Troutner, and Christine Hunefeldt, 35–59. Lanham, Md.: Rowman and Littlefield.

———. 2004e. "Quotas for Women in Elected Legislatures: Do They Really Empower Women?" Women Studies International Forum 27 (5).

———. 2003a. "Street Foods: Traditional Microenterprise in a Modernizing World," in "Toward Gender Equity: Policies and Strategies," edited by Nahid Aslanbeigui, Steven Pressman, and Gale Summerfield. Special issue, International Journal of Politics, Culture, and Society 16 (3): 331–49.

———. 2003b. "Utilizing Interdisciplinarity to Analyze Global Socio-economic Change: A Tribute to Ester Boserup." In Global Tensions: Challenges and Opportunities in the Economy, edited by Lourdes Benería. London: Routledge.

———. 2001a. "Economic Development and Women." In International Encyclopedia of the Social and Behavioral Sciences, edited by Neil J. Smelser and Paul B. Bates. Oxford: Pergamon Press.

———. 2001b. "Poverty, Women and Gender in Developing Countries." In International Encyclopedia of the Social and Behavioral Sciences, edited by Neil J. Smelser and Paul B. Bates. Oxford: Pergamon Press.

———. 2000. "Alleviating Poverty: Investing in Women's Work." Journal of the American Planning Association 66 (3): 229–42.

———. 1999a. "NGOs: An Alternate Power Base for Women?" In Gender Politics in Global Governance, edited by Mary K. Meyer and Elisabeth Prügl, 88–104. Lanham, Md.: Rowman and Littlefield.

———. 1999b. "Priority Shifts over Two Decades at the UN World Conferences for Women." In The Other Revolution: NGO and Feminist Perspectives from South Asia, edited by Renuka Sharma and Purushottama Bilimoria. New Delhi: Sri Satguru Publications.

———. 1999c. "Street Foods into the 21st Century." Food and Human Values 16 (3): 327–33.

Revision of remarks at the 1998 Joint Annual Meeting of the Association for the Study of Food and Society and the Agriculture, Food and Human Values Society in San Francisco in June 1998.

———. 1999d. "Women's Empowerment Through Rights to House and Land." In *Women's Rights to House and Land*, edited by Irene Tinker and Gale Summerfield, 9–26. Boulder: Lynne Rienner.

———. 1998. "Feeding Megacities: A Worldwide Viewpoint." *The Urban Age* winter: 4–7.

———. 1997a. "Family Survival in an Urbanizing World." *Review of Social Economy* 55 (2): 251–60.

———. 1997b. *Street Foods: Urban Food and Employment in Developing Countries*. New York: Oxford University Press.

———. 1996a. "Expectations of the Roles of Indigenous Nongovernmental Organizations for Sustainable Development and Democracy: Myth and Reality." Berkeley: IURD Working Paper no. 680.

———. 1996b. "Women in Development." In *Encyclopedia for the Future*. New York: Macmillan.

———. 1995a. "Beyond Economics: Sheltering the Whole Woman." In *Engendering Wealth and Well-Being*, edited by Rae Lesser Blumberg, Cathy A. Rakowski, I. Tinker, and Michael Monteon, 261–83. Boulder: Westview Press.

———. 1995b. "The Human Economy of Micro-Entrepreneurs." In *Women in Micro- and Small-Scale Enterprise Development*, edited by Louise Dignard and Jose Havet. Boulder: Westview Press. Revised and expanded from 1987 keynote address published in Jose Havet, ed., *International Seminar on Women in Micro- and Small-Scale Enterprise Development*, Ottawa: Canadian International Development Agency and Institute for International Development and Cooperation, 1988.

———. 1995c. "New Look at Energy." In *Women and Global Energy Policy: New Directions for Policy Research*, IFIAS International Federation of Institutes for Advanced Studies.

———. 1994a. "Urban Agriculture Is Already Here." In *Cities Feeding People*. Ottawa: IDRC.

———. 1994b. "The Urban Street Food Trade: Regional Variations of Women's Involvement." In *Women, the Family, and Policy: A Global Perspective*, edited by Esther Ngan-ling Chow and Catherine White Berheided. Albany: State University of New York Press.

———. 1994c. "Women, Donors, and Community Forestry in Nepal: Expectations and Realities." *Society and Natural Resources* 7 (4): 367–81. Reprinted in *Gender and Natural Resources*, edited by Carolyn Sachs. New York: Taylor and Francis, 1997.

———. 1993a. Global Policies Regarding Shelter for Women: Experiences of the UN Centre for Human Settlements." In *Shelter, Women and Development: First and Third World Perspectives*, edited by Hemalata Dandekar. Ann Arbor, Mich.: George Wahr.

———. 1993b. "The Street Food Project: Using Research for Planning." *Berkeley Planning Journal* 8: 1–20.

———. 1993c. "Women and Shelter: Combining Women's Roles." In *Women at the Center: Development Issues and Practices for the 1990s*, edited by Gay Young, Vidyamali Samarasinghe, Ken Kusterer. West Hartford, Conn.: Kumarian Press.

———, ed. 1992a. Special issue, "Urban Food Production." *Hunger Notes*.

———. 1992b. "The Political Context of Rural Energy Programs." In *Energy for Rural Development*, edited by M. R. Bhagavan and S. Karekezi. Zed Press for SAREC (Swedish Agency for Research Cooperations with Developing Countries).

———. 1991. "Expanding Social, Cultural, and Intellectual Exchanges." In *Proceedings, Second*

US-India Bilateral Forum. Berkeley: Institute of East Asian Studies, University of California, Berkeley.

———. 1990a. "A Context for the Field and for the Book." In *Persistent Inequalities: Women and World Development*, edited by Irene Tinker, 3–13. New York: Oxford University Press.

———. 1990b. "The Making of the Field: Advocates, Practitioners, and Scholars. In *Persistent Inequalities: Women and World Development*, edited by Irene Tinker, 27–53. New York: Oxford University Press. Reprinted in 1996, *Women, Gender, and Development Reader*, edited by Lynn Duggan, Laurie Nisonoff, Nalini Visvanathan, Nan Wiegersman, 33–42. London: Zed Press. Also reprinted in 2000, *Gender and Development: Theoretical, Empirical and Practical Approaches*, edited by Lourdes Benería. Cheltenham: Edward Elgar Publishing.

———, ed. 1990c. *Persistent Inequalities: Women and World Development*. New York: Oxford University Press.

———. 1990d. "Reaching Poor Women in Nepal: Do Literacy Programs Really Work?" Peace Corps *Visions*, Kathmandu, Nepal, summer 1988. Reprinted in *Newsletter for the Committee on Women for South Asia*, Spring 1990.

———. 1990e. "The State and the Family: Planning for Equitable Futures in Developing Countries." Keynote speech for Association of Collegiate Schools of Planning (ACSP). *Journal of Planning, Education and Research* 9 (3).

———. 1989a. "Credit for Poor Women: Necessary but Not Always Sufficient for Change." Special issue, *Journal of the Marga Institute*, spring, Columbo, Sri Lanka.

———. 1989b. "Equity for Women and Men: A Basic Need for USAID." *US Development Assistance: Retrospective and Prospects*, Center for Advanced Study in Development (CASID) Occasional Papers, Michigan State University.

———. 1989c. "Legalizing Street Foods in the Third World." *Whole Earth Review*, spring, 72–74.

———. 1987a. "The Case for Legalizing Street Foods." *CERES*, Rome: Food and Agriculture Organization, September/October.

———. 1987b. "Legalizing Street Foods in the Third World: The Right to Eat on the Street." *Howard Law Journal*, fall.

———. 1987c. "The Real Rural Energy Crisis: Women's Time." *Energy Journal* 8 (87): 125–46. A longer version was published in Ashok V. Desai, ed., *Human Energy*, New Delhi: Wiley Eastern, 1990.

———. 1987d. "Street Foods: The Fast Foods of Developing Nations." *VITA News*, January.

———. 1987e. *Street Foods: Testing Assumptions about Informal Sector Activity by Women and Men*. Special issue, *Current Sociology* 35 (3).

———. 1986a. "African Conundrum: Food Today and in the Future." Editorial. *Christian Science Monitor*, 23 April.

———. 1986b. "Feminizing Development: For Growth with Equity." *CARE Brief*, no. 6. Washington, D.C.: Overseas Development Council.

———. 1986c. "A Personal Review and Appraisal of Nairobi." *Signs* 11 (2), spring. Also published in *Journal of Women and Religion* 5 (1), summer, 1986.

———. 1985a. "Feminist Values: Ethnocentric or Universal?" In *Women in Asia and the Pacific: Towards an East-West Dialogue*, edited by Madeleine J. Goodman, University of Hawaii Press.

———. 1985b. "Street Foods as Income and Food for the Poor." *Dossier* 49 (September-October).

Tinker, Irene. 1985c. "Women in African Development." *Rural Sociologist* 5 (5), September.

————. 1984. "Mujeres, agricultura y modernizacion en America Latina rural." In *A Mulier Rural e Mudanças no Processo de Producão Agricola*, edited by C. Spindel, J. Jaquette, and M. Cordini. Instituto Interamericano de Cooperacão para a Agricultura, Serie: Proposicoes, Resultados e Recomendacoes de Eventos Technicos. *WID Working Paper*.

————. 1983a. "Women in Development." In *Women in Washington*, edited by Irene Tinker, 227–37. Beverly Hills: Sage.

————, ed. 1983b. *Women in Washington: Advocates for Public Policy*. Beverly Hills: Sage.

————. 1982. "Survival as an Obstacle to the Use of New Energy Technologies in Developing Countries." Published as a *WID Working Paper*, no. 04, Women in International Development. East Lansing, Mich.: Michigan State University, March, 1982.

————. 1981a. "A Feminist View of Copenhagen." *Signs* 6 (3): 531–37.

————. 1981b. "Issues of Women, Energy, and Appropriate Technologies in Developing Countries." In *Agriculture, Rural Energy, and Development*, edited by R. S. Ganapathy. Ann Arbor: University of Michigan.

————. 1981c. "Policy Strategies for Women in the 80s." *Africa Report*, March-April.

————. 1981d. "UN Energy Conference: Substance and Politics." *Science* 214, 4 December.

————. 1980a. "Changing Energy Usage for Household and Subsistence Activities: Some Implications for Information Collection. In *Important for the Future*. Geneva, Switzerland. UNITAR (UN Institute for Training and Research).

————. 1980b. "New Technologies for Food-Related Activities: An Equity Strategy." In *Women and Technological Change in Developing Countries*, edited by Roslyn Dauber and Melinda Cain, 22–34. Boulder: Westview Press.

————. 1980c. "Toward Equity for Women in Korea's Development Plans." *Social Science and Policy Research* 2 (2). In Korean.

————1976a. "The Adverse Impact of Development on Women." In *Women and World Development*, edited by Irene Tinker and Michelle Bo Bramsen, 22–34. New York: Praeger. Reprinted in *Peace Corps Program and Training Journal* IV (6) 1977. Translated as "Le developpement contre les femmes" in *Question feministes*, no. 6, September 1979.

————. 1976b. "Development and the Disintegration of the Family." UNICEF Quarterly Review no. 36, Geneva, Switzerland, October-December.

————. 1975a. "Pengaruh Pembangunan yang Merugikan Kaum Wanita." *Prisma* 4 (5, October) 33–44.

————. 1975b. "Widening Gap." *International Development Review*, January.

————. 1975c. "Women in Developing Societies: Economic Independence Is Not Enough." In *Economic Independence for Women: The Foundation for Equal Rights*, edited by Jane Chapman. Thousand Oaks, Calif.: Sage.

————. 1973a. "Federal City College: How Black?" In *Academic Transformation*, edited by D. Riesman and V. Stadtman, 99–126. McGraw-Hill/Carnegie Commission.

————. 1973b. "What's Happened to Progress?" In *Career Guidance for Women Entering Engineering*, edited by Nancy Fitzroy. New York: Engineering Foundation.

————. 1971. "Nonacademic Professional Political Scientists." *American Behavioral Scientist* 15 (2, December).

————. 1970. "Colleges and the Underprepared Student." *American Education*, November.

————. 1966. "Nationalism in a Plural Society: The Case of the American South." *Western Political Quarterly*, March.

————. 1956. "Malayan Elections: A Pattern for Plural Societies?" *Western Political Quarterly*, June.

———. 1954. "The General Election in Rajasthan, India." *Parliamentary Affairs* 7 (2).
———. 1953. "The General Election in Himachal Pradesh, India." *Parliamentary Affairs* 6 (3).
———. 1953. "The General Election in Travancore-Cochin, India." *Parliamentary Affairs* 6.

Coauthor or Coeditor

Tinker, Irene, and Arvonne Fraser, eds. 2004a. *Developing Power: How Women Transformed International Development.* New York: Feminist Press.

Tinker, Irene, and Patricia Blair. 1979. "Integrating Women in Development into ISTC's Programs." Paper prepared for USAID's planning office on a proposed Institute for Scientific and Technological Cooperation, October.

Tinker, Irene, and Michelle Bo Bramsen, eds. 1976. *Women and World Development.* Washington, D.C.: Overseas Development Council/American Association for the Advancement of Science. Reissued with annotated bibliography by Mayra Buvinic. Praeger: New York, 1980. Spanish translation, *Las Mujeres en el Mundo de Hoy: Prejuicios y Perjuicios.* Buenos Aires: Editorial Fraterna, 1981.

Tinker, Irene, and Cho Hyoung. 1981. "Participation of Women in Community Development in Korea." In *Toward a New Community Life*, edited by Man-Gap Lee. Seoul: Seoul National University. In English and Korean.

Tinker, Irene, and Monique Cohen. 1985. "Street Foods as a Source of Income for Women." *Ekistics* 310 (January-February).

Tinker, Irene, and Amitai Etzioni. 1971. "A Sociological Perspective on Black Studies." *Educational Record*, winter.

Tinker, Irene, and Jane S. Jaquette. 1987. "The UN Decade for Women: Its Impact and Legacy." *World Development* 15 (3, March): 419–27.

Tinker, Irene, and Lisa Prügl. 1997. "Microentrepreneurs and Homeworkers: Convergent Categories." *World Development* 25 (9): 1471–82.

Tinker, Irene, and Laura T. Raynolds. 1982. "Integrating Family Planning and Women's Enhancement Activities: Theory and Practice." Prepared for USAID Office of Population, June.

Tinker, Irene, and Gale Summerfield. 1999a. Introduction to *Women's Rights to House and Land*, edited by Irene Tinker and Gale Summerfield, 1–7. Boulder: Lynne Rienner.

———, eds. 1999b. *Women's Rights to House and Land: China, Laos, Vietnam.* Boulder: Lynne Rienner.

———. 1997a. "Background of the NGO Forum and Overview of the Family and Economic Transformation: Problems and Strategies." *Review of Social Economy* 55 (2): 196–200.

———, guest eds. 1997b. "The Family and Economic Transformation in Developing Countries: Impacts and Strategies, A Symposium Based on Issues Raised at the NGO Forum of the United Nations' Fourth World Conference on Women, Huairou, China August 30–Sept. 9, 1995." *Review of Social Economy* 52 (2).

Tinker, Irene, and Millidge Walker. 1998. "Indonesia: Chaos and Control." Editorial. *Christian Science Monitor*, 3 June, 20.

———. 1975. "Development and Changing Bureaucratic Styles in Indonesia: The Case of the Pamong Praja." *Pacific Affairs*, spring.

———. 1973. "Planning for Regional Development in Indonesia." *Asian Survey*, December.

———. 1959. "Indonesia's Panacea: 1959 Model." *Far Eastern Survey*, December.

———. 1956. "The First General Elections in India and Indonesia." *Far Eastern Survey*, July.

Contributors

EDITORS

JANE S. JAQUETTE is the Bertha Harton Orr professor in the Liberal Arts, professor of politics and chair of the Diplomacy and World Affairs Department at Occidental College. She served as a policy analyst in the Women in Development Office in USAID in 1979–80. Dr. Jaquette has published over fifty articles on women and development and the comparative political participation of women. She is an editor of and contributor to several collections including *Women in Development: A Policy Focus* (with Kathleen Staudt); *The Women's Movement in Latin America* (two editions); *Women and Democracy: Latin America and Eastern and Central Europe* (with Sharon L. Wolchik). Her most recent articles have appeared in *Foreign Policy*, *Journal of Democracy*, and *International Feminist Journal of Politics*. She is a member of the Council on Foreign Relations and the Pacific Council on International Policy.

GALE SUMMERFIELD is director of the Women and Gender in Global Perspectives Program and associate professor of Human and Community Development at the University of Illinois at Urbana-Champaign. She has written extensively on gender aspects of reforms in post-socialist and developing countries and global human security. Her articles appear in journals such as *International Journal of Politics, Culture, and Society*; *World Development*; *Journal of Economic Issues*; *Review of Social Economy*; and *Review of Political Economy*. She edited and contributed to the special issue of the *International Journal of Politics, Culture, and Society* on "Risks and Rights in the 21st Century." She is coeditor, with Nahid Aslanbeigui and Steve Pressman, of *Women in the Age of Economic Transformation*. With Irene Tinker, she edited *Women's Rights to House and Land: China, Laos, Vietnam*. Her current research interests address gender, global crisis, and human security (income, property rights, and health) and gender and transnational migration.

AUTHORS

MARUJA BARRIG, Peruvian activist and feminist writer, is currently a member of the board of Flora Tristán, a national center of research and promotion of women's rights in Peru. She obtained two Ford Foundation grants for research (1981; 1997) and was awarded a scholarship for senior researchers from the Consejo Latinoamericano de Ciencias Sociales (CLACSO) in 1999. Since 1979, when she first published *Cinturón de Castidad: La Mujer de Clase Media en el Perú*, she has conducted research on social movements and feminism. Her latest book, published in Argentina, is *El Mundo al Revés. Imágenes de la Mujer Indígena* (2001). Articles in English include "Women, Collective Kitchens and the Crisis of the State in Peru" in *Emergences: Women's Struggles for Livelihood* and "Female Leadership, Violence and Citizenship in Peru" in *Women and Democracy: Latin America and Central and Eastern Europe*.

SYLVIA CHANT is professor of Development Geography at the London School of Economics and Political Science, United Kingdom. She has carried out research in Mexico, Costa Rica, and the Philippines and has published widely on gender and development, migration, poverty, employment, household livelihood strategies, lone parenthood, and men and masculinities. Her recent books include *Women-Headed Households: Diversity and Dynamics in the Developing World* (Macmillan, 1997); (with Cathy McIlwaine) *Three Generations, Two Genders, One World: Women and Men in a Changing Century* (Zed, 1998); (with Matthew Gutmann) *Mainstreaming Men into Gender and Development: Debates, Reflections and Experiences* (Oxfam, 2000); and (in association with Nikki Craske) *Gender in Latin America* (Latin America Bureau/Rutgers University Press, 2003). Professor Chant is currently embarking on new collaborative research with Gareth A. Jones (also at LSE) on youth, gender, and livelihoods in sub-Saharan Africa (Ghana and the Gambia).

LOUISE FORTMANN is the Rudy Grah Professor of Environmental Science, Policy, and Management at UC Berkeley, specializing in forestry and agriforestry, land tenure, and gender issues. She spent eleven years in Tanzania, Botswana, Kenya, and Zimbabwe, working with villagers to better understand the interrelationships between natural resources and people living in resource-dependent households. She has extensively studied the roles of women and the obstacles they face in natural resource management. She has published numerous articles in journals such as *Rural Sociology, Science, Ecology Law Quarterly*, and *Public Administration and Development*.

DAVID HIRSCHMANN is professor in the School of International Studies at American University. Dr. Hirschmann specializes in development management, strategic planning and performance measurement, micropolitics of development, gender and development, bureaucracy, decentralization, and democracy. He has worked in several African countries as a professor and researcher and has undertaken consulting assignments in many countries in Africa and Asia and in transitional societies. He has published in journals such as *International Review of Administrative Sciences, Development and Change, Public Administration and Development, World Development*, and *African Affairs*.

DIANA LEE-SMITH, a resident in Kenya for over thirty-five years, holds a doctoral degree in Architecture and Development Studies from Lund University in Sweden. Along with her husband, Davinder Lamba, she was a founding member in 1978 of the Mazingira Institute, an independent research body in Kenya, where she was involved in research, development, and activist work on urban environment and development issues. She led an African network on human settlements issues for seventeen years and a global network on women and shelter for eight years. She has carried out independent research work on urban low-income housing, gender, transport, agriculture, and finance issues and has published widely on these. As a consultant, she has worked on implementation of low-income housing and urban development in

Kenya and Malawi for the World Bank and other international agencies. From 1998 to 2001 she was the Gender Focal Point for UN-HABITAT, while from 2002 to the present she has been the African Regional Coordinator for Urban Harvest, a program of the Consultative Group on International Agricultural Research (CGIAR) hosted by the International Potato Center. Dr. Lee-Smith is based in Nairobi.

AUDREY LUSTGARTEN is a recent graduate of the School of Law at the University of California, Los Angeles, and of Florida International University, where she earned her master of arts in International Studies. Her research interests include international labor law, workers' rights, and international migration, particularly as they are linked to gender and economic globalization. Her recent master's thesis looked at the conflict between international and domestic norms in relation to the issue of child labor in India.

DOE MAYER is the Mary Pickford Professor of Film and Television Production in the School of Cinema-Television at the University of Southern California, where she founded the Program in Development Communications at the Annenberg Center for Communication. She has consulted widely with international agencies and NGOs throughout Africa, Asia, and the South Pacific, specializing in the areas of reproductive health and girls' education. Mayer conceptualized and led the pilot project in Uganda for Women Connect! called Women Linking. Professor Mayer is an associate of the Pacific Institute for Women's Health.

FARANAK MIRAFTAB is assistant professor in the Department of Urban and Regional Planning at the University of Illinois, Urbana-Champaign. Her research spanning several countries of North America, Africa, and Latin America concerns social aspects of urban development. In particular she is interested in the issues of housing, gender, participatory community development, and urban governance. She has also served as a consultant to the United Nations Center for Human Settlements.

MUADI MUKENGE is program officer for Africa at the Pacific Institute for Women's Health where she is responsible for evaluation projects in reproductive health. She is manager of the Action Grants Program, which makes awards globally for reproductive health activities and women's empowerment initiatives. She also manages research activities for an initiative to prevent unsafe abortion in Kenya and is providing technical assistance to an affiliate in Burkina Faso in research design and monitoring for adolescent reproductive health interventions. For three years, Ms. Mukenge managed the communications capacity-building initiative discussed in her chapter. The project involved twenty-six women's NGOs in Zimbabwe, Zambia, and Uganda, aimed at strengthening NGO advocacy skills.

BARBARA PILLSBURY is a cultural anthropologist specializing in women's issues and the design and evaluation of health and development programs in developing countries. She received her Ph.D. from Columbia University in 1973, after which she moved into the field of international development, working with the U.S. Agency for International Development as Chief for Research and Evaluation for Asia and Women-in-Development Coordinator for Asia. In 1988 she established and became president of International Health and Development Associates, a women-owned consulting firm, and carried out a wide range of analyses in Asia, Africa, the Near East, and Latin America. In 1993 she co-founded and was program director of the Pacific Institute for Women's Health, a nonprofit organization working with women's NGOs around the world. Dr. Pillsbury has held teaching and research appointments at universities in the United States, Egypt, and Taiwan, and was founding president of the National

Association for the Practice of Anthropology. Her recent work has focused on HIV/AIDS, impacts of globalization on women's health, and use of the Internet for development and empowerment. She is currently director of The Synergy Project, implemented by Social and Scientific Systems, Inc., in Washington, D.C., which supports U.S. efforts to combat HIV/AIDS in developing countries.

AMARA PONGSAPICH received her Ph.D. in anthropology from the University of Washington, Seattle. She is now a professor in sociology and anthropology at the Faculty of Political Science, Chulalongkorn University. She is also the Director of Chulalongkorn University Social Research Institute (CUSRI). Her interests have focused on social development, gender, and ethnic studies. Her recent publications have been on the social impacts of the economic and financial crisis, and the role of social capital, social safety nets, and social protection programs in Thailand and Asia.

ELISABETH PRÜGL is associate professor of International Relations at Florida International University, Miami. She has written on the international regulation of female labor, in particular at the International Labor Organization and in the European Union, and on the intersections between feminism and constructivism. She is the author of *The Global Construction of Gender: Home-Based Work in the Political Economy of the 20th Century* (Columbia, 1999), coeditor of *Gender Politics in Global Governance* (Rowman and Littlefield, 1999), and *Homeworkers in Global Perspective: Invisible No More* (Routledge, 1996). Her articles are published in *International Studies Quarterly*, *International Studies Notes*, *International Feminist Journal of Politics*, *Global Social Policy*, *World Development*, and *Frontiers: A Journal of Women's Studies*. Her current research focuses on the effects of the European Union's common agricultural and equal opportunities policies on farm women in Germany and Austria.

KIRK R. SMITH holds the Brian and Jennifer Maxwell Endowed Chair in Public Health in the Environmental Health Sciences Division at the University of California, Berkeley. He conducts research on environmental issues related to the process of economic development in poor areas of the world. Currently, he focuses on air pollution, both in cities and in rural areas and both indoors and outdoors with a special but not exclusive focus on biomass fuel cycles. He is now working with groups in several countries to conduct large-scale epidemiological studies in Guatemala, Peru, and India of the health impacts of smoke from household use of solid fuels, a large source of exposure on a global scale. In the course of this work, he has developed new conceptual approaches to total exposure assessment and its use in regulatory policy. Since the late 1980s, he has also been conducting research on greenhouse gas emissions in developing countries, both at the level of field monitoring (India, China, Thailand, Brazil, and Kenya) and new concept development, i.e., the triple carbon-balance analysis technique. Dr. Smith has published in journals such as *Indian Journal of Pediatrics*, *Annual Review of Energy and the Environment*, *Epidemiology*, and *Indoor Air*.

KATHLEEN STAUDT received her Ph.D. in political science from the University of Wisconsin and is currently professor of political science and director of the Center for Civic Engagement at the University of Texas at El Paso. She has published twelve books, the latest of which include *Fronteras No Mas: Toward Social Justice at the U.S.-Mexico Border* (Palgrave, 2002) with Irasema Coronado and *Pledging Allegiance: Learning Nationalism in El Paso-Juarez* (Routledge/Falmber, 2002) with Susan Rippberger. Dr. Staudt is active in community and cross-border organizations and is currently conducting research on violence against women in Juarez.

IRENE TINKER's commitment to using research to alter policy has led to a career divided between university teaching and action research with nonprofit organizations. A professor emeritus from the University of California, Berkeley, she was a founder of the International Center for Research on Women, the Wellesley Center for Research on Women, and the Equity Policy Center. Current research focuses on women's accumulation of power through home ownership and electoral representation. Major publications include *Persistent Inequalities; Street Foods; Women's Rights to House and Land: China, Laos, Vietnam*; and *Developing Power: How Women Transformed International Development* (with Arvonne Fraser).

CATALINA HINCHEY TRUJILLO is a sociologist and social worker by profession. She was Executive Director for Fedevivienda, a National Federation of Self-Help Housing Organisations in Colombia, for seven years before her work at UN-HABITAT where she created, secured funding, and successfully managed the Women and Habitat Global Programme for ten years. She also developed the Comprehensive Gender Policy and Action Plan for UN-HABITAT and created and secured funding for the Gender Unit within UN-HABITAT. Currently she works with UN-HABITAT Regional Office for Latin America and Caribbean which is the focal point for the two global campaigns: Secure Tenure and Good Urban Governance and the Focal Point for Gender. She has more than thirty years experience in policy formulation, capacity building, and community management programs, and she has worked directly with peoples' movements on issues such as self-determination, housing as a human right, and citizen participation in local governance. She had the privilege of actively participating in the Earth Summit, Rio de Janeiro, Brazil, 1992; the Fourth World Conference on Women, Beijing, China, 1995; and the City Summit, Istanbul, Turkey, 1996.

Index

Library of Congress Cataloging-in-Publication Data

Women and gender equity in development theory and practice :

institutions, resources, and mobilization /

edited by Jane S. Jaquette and Gale Summerfield.

p. cm.   Includes bibliographical references and index.

ISBN 0-8223-3700-2 (cloth : alk. paper)

ISBN 0-8223-3698-7 (pbk. : alk. paper)

1. Women in development.

2. Women—Developing countries—Social conditions. 3. Women's rights.

I. Jaquette, Jane S.

II. Summerfield, Gale.

HQ1240.W6514 2006   305.4209172′4—dc22

2005029785

HQ 1240 .W6514 2006

Women and gender equity in development theory and pra